"Gentleman George"

Hunt Pendleton

"Gentleman George" Hunt Pendleton

Party Politics and Ideological Identity in
Nineteenth-Century America

Thomas S. Mach

THE KENT STATE UNIVERSITY PRESS · KENT, OHIO

Frontis: George Hunt Pendleton: This lesser known portrait of Pendleton seems to suggest his family's Southern heritage. (George H. Pendleton, n.d., George Hunt Pendleton Papers, Ohio Historical Society, Columbus, Ohio)

© 2007 by The Kent State University Press, Kent, Ohio 44242

All rights reserved

Library of Congress Catalog Card Number 2007021839

ISBN 978-0-87338-913-6

Manufactured in the United States of America

11 10 09 08 07   5 4 3 2 1

Library of Congress Cataloging-in-Publication Data

Mach, Thomas S., 1966–

"Gentleman George" Hunt Pendleton : party politics and ideological identity in nineteenth-century America / Thomas S. Mach.

    p.   cm.

Includes bibliographical references and index.

ISBN-13: 978-0-87338-913-6 (hardcover : alk. paper) ∞

1. Pendleton, George H. (George Hunt), 1825–1889. 2. Legislators—United States—Biography. 3. United States. Congress—Biography. 4. Diplomats—United States—Biography. 5. Democratic Party (U.S.)—History—19th century. 6. Civil service reform—United States—History—19th century. 7. United States—Politics and government—1861–1865. 8. United States—Politics and government—1865–1883. 9. Ohio—Politics and government—1787–1865. 10. Ohio—Politics and government—1865–1950. I. Title.

E415.9.P4M33 2007

328.73'092—dc22

[B]   2007021839

British Library Cataloging-in-Publication data are available.

Contents

Acknowledgments

Aproject that has spanned over a decade engenders a large number of debts. At the risk of omitting some worthy institutions and individuals, I would like to express my appreciation to some of those who have played vital roles in the process of bringing this project to completion. The staffs of the following institutions have worked very closely with me on numerous visits over the years: Cincinnati Historical Society, Ohio Historical Society, Rutherford B. Hayes Presidential Library, Western Reserve Historical Society, Bierce Library at the University of Akron, Thorne Library at Mount Vernon Nazarene University, Centennial Library at Cedarville University, the Library of Congress, and the National Archives. I sincerely appreciate the gracious assistance afforded to me during my research. Other institutions played important roles as well and I thank the kind staffs at the University of Cincinnati Library, Cleveland Public Library, Kenton County Public Library, and the Cartoon Research Library of The Ohio State University Library system. Finally, many others at archives and libraries scattered all over the country graciously assisted me via letter and long distance and I appreciate their help.

Numerous individuals volunteered to read portions or all of the manuscript at various stages along the way. Dr. H. Roger Grant, Dr. Keith L. Bryant, and Dr. Daniel Nelson were among the first to read and provide helpful insight. Dr. Bryant read through the entire document at various stages and I appreciate his professional and personal interest in this project. Dr. Charles Calhoun, Dr. R. Hal Williams, Dr. Frederick Blue, and Dr. George W. Knepper read portions of the work and gave me invaluable suggestions. No one, however, has read more drafts, provided more constructive criticism, or given me more encouragement along the way than Dr. Jerome Mushkat. Without his able guidance, assistance, and occasional fatherly advice, this book would not be a reality. His mentoring over the years on many matters has made me a better professor and a better person. Anything of value in this work is the product of the good counsel I have received from these readers; any errors are my responsibility alone.

I want to thank those who have worked with me in preparing this work or portions of it for publication. The editorial staffs of the *Ohio History* and *Ohio Valley History* journals were very helpful in preparing portions of this work for publication earlier. I appreciate their willingness to allow those articles to be included in this monograph. I also want to thank Joanna Hildebrand Craig, Mary D. Young, Tara C. Lenington, Dr. John T. Hubbell, and the rest of the helpful staff at the Kent State University Press for their encouragement during this process and insightful editorial pens. It has been a privilege to work with them.

Several institutions provided financial support for the research and writing of this biography. The University of Akron and Mount Vernon Nazarene University provided funds in various ways to help facilitate the early work. Cedarville University provided funding more recently to assist in bringing the work to completion. Along the way, Dr. Paul Mayle and Dr. J. Murray Murdoch, two men I have had the privilege of working under, have encouraged the process through word and their own modeling of what it means to be an historian. My thanks to Dr. Mark Caleb Smith, Director of the Center for Political Studies at Cedarville University, for supporting the endeavor. I appreciate the willingness of Dr. Smith, Dr. David Hoffeditz, Prof. Michael Thigpen, Dr. Gary Yates, and Dr. Marc Clauson in letting me commandeer numerous get-togethers and casual lunches and turn the conversation over to the serious business of Gilded Age politics. Their insightful comments, challenging questions, and good-natured ribbing helped me focus my thinking and encouraged me in the endeavor. It is indeed a privilege to count among my friends individuals who value the life of the mind. In the end, their friendship means even more.

Finally, I want to thank those to whom I am most close for their support through this long project. One of my greatest regrets is that my grandfather, Charleton D. Hull, is not living to see this work completed. He passed along his keen analytical mind and ideological bent to my mother and I like to think that she has passed it on to me. I appreciate her and my step-father's unfailing support throughout every stage of my career. Thanks to my mother-in-law and father-in-law for their faith in me and for the many ways they have invested in my family. Thanks to my dad, who undoubtedly knows more history than I ever will, and shares my love of it. Thanks to Jennifer Chaplik, Robert C. Mach, Eric Kuivinen, and Julie Kadamus. They and their spouses have always taken an enthusiastic interest in this work. In spite of one well-crafted prank where I was led to believe that Pendleton's papers had been found, I still appreciate each of them. There will come a day of recompense for that, however!

Thanks to my students in HIST-1120 United States History over the years, for letting me drone on about Pendleton and the Gilded Age. I do not know if I convinced them of the importance of such topics, but I have appreciated their challenging insights, patient attentiveness, and desire to integrate what they believe with their understanding of the past. Indeed, teaching will always be my first love. My thanks and adoration belong to the Creator God, in whose existence is found the ultimate meaning for the study of history. It is His Greatest Gift to mankind that is the wellspring of all that is significant in human history. And last, but certainly not least, I want to express my thanks to my wife, Christine, and my children, Jacob and Kiley. They have had to live with an uninvited guest in our home for years. Thanks to them for understanding why this project was important and for providing needed perspective in my life. Years from now when they look back at this time, I hope that they will say that the history we made as a family was my greatest achievement. Any accomplishment represented in these pages is due to their support. It is for this that I dedicate this book to them.

Introduction

George Hunt Pendleton's life spanned most of the nineteenth century. He came of age in the burgeoning city of Cincinnati in the early 1840s, just prior to the political conflict that would end in civil war. His was well-established stock, but, independent minded from the start, young George chose the Democratic Party over his father's Whig Party. His biography provides not only a microcosmic view of Democratic Party operations during his lifetime but also a case study of the longevity of Jacksonian principles and their political adaptation during some of the most critical periods in the nation's history. Pendleton served as a congressman during the Civil War, Gen. George B. McClellan's vice-presidential running mate in 1864, U.S. senator from Ohio, father of the first major civil service reform legislation—the Pendleton Act of 1883—and diplomat to Germany.

Like too many important nineteenth-century politicians, Pendleton is a significant but neglected figure. The reasons why are numerous and varied, but the main reason for the neglect of Pendleton in historical literature is the sparseness of source material. He left no memoirs, diaries, or journals. Nor did Pendleton or his family deposit his correspondence in a public archive. If any personal letters survived, his descendants believe that a house fire in 1926 destroyed them.[1] Consequently, no complete academic biography of Pendleton exists. With his few remaining letters scattered in depositories throughout the United States, there was a marked lack of scholarly interest in Pendleton's life. Historians have taken at face value what Pendleton's political opponents said and wrote about him. Thus the historical record of his life and accomplishments is skewed and negative. No wonder, then, that the modern interpretation of Pendleton is at best incomplete and at worst simply inaccurate. Such views demand balance and demonstrate the need for a complete biographical study of Pendleton, who was a major figure in his party and the nation during four critical decades.

Certain questions about Pendleton come to mind after even a cursory reading of the historical literature. Why, for example, did the Democratic Party provide him such significant roles? Why did Democrats disavow Pendleton during his later years? What principles guided his political career? What was his lasting legacy? Why is there no biography of him?

In attempting to answer these questions, I have reconstructed Pendleton's life based on the sources available. Beyond the relatively scarce correspondence that is extant, I have depended on newspaper accounts; the *Congressional Globe* and the *Congressional Record;* political tracts and speeches; periodicals; newspaper editorials; and references in the manuscripts of his peers, both Democrats and Republicans. Using the methods of community study historians, I have ferreted out town records to elucidate the workings of Pendleton's community and how he interacted within it. Using quantitative data, I have reconstructed and analyzed Pendleton's votes in Congress to place him within his political context and evaluate how his actions represented his constituency. While some of this material allows Pendleton to speak in his own words, the picture is admittedly limited. Nonetheless, the portrait of George Hunt Pendleton that emerges is enlightening and instructive.

This investigation of Pendleton reveals a much different man from the one historians have previously depicted. Indeed, the image that comes into focus throughout this study is one of a man who defied expectations. Unlike his father, Pendleton entered politics as a Jacksonian Democrat and quickly established himself as a rising politician in Ohio. In analyzing his career, three basic themes emerge. First, Pendleton was consistent in his efforts to unite the divided party around its traditional Jacksonian principles. What caught some of his contemporaries off guard, however, was his willingness to reinterpret Jacksonianism, allowing for new means of implementation, to address changing political issues. Second, he developed this strategy in terms of party loyalty. The Democratic Party, he believed, was worth saving because it provided ordinary Americans, far more than did the Republicans, with a mechanism to shape government operations, administer the nation, and implement sound public policies. Pendleton was a man of his times, however, and did not conceive of complete equality among ordinary Americans. Though there were forward-thinking individuals in the nineteenth century, most of Pendleton's contemporaries rejected the notion of racial equality. His commitment to white supremacy prevented him from seeing a place for African Americans in the political system. Because of his racism, while there is much to be lauded in the ideologue and the partisan, he is hard to praise where his principles or his party are flawed. Nonetheless, the ideologically driven partisan, and party, present a clearly identifiable agenda for the electorate. When this is true, the voters can easily fulfill their role as agents of accountability when they go to the polls. Third, Pendleton's faith in traditional principles and his devotion to perpetuating the Democratic Party served his personal ambitions. At every stage of his activities, Pendleton was conscious of the rewards that the party would bestow on a leader who could restore the organization to its former position as the majority party in the United States.

Though a biography of Pendleton is worthwhile and valuable by itself, a look at his life provides much more than a study of an important and neglected nineteenth-century politician. Pendleton's experiences cover the expanse of the nineteenth century. In his childhood, he encountered life in a frontier town, vibrant with commercial activity. He cut his political teeth in a turbulent era that eliminated several parties and created the two-party system that would dominate politics from the mid-nineteenth century to the present. He served in Congress during the Civil War and participated in the wave of industrialization that followed. Though no longer in office in the Reconstruction Era, he drove Democratic policy through his speech making and campaigning. Then, in his sunset years, while most men experience decline, he ascended to his loftiest position as a U.S. senator and fathered the first major civil service reform legislation. The length and breadth of his involvements and experiences not only give us a look at one man's political ambitions but also open our eyes to the broader American political milieu in the nineteenth century. Americans in this era, much more so than today, defined themselves by their partisanship. This study uses an investigation of Pendleton and politics to examine what drove Americans in the nineteenth century. Political history is not the ending point of this work, however; it is the starting point—the lens through which to view a rapidly changing American society. Pendleton shows us change over time, and in many cases the lack of change, in the society in which he lived, from the antebellum era through the Gilded Age.

Pendleton's actions both shaped and reflected the fortunes of the Democratic Party during much of the nineteenth century. By challenging expectations, he represents a type of Democrat that historians have not clearly defined. As a party ideologue in a transitional time, Pendleton was committed to the ideals of Andrew Jackson. Along with other midwestern Democrats who shared his principles, Pendleton visualized Jacksonianism as the foundation of his party. That body of ideas provided the clearest demarcation between Democrats and Republicans. Pendleton developed a distinct midwestern Democratic ideology that he attempted to use to unify the party. It welcomed ethnic diversity and opposed government interference in areas of private conscience. It valued states' rights, limited federal authority, political partisanship, and a democratic system involving all white men. Pendleton and his followers worried that the developing market economy and government-sanctioned privilege or monopoly would reduce the opportunities of the Common Man to survive in America. Yet Pendleton's ideology was also influenced by his father's Whiggism. Pendleton consistently viewed the government as a vehicle for political and social reform throughout his career. His reform initiatives ran the gamut, including building public parks, improving orphanages, reorganizing Ohio's judicial structure, securing government efficiency, introducing the merit system into military promotions, giving cabinet members seats in Congress, and reforming the federal civil service system. Pendleton employed this reform impulse to accomplish Jacksonian goals.

Pendleton's adherence to a Jacksonian emphasis on advancing democracy and a concern for protecting the opportunity of ordinary Americans from the exploitation of a powerful elite influenced his political pursuits. Jackson's commitment to states' rights molded Pendleton's opposition to Republican centralism during the Civil War. Jackson's financial policies influenced Pendleton's view of the government's role in economic development. Though seemingly contradictory, Jackson's ardor to expand opportunities for ordinary Americans buttressed Pendleton's efforts to institutionalize civil service reform.

So Pendleton used the foundation of Jacksonian ideology as the basis of his political activity. The continuity of this activity throughout his career is due to this foundation, and an analysis of his career, if left there, would give added credence to the notion of stability rather than change in the antebellum to postwar American political milieu. Indeed, there is much to be said in favor of this argument.[2] Yet Pendleton's political career provides a case study to evaluate this position. Perhaps there needs to be a more nuanced understanding of this time. The possibility of political realignment and the threat of third-party movements reinvigorated a party leader such as Pendleton to solidify the Democratic fold.[3] Working from a foundational political ideology, and influenced by reform impulses stemming from his father's Whiggism, Pendleton faced the new and complex issues of Reconstruction and Gilded Age America with a fresh perspective. Time and time again, in an effort to unify his party's power and push it forward, he reinterpreted and adapted Jacksonianism to meet the new challenges. In the final analysis, Pendleton's career provides a lens for viewing a more complete picture of what remained the same within the Democracy, allowing the party to reemerge from the ashes of the Civil War, and what evolution was necessary for it to truly rebuild and regain national ascendancy. The Democracy, then, remained a clearly identifiable party for Americans following the war, but not one hopelessly locked in the past. Although

Pendleton did pursue Jacksonian goals, he does not represent stasis alone. His willingness to adapt worn-out Jacksonian methodologies with reform impulses represents a fresh approach. To the extent that Democrats followed his lead, they found a new means of implementation and new tactics to address current problems while still pursuing goals anchored in an old and defining ideology.

Democrats frequently failed to follow his lead, and political success did not come easily to Pendleton. Some misunderstood his actions or believed that Jacksonianism was no longer relevant to their needs. Some, like Conservative "Bourbon" Democrats, held onto traditional understandings of Jacksonianism on certain issues, while totally disowning them on others. They fell short of seeing the need for adaptation, choosing rather to be inconsistent. As a result, the Democratic Party was severely factionalized for much of Pendleton's career. Traditionally, the country had been divided, East and West, over political issues. Questions related to tariffs, internal improvements, and banking issues frequently split the sections during the first half of the nineteenth century, at times even overcoming partisan affiliation. On a more local level, Pendleton experienced significant factionalization in Cincinnati over issues related to nativism, fusion with various third-party movements, and the Nebraska issue in the 1840s and early 1850s. During the same time, the national party faced geographic expansion and the extension of slavery out west, causing the East-West division to fade and North-South differences to become more visible. The split at the Democratic convention in 1860 represented the failure of probably the last great bulwark preventing secession. During the Civil War, the Northern Democrats split between War Democrats and Peace Democrats—those willing to support Lincoln's administration of the war and those who were not. After the war, Democratic divisions remained over economic matters. The East-West divisions reemerged occasionally, but the factionalization of the postwar period cannot be portrayed that simply. A good example of the postwar split is found in the debate over payment of the Civil War debt.

Democrats demonstrated ambivalence in their reactions to the Ohio Idea, Pendleton's controversial plan to redeem in greenbacks the Civil War bonds known as "five-twenties." In this case, as in others, Pendleton construed Jacksonianism in a fresh manner. Although economic conditions had changed markedly since the 1830s, those who were later called Bourbon Democrats continued to pursue old perspectives of Jacksonian hard-money solutions. Bourbons tended to be eastern Democrats—though there were some in the Midwest and the South as well—and represented the commercial and manufacturing interests. They held to Jackson's hard-money policies, though they conveniently neglected his opposition to a national banking system and government support of economic growth. Pendleton, operating on the same principled foundation, argued that the methods had to change if the greater Jacksonian goal of equal opportunity were to be obtained. Greenbacks could be used to pay down the debt, he argued, as long as the plan provided for their eventual withdrawal. Pendleton's plan also would destroy the national bank system. Though he was "represented as an apostate from the Jacksonian Democratic tradition of specie," Pendleton rightly charged his Bourbon critics with this "crime."[4] Because he was seeking the same goals as Jackson—supporting the Common Man and eradicating privilege in the form of the national bank—he argued that he was the one remaining true to Jacksonianism, even if his implementation differed.

Pendleton's persistent Jacksonianism built a significant base of support, both in Ohio and nationally. It was a base he used to pursue his second goal, the revival of the fractured Democratic Party. Although other Democrats chafed at his leadership, Pendleton set the party's agenda throughout most of his career. Working tirelessly, he tactfully articulated the Democratic Party's position of "loyal opposition" during the Civil War, and he formulated the Ohio Idea after the war. Moreover, Pendleton traveled throughout the nation to advance Democratic doctrines, many of which he inaugurated. Even after he assumed the presidency of the Kentucky Central Railroad in 1869, an office he held for ten years, Pendleton continued to lead the Democracy and remained a masterful figure in state party conventions, serving as chairman, drafting party platforms, and canvassing the electorate. But in the end, Pendleton failed to reach the goals he set. The Ohio Idea created division among Democrats rather than the unity he had sought. The party also fractured over Pendleton's greatest achievement, the Pendleton Act, which reformed the federal civil service. While unsuccessful in unifying the various factions of his party, Pendleton did succeed in forcing his fellow Democrats to recognize the necessity of acting in unison to promote Jacksonian goals, even if they differed on the new approaches to be used.

These failures thwarted Pendleton's ambitious dream of high office. When he gained the vice-presidential nomination in 1864, the brass ring seemed within his grasp, but the electorate rejected the Democratic ticket. Still hoping for the presidency, Pendleton was a leading candidate four years later, but the Bourbon Democrats prevented his nomination. Other disappointments came his way, culminating in the loss of his Senate seat and his selection as a diplomat to Germany when many expected he would be given a cabinet post.

On the surface, it might appear as though Pendleton could have fulfilled his personal ambitions if he had been willing to bend his principles, but he refused to compromise to achieve success. He believed that in order to succeed the party had to be built around Jacksonian goals. His ambitions could not be served, therefore, without maintaining his principles. By refusing to bend to what was expedient and, conversely, by his unwillingness to be stagnant, Pendleton, at times unknowingly, sacrificed his ambitions for a larger end, the survival of the

Democracy and what defined it—Jacksonianism. Time and again, he suffered political losses when his ideology was pitted against factional politics and compromise. Democratic factionalism continued, and the party failed to achieve the power it sought until well into the twentieth century.

In the long run, however, Pendleton's efforts succeeded. After his death, the Democratic Party recognized his lasting legacy. He had been correct on one level. Pendleton's midwestern Democratic ideology, a mixture of Jacksonianism and reformism, became the means to unite the Democratic Party and set its course. In short, Jacksonian principles were the adhesive that kept the party together and allowed it to survive. Before the party coalesced around these principles, however, some of them found expression in third-party movements. Pendleton's philosophy focused on elevating the Common Man and squelching privilege and monopoly, much as the Populists and political factions such as the Progressives would later do. Eventually, the African American would also be included as a Common Man—something Pendleton was never willing to grant. In the 1930s, these principles served as part of the philosophical foundation for Franklin D. Roosevelt's concern for the suffering of the American people, and his legislative response, the New Deal. Although the link is neither direct nor total, Pendleton's influence is evident. In his tenacious espousal of Jacksonianism, Pendleton played a significant role in sustaining the party and maintaining its traditional philosophic roots. On a broader spectrum, he continues to speak to America today about the value of a principled approach to politics. Pendleton understood the importance of staying firm against the whims of public opinion and the necessity of providing voters with a clear choice. Pendleton's ideological approach superseded partisanship and crass economic or personal motivation. In the end, Pendleton encouraged the parties to function responsibly and the voters to keep their leaders and the government accountable.

An understanding of George Hunt Pendleton provides historians with a window into the Democratic Party during the nineteenth century. Around him circled a constant flurry of debate and discussion about where the party should go and how it should revitalize itself during and after the debacle of the Civil War years. Sometimes Pendleton was instrumental in directing the Democracy, sometimes factionalism defeated him. Yet his political career provides insight into the internal turmoil of the Democratic Party.

In sum, Pendleton's successes far outweighed his failures. He had a number of shortcomings, but he operated in a manner that allowed the system to overcome them. As a result, Pendleton was a significant figure in American politics. Yet he was more than a mere politician. A study of his life shows a person of great consequence, living in a significant period of American history. He was a man who defied expectations. This biography tells his story, a story that illuminates our understanding of nineteenth-century America.

The Early Years

The mighty Ohio River brought much more than life-giving water to the burgeoning city of Cincinnati in 1825. Indeed, the river provided the very means for maintaining the Queen City's most important economic activity, commercial trade. But beyond the farm produce that was shipped south and the finished goods brought in from the East, Ohio's fastest growing city relied on the river to transport to the city immigrants who would comprise a significant portion of the city's population. As Cincinnati gained economic prominence, her citizenry began to make a political impact not only on the state of Ohio but also on the nation.[1] The Pendletons, one of the prominent families in Cincinnati, came west down the Ohio in 1818. Already having made a significant impact on the national political scene, the Pendleton family introduced its latest addition on July 19, 1825, George Hunt Pendleton, who would continue to place the family's mark on the development of the Republic. Although Pendleton's father was a Whig, Pendleton chose to become a Democrat in the early 1850s when he began his political career. As a young man, this pivotal decision set the stage for his role in developing the midwestern Democratic political ideology in the middle of the nineteenth century. Pendleton's choice of party affiliation was a difficult one influenced by a number of factors, some of which are already recognized as part of the historiographical discussion of partisanship in this era and some of which are not. An examination of his decision and his early political career provides a window for viewing the changing political arena in Cincinnati and Ohio, the variety of factors involved in making such choices, and the continuity of political ideology in the face of a dynamic party system.

The fourth of seven children, George Pendleton entered the world as a member of a founding family not only of Cincinnati but also of the United States. The Pendletons emigrated from Norwich, England, in 1674 to New Kent

County, Virginia. Philip Pendleton was its first representative in the New World and eventually brought the family to high economic and social status. One of his grandsons, Edmund Pendleton, served in the Virginia House of Burgesses and the Continental Congresses of 1774 and 1775. George's grandfather, and the nephew of Edmund, Nathaniel Pendleton, was an aide-de-camp to Gen. Nathaniel Greene during the American War for Independence. Following the war, Nathaniel Pendleton served as delegate to the Constitutional Convention in 1787. President George Washington named him judge of the U.S. District Court for the state of Georgia where, in 1793, Nathaniel Greene Pendleton was born. An ardent Federalist, the elder Nathaniel was a close friend and confidant of Alexander Hamilton, serving as Hamilton's second in his fateful duel with Aaron Burr. Nathaniel Pendleton eventually moved his family to Dutchess County, New York, where he rubbed elbows with some of the most respected men in the young republic. He practiced law there until his death in 1821.[2]

Young Nathaniel Greene Pendleton left his family in New York and migrated west to the Queen City. Within two years, he met and married Jane Frances Hunt, daughter of Jesse Hunt, one of Cincinnati's earliest settlers. Together with William Henry Harrison, Arthur St. Clair, Jacob Burnett, and Nicholas Longworth, Hunt had helped to create the city. Born in Savannah, Georgia, Nathaniel Greene Pendleton graduated from Columbia College in New York and served in the War of 1812. He entered local politics and won a seat in the Ohio Senate, where he served for four years. In 1841, voters sent him as a Whig to the U.S. House of Representatives for one term. He rejected renomination and practiced law in Cincinnati until his death in 1861.[3] Pendleton's economic and political success provided his seven children a respected family name and all the benefits that wealth could provide. Yet those same blessings brought with them high expectations and responsibility.

Reflecting their status, the Pendletons sought the best secondary education possible for their son, George Hunt. They considered the state's common school system, which the state legislature had organized in 1828, inadequate. Instead they selected Woodward High School, a small college preparatory institution, founded by William Woodward and his wife. This school did not meet the goals of the Pendletons, however, and in 1835 they sent young Pendleton to a more rigorous school operated by Ormsby Macknight Mitchel, a graduate of the U.S. Military Academy.[4]

Mitchel had left West Point to teach mathematics, natural philosophy, geography, and astronomy in Cincinnati. He was best known for his love of astronomy. Mitchel traveled extensively throughout the nation raising $40,000 in subscriptions to construct the Cincinnati observatory in 1845. When it was built, the telescope was the largest in the United States and second largest in the world. When Cincinnati College was organized, both Mitchel and Pendleton entered but in different capacities. Mitchel became a professor of mathematics, while Pendleton began studying foreign languages and mathematics. The college, headed by President William H. McGuffey, later famous for his primary readers, was nonsectarian and had a curriculum heavy in classical studies, medicine, and later, law. Pendleton found that even this institution did not suit his needs, and he left in 1841 to continue his studies under private tutelage.[5]

For the next three years Pendleton studied at home, continuing to improve his mastery of French and German as well as classical studies. While the city in the 1830s and 1840s was populated by hardworking families who had little time or money for either leisure or the extravagance of a private education, the Pendleton family was an exception, and private tutors were available to wealthy families in Cincinnati. Nathaniel Greene Pendleton provided his children benefits that were not accessible to most families in the nineteenth century, and his son George took full advantage of them. He and his brother Elliot Hunt would spend two years traveling throughout Europe as part of their education.

In 1844, five years after the death of his mother, George Hunt Pendleton bid his family farewell and ventured off to see the world. Initially visiting Paris, he then traveled south to winter in Italy. During the following spring, he journeyed north through the German states, spending some time in Berlin, and continuing on to Great Britain. In the 1840s, Europe had yet to develop an extensive railroad system, so much of Pendleton's traveling was slow and difficult. He persevered, however, and made a learning experience of his journey. He spent a considerable amount of time in the galleries of the British Parliament in London, absorbing the rules of order and the interworkings of government. The knowledge gained there provided him with an expertise that he would use time and again as a member of the loyal opposition during the Civil War. After his stay in the island nation, he returned to Heidelberg where he enrolled in the university.[6]

Pendleton matriculated on May 13, 1845, at the age of nineteen. His mastery of the German language allowed him to study the philosophy of law for two semesters.[7] After a summer and winter of formal study, he resumed his experiential learning through travel, departing for Greece. There he surveyed the ruins of classical civilization. Still yearning for more, he journeyed east to the Holy Land, contemplating sacred places. Continuing his circumvention of the Mediterranean Sea, he traveled to Egypt and crossed the desert by camel to view the remains of that ancient society. He concluded his European trip by traveling through France, Great Britain, and Ireland before returning to the United States in the summer of 1846. Having seen more of the world than the vast majority of his countrymen, and having visited many of the national capitals en route, Pendleton stood above his peers in his knowledge of world affairs.[8]

Upon his arrival home in Cincinnati, he met, proposed to, and married Mary Alicia Lloyd Nevins Key, generally known as Alice Key. Little is known of their courtship, but recognizing the Southern heritage and high standing of both families, the parents probably played a role in bringing them together. Nonetheless, by all accounts the young couple was truly in love. Alice was the daughter of Francis Scott Key, author of "The Star-Spangled Banner," and the niece of Roger B. Taney, chief justice of the United States Supreme Court. They were married in Baltimore in 1846 but took up residence in Cincinnati. The newlyweds lived with Nathaniel Greene Pendleton while they looked for a home in the Queen City. Over the next decade they started their own family. By the time Alice's brother, Philip Barton Key, district attorney for the District of Columbia, was murdered by New York congressman Dan E. Sickles, the Pendletons already had two children of their own. The first was a son, Francis Key, and the other a daughter, Mary Lloyd. After the funeral, they took in Philip's son and daughter to rear as their own.[9]

Pendleton now focused his studies on the reading of law in the office of Stephen Fales, the former partner of Nathaniel Greene Pendleton. Pendleton's genteel manner and quick mind allowed him to stand out in a crowd where his physical appearance might not. A newspaper report described him as "a fine-looking man, with dark hair, inclined to curl; dark expressive eyes, a handsome face, well rounded head generally, and set upon a well-formed trunk."[10] He stood about five feet nine inches tall and weighed in the neighborhood of 170 pounds. Admitted to the Ohio Bar in 1847, young Pendleton soon formed a business partnership with a boyhood schoolmate, George Ellis Pugh.[11] Through much of this partnership, Pugh was serving in the army during the Mexican War with the 4th Ohio Volunteer Infantry. He returned to Cincinnati only to be promptly elected to the state legislature. The partnership of Pugh and Pendleton lasted only five years; Pugh was elected attorney general of the state of Ohio in 1852, and the firm dissolved. The few extant records reveal little of their day-to-day activities.[12] Pendleton then apparently focused some of his attention on rental and mortgage claims, but his law career slowed as he launched his political career in 1854.[13]

Although Edward D. Mansfield, journalist, editor, historian of Cincinnati, and a contemporary of Pendleton, believed that men obtained their political affiliation from their fathers, Pendleton defied expectation and broke from his father's Whiggish background to become a Democrat. An investigation of this break provides an opportunity for examining party identification in Ohio during the 1840s and 1850s. It also illustrates the variety of influences that went into creating the western Democratic political ideology that Pendleton represented and, in many ways, helped form in this period. In the end, this is a story that highlights the importance of family ties over family status, party realities over party nostalgia, and political ideology over political rhetoric in the process of choosing a partisan affiliation.[14]

The factors in George Pendleton's decision to become a Democrat vary and provide some insight into the political composition of parties in this era. Historians have grappled for decades with the issues that induced Americans of the early nineteenth century to form and reform their political alignments. Some voters were influenced by economic determinants in choosing their party affiliation. Political rhetoric of the era frequently equated the Whig Party with business, commercial, and property interests, while the Democratic Party was portrayed as representing the poorer elements of society or those not directly benefiting from the changing economy.[15] With the advent of the Market Revolution, the disparity between the economic groups seemed to solidify.[16] Those benefiting from the new commercial systems developing in the country tended to be Whigs, whereas those who were not tended to be Democrats. While Pendleton's Cincinnati was a commercial city and should have been strongly Whig, it was an exception to the rule, likely because the Queen City residents had suffered disproportionately during the Panic of 1819 and blamed the Second Bank of the United States for it. Economic factors, or at least the perception of those factors, were causative agents in party affiliation. Nonetheless, power vacillated back and forth between the parties.[17]

Other factors played a role as well. That economic issues were not the sole determinants is evidenced in the makeup of the Democrats and the Whigs. Both parties had members from all economic strata. Ethno-cultural and religious differences played a role in political preference, such as national origin, region and era of birth, and religious inclination. Immigrants from the British Isles tended to vote for Whigs; those from the rest of Europe tended to vote for Democrats. Native-born citizens from New York tended to be Whig, while those from Virginia held to Democratic ideals. With reference to religious beliefs, Evangelicals, comprised of Baptists, Methodists, Presbyterians, and Congregationalists, who wanted to maintain the moral fiber of society and who sought the eradication of evils such as alcohol, prostitution, and slavery, tended to vote Whig. Anti-Evangelicals, who were mainly Catholics, Episcopalians, Campbellites, Unitarians, Universalists, free-thinkers, deists, or atheists, and who focused on the individual rights of men (and thus eschewed increased state power for the purpose of maintaining a set of morals), were generally Democrats.[18]

Although ethno-cultural influences were important for many, ideological emphases cannot be ignored.[19] For example, the "two great principles of Whig social thought, order and philanthropy" tended to differentiate the two parties.[20] This focus was a key distinction from the Democratic Party, which could not accept the

"Gentleman George" Hunt Pendleton, 1825–1889. (*History of Cincinnati and Hamilton County, Ohio; Their Past and Present, Including . . . Biographies and Portraits of Pioneers and Representative Citizens, etc.* Cincinnati: S. B. Nelson, 1894)

notion of government controlling the individual. As an example, Abraham Lincoln had been a Whig because he believed Whiggery promoted a more civilized lifestyle. Whigs accepted modernization with restraint, and according to their values, economic advance was to be embraced and encouraged with governmental support, but they rejected "socioeconomic equality, toleration of diversity, and acceptance of political conflict."[21] The Whig "ideological core [was] built around beliefs in social order, Unionism, activist domestic governance, a non-aggressive foreign policy, and opposition to executive tyranny."[22] Democrats, conversely, pursued greater economic equality, embraced diversity and political partisanship, and preferred state sovereignty, rather than federal involvement, over most domestic issues. The prevalence of these themes in political speeches and editorials of the era suggest that they resonated with voters.

With the multitude of variables that determined political partisanship, ascertaining the reasons for Pendleton's party choice proves complex. The Pendleton family was part of the wealthy elite of Cincinnati, and George Pendleton had the benefits of this esteemed family name in addition to an inherited family fortune. He traveled extensively and obtained an excellent education. As testimony to the family's affluence, the censuses of 1850, 1860, and 1870 enumerate at least one and generally two domestic servants in the employ of Alice Key and George Pendleton. His holdings in 1860 amounted to $75,000 in real estate and $3,000 in personal property. By the next census, he had accrued through inheritance and accumulation real estate worth $250,000 and personal property totaling $25,000. If economic considerations were decisive for the Pendletons, Nathaniel Greene would have been a Whig, and indeed he was. On that basis, his son should have followed his father's footsteps into the Whig fold, yet George became a Democrat.[23]

For the Pendletons, economic factors were not primary in determining partisanship. In evaluating ethno-cultural factors, George Pendleton is again an enigma. The Pendletons were native-born citizens who migrated from the New York region, suggesting that Nathaniel Greene and his sons would probably become Whigs. Again, only the elder Pendleton fits the model. It is clear, however, that the family's Southern heritage influenced the elder Pendleton's political ideology and eventually George Pendleton as well. The family was Episcopalian, which placed it within the anti-Evangelical group of partisans who tended to vote Democratic. This partially explains the younger Pendleton's decision to be a Democrat, but does little to reveal his father's motives for remaining a Whig. Either George Pendleton is an exception to the rule or he is an example of the struggle many Whigs faced as their party began to disintegrate.[24]

Introducing the ideological factors in antebellum partisanship as well as the question of party viability adds to an understanding of Pendleton's choice but does not address all potential variables. The Ohio Whig Party was losing power in 1850. Internal state turmoil and conflicts due to national issues, such as the Compromise of 1850, may have signaled to Pendleton that the Whig Party was in decline.[25] Yet Pendleton was no neophyte and undoubtedly understood the ebb and flow of political power. The difficulties of the party did not cause his father to jump ship. Indeed, even if George Pendleton did sense the Whig demise, there were other options available to him than aligning with the opposition. Whig ideological distinctiveness may shed more light on Pendleton's decision. The Whigs' focus on order and control undoubtedly concerned Pendleton, for during his long career he maintained a strong adherence to the concept of private conscience, believing that the government should not regulate private behavior. In addition, his Southern heritage lent itself to a states' rights concept of governance, including the idea that states should decide internal matters such as slavery. Perhaps the Ohio Whig support for abolitionist Benjamin Wade as senator solidified his resolve to be a Democrat. Yet even here, the partisan indicators are not clear. A nuanced analysis recognizes that neither of the major parties could easily align, even on as potent an issue as slavery. Perhaps this discourse shows how a multitude of factors played some role in influencing Pendleton's choice of party affiliation.

In evaluating the causes of Pendleton's decision to become a Democrat, it is important to understand his family's partisan background. Nathaniel Pendleton, George's grandfather, had been a close friend of Alexander Hamilton and a fellow Federalist. Nathaniel Greene, his son, represented the Whig Party in both the Ohio Senate and the U.S. House of Representatives. He was a confidant of William Henry Harrison and campaigned hard in Ohio for his friend during the presidential election of 1840. Harrison's home was in Hamilton County, and so close was the association between Harrison and Nathaniel Greene that Ohio Whigs assumed that the new president would name him to a cabinet post. Though Harrison served less than a month, he had selected his cabinet even before his inauguration, which did not include Nathaniel. His successor, John Tyler, initially made no changes in the executive department, but when he did he also passed over Nathaniel for a post. When both men failed to recognize the contributions of Nathaniel Greene Pendleton, the Ohio Whig Party believed it had been done a disservice. Pendleton did not become embittered or leave the party, and other politicians recognized him as one of the leading Whigs in the state throughout his life.[26]

Beyond the damage done by Harrison's seeming indifference, the Ohio Whig organization had many internal conflicts, similar to those of the national party. The Whigs were comprised of four major factions. In the North, "Cotton Whigs," who were reliant on the cotton trade, advocated the expansion of slavery. In contrast, Northern "Conscience Whigs" sought to prevent the spread of the "evil" institution of slavery. They believed that slavery was constitutionally protected in the South but did not think it should be allowed to expand into the western territories. In the South, the Cotton Whigs, generally slave owners, opposed the extension of slavery because of the principle of supply and demand. Slave prices would go up, they thought, and cotton prices would go down if the institution spread to the West. The "Union" or "National

Whigs" feared the slavery issue altogether and wanted the party to avoid the question. Because of the variety of views, the very existence of the national Whig organization depended on the success of the Unionists in squashing the issue. The Whig principles that tied these factions together were order and philanthropy.[27] Practical application of these ideals resulted in numerous Whig issues outside of slavery including neomercantilism, white supremacy, political piety, temperance, and xenophobia.[28] The Whigs had to maintain a delicate balance to prevent factionalization of the many disparate groups within its organization, even to the point of remaining silent on major issues such as the extension of slavery.[29]

This fragile coalition had little internal strength to weather the storms of the 1840s and 1850s. After Harrison's death, Tyler, a slave owner, assumed the presidency with little regard for party unity. When Henry Clay, the Whig leader in Congress, proposed his "American System," President Tyler vetoed the national bank portion of the package and created considerable division within the party. Further factionalization of the party continued throughout the decade and accelerated when the territories gained from the Mexican-American War sought statehood. Now the Whigs could not avoid the issue of slavery expansion. They had hoped that the issue had been settled by the Missouri Compromise, but after struggling through the Compromise of 1850, they felt far less secure. The Kansas-Nebraska Bill of 1854 repealed the 36° 30' line of the Missouri Compromise that separated free and slave territories, jeopardizing the future of the Whigs. As with many compromises, groups on both sides were left disgruntled. Slavery extension was a major issue that brought about the disintegration of the national Whig organization, but there were other important issues that hastened the end. Most of them are revealed more clearly through an examination of state and local elections.[30]

There was among some Whigs in this period a growing sense that the major parties were not directly confronting the issues of greatest political importance to the mass of the electorate. Often those issues were more local in nature or expression and thus made them more difficult for the national organization to address. This frustration resulted in what some historians have referred to as "antipartyism." Driven by the sense that parties were more interested in "office-chasing and wire-pulling" than the ultimate success of the Republic, these Whigs began to seek redress in what became known as Know Nothing fraternal organizations, completely outside the two-party political system.[31] These disaffected citizens focused their attention on ethno-cultural issues such as "temperance, nativism, anti-Catholicism."[32] They pursued legislation to protect the use of the Protestant Bible in schools, extend the naturalization process, bring labor and political reform, and support Sunday and prohibition laws such as the Maine Law of 1851.

The seeming indifference to these concerns at the national organization level and the growing economic prosperity of the late 1840s and early 1850s made the Whig party appear unnecessary in their eyes. When combined with the centrifugal force of the antiextension issue, the Whig party appeared doomed. By the mid-1850s, the Know Nothings came into their own as a separate party while the Whigs began to disintegrate.[33]

In early 1841, Ohio Whigs had cause for optimism when President Harrison appointed Ohioan Thomas Ewing as secretary of the treasury, but Harrison's untimely death brought doubt and disillusionment to Buckeye Whigs. They seriously wondered if the party would consider the interests of the West, especially after a Southerner, John Tyler, assumed the executive office. The conflicts within the party attributable to Tyler's opposition to Henry Clay's American System, and the resulting decline of the organization, accelerated during the early 1840s even as George Pendleton was determining his political loyalties. If he looked realistically at Ohio politics without concern for his political heritage, he might have been able to predict the eventual doom of the Whigs. He doubtless considered it unwise for a young, ambitious attorney to step aboard the sinking vessel that was the Whig Party.[34]

In weighing the political strength of the Whigs versus the Democrats, Pendleton also looked realistically at his potential constituency. In examining the composition of the Cincinnati electorate, Pendleton could not help but notice the high percentage of foreign-born Cincinnatians who tended to vote Democratic. Hamilton County had traditionally voted Democratic in the 1830s. As early as 1825, there were 2,411 names on the register of gainfully employed Cincinnatians, with 533 immigrants, including 210 English, 166 Irish, 51 Germans, 40 Scots, and a variety of other nationalities. The numbers of Irish and Germans, who were largely Catholic, continued to grow, and they became, after 1830, a significant voting bloc. By 1850, 27 percent of the people living in Cincinnati had been born in Germany. Seven years earlier, the Germans, realizing their growing political clout, had organized the German Democratic Union of Hamilton County.[35] The following year, Cincinnati elected the first German-born representative to the Ohio General Assembly. Later, he was elected to the Ohio Senate and served as a delegate to the Ohio Constitutional Convention in 1850 and 1851. His understanding of the electorate in Cincinnati deterred Pendleton from considering associating with the Whigs, who used nativist tactics, and later the American Party, another name for the nativist Know-Nothings.[36]

Yet simply because a voter was foreign born did not mean he would vote Democratic. Political debate in Cincinnati in this period did not always revolve around traditional party issues. Rather, nativism drove much of the conflict. Consider, for example, the political behavior of Germans in Cincinnati in the

1853 municipal elections. In early 1853, Archbishop John Purcell asked for state funds to be shared with parochial schools in the Queen City. Local Catholics were concerned that the public school curriculum was Protestant in flavor or excluded religious instruction altogether. Purcell's request unleashed a firestorm. Simple prejudice drove part of the backlash, but an underlying belief that the common school system inculcated in the next generation the values and ideals necessary for citizens of a republic also caused Protestants to eschew any curriculum that might encourage the spread of Catholicism. Sensing that neither of the two major parties, the Whigs or the Democrats, was responding appropriately to this threat to the common school system, native-born Cincinnatians and Protestant Germans formed independent parties.[37]

Although the Democrats dominated the city by this time, owing in part to the support of its foreign-born population, the issue of foreign ascendance threatened to eat away at its power base. Some native-born Democrats formed a secret society within the Democracy to prevent Germans from obtaining public office. The Miami Tribe, as it eventually became known, apparently made little distinction between Catholic and Protestant Germans. When word of the organization leaked out, German Democrats of all faiths felt alienated from the party. The main Democratic organization tried to maintain its support base among immigrants by opposing the open nativism of many of the Whigs, but because of anti-German sentiment within its own ranks, it lacked a strong resolution on the issue. Even further complicating matters, German Protestants had no love of German Catholics, representing one of various shades of nativism apparent in Cincinnati in the early 1850s.[38]

The Whig Party in Ohio had a history of being unable to garner much of the immigrant vote. Many Whigs were nativists, and as the party disintegrated, Irish and German immigrants who went to saloons on the sabbath offended many Whigs' politicized sense of piety. Whig anti-Catholicism, xenophobia, and prohibitionism tended to push immigrants, particularly Catholic immigrants, into the Democratic fold.[39] Because of Cincinnati's large immigrant population, Pendleton clearly recognized the need to secure their support to be successful politically. His speeches indicate that he deprecated nativism and religious discrimination. This position is consistent with his ideological support of the inviolability of the private conscience. Whether his words were due to ideals of tolerance or simply political opportunism is unclear.[40] Nonetheless, Pendleton did remain consistent in his opposition to nativism throughout his career.

Pendleton's antinativism demonstrated a cognizance of Cincinnati's growing immigrant electorate. Yet this cannot be the decisive factor for Pendleton because the immigrant community did not vote as a bloc during the early 1850s. Another factor that played a role in George Hunt Pendleton's decision to become a Democrat was his relationship with Ohio's attorney general and soon-to-be U.S. senator, George Ellis Pugh. Born into a Quaker family, which according to the ethno-cultural historians' interpretation would place him within the Whig Party, Pugh held no prejudice against those of other nationalities or faiths. As a young man, he became a Baptist and considered becoming a minister. He later married Theresa Chalfant, who was a Catholic, and after her death in 1868, converted to Catholicism.[41] Interestingly, Pugh had been a Harrison Whig in 1840, but the *Cincinnati Commercial* noted that he became a Democrat when the Whigs became a "hopeless minority in Hamilton County."[42] Pugh grappled with this decision concurrently with his friend, Pendleton, and both apparently came to the same conclusion about their own political philosophies and which party would provide the greatest personal advantage.[43]

One must consider a final and decisive factor in attempting to explain Pendleton's decision to become a Democrat. Although Nathaniel Greene Pendleton was unsuccessful in passing along his political partisanship to his son, he was much more effective in bestowing upon him his political ideology. The younger Pendleton had more than one choice of political philosophy as the 1850s began. He rejected the Know Nothings because of their nativism, preferring instead a society based on "cultural heterogeneity, ethnic diversity, and *laissez-faire*."[44] He also objected to their willingness to abrogate liberty and equality by allowing government to infringe on matters of private conscience, such as temperance and sabbath laws. Finally, unlike Know-Nothings, he believed in the value of the political party. It was a positive good, a tool to be used to protect the liberties of individuals from forces seeking to limit them.[45] Pendleton could have joined former Whigs such as Abraham Lincoln and others of the Free Soil philosophy who eventually formed the Republican Party. Like former Whig Alexander Stephens, however, he could not support its association with abolitionism. His racial prejudice was "so visceral and powerful that it . . . required no justification, no supporting reason, at all."[46] In addition, association with the subsequent Republican Party would have run counter to his family's Southern heritage dating to the colonial period. The Southern political philosophy of states' rights, limited federal authority, and concern for a truly democratic governing system—though reserved for white men—remained a part of Pendleton's ideology throughout his career and would ultimately influence his decision to become a Peace Democrat and oppose the Republican prosecution of the Civil War. His father was dedicated to these principles, though surprisingly Jacksonian in concept, and he passed them on to his son.[47] They formed the basis of the midwestern Democratic ideology that would dominate the party in this region for the decade to come. That Pendleton's father previously held these views further demonstrates the amalgamated nature of the Whig Party.

Early in his career, George Pendleton's political beliefs evolved to include other Jacksonian tenets such as a strict construction of the Constitution, the elevation of the Common Man by instituting a delegate view of representation in Congress, strict economy in appropriation of public funds, and opposition to concentrated power, particularly government-sanctioned monopolies or privilege.[48] Pendleton believed that the power of the central government should be limited so as to prevent the trampling of individuals' and states' rights. The southwest portion of Ohio was inhabited by many farmers and laborers—common men who "were deeply unsettled by the emergence of an individualistic social order" associated with the emerging market economy.[49] Some of the farmers still held onto the agrarian myth, believing that the very essence of the Republic was at stake if the economy evolved too much. Both farmers and laborers alike feared the institutionalization of society, the growth of impersonal corporations, and government-condoned privilege or monopoly. They longed for a "simpler, arcadian past" where personal relationships predominated and the disparity between economic groups was less noticeable.[50] Unwilling to tolerate (as his father had) such emphases as neomercantilism, Pendleton's developing ideology precluded association with the Whig Party. Much of this evolution took place due to Pendleton's focus on national rather than just local issues. His father had served in Congress, allowing him to recognize the importance of local concerns in light of national initiatives. In examining the inability of President John Tyler to become the leader of the Whig Party in the early 1840s, for example, Pendleton realized that no further impediments stood in the way of Henry Clay's becoming that party's clarion voice. The Whigs, under Clay, had less and less room for those holding to Pendleton's, and his prospective constituents,' ideals. To be successful politically, Pendleton understood that he had to temper his personal ambition with his desire to remain true to his political beliefs and his recognition of the direction of the national party organizations.[51] Even his desire for success fit within the confines of this emerging Jacksonian midwestern Democratic ideology. The common midwesterner was willing to follow a well-to-do and respected man such as Pendleton if he melded his personal ambition with the public interest. Midwesterners were searching for a leader of "honesty, manliness, and wisdom," and one untainted with the alloy of unmerited privilege.[52]

The complexity of the antebellum political parties is evident in this seemingly strange mixture of positions that Pendleton brought together. Yet his philosophy was clearly rooted in Jacksonianism. Pendleton's later partisanship seems to support the idea that his father's ideology heavily influenced him, leaving him in the given time period little choice but the Democratic Party. By the Reconstruction era, the party "bore certain similarities to prewar Whiggery."[53] Pendleton represents that fusion of ideas well: he upheld his father's Southern heritage, including his support for white supremacy, states' rights, and strict construction of the Constitution. Pendleton maintained those Jacksonian principles throughout his career, leading the western Democracy through the Civil War and attempting to direct it beyond. Yet he found justification for some Whig objectives in a Jacksonian ideology reinterpreted, of necessity, because of a changing political milieu. During the war, consistent with Whig tradition, Pendleton frequently fought to limit the expansion of executive power at the expense of legislative prerogative. One cannot interpret his attacks on Lincoln's administration as anti-Jacksonian, however, because Pendleton based them on a concern for the maintenance of personal liberties. In his final initiative in the House before leaving his seat, Pendleton furthered this objective by introducing a bill to authorize cabinet members to have nonvoting seats in Congress—in his mind, another means of keeping tabs on the executive branch. In the end, Pendleton took many of his father's ideals, reinterpreted them within the context of Jacksonianism and in light of new political issues, and developed a political ideology that defined the midwestern Democracy for decades.[54]

The amalgamated nature of the Democracy in the mid-nineteenth century extended beyond Pendleton and his midwestern Democratic supporters, but he did not believe the eastern wing of the party maintained its roots in Jacksonian ideology. Pendleton never strayed far from his Jacksonian principles. It was the foundational political philosophy through which he evaluated all political issues. Pendleton and his midwestern Democratic followers differed from most eastern Democrats, later know as Bourbon Democrats. Both wings of the party supported the long-standing ideals of white supremacy and states' rights, and neither could condone expansion of the central government. Yet on economic issues they parted ways. Bourbon Democrats harkened back to Whig neo-mercantilism. Pendleton parted with his father's Whig heritage here because it contradicted his chosen Jacksonian foundation. Government involvement in support of economic interests smacked of monopoly and privilege and was anathema to any consistent Jacksonian. In his final analysis, Pendleton argued that the Bourbons had left the Jacksonian tradition behind, and he therefore felt compelled to lead the midwestern Democracy in a different direction. He hoped to convince the Bourbons of the error of their ways.

Pendleton never turned his back on the political legacy handed down to him by his father. This legacy became the centerpiece of midwestern Democratic politics during the rest of the nineteenth century. Pendleton developed this political ideology throughout his career, reinterpreting Jacksonianism to address contemporary issues, but never straying from his ideological roots. In the end, wealth, family status, place of birth, and denominational affiliation were necessary causes but not sufficient in and of themselves. The political environment of his city and his time must be factored into Pendleton's decision. Cincinnati's inhabitants and the demise of the Whig Party certainly played a role. National debates over the expansion of slavery and state squabbles over political dominance had left the party in Ohio in turmoil. Though the Democrats dominated Ohio's politics in the early 1850s, the complex interplay between political factions and ethnic voting blocs within Cincinnati precluded certainty about the future. All of these factors, including Pendleton's relationship with Pugh, had their place: they laid the groundwork for the most decisive influence in Pendleton's choice of political party. Although Pendleton was principally influenced by his father's political ideology, in the changing political milieu of the 1840s and 1850s, many of those beliefs could no longer find a comfortable home within the Whig Party. Edward Mansfield seems to have been partially correct when he argued that fathers influenced the partisanship of their sons. Though partisanship was not always passed down from father to son, political ideology often was.

Emerging from and through this process of choosing partisan affiliation, George Pendleton soon joined his law partner, Pugh, in a meteoric rise to political prominence. The people of Cincinnati took notice of Pendleton as well and, in 1853, nominated him for the office of state senator with little effort on his part. William F. Converse and John Schiff also won nominations to represent Hamilton County as Democrats in the Ohio Senate. In the fall of 1853, the Ohio Democracy reiterated its oft-repeated principles in state elections. They sought to prevent the repeal of the bank tax; to preserve a "just" tax system, which meant that corporations and banks paid a significant share; and to support President Franklin Pierce's policies in lowering the tariff and seeking free trade. Statewide, key races pitted three candidates against each other. These men represented the Whig, Democrat, and Free Soil parties. An editorial in the *Ohio Statesman* on the lieutenant governor's race, for example, accused the Free Soil candidate of being an abolitionist and told Democrats with Free Soil leanings not to be deceived. The Free Soiler eventually dropped out of the race in an effort to push Free Soil voters over to the Whig candidate, leaving the Democratic and Whig candidates to battle for the office. The Whigs, however, faced an uphill climb.[55]

After the presidential election of 1852, the Whig Party in Ohio lost much of its strength. Divided by the platform's acceptance of the Fugitive Slave Law, the national Whig Party had been unable to elect Gen. Winfield Scott. Northern Whigs had been unhappy with the inclusion of the law in the platform, while Southern Whigs feared that Scott would not seriously uphold it if elected. The result was a large Whig voter bloc that was unwilling to vote at all, giving Franklin Pierce and the Democrats the election. In the state elections of 1853, the Whigs in Ohio were little threat to the Democrats. In spite of their own recent factionalism, the Democrats managed to unite for the sake of victory. They ran no campaign whatsoever, relieving them of having to deal directly with such issues as temperance, which the Free Soilers, now called Free Democrats, had espoused. The Whigs gave up the fight early in the race, handing the Democrats a majority across the state. Democrats won the crucial governor's and lieutenant-governor's races and gained decisive control of the General Assembly, leaving the Free Democrats without the determining influence they had sought. In the state senate race in Hamilton County, Pendleton and the entire Democratic ticket won.[56]

An event prior to Pendleton's entrance into the Ohio Senate made his term especially important to the future of the state. The Constitutional Convention of 1850–51 caused a great deal of dissension within Ohio and even disrupted the Democratic Party. Working as an attorney at the time of the convention, Pendleton had no influence on its decisions, but the revised constitution provided a number of issues that the incoming legislature would have to address. One of the key questions was the regulation of banks and corporations. Whigs tended to be probank and probusiness, seeing little need for more regulation. Free Soilers generally agreed with the Whigs. Democrats split between two viewpoints. The more agrarian areas of the state combined with the laboring class of Cincinnati to generate the "Locofoco" faction that sought to stiffen regulations on businesses and abolish state banks. This radical group, which in Cincinnati was comprised largely of what were called old anti-Miami men, supported hard money and believed that the corporate sector did not pay enough taxes.

Moderate Democrats disagreed, arguing that the system of state-chartered banks was acceptable and only in need of a little more regulation. The moderates combined with the Whigs to defeat the more radical goals of the Locofocos, but the compromises in the revised constitution did allow for more taxes on corporations and banks. The next session of the General Assembly would determine which faction would ultimately be successful. In 1853, Ohioans voted to determine the composition of the second assembly under the revised constitution. Due to the strength of the Locofocos in Cincinnati, Pendleton was mindful of their concerns, but he did not allow them to manipulate his position on financial matters while he served in the state senate. Perhaps motivated by his father's Whig past or by his own interaction with business and bank men as a lawyer, Pendleton stood for moderation on such issues. As he would do throughout much of his career, Pendleton interpreted Jacksonianism through fresh eyes. The issue at hand was the state bank system, not the national bank system that Jackson had opposed. Gradually the strength of the Locofocos began to diminish, due to a conservative business reaction.[57]

One of the major tasks facing the new state assembly was the election of a new U.S. senator. The Democrats had a large majority, but quarreling factions within the party hampered the electoral process. The old Miami Tribe prejudices against the anti-Miami or radical Democratic group resurfaced. The former supported George Manypenny; the latter voted for William Allen. Allen opposed the Kansas-Nebraska Bill presently being debated in Congress. Manypenny refused to take a position, though many of his supporters were considered "pro-Nebraska." George Pugh controlled thirteen vital votes in the legislative caucus, one of which was Pendleton's, and was unwilling to give the victory to either man. Manypenny withdrew in favor of Judge Thomas Bartley of the state supreme court, but the caucus remained deadlocked. Finally Allen withdrew, and Pugh won as a compromise candidate. His views regarding the Nebraska bill were unknown until after his selection, but he ultimately supported the proposal as did George Pendleton. The resolution of the senatorial decision did not end the conflict and divisions, adding to the dissension produced by Locofocoism. These were signals that the Democratic Party was not a strongly unified whole, and the divisions reappeared in the 1854 elections.[58]

Pendleton enjoyed a successful term in the Ohio Senate from January 1854 until late in 1855. He made a significant impact despite his youth and inexperience. The chairman of the senate designated Pendleton, the youngest senator at age twenty-eight, as clerk pro tempore. Though subsequently appointed chairman of the Standing Committee on Federal Relations as well as a member of both the Judiciary Committee and the Committee on Municipal Corporations, Pendleton recognized his status as a junior senator and did not overstep the boundaries imposed by his position. Though he rarely addressed the Senate, he gained a positive reputation through hard work on his committee assignments. Specifically, his work on the Committee of Municipal Corporations exemplified a concern for governmental efficiency and reform that would distinguish much of Pendleton's career. His interest in general improvement, even in the early days of his political career, suggests that he viewed government as an instrument for political and institutional reform.[59]

Pendleton seldom reported to the Senate for the Committee on Federal Relations. One case that arose immediately upon his being seated, however, concerned the disruption of the mails from Ohio through Pennsylvania on the Lake Shore and Michigan Southern Railroad. Pendleton introduced a resolution from the committee declaring that it was the duty of the U.S. Congress to make sure that the mail got through safely. Pendleton gained more opportunities to address and influence the Senate from the work he did on the Judiciary Committee.[60]

The revised constitution initiated many changes in the state's judiciary system. Pendleton's legal background made him well suited for his responsibilities on the Judiciary Committee. He created a board of commissioners to commence work on reforming the practices of courts in criminal cases, as well as reclassifying the law for the punishment of crimes. The Judiciary Committee also proposed expanding the role of the justices of the peace to encompass claims not exceeding one hundred dollars. Claims of more than that amount up to three hundred dollars would be assigned to the concurrent jurisdiction of the justice of the peace and the court of common pleas. Pendleton's efforts on behalf of these two measures proved successful and indicated that the Judiciary Committee sought to recreate the judicial system under the guidelines of the revised constitution. Even though three years had passed since its inception, many areas in the legal system still needed to be refined and codified.[61]

Much of Pendleton's labor on the Judiciary Committee involved improving laws dealing with such issues as child-centered reforms and efficiency in government expenditures. For example, Pendleton reported to the Senate a list of amendments to a probate act regarding the appointment of guardians for orphaned children. The amendments, which eventually passed, required guardians to report to the court about how they were managing the estates of dependent children and instituted strict guidelines regarding how long the guardianship would last.[62]

Pendleton's activities on the Committee of Municipal Corporations also promoted reform and change. For example, he reported and supported a bill allowing municipalities to use bonds to purchase land within city limits to be converted to public parks. Such recreation facilities provided urban dwellers with a much-needed respite from the squalor of the city. Pendleton laid the legislative groundwork for this reform, exemplifying a Jacksonian concern for the Common Man. Pendleton also supported legislation to improve the management of orphan asylums. In spite of these progressive positions, Pendleton showed little sympathy for the developing women's rights groups in Ohio. For example, he voted to strike the female gender pronouns in a bill to regulate the admission and practice of attorneys in Ohio. Still, in most issues, he exemplified reformist ideas in the decade before the outbreak of the Civil War.[63]

In addition to his focus on reform, Pendleton concerned himself with the affairs and views of his constituency. His focus on these issues should be seen as another example of his Jacksonian heritage. As a representative, Pendleton believed that it was his responsibility to act as a delegate, or a direct agent, of the people before the state legislative assembly. For example, he often presented petitions from Cincinnatians to the General Assembly.[64] Concerned about the various economic interests within the city, his political positions exemplified a moderate approach in light of the growing reaction of Cincinnati businessmen against the Locofocos. These radical Democrats wanted to rid Ohio of state banks, increase the regulation of corporations, and eliminate paper money. As a Jacksonian, Pendleton supported some of the regulations they desired, but he refused to neglect the needs of his other constituents, the business community, which feared stifling regulation and constriction of paper money. After all, this was a state, not a federal bank system. In addition, he recognized that regardless of his personal view of paper currency, it was the lifeblood of Ohio's commercial economy. As a result, he fostered a policy of moderation. For example, Pendleton served on a select committee to analyze the insurance business in Ohio and to recommend improvements. He supported regulations that ensured payment of claims, but opposed an amendment that required insurance companies to provide the state auditor with a $50,000 security deposit before entering into business. This proposal, he believed, placed too much restraint on free enterprise and would close the insurance field to all but the largest and wealthiest insurance companies. This bill would have had the effect of granting control of the insurance industry to a small pool of privileged companies, an obviously anti-Jacksonian goal. Pendleton also opposed an amendment to a bill dealing with banking regulation that would have prevented state banks from recirculating notes that they had redeemed with specie. Pendleton recommended that the bill be resubmitted to the Committee on Currency because the wording was vague. He also wanted to prevent the bill from being applied to corporations. If it were, he feared that it would prohibit companies from paying their employees with the paper money they received as income. His proposal lost. While he was mindful of the Locofocos' concerns about currency and corporations, he tried to pursue a compromise position as business opposition to this radical group developed.[65]

Pendleton's attentiveness to his constituency received widespread acknowledgment though he almost did not complete the session. His role in the Senate so impressed local Democratic leaders that they nominated him for the First Congressional District in Hamilton County in 1854, only one year into his Senate term. The seat had been held by his father thirteen years earlier, and most recently by David T. Disney, a Democrat. Four men ran for the Democratic nomination: Pendleton, Disney, Jacob Flinn, and George W. Holmes. The primary race, which focused largely on front-runners Pendleton and Disney, gave Pendleton a majority. Disney claimed that there was corruption in the fourth and thirteenth wards of the district but decided not to contest the election because Pendleton would have won even if the votes in those wards were thrown out. The young lawyer's upset of the three-term incumbent signified Pendleton's rising reputation.[66]

Pendleton's general election opponent, Timothy C. Day, previously a Democrat, had become disgruntled with the party over the Kansas-Nebraska Bill. Western expansion had compelled Congress to address the organization of the

Nebraska Territory. Exacerbating the struggle between Northerners and Southerners was the route of the proposed transcontinental railroad. Illinois senator Stephen A. Douglas wanted, for personal and political reasons, the railroad to be built west from Chicago. In order to garner Southern support for this route, Douglas introduced the Kansas-Nebraska Bill, which annulled the Missouri Compromise and split the Nebraska Territory. Under his plan, the two territories would enter the Union as either slave or free states based on popular sovereignty rather than the prescriptions of the Compromise of 1820. Senator Douglas assumed that the northernmost state would be free and the southernmost would be slave, effectively maintaining the existing balance. By focusing on a democratic choice by the population of the territory, he hoped to find a workable solution to the slavery expansion question that Northerners could support. By opening up a previously free territory to the possibility of slavery and emphasizing states' rights, he hoped to gain Southern support. In return, he wanted to obtain the northern railroad route with Chicago as the eastern terminus.[67]

Day had been a member of the Democratic Party faction that opposed the Douglas plan and therefore condemned the Pierce administration for supporting it. Day, and others like him, left the Democratic Party after Pugh won the U.S. Senate seat instead of the "anti-Nebraska" man, William Allen. The *Cincinnati Commercial* listed Pendleton as a "Nebraska" man, meaning he supported the Douglas plan, while Day, who now openly espoused the ideas of the Know-Nothings, was the anti-Nebraska candidate. The Nebraska issue had precipitated further division within the Democratic Party, and even after the Douglas bill passed, the factions remained. The different political groups emerging took on other distinguishing characteristics, which became the focus of political battles in Ohio in 1854. The underlying agitation over the Nebraska issue, however, remained crucial and forced Democrats such as Pendleton to dodge the question in an effort to entice disgruntled Democrats back to the fold.[68]

Day made an issue of the disputed primary election, saying that Pendleton won due to corruption. Beyond that accusation, Day attempted to resurrect the old factionalism within the city of Cincinnati by charging that his opponent was a member of the Miami Tribe. Day asserted that a combination of the "Miamis" and the "Jesuits" gave him the primary and that the *Cincinnati Enquirer*, which supported Pendleton, was guilty of appealing to voters on this basis. Pendleton responded by denying any affiliation with the Miamis and denouncing the religious prejudices of Day and his supporters.[69]

After abandoning the Democratic Party, Day represented the American Reform ticket in the general election. That party was a fusion of radical Democrats who opposed the Kansas-Nebraska Act, Free Soil Democrats and abolitionists who fought any extension of slavery, old Whigs who resisted the reopening of the slave question, and Germans who feared that the extension of slavery would limit their economic opportunities in the territories. The Know-Nothings also joined the fusion, however, causing some Germans to jump ship.[70] The Know-Nothings feared that foreigners, especially Catholics, whose allegiance to the Pope allegedly threatened their loyalty to the United States, were taking over America. The Know-Nothings supported religious and nativist tests to prohibit Catholics and other minorities from running for office or even from voting. The xenophobia of the new American Reform ticket was especially repulsive to the large immigrant population in Cincinnati. Believing that bigoted Whigs used nativism as a smoke screen, Pendleton focused his attacks on this issue. The *Enquirer* told readers that the Democratic Party upheld its Baltimore platform of 1852, based on the spirit of national reconciliation, as well as support for the Pierce administration. As part of its election strategy, the newspaper followed closely Pendleton's tactics and focused its assault on Day's association with the Know-Nothing Buntline organization.[71] The editor was incensed that Day would not respond to repeated questions concerning his nativism.

Another Democratic paper, the *Statesman,* attacked Day's withdrawal of support for Pierce, saying that Day shifted his allegiance when Pierce did not appoint him postmaster. Once again, the party attempted to divert attention from the divisive Nebraska issue. In spite of the concerted effort of Democratic newspapers and party leaders, the fusion party carried Ohio by some eighty thousand votes. The combination of Whigs, Know-Nothings, and disaffected Democrats was too much for the diminished Democratic Party. In the First Congressional District, Pendleton lost to Day by more than three thousand votes. Even in Cincinnati the American Reform ticket won a majority, though it was unable to gain more than a small minority of German voters. Pendleton lost little in the election, because the party as a whole had done so poorly. In addition, fusion could not last for long, and Pendleton was young enough to rebound from defeat.[72]

Though he entered his second year as a state senator, bruised but not beaten, the following September Pendleton apparently suffered another defeat. The Democratic County Convention nominated George Holmes, William F. Converse, and Stanley Matthews for the state Senate without even mentioning Pendleton's name. The fact that he was not renominated suggests that, rather than a defeat, it was an opportunity, as the party planned to run him for Congress again in the 1856 election. In the October elections of 1855, the Democrats won handily in Hamilton County, electing the entire ticket and giving gubernatorial candidate William Medill a large majority. After losing Hamilton County by 7,500 votes the year before, Medill and the Democrats won it back by more than 8,000 votes.[73] The *Enquirer* lauded the dramatic downfall of the Know-Nothings in Cincinnati earlier in the year. They had been overwhelmingly defeated in the April municipal elections and further stained their reputation with the blood of those injured in riots that followed.[74] Within the state as a whole, however, the Know-Nothings remained a threat and won the governor's seat for Salmon P. Chase, a Free Soil Democrat. Yet Chase's candidacy further seemed to weaken fusionism. He angered many of the Whig Know-Nothings because of his association with the Democrats and because he was strongly antislavery. Regardless, Chase had been nominated on a ticket filled almost entirely with Know-Nothing candidates. The fact that there were so few Free Soil candidates upset the Free Democrats who supported Chase, but not the rest of the ticket. The Democrats initially encouraged the Free Soilers in their attacks on the Know-Nothings, hoping some of them would rejoin their party. When this proved futile, the Democrats changed tactics, encouraging a group of Cincinnati Know-Nothings who had bolted from the fusion party and nominated Allen Trimble for governor. While the goal was to split the opposition, the Democrats were tainted with Know-Nothingism, a point not lost on the foreign element in Cincinnati. Chase won the election, though he did poorly in southwestern Ohio.[75]

In the fall of 1856, the Democratic Party indeed selected Pendleton as their candidate for Congress from the First District and William Groesbeck from the Second District just as they had two years earlier. The *Enquirer* remembered the 1854 contest in its columns by calling Pendleton the candidate representing "the cause of civil and religious liberty and political equality." The newspaper contended that Pendleton was a Democrat of "excellent attainments . . . unblemished private character . . . principle and conviction . . . [who has] the hearty support of our business and commercial men."[76] Even before the opposition, which had previously been the fusion party and was now the Republican Party, had named a candidate, Pendleton took the stump. In Georgetown, Ohio, he argued that the Compromise of 1850 and the Kansas-Nebraska Act were analogous, agreeing with the popular sovereignty aspects of both laws, which represented deep-seated Jacksonian principle. While the Ohio Democratic Party had retained up to this time a platform plank in opposition to the expansion of slavery, it recognized that the federal government did not have the power to interfere with the institution where it previously existed. By the 1856 election, however, the party abandoned this position and accepted the principle of popular sovereignty in the territories. Pendleton supported both the Democratic presidential candidate, James Buchanan, and the revised party platform.[77]

Meanwhile, the Republicans selected a congressional candidate. Timothy Day had occupied the seat for two years, but he suffered from severe physical afflictions and declined a second term. Confiding in his friend Frederick Hassaurek, a German Cincinnatian, he said that he would rather not run, and "nothing but the direst necessity on which my honor, my friends and the cause shall be involved, will make me consent."[78] The *Enquirer* accused Day of being a "Black Republican," or an abolitionist, and said that he was using health as an excuse not to run because he knew he would lose. Nevertheless, Day maintained that he had heart problems. With his withdrawal as a candidate, the Republican Party nominated Alphonso Taft, a prominent Cincinnati lawyer and judge.[79] Taft's party nominated John C. Frémont for president on a platform committed to fighting the extension of slavery. The specter of nativism remained alive in this election, and the Know-Nothings, upset at Republican emphasis on the slavery extension issue, nominated Millard Fillmore as their candidate on the American Party ticket.

Pendleton organized his campaign somewhat differently from his previous effort. Hamilton County Democrats planned some twenty-five meetings for the campaign in the First and Second Districts alone. They continued to attack the Republicans as they had in 1854, associating them with the Know-Nothings. In this election, however, Pendleton and the Democrats directly addressed the slavery issue. They accused their opponents of exploiting the atrocities in Kansas in an effort to dissolve the Union and give the Northern states control of the federal government. In an effort to confuse the voters, the Republicans charged Pendleton with making Free Soil speeches. Pendleton stood to gain from portraying himself as a Free Soiler, as many Germans voters supported that position. He could only do so, however, at the risk of offending the majority of his own party and losing the support of the *Enquirer*. The *Enquirer* reported that his speeches confirmed his support of popular sovereignty.

The *Commercial* also accused Pendleton and the Democrats of working in collusion with the Know-Nothings. It reminded voters of Democratic tactics in the 1855 election. In addition to trying to associate the Democrats with the Know-Nothings, Republicans such as Timothy Day tried to convince the Germans that any Know-Nothingism left in the Republican Party was harmless. Day tried repeatedly to assure his German friend Hassaurek that the Know-Nothings were not to be feared. In fact, Day said that Hassaurek's own prejudice against Catholics made him a "half K[now] N[othing]." Day suggested that the faction would eventually "be transferred to the South, and become allied to the present Democratic Party."[80] Speaking as a Republican, Day exemplified the efforts of his party to gain the German vote. Hassaurek and other Germans did vote Republican because they advocated Free Soil, but they had to overcome their concerns about the party's past connections with Know-Nothingism. Pendleton could gain very little from associating with the Know-Nothings, as that would estrange the predominantly Democratic immigrant population. In 1855, the campaign tactic had attempted to split the Republicans rather than unite the Democrats with the Know-Nothings. Besides, the Know-Nothings had nominated John Torrence to run against Taft and Pendleton. The Democracy stood to gain from the split within the old fusion party and would not jeopardize itself by fraternizing with the nativists.[81]

The Democrats broadened the scope of the election by exposing what they considered to be the deleterious goals of the Black Republicans. Pendleton and his partisan brothers condemned the Republican program for including temperance laws, personal liberty laws to circumvent the Fugitive Slave Law, naturalization laws limiting the power of state courts to bestow citizenship, and national civil liberty laws granting African Americans the right of citizenship. Each of these issues meant the enhancement of the federal government's power to the detriment of states' rights. In addition, each of these issues represented one of the various factions in the Republican Party. The temperance, personal liberty, and civil liberty laws exemplified the "Puritan" aspect of the old Whig platform, while the nativist plank appealed to the Know-Nothings. As the two major parties emerged from the political turmoil of the late 1840s and early 1850s, they solidified around two very distinct sets of principles.[82]

Pendleton won the election, garnering 6,134 votes to Taft's 4,256. The Know-Nothing candidate obtained only 2,648 votes. While Pendleton and Groesbeck won, the Republicans made gains over their 1855 showing in Cincinnati. Much of that increase resulted from Germans voting for the Republican ticket. The *Enquirer* lamented this outcome, wondering how they could support the nativist-tainted Republicans while the Democrats had worked for so long to oppose the Know-Nothings. In spite of some losses, the Democrats of Hamilton County stood solidly for Buchanan, who won the region by some 3,500 votes. Following receipt of the official notice of victory, Pendleton looked ahead to taking his seat in the U.S. Congress, the seat his father had held sixteen years earlier. At thirty-two, he faced impending turbulent times, the worst in the young country's history. Holding to the Jacksonian principles he espoused in the 1856 campaign, Pendleton formed a lasting political philosophy, one that would eventually form the basis of the midwestern Democratic political ideology and one that made him much more than a parochial Ohio politician.[83]

The Young Politician
from Cincinnati

T he significance of judicial and municipal reform in Ohio paled in
comparison with the gravity of the issues the state's youngest congressman faced when he took his seat in the House of Representatives
in Washington, D.C. George Pendleton ran for office in 1856 in support of the
Democratic national platform and its candidate, James Buchanan of Pennsylvania. In previous years, the Democracy of Ohio had denounced the institution of slavery and considered it their duty "to see all power clearly given by
the terms of the national compact to prevent its increase."[1] At the same time,
Democrats recognized the rights of states to control their own internal institutions. In 1856, Ohio Democrats altered their platform to adopt Sen. Stephen
A. Douglas's position on the Kansas-Nebraska Act providing for popular sovereignty in the western territories.[2]

These changes placed Pendleton in a difficult position, but one that ultimately helped propel him from being a local politician to becoming an important national player from his first day in Congress. He accepted his state party's
official position and supported Buchanan in the campaign, yet Pendleton's position proved perilous. Buchanan personally opposed the doctrine of popular
sovereignty in the territories because it suggested that Congress was unable to
rule them effectively. He distrusted the resolution of important issues, such
as slavery, by poorly educated frontiersmen who knew little of such political
complexities. After his nomination, however, Buchanan believed he had to represent the party's platform and professed his support of the Douglas plan. After
his inauguration, Buchanan abandoned this commitment. As a result, the Democracy split between Douglas men and administration supporters, each side
courting the support of those who had yet to embrace a position. Pendleton
was one of those pivotal votes, and both sides had high expectations of him.[3]

Conflicts in Kansas Territory heated up when the territorial legislature called for a constitutional convention. In response to complaints that Missourians had commandeered the political process in Kansas and formed the bulk of the proslavery movement, the legislature instituted a strict deadline by which emigrants would have to enter the territory to be allowed to vote. Free-state Kansans viewed the deadline as detrimental to their cause because they would have a hard time getting like-minded settlers into the area in time, whereas proslavery Kansans could get Missourians to cross the border easily enough. As a result, free-state Kansans boycotted what they believed would be an unfair election of delegates for the constitutional convention. Not surprisingly, pro-slavery settlers won handily and began work on a constitution at Lecompton. Free-state Kansans, who had previously established an antislavery government at Topeka, complete with a constitution of their own, had acted without the sanction of government. They had failed to obtain congressional approval for admittance to the Union due to pressure from Southern members of Congress who supported the expansion of slavery. President Buchanan accepted the legitimacy of the Lecompton government because it was the result of action by the territorial legislature. As a result, he ignored the Topekans and refused to recognize that the Lecompton gathering failed to adequately represent the territorial settlers. Neither side relinquished its respective capital, and a series of bloody conflicts commenced. These episodes of violence set the scene for Buchanan's early days in office.[4]

One of Buchanan's first appointments was a new governor for Kansas Territory. Previous governors had been unable to stem the tide of violence. Buchanan's choice, Mississippian Robert J. Walker, wanted a popular vote, free of corruption, on the issue of slavery. Buchanan concurred, but in his inaugural address in Lecompton, Walker added that he would pursue an election on the entire constitution, not just on the issue of slavery. Northern Democrats were cautiously optimistic about Walker's speech, but Southerners lashed out against his argument that Kansas's climate would not sustain slavery. Walker was an expansionist and a friend of Douglas, making his selection by Buchanan politically shrewd. Buchanan tried to appeal to both Southerners and Northern Douglasites with this choice. Walker agreed with popular sovereignty because it rejected the idea that Congress had any authority over the question of slavery in the territories.[5] Because of his commitment to popular sovereignty and his belief that Kansas was not suited for slavery, Walker continued to favor the free-state Kansans in speeches even as the Lecompton government called for a constitutional convention, thus placing Buchanan in a difficult position.[6]

Before the convention gathered, Kansans had to determine the method to elect its members. To that end, the territorial legislature conducted a census to allocate delegates proportional to the population of each section of the territory. The census effort failed. Many settlers feared that census takers were actually assessing taxes or checking land claims and refused to record their names. Some towns were not even visited. Most importantly, free-state Kansans did not participate in the census in large numbers in order to protest the authority of the Lecompton government. The constitutional convention, based on this "census," was "irregular" at best and probably fraudulent.[7]

Representing only a minority of the population, the proslavery delegates dominated the Lecompton constitution convention in September 1857. The document they drafted required that governors be citizens for twenty years prior to their election. It also allowed the legislature to incorporate only one state bank. The proposed constitution prohibited free blacks from living in Kansas. As part of their plan for admission to the Union, the Lecompton drafters requested a huge grant of land from the federal government for railroads and public properties, four times the size of ones previously allocated to new states. The key aspects of the document, however, revolved around slavery. It contained a clause allowing new slaves into the territory, but apparently to appease popular sovereignty advocates, voters had the right to vote for the constitution with or without that clause. If Kansans voted against the clause, those holding slaves in the state at the time of its admission would still be allowed to keep them. The children of those slaves born in Kansas would eventually be free, and no additional slaves would be brought into the state. There was also a clause that prohibited tampering with the section of the constitution dealing with the current slaves until 1864, and then only by a vote of two-thirds of both houses of the legislature. In essence, this process protected current slave owners, a fact that angered antislavery advocates who wished to bar slavery, both in the present and in the future. This provision also outraged Senator Douglas and his followers, though it assuaged the concerns of Southerners. In the final analysis, the Lecompton constitution was proslavery and appealed to most Southern Democrats and some Northern Democrats. The nation awaited President Buchanan's response.[8]

In his first days in office, George Pendleton watched closely as events unfolded in Kansas, and he appeared to vacillate. He had more than a year from the time of his election until he took his seat to contemplate his position. He recognized the potentially divisive impact the Lecompton constitution could have on the Democrats, the sole remaining national political party. The Thirty-fifth Congress consisted of 128 Democrats, 92 Republicans, and 14 Know-Nothings. Of the Democrats, only 53 were Northerners.[9] Early business in December 1857 included the election of House officers, particularly the speaker and the clerk. Because the choice hinged on the party's internal factional struggles, Pendleton was caught in a monumental crisis. Buchanan supported James L. Orr of South Carolina, against the Illinois Douglasite Thomas L. Harris. Harris's supporters agreed to vote for Orr, fearing the nomination of a Southern Democratic contender, Georgian Alexander H. Stephens, in return for administration backing for a Douglas man for House clerk. Pendleton acquiesced to the deal, voting for Orr for speaker and James C. Allen for clerk, thus splitting the two important positions between the factions. While some Northern Democrats felt more secure with Orr than with Stephens, the two varied little on important issues such as Kansas. Speaker Orr stacked the ten most important House committees with administration supporters, naming six Buchanan men as committee chairs. Not considered an administration man, Pendleton landed on the Committee of Military Affairs, an assignment that neither enhanced nor injured his reputation.[10]

As the Kansas issue evolved, Pendleton developed a position that focused less on factional leaders and principle than on expediency. As a result, he appeared to be buffeted about by the winds of political infighting. Frequently those winds blew in from Cincinnati in the form of scathing editorials in the *Enquirer,* but even now Pendleton was becoming his own man. In the end, Pendleton evaluated each vote in light of a desire to maintain Democratic unity and the Jacksonian ideology he had clung to as a young partisan.

Pendleton's first term in the House began with the critical vote on the Lecompton constitution that riveted national attention. Free-state voters boycotted the polls to negate the legitimacy of the fraudulent convention. The result was predictable: more than six thousand proslavery men voted for the Lecompton constitution with slavery against fewer than six hundred dissenters. Meanwhile, the free-state legislature called for a territorial referendum on January 4, 1858. In spite of the obvious fraud in the December election, which an investigative committee had found to include not only the unsatisfactory census but also "stuffed" ballot boxes, President Buchanan accepted the vote affirming Lecompton. Governor Walker resigned in protest. He believed the vote was unfair, but he lacked the power to rectify the situation because of the president's position. The second vote, held under the new governor, James W. Denver, would have pleased Walker. The referendum gave voters three choices: accepting the constitution with or without slavery, or rejecting the constitution altogether. The results were overwhelming. With a majority of more than ten thousand, the citizens of Kansas repudiated Lecompton. The vote forced Buchanan to choose between principle and expediency, leaving many congressmen simply confused and frightened.[11]

Prior to the two votes on the Lecompton constitution, President Buchanan had endorsed the proslavery government. Buchanan accepted the Lecompton constitution because he was a legalist.[12] The Lecomptonites had formed their convention and proceeded to create a government under the authority of the territorial legislature. If the free-state men did not wish to send delegates to the convention or to vote in the December ratification election, such was their prerogative. In addition, Buchanan, who owed his election in large part to the South, read the Dred Scott decision of the previous year to mean that Congress could not decide the issue of slavery in the territories and that the territorial legislatures themselves did not have this right. By his endorsement of this decision, he ruled out both the Republican notion of congressional authority over the territories and the Democratic concept of popular sovereignty. The decision about slavery should be made, he believed, after statehood was attained. Buchanan also faced secessionist threats from Georgia and Alabama if the Kansas Territory did not enter the Union under the Lecompton constitution. In an effort to maintain the Democracy, as well as the Union, the president ignored his Northern supporters' wishes in order to mitigate the threatening voices of many Southerners. He just wanted the issue settled. As the battle lines began to solidify, Pendleton and his fellow congressmen grappled with their own positions.[13]

Sen. Stephen Douglas had made his view on Kansas known in 1854 through the Kansas-Nebraska Act and maintained his support for popular sovereignty throughout the conflict. The anti-Lecompton bloc in the House formed around Douglas's principles. The group included five representatives from Illinois, six from Ohio, six from Pennsylvania, three from Indiana, two from New York, and one each from California and New Jersey. Pendleton occasionally allied with this group, although his vote sometimes strayed to support the administration. Of the eight Democratic congressmen from Ohio, only one was strictly a Buchanan man. The contest in the House was much closer than in the Senate, where the bill to admit Kansas under the Lecompton constitution passed easily. Republicans began to support Douglasite Democrats and viewed popular sovereignty as the only available route to a free Kansas after the administration Democrats got the bill through the Senate. In a series of votes in the House, the battle lines emerged.[14]

George Pendleton's voting record on the admission of Kansas did not indicate a strong adherence to one side of the issue or the other. Variations and apparent contradictions suggest the tug-of-war going on in the House for the swing votes of men such as Pendleton. Rep. Alexander Stephens, supported by the administration, took the lead in the House to push the bill through. He proposed to refer the bill to the Committee on the Territories over which he presided. Pendleton voted against Stephens. When the anti-Lecompton Thomas Harris of Illinois suggested sending the bill to a select committee with instructions to investigate the situation in Kansas, Pendleton voted in the negative again. The

Harris proposal would have delayed consideration of the bill for some time and risked further revelations of fraud in Kansas. Finally, James Hughes of Indiana moved to assign the bill to a select committee, chosen by Speaker Orr, with no instructions. Pendleton supported the Hughes resolution. These early votes indicate that Pendleton generally supported Buchanan, probably due to a similar desire to see the issue settled quickly, to preserve the party, and to maintain national unity. Even so, Pendleton could argue that Douglas's principle of popular sovereignty was consistent with the Jacksonian perspective of democracy, which explained his other votes. In addition to being pulled in these opposing directions, Pendleton also faced several other pressures.[15]

While new to the House, Pendleton recognized a political milieu that could catapult him from obscure Ohio politician to a figure of national stature, provided he made no false steps. Pendleton caught on very quickly. He saw that he needed to court the favor of men in power, particularly Speaker Orr, who had the influence to make or break his political career. But Pendleton was no mere sycophant. With each vote critical, he understood that his position was personally advantageous because each side needed his support.

As a Northern Democrat, Pendleton anticipated the impending crisis within his party and within the Union. He had two strong reasons to support efforts to avoid disunion. First, he was passionately committed to the Union and believed it could be preserved if the Constitution were interpreted correctly. Second, if the Union were to split, his party would lose a substantial portion of its strength because Democrats dominated the South. In light of these considerations, he tried to assuage the conflicts within his party that threatened not only the party and the Union but also his career.

Pendleton understood the tensions among his constituents and the need to serve them. Midwestern Democrats predominantly supported popular sovereignty, and Pendleton had run his campaign based on that principle. He tried to balance the seemingly incompatible positions within the party in his voting, and the result was sometimes confusing to his friends and foes. Pendleton would spend most of the next campaign explaining his record in response to the charge of inconsistency made by his Republican opponent.[16]

While Pendleton pondered his options, lobbyists used any pretext to influence swing voters, especially those among the Ohio delegation. Along with his friend and fellow Ohioan William Groesbeck, Pendleton found himself a center of attention at numerous parties during the Washington social season. Members on both sides of the issue attended these functions to persuade, pressure, and cajole. President Buchanan was equally active in subtle arm-twisting. He met with key men individually to discuss his fears about the threatened secession of some Southern states if the question were not resolved in their favor. At the same time, he explained his reasons for supporting the Lecompton constitution. The president also wielded raw political power. He dismissed Douglasite postmasters in Chicago, Cleveland, Columbus, and Cincinnati and replaced them with men committed to the administration. In spite of his influence and that of the House leadership, many Northern Democrats remained loyal to Douglas.[17]

While considering the Senate bill to admit Kansas, William Montgomery, a Democratic representative from Pennsylvania, offered an amendment to re-submit the constitution to the people. Buchanan did not accept the results of the January 4, 1858, vote in Kansas. Indeed, revealing his Southern minded-ness, both he and a majority of the Senate supported admitting Kansas under the Lecompton constitution in spite of the overwhelming vote against it. The Montgomery amendment proposed that, if the people of Kansas accepted the constitution in yet another vote, the state would be admitted immediately. But if they did not agree, they could draft a new constitution. Kentucky senator John J. Crittenden had previously offered the same amendment in his cham-ber, but without success. In spite of a renewed effort by the administration, Montgomery's amendment passed, though a majority of Democrats opposed it. The bill for admission now returned to the Senate for reconsideration. Pend-leton had voted for the Montgomery proposal.[18]

The *Cincinnati Enquirer* responded angrily to Pendleton's vote and to the twenty-one other Democrats who supported the Montgomery amendment. Pendleton defended himself, contending that this proposal was consistent with the principle of popular sovereignty. Indeed, Senator Douglas supported the Crittenden and Montgomery amendments. The *Enquirer,* now squarely be-hind the Buchanan administration, declared that the votes of the twenty-two Democrats were disloyal to the party because they had sided with the sectional Republican Party. Yet the newspaper was not as principled as it appeared. The editor, James J. Faran, denounced the representative of his own district, whom he had supported in the last election, for purely personal reasons. President Buchanan rewarded Faran by appointing him postmaster of Cincinnati.[19]

Buchanan offered political rewards to congressmen who supported the ad-ministration. He focused his attention on the twenty-two Democrats who had failed to vote consistently for his position. He promised that if they voted to send the amended bill for admission to a conference committee made up of members from both houses of Congress, it would include a version of the Montgomery amendment. Buchanan even promised Ohio's congressional caucus that he would accept two Ohio volunteer regiments for the Utah expeditionary force, which had widespread public support. The president was sending to Salt Lake City a large military force to quell the Mormon rebellion. Mormon leader Brigham Young had armed his men, fearing that a federal presence in the territory would bring to an end the society of saints. Buchanan's acceptance of the Ohio regiments was predicated on the support of Buckeye representatives. Pendleton, Groesbeck, and Samuel S. Cox received letters from prospective officers for the two regiments that endorsed the president's plan. The pressure on Pendleton from these Ohioans to abandon Douglas and popular sovereignty became acute.[20]

Senators rejected the Montgomery amendment and voted to create a Committee of Conference to draft a compromise measure. Senate leaders delayed returning this proposal to the House until after the spring elections in Connecticut, Rhode Island, and Ohio took place, hoping that administration men would win. They lost. The House then voted again to return the bill with the Montgomery amendment to the Senate. Pendleton favored this move, but the Senate proved intractable. When the House voted on the Senate proposal to create a conference committee, Pendleton sided with the administration men in its support. The House stalemated, but Speaker Orr broke the tie in favor of the conference committee. It is not difficult to speculate on Pendleton's motivations for advocating the conference committee. The party factions were no longer so easily defined. The Lecompton constitution was now dead. Though Douglas ultimately opposed the conference committee idea, it was not clear that the compromise would have been totally distasteful to him. The pressure from the *Enquirer,* which had considerable influence in Cincinnati, may have affected Pendleton. Another possible explanation for Pendleton's vote was his belief that the deadlock served only to hurt Democrats, driving him to seek a compromise. In any case, his decision facilitated the conference committee compromise.[21]

Speaker Orr appointed the House members of the Kansas Committee of Conference, including Alexander Stephens and William H. English of Indiana. An ambitious young representative, English eagerly desired the approval of President Buchanan and the powerful administration men of the House. The president and his supporters planned to make English the author of the committee bill because he was not closely tied to either faction. If Stephens's name were attached to the bill, it would encounter the opposition of Northern Democrats preventing its passage. Stephens wrote much of the bill, however, and when the committee adjourned, he was very happy with the results.[22]

The committee proposal, known as the English Bill, called for some changes in the Lecompton constitution. The Lecomptonites had requested a huge land grant from the federal government, more than 23.5 million acres. This grant was equal to the size of Indiana and four times larger than that given other new states. The English Bill reduced the grant to 25 percent of the original request. In return, Kansas could enter the Union as a state if the voters ratified the Lecompton constitution. If they rejected the constitution again, Kansas would have to wait until its population rose to 93,000, the required number of people for representation in Congress, before being eligible for statehood. Stephens attempted to place the focus on the land grant, not slavery. He further sought to pacify anti-Lecomptonites by resubmitting the constitution to the people, while conciliating Southerners by delaying statehood if voters rejected it. As an administration man, Stephens kept Buchanan abreast of the contents of the bill, maintaining his approval. He was unsure, however, how Douglas and the anti-Lecomptonites would respond.[23]

Senator Douglas agonized over the compromise for some time. He thought that possibly, if he unified the party by accepting it, he would bolster support for his presidential bid. On the other hand, some of his supporters argued that the inequity of allowing either immediate admission under Lecompton or delayed admission provided for popular sovereignty in principle, but not practice. He also had his own Illinois constituency to consider. After the Illinois Democratic Convention soundly rejected the compromise idea, Douglas stopped leaning toward acceptance and decided to oppose the compromise. He could not turn his back on those who held the keys to his political future. In spite of Douglas's opposition, the English Bill passed the Senate 31 to 22, and the House 112 to 103.[24] Although the Republicans had supported the Montgomery proposal as the best means to obtain a free Kansas, they did not accept the new compromise. They viewed the land grant and promise of immediate admission under the Lecompton constitution as bribery. Pendleton, who had stood with Douglas on the Montgomery amendment earlier, now voted in support of the English Bill. While the *Enquirer* praised his vote as regaining the confidence of Ohio Democrats, Republicans attacked his support of political bribery. Pendleton believed he had been consistent throughout the process and responded to the allegations in a public letter to his home district and in a speech before the House.[25]

In the May 10, 1858, letter to his constituents, Pendleton summarized his position on the English Bill. He asserted that the Lecompton constitution, while it had been created under "the forms of law" by a territorial constitutional convention, did not have public support. The Topeka government, however, was without any legal foundation.[26] Pendleton argued that the free-state Kansans easily dominated the proslavery element in the territory but that they did not wish admittance under the Lecompton constitution. Yet if Kansas did enter, the free-state men could make any changes they wished after gaining statehood, as they had such a large majority. If they did not want to enter the Union under it, they had the right to call another constitutional convention and write a new constitution. When they reached the requisite population, they could enter the Union under these new terms. He did not consider this portion of the bill to be a bribe, because the free-state men would control the government. If anything, he suggested, it favored that political group, "for to that majority is given the right and the power to decide whether their interests . . . require them to avail themselves of [immediate statehood]."[27] The option, which caused a delay in statehood, was constitutionally offered to any territory.

Pendleton also addressed in this letter and in his speech to the House of Representatives the Republican assertion that the land grant was a bribe. He countered their attacks by stressing that the Montgomery Amendment, which Republicans supported, contained the same land grant as the English Bill. If that was a bribe, then they were equally guilty. Continuing, he argued that the federal government gave no land or money to any individual, but to the entire state, a precedent Congress had established in Minnesota. Growing more acerbic, he queried if that had been a bribe as well. If the people had rejected the Lecompton constitution, which demanded more than 23 million acres of land, "will it bribe them to accept it when you offer them only six millions?"[28] Pendleton concluded his letter by illustrating how the English Bill was similar to the Montgomery Amendment. Both allowed admission under Lecompton if Kansans had accepted it. Both provided a land grant. While the English Bill delayed statehood if the voters rejected the Lecompton constitution, the Republicans had originally introduced the idea of delay. He concluded by summing up his thoughts regarding Republican criticisms of his vote: "I would suggest . . . that when they voted for the Montgomery Amendment they took up their residence in a glass house, out of which it is very dangerous to throw stones at those who voted for the conference bill."[29]

In the end, Pendleton clearly believed that, while he appeared to be an administration man at times, he had adhered to the democratic principle of popular sovereignty, a position easily accommodated by Jacksonian ideology. The emphasis on Kansans deciding their own fate in the English Bill demonstrated this doctrine. Pendleton believed that he had been consistent to principle, if not to individuals. While a master at argumentation, even Pendleton could not explain away his early inconsistency. Douglas saw things differently and decided to reject the English Bill, which angered the *Enquirer.* In a hard-hitting editorial, the paper pitied Douglas for digging up the bribery issue, an attack originated by the "Black Republicans." By contrast, Pendleton was back in Faran's graces, even as Pendleton made it clear he was his own man. Consequently, the *Enquirer* supported him on most other issues that arose during his first term in Congress.[30]

The *Enquirer* was especially pleased with Pendleton's continued concern for Cincinnati issues. As a state senator, he had been mindful of local matters, a practice he continued in Washington. In the Thirty-fifth Congress, he introduced a bill to make Cincinnati a port of entry. Cincinnati merchants had long desired this status to circumvent the expensive procedure of hiring agents in New York City to buy commodities from the European market. In addition, the extra costs involved in the storage of goods in eastern warehouses prior to transportation west were also oppressive. Yet Pendleton's fight for this change in designation made little headway during his first term.[31] Pendleton further worked to aid Cincinnati merchants by lowering the tolls on the Louisville and Portland Canal to the Ohio River.[32] One final example of Pendleton's focus on local issues was his resolution regarding Ohio judiciary districts. He proposed to divide the state into two districts to afford more efficient execution of federal court proceedings. The reason, he explained, was that Ohio's growing population demanded changes to keep up with increasing judicial needs.[33]

At the same time, Pendleton maintained his focus on government reform. Returning to an issue that had evolved when Timothy Day defeated him in the election of 1854, Pendleton condemned the franking privileges of congressmen. Day had encountered accusations during his term that he abused his franking privilege. As a state senator, Pendleton had thought it was not the duty of the Ohio treasury to pay the postage fees of members of the General Assembly.[34] In the Congress, he continued his quest for government economy and efficiency by voting for a proposal to abolish the franking privilege. Although the vote was close, the bill failed to pass. Pendleton feared that such provisions gave an unfair advantage to incumbents and smacked of the type of privilege Jacksonians detested. Yet he was also motivated by a concern for governmental fiscal responsibility. To further prove his reputation as a watchdog of the treasury, Pendleton also voted against a Senate amendment to provide congressmen with reimbursement for travel expenses to and from Washington, D.C. Throughout his career Pendleton maintained a belief in government efficiency and a perception that a public office was a public trust.[35]

Apart from his focus on local and reform issues, Pendleton did not stint his other duties. As a member of the Committee on Military Affairs, he examined closely the potential threats facing the nation during his first term and considered a bill to enlarge the army. In his first significant speech to the House, Pendleton addressed the issues pertaining to this proposal and used the occasion to deal with a variety of related topics. He agreed with the views of an administration man, Charles Faulkner of Virginia, who desired to increase the size of the regular U.S. Army. In particular, Pendleton described the vast area that the army, numbering just over seventeen thousand men, was required to protect from enemy invasions and Native American uprisings. Indeed, the government expected this thin force to secure an area "larger than all Europe together," a task that an army of 100,000 would find difficult.[36] While he had assumed, prior to reading reports on the military, that the administration simply wanted to enlarge an already bloated federal government, he now realized that more than a temporary volunteer force was necessary to meet national security needs. In addition to enlarging the army, he hoped that appropriate officials would alter the process of promotion within the military. No longer should ranks be awarded on the basis of simple seniority, he argued, but on merit. Later in his congressional career, Pendleton would apply this same principle to civil service positions.[37]

Pendleton continued by addressing each of the national concerns that could require military intervention. Expressing the common misconceptions and bigotry of the time, he referred to the Great Plains as "inhospitable for man and beasts" and queried whether the Digger Indians, who lived there, were truly men. Those Indians, whose humanity was in question, posed a real threat to western expansion, and, he asserted, the army's job was to subdue them. With 250,000 Indians in the West who threatened settlements from the Mississippi to Washington territory, he concluded that Congress needed to enlarge the army.[38]

Pendleton also mentioned the most recent military foray on the frontier, the Mormon Rebellion. After trying to live amidst those who viewed their lifestyle practices as antithetical to American values during the 1830s and 1840s, the Mormons followed their leader, Brigham Young, west to create their Zion. They established the State of Deseret that remained independent of federal control until after the Mexican Cession in 1848. The U.S. government made Young the governor of the new Utah Territory, but a chorus of opposition that disdained the Mormons for practices such as polygamy persuaded President Buchanan to establish greater control over the territory. Then, too, the threats of secession from Southern states made Pendleton acutely aware that the federal government could not allow any segment of the country to act independently of the Union. Federal justices with little tact and a personal dislike for the Mormons only exacerbated an already tense situation. Territorial justice William Drummond abruptly resigned after Buchanan's inauguration, stating that Young had continually resisted him and committed crimes against the country. In reality, Drummond was a gambling adulterer whom the Mormons could hardly stomach, but more importantly, he had attempted to systematically aggrandize control of Utah under his own authority. Buchanan responded without investigation and had Gen. Winfield Scott send 2,500 troops westward to install a new governor to replace Young. Young responded by raising his own army, fearing that the federal government would restrict Mormon religious and political practices.[39]

Pendleton reacted harshly to the taking up of arms by the Mormons. He lashed out at Young, who retained both "the powers of the government and the church."[40] The Mormons had repudiated the government of the United States and deserved subjugation, Pendleton maintained. Because they refused to accept their duly appointed governor, it was the "duty of the Government of the United States to . . . vindicate its own dignity, and the power of its law."[41] He agreed with Buchanan's decision to dispatch a force carrying an "olive branch," but with sufficient strength to crush the rebellion "even if it should be with the entire extermination of the rebels."[42] Young finally acquiesced to federal authority and allowed the new governor into Utah. He wanted peace above all other concerns. Pendleton clearly supported the right of the federal government to control the territories and to use military force if necessary. His position in this case could be seen in contrast to his views on Kansas, where he sought a peaceful resolution through popular sovereignty. This distinction can be explained by Pendleton's prejudices against the Mormons and his belief that their practices threatened American society. Further, Pendleton perceived the Kansas debate as one pitting differing constitutional interpretations against another and one that could not and should not be handled by force.[43]

In addition to subduing a rebellious territory, Pendleton sought to bolster the military to foster national expansion, a goal that both of the Democratic fathers, Jefferson and Jackson, sought. Pendleton was quite interested in Cuba. The Spanish owned the island, whose proximity to Florida allowed pirates to capture American goods and interrupt commerce by using Cuba as a base. Pendleton's expansionist desires encompassed Central America as well. In that regard, he desired to terminate the 1850 Clayton-Bulwer Treaty with Great Britain that provided for joint control of any Central American canal. President Zachary Taylor's secretary of state, John Clayton, offered the British the treaty, hoping the promise of joint control would allay British concerns about the region and encourage them to withdrawal their troops. The treaty backfired on the United States and only solidified British control of the region when their forces did not leave.[44] Now the time was ripe, Pendleton asserted, for the United States to begin securing control of the Western Hemisphere, for "the interests of this continent require that American influence, American interests, and American policy should predominate throughout the land covered by the treaty."[45]

Even more, Pendleton argued, ownership of Cuba would provide the federal government with a means to more effectively uphold the 1808 legislation that prohibited the African slave trade. Smugglers used Cuba as a stepping stone to Southern states to sell their human commodity. Pendleton backed efforts during his first term to stop smugglers. Twice he voted against Southern Democrats to prevent the reduction of appropriations for combating the slave trade. He supported a resolution advocating the government's duty to enforce the slave trade ban. While the Republicans attacked Democrats who supported the annexation of Cuba as an attempt to continue the slave trade, or even abolish slave trade laws, Pendleton's voting record on the issue denied that assertion.

Nonetheless, Pendleton recognized that annexing Cuba would have the effect of increasing the slave territory of the United States, a boon for the political and economic interests of the South.[46]

Congress adjourned until after the fall elections of 1858, a month and a half following the vote on the English Bill. Pendleton planned to run for reelection, and the major issue of his first term shaped the key elements in the contest. He faced a more difficult challenge this time. The Know-Nothing Party had fused with the Republicans, no longer dividing the opposition vote as it had in 1856. Delegates at the Hamilton County Democratic Convention renominated Pendleton from the First District, as well as Groesbeck, his fellow partisan from the Second District.[47]

Portents for the coming election were not particularly hopeful for the Ohio Democracy. The conflict within the party over the admission of Kansas had caused deep wounds that did not heal quickly in spite of a relatively uneventful state convention. The platform endorsed the English Bill and stated that the Lecompton question was a dead issue. Though the party had done well in the 1857 state elections, gaining control of the General Assembly and mounting a strong if unsuccessful challenge to Gov. Salmon P. Chase's reelection bid, the factionalization begun in 1858 over Kansas remained unhealed. Key newspaper editors, such as Faran of the *Enquirer* and J. W. Gray of the *Cleveland Plain Dealer,* took opposing sides in the debate. Faran and other administration supporters won federal patronage rewards while Gray and the Douglasites did not. The debates in Illinois between Douglas and Republican senatorial hopeful Abraham Lincoln kept Douglas's name in the paper and added fuel to the smoldering embers of dissension in Ohio.[48]

The Republicans exploited Democratic divisions to the fullest in their campaign. Timothy C. Day, their nominee for the First District of Ohio, had defeated Pendleton for the seat in 1854. Still suffering from poor health, which had kept him out of the race in 1856, Day could not campaign extensively. Instead, he attacked Pendleton's record through a series of public letters. The *Cincinnati Commercial* provided Day with an editorial forum from which he accused Pendleton of vacillation on the Lecompton constitution. In recounting Pendleton's voting record, Day censured him for indecision and leveled the same bribery charges over the English Bill that Pendleton had addressed in his speech before the House. In these columns, Day questioned who represented the true Democracy, Douglas or Buchanan, and tried to exploit Democratic factionalism. Day even suggested that Pendleton had favored free-soil principles in the 1856 election but had changed his mind. Pandering to the Know-Nothing faction of the Fusion Party, the *Commercial* referred to Pendleton's supporters as the "Celtic District."[49] Pendleton deigned not to reply to these tired and baseless criticisms. He was satisfied that he had addressed these issues before and felt no need to reiterate his position again. Rather, Pendleton made the rounds in the district, speaking on several occasions and standing on his legislative record. His tactics were so successful that noted Republican Rutherford B. Hayes believed he would win reelection in spite of the fusion.[50]

The *Enquirer* defended Pendleton against Day and the Republicans by emphasizing Day's own inconsistencies while in the House. The Congress in which Day participated grappled with the Dunn Kansas Bill. That bill would have expanded the Fugitive Slave Law to cover the territory, extended slavery there until at least 1858, and designated all children born to slaves in Kansas as slaves. An issue of this importance, Faran noted, demanded Day's attention, and yet he failed to vote one way or the other. He also dodged votes on other important items such as the Legislative Appropriations Bill, the Naval Appropriations Bill, and the Civil Appropriations Bill. Faran reiterated Pendleton's defense of the English Bill, citing its similarities with the Montgomery Amendment, which most Republicans supported. Finally, Faran attacked Day's desire to make African Americans politically equal with whites, thereby enhancing sectional strife and raising the specter of racial discord.[51]

The divisions in the Ohio Democracy resulted in dramatic Republican gains. Democrats won only six of the twenty-one congressional districts. William Groesbeck was among the victims. Clement L. Vallandigham, whose election in 1856 was so close that his right to a congressional seat was contested and resulted in his missing most of the Thirty-fifth Congress, won his campaign in the Third District. Vallandigham was a Democrat who, along with Pendleton, would rise to prominence in the Thirty-sixth and Thirty-seventh Congresses as a leading midwesterner. Pendleton won his reelection bid as well, defeating Day with a 346-vote majority.[52]

In resisting the public surge for Republicans, Pendleton maintained his primary support base due to his habitual attention to constituent concerns. Moreover, he proved that he could rise above party factionalism and political coercion while maintaining a commitment to principle. Just as important, Pendleton was the beneficiary of Day's illness, which blunted his prospects. The jubilation of victory was short-lived for Pendleton, however, as he pondered the coming term. The Union had almost dissolved over the admission of Kansas, and he was not naive enough to discount Southern threats of secession. The days when he was merely a parochial politician had passed, and Pendleton longed for their simplicity.[53]

The Pendleton family was rocked with scandal and tragedy during the final session of the Thirty-fifth Congress. Alice's brother, Philip Barton Key, had been carrying on an affair with the wife of Daniel Sickles of Washington, D.C.

At the time, Key was the U.S. district attorney for the district. When Sickles found out, he shot and killed Key in Lafayette Park. After burying her brother, Alice and George returned to Cincinnati for the break between sessions to mourn their loss and escape the whispers in Washington.

The atmosphere at the opening of the Thirty-sixth Congress was tense from the start. Three months prior to the first day of the session, John Brown had attacked the federal arsenal at Harpers Ferry, Virginia. Planning on seizing arms, Brown had hoped to gain the support of rebellious Virginian slaves along with antislavery groups in the state's far-western counties, establish a foothold in the mountains, and foment a series of slave insurrections throughout the South. That effort failed. Captured by federal and state militia, Brown was executed for treason. To House Southerners, this seemed the direct result of a book, *The Impending Crisis of the South,* written two years earlier by Hinton R. Helper. Helper instructed Southern yeomen farmers about how slavery hurt them economically and called upon them to assert their rights against oppressive plantation owners. Some Republicans financed the printing and distribution of this work for campaign purposes. When they mailed a circular to the nation's Republicans requesting funds for the project, the Democrats fired back that such revolutionary ideas had inspired John Brown. To distribute this book would cause more violence. The upshot was that Southern representatives came to the first session of Congress late in 1859 with little trust in their Republican colleagues.[54]

The battle over selection of congressional leaders dragged on for two months as a result of the consternation among many of the members. The Democrats had 101 votes, but 13 of those were anti-Lecompton men who had been ostracized from the party in the last Congress. The Republicans had 109 votes, but they too were short of a majority by 10 votes. There were 27 other members, mostly Southern American-Whigs. Pendleton originally voted for an administration man for speaker, as did the majority of Democrats, but no candidate gained a majority. As days became weeks, the Thirty-sixth Congress addressed no business. Members began forming coalitions to create a compromise on the House offices.[55]

The Republicans wooed the anti-Lecompton men and some of the American-Whigs, hoping to elect John Sherman of Ohio as speaker. The John Brown raid prevented many of the American-Whigs from voting with the Republicans. At one point, the Republicans tried to change the election rules so that a candidate with a plurality would win. Pendleton and Clement Vallandigham rose to speak against this suggestion and castigated it as unconstitutional. Days dragged on with no resolution, and legislation stalled. In an effort to break the impasse, Pendleton voted for an anti-Lecompton Democrat, John G. Davis of Indiana. When that proved unsuccessful, Pendleton switched his vote to an old-line Whig from North Carolina, William N. H. Smith. As a justification,

Pendleton explained that Smith told him that he had never been a member of the American or Know-Nothing Party. To further defend himself, Pendleton noted on the floor of Congress that because his constituency included a large number of Germans and Irishmen, he had ascertained before voting that Smith had never had any connection with the nativist group. After continued debate and a couple of potentially violent moments, the partisan opponents struck a deal to elect Republican William Pennington of New Jersey as speaker and an anti-Lecompton Democrat, John W. Forney of Pennsylvania, as clerk. With that question settled, Congress finally could take up the business at hand.[56]

While the country's concerns occupied most of Pendleton's time, he did not neglect the needs of the First District. Soon after the resolution of the speakership, Pendleton reintroduced his bill to make Cincinnati a port of entry. He advanced another bill to inquire into and set the salaries of Ohio's district court judges. Both bills went to committees. When the tariff came up for debate, Pendleton responded to a petition of nineteen Cincinnati businessmen calling for an increase in the duty on flaxseed, which was used in the production of linseed oil. The petition argued that if the tariff was not raised, western farmers would not be able to compete with the European flaxseed imports. Congress rejected Pendleton's proposal for a four-cent-per-bushel increase in the tariff, however.[57]

Pendleton also actively pursued legislation to benefit Ohio. In that regard, he delivered a speech concerning the enlargement of the Louisville and Portland Canal. He emphasized that he was not asking for federal funds to accomplish this request. The Democratic Party had long opposed the use of federal monies for internal improvements. Instead, the people of the Ohio Valley wished only for approval to use the tolls collected on the canal for improvements. Ever mindful of time limits on addresses in the House, Pendleton nonetheless used the opportunity to expound his views on the interrelationship between the Old Northwest and the Union. The canal serviced more than just the Northwest; allowing the tolls to be used as requested would benefit the entire country. Explicating the importance of his region, Pendleton continued, "The next census [would] tell of the power of the Northwest." As the area proceeded to grow in size and political strength, the federal government could serve the nation by addressing these local concerns.[58]

Continuing to clarify the importance of his section of the country, he maintained that the Midwest would preserve "those guarantees of liberty which are written in the Constitution . . . [and] it will tolerate no sentiment of disunion, because it will permit no infraction of the Constitution."[59] Even at this early time, Pendleton recognized the possibility of disunion and declared his own position and that of his constituents. He believed that adherence to the Constitution, viewed through the lens of a strict constructionist, would prevent secession.

An early controversy in the House followed the struggle for the speakership—the selection of the government printer. The Democrats had installed a Democratic printer in the Thirty-fifth Congress through promises to disperse excess profits to the Democratic Party. In the following Congress, the Republicans used the scandal to their benefit but subsequently engaged in similar practices. Pendleton denigrated this alleged Republican reform and questioned his fellow Buckeye representative, John Gurley, on the plan to divide the work between Senate and House printers. Pendleton believed that the Republicans planned on the two printers forming a partnership so that one printer did the work while both received pay. The party, he contended, would siphon off the excess profits for partisan use. While undoubtedly motivated by political concerns, Pendleton continued his first term's quest for efficiency in government. And he again voted to eliminate franking and the payment of travel expenses of congressmen.[60]

Because the Democrats had lost their position as the majority party, Pendleton supported an amendment to the House's rules ensuring all members the right to speak on topics they introduced. Too often, Pendleton asserted, the speaker cut off discussion after one member had spoken for only five minutes. The rules allowed debate on topics for five minutes per individual, but the debate could be cut off by a vote any time after the first five minutes. By manipulating the rules, Republicans often succeeded in abbreviating debate. Pendleton did not believe this was conducive to good lawmaking. He wished to see an amendment passed that guaranteed members time to speak or to add their own amendments. The amendment never came to a vote. When Vallandigham proposed that the rule limiting speeches to one hour be eliminated, Pendleton supported that change, but it failed as well.[61]

Two of the important issues of the previous Congress carried over into Pendleton's second term in the House, the admission of Kansas and the expansion of the army. Once again, a request of the Kansas Territory to join the Union caused dissension. In July 1859, Kansans met at Wyandotte to write a new constitution and then submitted it to Congress for admission following ratification. The English Bill required that because Kansans had rejected admission under the Lecompton constitution, they had to wait until the territory had enough people for representation in Congress, or 93,000 inhabitants. Congress had omitted federal appropriations for a census from the final draft of the appropriations bill in the previous session, so the territorial legislature conducted their own. The result was as inconclusive as the Lecompton census; the total reached only 60,000.[62]

Pendleton spoke on this question to defend his vote for admission under the Wyandotte constitution. He recognized that the census did not indicate that Kansas had reached the required number of citizens but stated that the census was void due to its poor execution. Several counties were not included, and the results in many other counties were incomplete. Based on his calculations, Pendleton told Congress that if the figures included those portions of the territory neglected by the census, "the population [would] not fall far short of the population estimated by the chairman of the Committee of Territories—one hundred and ten thousand."[63] As the population was far more than necessary based on this figure, Pendleton believed that he was consistent in voting for the English Bill and in supporting the admission of Kansas under the Wyandotte constitution. Even so, the state of Kansas was yet to be.[64]

Again a member of the Committee of Military Affairs, Pendleton faced the second ongoing issue from the last term, the question of enlarging the army. The issue took new shape because of the need to secure the borders of Texas. The majority on the committee believed that no need existed for more forces in Texas. Agreeing with President Buchanan, Pendleton believed a requirement existed for more troops, and he wanted to expand the regular army rather than muster volunteer regiments. The president and Pendleton shared an uneasiness caused by the robbing and killing of American settlers by marauding bands of Comanches, other Native Americans, and some Mexicans. Disturbed by the accusation that he and others who supported enlarging the force were intent on eradicating the Indians, Pendleton contended that the Indians should be punished but not annihilated. He reminded the House of the prudence the president had shown in his use of force in Utah and recommended that Buchanan be given the armed forces required to end depredations in Texas. Indeed, Pendleton feared that war with Mexico was again possible and that the United States was woefully unprepared.[65]

While Pendleton's concern about war with Mexico was misplaced, he and other Democrats looked ahead as Congress adjourned to the conflict that was sure to arise between the Southern and Northern wings of their party. It was that conflict that would eventually lead to war, not with another nation, but within the nation.

Ohio Democrats met early in 1860 in a state convention to elect delegates for the national convention at Charleston, South Carolina, scheduled for late April. Senator Douglas had cultivated the state of Ohio during the preceding months, visiting Cincinnati, among other places, in September 1859. Pendleton promoted Douglas's canvass of Ohio and was named an honorary vice president of his Cincinnati meeting. Douglas's spadework bore impressive fruit. When Hamilton County Democrats met in December, they voted overwhelmingly for Douglas. The state Democratic convention followed suit. Delegates endorsed the principle of congressional noninterference in territorial slavery, essentially endorsing popular sovereignty. Under that formula, when the people of a territory organized a legislature, they could decide on issues of domestic policy. As a sop to administration men, the convention included a phrase stating that any questions arising regarding the rights of property would be directed to the Supreme Court of the United States. Attempts by the few administration men elected to the convention to pass resolutions commending Buchanan on his presidency met resistance. Following the struggle between Northern and Southern Democrats over the Lecompton constitution, Ohio Democrats knew that the decisions made at Columbus would encounter opposition within the party. George E. Pugh, Pendleton's old law partner, now a U.S. senator, wrote to a friend concerning Douglas's chances in Ohio. Both native-born and foreign-born Buckeyes favored his nomination, according to Pugh, and he added that any man nominated at Charleston would gain the vote of Democrats in Ohio. If Douglas was not the nominee, however, he believed Ohio was lost in the general election. If that occurred, Pugh feared that the Southerners would have to "eat their own words" or secede. That worst case scenario was a "woeful alternative."[66]

Northern Democrats traveled south to the convention amidst Republican denunciations that they were "Doughfaces" in the service of Southern Democrats. Pendleton was not a delegate to the convention, and his presence at home allowed him to greet the latest addition to the family, a baby girl they named Jane. While the Pendletons rejoiced, the convention opened. Southern Democrats were in an intractable mood. Senator Pugh, hoping for moderation, made a lengthy speech castigating Southern reluctance to compromise. But Southerners demanded that the party adopt as a plank in the platform the principle that neither Congress nor a territorial legislature had the right to prohibit slavery in a territory. In addition, Congress must protect the private property—or enslaved African Americans in this case—of individuals within the territory through slave codes. Pugh countered that the Constitution prescribed no such right upon Congress to legislate in a territory once its legislature was elected. On the basis of constitutional proscriptions and previous Democratic platforms, Pugh argued that compromise was impossible. When other Northern Democrats followed Pugh and assumed the same position, Southerners left the convention and met at another hall in the city. The remaining Democrats did not extend an invitation for the bolters to return, and the convention adjourned for two months with neither a nominee nor a platform.[67] Pendleton must have read the press reports arriving in Cincinnati in great frustration. His diligent labors in the House to appease the Democratic factions and his efforts toward compromise in supporting the English Bill appeared to have been for naught. He endorsed the position of Pugh, however, and Pendleton's unwillingness to accept the Southern demands was evidenced by his identification with popular sovereignty during the 1859 Douglas tour. Personally, Pendleton agreed with Pugh's interpretation of the Constitution and would not allow those principles to be compromised. With great anxiety, therefore, Pendleton awaited the reconvening of the Democrats.

When the convention reassembled in Baltimore in late June 1860, delegates from both the Northern and the Southern states returned to the assembly, except for those from South Carolina. They refused to travel north for the convention. Some delegates from the Deep South were excluded, however, because of their disruptive role in the previous convention. Once again neither side proved willing to compromise. In spite of a public letter by Alexander Stephens of Georgia in favor of the Northern position of congressional noninterference, Southern Democrats refused to accept compromise. Senator Douglas twice sent messages to his convention lieutenants that he would be willing to withdraw as a candidate in favor of another noninterventionist Democrat, but the Southerners could tolerate scarcely such a candidate any more than Douglas himself. After his nomination, Douglas said that he would have advocated Stephens, but his supporters did not make such a proposal public. After compromise proved impossible, the Southerners bolted a second time and nominated John C. Breckinridge of Kentucky, Buchanan's vice president, for the presidency. Their platform demanded that Congress protect slavery in the territories. The Southerners held a formal convention later in Richmond that simply reaffirmed the earlier decision at the rump convention in Baltimore. The Northern Democrats who remained in Baltimore nominated Stephen A. Douglas on a platform of congressional noninterference, leaving questions regarding private property up to the Supreme Court. Ohio's Democrats supported the decision.[68]

The 1860 election entailed congressional contests as well, including Pendleton's reelection bid. He easily won the Democratic nomination over two competitors. Pendleton supported the decision of Northern Democrats to nominate Douglas in accord with the Ohio state and Hamilton County conventions. The platform was perfectly suited for Pendleton. He had been his own man while in Congress, rather than aligning solely with either Douglas or Buchanan, and welcomed the platform as a compromise of the two men's positions. Douglas's idea of popular sovereignty formed the foundation of the Democratic doctrine, whereas Buchanan's push to take the issue out of the halls of Congress and leave it to the Supreme Court was added. Pendleton's Republican opponent was a well-respected judge, Oliver M. Spencer. The *Cincinnati Commercial* testified to the high standing and character of both men running for the seat but supported Spencer because of his position on slavery. The judge was not closely associated with the Republican radicals, and the *Commercial* labeled him an "independent." On the slavery issue, however, he clearly stood with his party. He believed that blacks were human beings and could not be property. He upheld the right of Congress to legislate on slavery in the territories; he upbraided Douglas for his Kansas-Nebraska Bill. In Spencer's eyes, he had encouraged disunion by negating the Missouri Compromise.[69]

The focus of most Cincinnati voters was on the presidential election, but Pendleton diverted some of that attention by addressing the issues raised by both the Republican and Democratic platforms. He upheld his party platform and criticized Spencer's position on slavery. Accusing Spencer of being an abolitionist, Pendleton attacked the constitutionality of Spencer's plan to allow Congress to decide on slavery in the territories. Beyond this national perspective, Pendleton had two terms of service in the Congress on which to draw during the campaign. His growing reputation for oratory in the House and his constant attention to constituent needs also helped his cause. Another factor in the race was Spencer's poor health, which hampered his ability to campaign. The frequency with which Pendleton's opponents succumbed to illness must have led observers to wonder if opposition to him was hazardous to one's health. Finally, the fusion between the Republicans and the American Party had broken down between the 1858 and 1860 elections, and the American Party ran a separate candidate in the First District. Their candidate withdrew from the contest, however, before the election.[70]

Pendleton's strength in Hamilton County became apparent when the results of the election in 1860 were known. In the presidential election, Lincoln received a majority in Hamilton County and Ohio as a whole, with Douglas running a close second. Douglas lost by just over seven hundred votes in the county. Pendleton withstood this Republican tide. Hamiltonians returned him for a third congressional term by a margin of 7,485 to 6,582. The American candidate, A. K. Jones, polled 1,250 votes in spite of his withdrawal from the race.[71] Other important Democrats who won their contests included Clement Vallandigham, Samuel S. Cox, and William Allen. While the state's electoral votes went to Lincoln, the Democrats gained two additional seats in Congress, yet remained a minority with only eight seats out of twenty-one. Nationwide, Lincoln won the White House. Pendleton and the Northern Democrats now awaited the response of the South, which had threatened secession if Lincoln won.[72]

On December 20, 1860, South Carolina seceded from the Union. That day, the *Cincinnati Enquirer* editorialized for compromise. The newspaper placed total responsibility on Republican leaders who would not concede any ground to Southerners.[73] Pendleton expressed a similar opinion in a letter to fellow Ohio attorney, Rufus King, but broadened the focus of blame. Pendleton informed King that he was distributing a speech concerning compromise and was gratified by a groundswell of public support. Yet he confided to King that the speech "would not have much effect. . . . They [Northern and Southern men he had talked to] mean . . . it is not vindictive enough—it distributes too equally and justly both the blame and censure." Pendleton explained their position, saying that if they accepted any compromise, they could "not play abolitionist or fire-eater anymore."[74] Pendleton believed that extremists on both sides of the slavery expansion issue were fostering disunion. Along with most Ohio Democrats, he did not support coercion and sought compromise.[75]

As the second session of the Thirty-sixth Congress began in December 1860, Congress considered a number of compromise measures to avoid impending violence. The most promising was the Crittenden Compromise, offered to the Senate on December 18. This proposal called for the reinstatement of the Missouri Compromise line dividing slave and free territories. Popular sovereignty was not granted to the territories, though any state could choose to be free or slave. The compromise also afforded indemnification of slaveholders in territories north of the proposed line. While even Senator Douglas supported the compromise, it failed to pass the upper House because Republicans and President-elect Lincoln stood for a platform opposed to the extension of slavery. Speaking to a crowd in Washington, D.C., the day after Senator Crittenden introduced his plan, Pendleton endorsed the idea. He asserted that the Founding Fathers had built the nation on a foundation of compromise and evoked that memory to avoid war. Deprecating the idea that force could compel the seceded states to return to the Union, he called for peace.[76]

On January 18, 1861, Pendleton addressed the House of Representatives on the same topic. He presented a petition to the House with the signatures of ten thousand Cincinnatians who requested that the government adopt the Crittenden Compromise, and then proceeded to explain why using force against the seceded states was impractical and contrary to the spirit of the Constitution.[77] The case in point was consideration of enforcing revenue collection at ports in South Carolina, which would require the use of the military, as the state had officially declared its independence from the United States.[78] Pendleton noted that the revenue collected would not recoup more than a fraction of the cost involved to obtain it. Beyond this very practical reason, he wondered why House Republicans could agree to forego delivering the mail or maintaining federal courts in the state, but could not accept termination of the collection of duties. Striking directly at the heart of the question of coercion, Pendleton continued,

> Sir, if armies could preserve this Union, half a million of armed men would spring up in a night. . . . But, sir, money, armies, blood, will not maintain the Union. Justice, reason, peace may. This Union, Mr. Chairman, is a con-

federation of States. The Constitution is the bond. In order to attain certain ends beneficial to all, these States came together in voluntary association. . . . In order to maintain this Union, in order to preserve this Constitution, it is necessary that every agency of this complicated machinery—the General Government, the States united, the States severally—should perform the functions allotted to them by the Constitution.

Now, sir, what force of arms can compel a State to do that which she has agreed to do?[79]

Any such use of force, he continued, would change the nation from a confederation to a "consolidated empire."[80]

Changing his focus slightly, he exhorted Congress to accept compromise. The House should address the concerns of the Southern states, and if the differences were so great that conciliation could not be gained, then they ought to let the "seceding States depart in peace."[81] Benjamin Stanton of Ohio interrupted Pendleton after this point and stated that the Southern states had already precluded any chance of compromise. Pendleton responded that it was little wonder, considering the numerous resolutions that Congress had passed threatening to use force against them. He reiterated that his constituents loved "the Union above all things; but if dissolution [wa]s inevitable, they want[ed] it in peace."[82] If the country should split in peace, the Cincinnatians believed that the door would be left open for eventual reunification. Pendleton concluded with the warning that if the North proceeded into war that it must prepare well, for every wound inflicted on Southerners would "rankle in their breasts until they wash[ed] out the last stain in your blood and mine, or it may be, in that of our children."[83]

John Sherman, a Republican representative from Ohio, responded to Pendleton's assertions by claiming that the U.S. government had the right to exact the payments due it from imports into South Carolina. The federal government was obliged to follow the law and maintain its "ports, arsenals, navy-yards, vessels and munitions of war."[84] Sherman maintained that the government had the right to protect itself and in so doing had not infringed on the rights of any residents of South Carolina. He concluded by referring to secession as a "revolution." As such, the Southern states composed a "domestic enemy."[85]

There was a great deal of confusion between and within both parties as to the correct path to follow in this early period. While Sherman professed that the government had a right to use force, the Republican *Cincinnati Commercial* differed and announced that the Northern states ought to recognize the South as a separate nation. "There is room for several flourishing nations on this continent," it pontificated.[86] The reaction was no different among Democrats. A friend of Democratic congressman Samuel Cox kept him abreast of the political mood in Ohio. He wrote Cox that some Democrats might reject the Crittenden Compromise if it forced slavery on territorial residents who opposed the institution. In a subsequent letter, he reminded Cox of the economic interests many Ohioans had in the South, saying that they could not afford to pay duties on trade with a Southern nation.[87] Exposing his own uncertainty, Pendleton, shortly before his address about the evils of coercion, backtracked by voting to table a resolution calling the use of force to preserve the Union impractical. Representative Cox voted with him in this case, showing that there may have been pressure from Ohio to reject the compromise because it did not uphold the principles of popular sovereignty. It may also have reflected the difficulties Pendleton and his colleagues faced as they grappled with the dissolution of the Union. In either case, Pendleton soon settled the matter in his own mind. In his voting record and speeches, Pendleton became consistently opposed to President Lincoln's use of force against the South while at the same time voting to provide for the needs of the Union soldiers. The different roads that members of the Democracy followed thereafter led to divisions that became much more apparent in the Thirty-seventh Congress.[88]

Early in the second session, Pendleton and a majority of the congressmen voted to create a Committee of Thirty-three to propose solutions to the crisis. While they worked to formulate yet another compromise, the House voted on a variety of resolutions to establish the position of the government toward the seceded states. Many of these resolutions restated portions of the Crittenden Compromise while omitting the more divisive aspects. Pendleton consistently upheld his view of the Constitution, reprimanding those who in his opinion had disobeyed it. He voted in favor of a resolution that Congress recognize the institution of slavery, but it was tabled. When a Peace Conference, referred to as the "Old Gentlemen's Convention," proposed an amendment to the Constitution, Pendleton voted to suspend the rules of the House to consider it. The amendment would have reestablished the Missouri Compromise line between free and slave territories. The amendment further prohibited Congress from interfering in state domestic institutions and called for federal reimbursement of slave owners whose runaway slaves had eluded the Fugitive Slave Law with the help of abolitionists. Congress rejected this compromise as well.[89] Regarding the president's power to enforce the laws of revenue collection, Pendleton voted to prevent consideration of a bill in support of coercion. He was so opposed to using military force against the Southern states that he even voted against organizing the militia of the District of Columbia, an idea ostensibly aimed at protecting the capital.[90]

Pendleton's voting record evidenced a commitment to preserving the Jacksonian philosophy of states' rights and limited government, key aspects of his midwestern Democratic ideology. Yet in marked contrast to Jackson's own willingness to use troops during the Nullification crisis because of South Carolina's defiance of federal law, Pendleton was unwilling to give Lincoln authority to use military power to bring the seceded states back into the Union. Jackson faced a single state that was breaking a law. As a congressman, Pendleton did not face the same pressures that President Jackson had. In addition, during Pendleton's time the federal government was facing the secession of most of the South. It was constitutionally unclear what the federal government could do. Jackson believed in the notion of states' rights and favored slavery. Pendleton could rationalize Jackson's actions with South Carolina on the basis of his role as chief executive. He feared the abuse of governmental power and the restriction of individual liberties. Pendleton viewed Lincoln's situation as quite different. He questioned the notion of coercing the South back into the Union as constitutionally suspect and wanted to protect the Jacksonian notion of states' rights and individual liberties as well as the institution of slavery. At the same time, his love of the Union caused him to seek a peaceful split, if it was necessary, to allow for eventual reunification. The differences between Jackson's and Lincoln's predicaments were significant enough for Pendleton to allow similar philosophies to arrive at different conclusions.

When the Committee of Thirty-three reported to the House, Pendleton was absent. He missed sixteen days of debate in the House, probably due to illness. The committee recommended a series of proposals, including repealing the personal liberty laws in the North, which circumvented the Fugitive Slave Law; passing a constitutional amendment to protect slavery in states where it existed; admitting New Mexico as a state; providing jury trials for fugitive slaves; and forcing extradition of fugitives to states in which they were sought. Of those proposals on which he was able to vote, Pendleton favored only the constitutional amendment. He opposed the admission of New Mexico as a state, jury trials for fugitive slaves, and forced extradition of runaways. The Democrats in Congress inexplicably divided on each of the proposals. Only the amendment preventing federal interference in slavery was considered in the Senate, which voted not to concur. While efforts at compromise failed, attempts to increase the president's power or to support the use of force against the South also failed.[91]

While Pendleton pushed for compromise, others suggested more radical solutions. His father, Nathaniel Greene Pendleton, in a public letter to Sen. John J. Crittenden, suggested that if compromise failed, then the border states ought to form a "Central Confederacy." This proposal would alleviate conflict over fugitive slaves because the Central Confederacy would have a fugitive slave law. The central states would form a buffer zone between the two countries, which otherwise would be constantly at war. While the elder Pendleton endorsed this solution, he still hoped that the Union would not dissolve.[92] Clement Vallandigham proposed a similar settlement modeled on an idea that John C. Calhoun had proffered years earlier.[93] He suggested that representation in Congress be divided to correlate with four distinct sections: North, West, Pacific, and South. The plan would, he hoped, eliminate the natural enmity between the North and South over slavery. Each section would be protected by a veto in the Senate. This element of the plan would not only alleviate the strife between the North and the South, he contended, but also elevate the Northwest to a position equal to that of the East. Ohioans had long believed that the eastern states held too much political power. While Republicans and even some Democrats suggested that he was advocating a dissolution of the Union, Vallandigham countered that he wanted only a reorganization of representation to eliminate conflict and to preserve the nation.[94] Pendleton later defended the proposal but gave no immediate public profession of agreement. When the Thirty-sixth Congress adjourned, he went home for an abbreviated break, cut short by the outbreak of war in the South.

Immediately upon his inauguration, President Lincoln faced a critical policy decision regarding federal forts in the seceded states of the Deep South. Southerners had taken over federal installations in these states, but a handful remained under Washington's control. The most important of these was Fort Sumter, near Charleston. Maj. Robert Anderson had moved his troops from Fort Moultrie to Fort Sumter to maintain a more defensible position two months prior to Lincoln's inauguration. Congress voted to approve Anderson's move and affirm the president's power to preserve the Union, but Pendleton refused to support this cloaked provision for the use of force.[95] A little more than a month after he entered the White House, Lincoln decided to support the fortress by sending supply vessels. He made it clear to the Confederates that the ships carried only provisions, not reinforcements. South Carolinians viewed Lincoln's move as an act of aggression, and early on April 12, 1861, they began bombardment of the fort that lasted for thirty-four hours. Though he lost only one horse in the barrage, Major Anderson knew his position was untenable and surrendered. Anxious Cincinnatians, their fears realized, withdrew into a state of incredulous shock at this aggression. Pendleton's hopes for reconciliation seemed crushed under the weight of the rebellion's cannonballs. For many Ohioans of both parties, secession had been a grave disappointment, but it was tolerated. They could not countenance, however, the firing on the U.S. flag. It was unconscionable, compelling many to resolve that war held the only possible solution. As a result of the attack on the U.S. government, Pendleton gave limited support to the Lincoln administration so the country could defend itself. Pendleton remained steadfast, however, that coercion should not be used to seek reunification and strong in his conviction that compromise and peace could prevail.[96]

During his stay at home, Pendleton was asked to present a horse to the colonel of the 6th Ohio Regiment, known as the "Guthrie Grays."[97] In his presentation speech, he exemplified yet another aspect of his position throughout the war. He was always willing to provide for the military, especially troops from Ohio, even when he disagreed with the way the president employed them. He told Colonel Bosley to lead his men in an honorable fashion, "that they should have no other purpose than to uphold the Constitution, to reinvigorate the Union, and to maintain the true dignity of the banner of the Stars and Stripes" against which the Southerners had "raise[d] an unhallowed hand."[98]

Pendleton chose his words carefully, noting that the troops should act in moderation. His position differed sharply from when he proposed the destruction of the rebellious Mormons if they did not acquiesce. He understood the Southerners; his city had numerous economic ties with them. His own relatives came from the South, and he shared many of their political principles. When Pendleton returned to Congress in July 1861, he was pulled in several different directions. He was devoted to the Union and the men fighting for it, yet he could not justify constitutionally the use of force against the seceding states because of his Jacksonian belief in states' rights. At the outset of the Thirty-seventh Congress, he upheld the principles of the Democratic Party, now a minority in the House. He became a leading light in the faction of Congress that would oppose Lincoln's conduct of the war, the Peace Democrats.

The Tortuous Course

Pendleton and the Peace Democrats

I n examining the Peace Democracy during the Civil War, contemporaries
and historians alike have often accused it of "treasonous" positions. While
some Democrats supported Lincoln's administration in its effort to restore the Union, George Hunt Pendleton and a large portion of the party dis-
sented. Republicans stigmatized Pendleton and the Peace Democrats as "Copperheads," poisonous snakes with protective coloring, because they pursued
compromise and conciliation after Lincoln's election and throughout the war
years. Pendleton and like-minded Democrats decried Lincoln's alleged aggrandizement and misuse of power, as well as his administration's perceived trampling of the Constitution, in conducting the war and even the war itself, especially after the Emancipation Proclamation. Conversely, Republicans viewed
these Democrats as sympathetic with the Rebels.[1]

This categorization is inaccurate. Contemporaries and some historians have
equated loyalty to the Union with sustaining the war and the Lincoln administration. While there were Copperheads who sympathized with the South
and even committed acts of treason, they comprised a very small minority
of Northerners. Pendleton and his allies formed a loyal opposition, based on
legitimate dissent, against the Lincoln administration and its war policies. In
so doing, the Peace Democrats acted as a check on the use of power by the Republican administration. Examination of Pendleton's activities during the war
years opens new avenues for analyzing the Democratic Party and questioning
the "loyal versus traitor" dichotomy.

George Hunt Pendleton loved the Union. He was an American who wanted
the Union maintained and the conflict ended. He was also a partisan motivated
by the conservative ideals of a Jacksonian strict construction of the Constitution. Perhaps his proposal to guard and protect the Union through conciliation

was idealistic, but that did not detract from his devotion to the Republic. His supporters tended to be of immigrant stock, particularly Irish and German American Catholics; butternuts, a term given to Southerners who had settled north of the Ohio River; and middle-class Jacksonians.[2] Other Democratic issues, included exploiting fears of free blacks moving to the North, New England dominating the Midwest politically, and the Republican administration's usurpation of power, formed the foundation of Democratic platforms that appealed to all midwestern antebellum Democrats. Certainly these were not treasonous positions. While some War Democrats supported Republican measures without reservation as part of the Union Party, most Democrats, especially Peace men, endorsed the traditional party positions. Pendleton and the Democrats were simply the conservatives of the Civil War era.[3]

Pendleton and the Democracy can also be viewed as fulfilling the role of the loyal opposition. Traditionally, minority parties adopt some of the majority party's views in an effort to make themselves more appealing to voters. The Democrats remained consistent in their traditional positions, forfeiting the possible rewards of compromise. They constituted a "respectable minority" and sustained faithful party members.[4] Yet the Peace Democracy cannot be construed to be monolithic. It was deeply divided, particularly early in the war, and these divisions added to the complexity of Civil War politics. They also provide more fodder for those who have portrayed the Peace men as disloyal. Contemporary opponents could not be rid of them by such dismissals, and historians cannot be so cavalier with them either. The Copperheads should be divided into three main groups: the peace-at-any-price men, the Extreme Peace Democrats, and the Moderate Peace Democrats. Pendleton was a leading Extreme Peace Democrat.[5]

The peace-at-any-price men were the most reactionary of all the Peace Democrats. They were willing to accept anything to end the war, even if that meant the dissolution of the Union. Alexander Long, a representative from Ohio, is an example. He was almost expelled from Congress for his virulent acceptance of secession in the interest of peace.[6] While Pendleton was frequently lumped together with men like Long, and the two Ohioans did work together in Congress on some issues, there was a clear demarcation between them. The majority of the Peace men did not fit Long's mold.[7]

A second group within the Peace Democrats, known as the Extreme Peace Democrats, consisted of individuals such as Pendleton and Clement L. Vallandigham.[8] After the firing on Fort Sumter, the Extremists supported only those war measures and appropriation bills that conformed to a strict constructionist interpretation of the Constitution. While they did not believe coercing the Southern states back into the Union was constitutional, they conceded that a response to the Fort Sumter aggression was necessary. Extreme Peace men such as Pendleton worried as well about the economic effects of the war. Midwestern reliance on the Southern states as markets for farm goods compelled many agrarians to support Democratic appeals for peace. Democratic laborers from Ohio, Indiana, and nearby states saw only high prices and low wages in the early years of the war, providing further opposition to Lincoln's administration. As a Democratic "extremist," Pendleton's major concern was Lincoln's aggrandizement of power, which he believed limited personal liberties. The extremists consistently sought a negotiated end to the Civil War and fought legislation that they considered unconstitutional. All the while they maintained their allegiance to the Union, however, believing compromise could save the United States. They doggedly expressed their unwillingness to see the Union permanently dissolved. Their mantra became "the Constitution as it is, the Union as it was."[9]

The most conspicuous of the western Extreme Peace Democrats was Vallandigham, and his fanatical sectionalism and alleged dealings with Southern Rebels led to his traitorous reputation. To the public, Vallandigham appeared quite different from Pendleton. While both men were from Ohio, Vallandigham exercised less tact, was more outspoken, and was generally attacked as the representative of the Peace Democrats early in the war. Pendleton consistently supported his colleague, but gained less notoriety. He pursued dilatory tactics in Congress and gave emotional, but more cogent speeches, gaining a reputation for fine oratory. He also tempered his personality, which, when juxtaposed against Vallandigham's demagoguery, allowed him to acquire the moniker "Gentleman George." Well known as a "dashing political leader" and for his stylish hats, Pendleton personified gentility.[10] His family's Southern aristocratic paternalism, though tempered by the move to Cincinnati, was not completely erased. Pendleton was congenial but remained reserved, cool, and aloof. Such "manliness embodied many of the virtues midwesterners looked for in their candidates, while gentlemanliness provided a leavening of decorum to what might otherwise verge on a contest of brute strength."[11] Pendleton would often dodge an issue rather than appear too obdurate by voting "nay." He was pragmatic enough to recognize that his party was comprised of more than just Extreme Peace Democrats. If Pendleton intended to seek higher political offices, he needed to maintain an acceptable and moderate image.[12] Yet Pendleton did not forfeit principle for moderation. His commitment to Jacksonianism, for example, only increased over time. But his strategy paid mixed returns. Pendleton maintained political leadership and influence and even created a positive legacy, however, long after the war. Vallandigham did not. Though partially due to his untimely death in 1871, Vallandigham's behavior and positions won him notoriety and ruined his subsequent political career.[13]

A third group of Peace men included the Moderate Peace Democrats. They were willing to support Republican measures concerning the war, at least until the Emancipation Proclamation.[14] A member of this group, Ohio congressman Samuel S. Cox, had been closely associated with men such as Pendleton and Vallandigham: "He made up his mind . . . that secession was impossible and that the use of force, although a calamity, was necessary under the circumstances." "Force," according to Cox, was to be employed for as short a time as possible and in conjunction with ongoing peace efforts. Cox feared that Democratic opposition to war measures would damage the party's image and make it appear disloyal to the Union; at the same time, Cox had "no use" for War Democrats who left the party in support of the war.[15] He believed his party should support the war but maintain traditional principles in defense of limited government, strict construction of the Constitution, civil liberties, and states' rights. Yet according to Pendleton's philosophy, Cox's moderate position compromised those principles by accepting the administration's constitutional right to coerce a state back into the Union. Once Lincoln declared emancipation as a war aim, however, Cox and the Moderate Peace men began to withdraw their support, fearing the president had overstepped his constitutional authority. Even after the proclamation, however, Cox did not consistently oppose Lincoln as Pendleton did. Cox's moderate and at times inconsistent support for Lincoln's administration of the war represents and clearly delineates the position of the Moderate Peace Democrats.[16]

While the three-group categorization is helpful for examining the Democratic Party during the Civil War, it is generally artificial and frequently breaks down in the case of Pendleton. As seen in the distinctions between Vallandigham and Pendleton, there were significant variations even within the groupings. In addition, while Pendleton was identified with the extremists, he occasionally acted with the moderates, voting to supply troops with military goods and supporting appropriations bills. He never accepted the constitutionality of coercion, however, as most moderates did. Historians have traditionally placed Pendleton with more reactionary men such as Long or Vallandigham because the information available about him was generally tainted with Republican bias.[17] With the advent of a federal victory in 1865 and the subsequent "waving of the bloody shirt," distinctions between Southern sympathizers and Peace men blurred in the public mind. Not allowed to stand on his record, the historical perspective of Pendleton has been either that of a traitor or a reactionary Copperhead. Both views are inaccurate. Pendleton was neither a Southern supporter nor a demagogue like Vallandigham. Instead, he forged ahead on his own, with an eye to maintaining principled consistency, to become a leader of the Extreme Peace men. He represented many Democrats who were unwilling to blindly follow the Lincoln administration. The result for the Democratic Party was a variety of loosely defined factions and the absence of a national party leader.[18]

The emergence of these differences within the loyal opposition evolved with the passage of time. Immediately following the fateful attack on Fort Sumter, the newly inaugurated president called for the enlistment of 75,000 volunteer troops. Stephen Douglas visited his old political nemesis and encouraged Lincoln's preparations for war.[19] In the ensuing months, with the newly organized troops drilling outside Washington, Lincoln seized upon the swelling tide of Northern unionism to call a special session of Congress, scheduled for July 4, 1861. Undoubtedly, Pendleton and like-minded congressmen rode trains back to the capital filled with trepidation. Passing by the mustering camps, with their callow, Union-minded men, Pendleton feared that the failure of compromise in the Thirty-sixth Congress had brought the young Republic to the brink of disaster.

Days later Pendleton read President Lincoln's request of Congress for 400,000 men and $400 million to ensure a short and victorious war.[20] Pendleton resolved to support the president's request. As he had exhorted the 6th Ohio Regiment before leaving Cincinnati, he hoped the Union forces would "achieve an honorable victory, and restore an honorable peace."[21] Pendleton was indeed a Union man. Yet he had sought peace through compromise and would consistently do so in the future. His family had a Southern heritage, as did many of his constituents, and Cincinnati had strong economic ties to the South that the war had disrupted.[22] He deplored the thought of bloodshed between members of the same nation. Pendleton believed that in large part the Republicans had precipitated this conflict. In spite of these concerns and fears, he acquiesced in war measures after the Southern aggression at Fort Sumter. If war could save his beloved Union, then he would back a narrowly defined war plan. As thousands of Ohioans and hundreds of his own constituents marched off to fight in the whirlwind of patriotism during the spring of 1861, Pendleton vowed not to abandon them. Even so, he warned his political opponents that his support was conditional.

In a speech shortly after the start of the special session of Congress, Pendleton articulated his conditions. "I will heartily, zealously, gladly support any honest efforts to maintain the Union and invigorate the ties which bind these States together. But, sir, I am not willing to vote for more men or money than the Administration asks, more than it can fairly use, more than General Scott—who advises and controls the Administration—tells us he thinks necessary."[23] Pendleton objected to raising the number of regular army troops. Increasing the number of regulars was significantly different in Pendleton's mind than calling for volunteers. The latter served for a specific period of time and returned home. The former added to the size of the permanent army, and therefore the government. Any increase in the regular army would only add to the president's patronage powers and facilitate a longer war. The immense response of volunteers to Lincoln's call was sufficient, Pendleton argued, to supply the needed troops. Concluding his comments, Pendleton informed Congress that his backing would cease when bills to expand presidential power, obviate proper adherence to the Constitution, or interrupt personal liberties came before the House.[24]

A number of issues that surfaced during the special session illustrate Pendleton's willingness to sustain the war effort. John J. Crittenden of Kentucky introduced in Congress a conservative resolution blaming the Southern states for disunion and proposing to "defend and maintain the supremacy of the Constitution and to preserve the Union unimpaired."[25] The July resolution was more telling for what it prohibited than for what it proposed. Crittenden and his supporters, including Pendleton and most Democrats in the House, were sending Lincoln a message that they would condone the war only as long as he did not interfere with domestic institutions such as slavery.[26] Early in the session, Pendleton reported a bill from his new seat on the Committee of the Judiciary seeking the relief of Ohio volunteers. The bill requested their full payment from the time they responded to the president's call to their mustering into service. Samuel Cox amended the bill to include all states that did not pay their troops during the intervening period. The measure passed without much opposition. Later Pendleton worked to match the pay schedule of volunteer officers with that of regular army officers.[27] At the same time, Pendleton did not wholeheartedly embrace the administration's war efforts. When Radical Republican Thaddeus Stevens proposed an increase in the number of cadets admitted to West Point, Pendleton balked. He was not interested, he repeated, in bolstering the ranks of the regular army and empowering the president with a large military patronage.[28]

In a resolution introduced in the House, Pendleton reiterated the conditional nature of his support and called for the maintenance of the equality of the states.[29] All efforts to sustain the Union, he argued, must be made with regard to this equality and within the limits set by the Constitution. They should not be designed "to reduce to a position of inferiority any of the States, or to interfere with their State governments, or to abolish slavery within their limits."[30] Pendleton's statements implicitly accepted the use of force as a necessary evil to preserve the Union due to the attack on Fort Sumter but rejected the subjection of Southern states to territorial or inferior status after the war ended. Reinforcing the Crittenden resolution, he hoped to warn the abolitionists from seeking to make the end of slavery a war aim. Though ultimately unsuccessful, Pendleton set the course for himself and the Extreme Peace Democrats throughout the conflict. The *Cincinnati Enquirer*, agreeing with Pendleton's stand, expressed dismay over the Republican president's unwillingness to appoint a Peace Democrat to his cabinet. Because the Republicans comprised a sectional party with many abolitionists within its ranks, the newspaper argued that the Democrats needed to be on the defensive. The editorial closed with a plea that "in defending the flag of the Union, let us carry along with it the olive branch."[31]

Pendleton agreed. While supporting initial war measures, he did not abandon the possibility of peace through compromise. Peace men endeavored to hold several conventions whose goal was formulating compromise legislation. Early in the session, Republicans tabled a Democratic resolution calling for a national convention of delegates from each congressional district. Pendleton opposed the tabling.[32] Two weeks later, Samuel Cox offered another peace resolution. Cox said that although the administration had used military force to "maintain the integrity and stability of the Government," the fact that the belligerents were comprised of people of the same ancestry and history demanded continued efforts for peace.[33] He proposed a convention with one delegate from each state to hammer out a compromise constitutional amendment dealing with the issues of secession for submission to Congress. While Pendleton and most Democrats supported the idea, it failed. A third peace effort, also tabled by the Republicans, proposed a joint congressional committee to find constitutional amendments aimed at reuniting the Union. Again, Pendleton's support proved futile.[34]

Other legislation considered during the special session included increasing government revenue and a confiscation act. The first brought before the House the tariff question. Lincoln's secretary of the treasury, Salmon P. Chase, suggested some changes in the 1861 Morrill Tariff to increase revenue. He favored removing some items from the free list, yet simultaneously appeared willing to see some highly protective duties lowered. This latter provision angered leading Radical Republicans, chiefly the chairman of the House Ways and Means Committee, Thaddeus Stevens. High tariff schedules were not only a wartime means of raising revenues but also a key political aim of the Republican Party. Pendleton seized the opportunity to advance both Democratic and midwestern interests. Ohioans had long believed that the Northeast benefited unfairly from high tariffs that seemed only to raise costs for midwesterners on important products such as iron and farm machinery. Pendleton introduced an amendment to lower the proposed duty on tea and the highly protective tariff on iron. Stevens represented Pennsylvanian iron interests who wanted the iron duty left high. Pendleton retorted that the estimated income from the tea tariff was only half of what could be realized from simply lowering the duty on iron. Moreover, lowering the cost of tea would benefit Northern workers on whose backs the Union war effort largely rested. The committee refused Pendleton's amendment, and he voted against the tariff, which passed on a largely partisan and somewhat sectional vote. Partisanship played the more important role, as many Republican midwesterners favored the tariff.[35]

The other nonmilitary issue, confiscation, engendered much debate. Crittenden spoke at length detailing why the Republican measure was unconstitutional. He stated that the Constitution did not afford Congress the right to take the property of belligerents on the offense of purported treason. He also feared that because much of the property seized would be slaves, the few remaining Southern unionists would rally to the Confederate cause to protect their investment capital and state sovereignty. Pendleton spoke briefly on the topic, saying that Congress needed to determine if Southerners were enemies or citizens of the United States entitled to the constitutional protection of property rights. Beyond that question, he directly attacked the bill for its vague wording. The proposal left open the possibility that any citizen who suspected a neighbor of aiding the rebellion in any fashion could conceivably take the property of the accused. This would lead to false accusations and illegal seizures. Pendleton surely knew this was not the intent of the bill, but he did not want to see the federal government's power expand or create a pretext for freeing slaves. He introduced an amendment to ensure that a legal warrant was issued if the property in question were in a Northern state. If in a Confederate state, a designated officer of the executive department was responsible for the seizure. Pendleton successfully had the bill recommitted to committee to consider his amendment, but it later passed the House without his addition.[36]

Congress adjourned in early August, and Pendleton spent a few months at home in Cincinnati. War hysteria remained high, but Cincinnatians began to realize that there would not be a short, swift victory. Union forces failed to win any decisive battles in 1861. The "Trent Affair," in which a U.S. naval vessel detained a British ship carrying two Confederate envoys, caused more concern among Northerners with its portents of British intervention in the conflict. When Congress reconvened in early December 1861, it would have to wrestle once again with the issues raised in the special session.[37]

When Pendleton returned to the District of Columbia, he found the capital shrouded in somberness and uncertainty. While his private residence insulated him from the spirited and sometimes raucous deliberations of boardinghouse politicos, it could not shield him from the ravages of war. Washingtonians daily faced the consequences of armed conflict. What had once caused patriotic exhilaration now produced only casualties that were brought into the city for care and convalescence. Their numbers grew so rapidly that by January 1862, the provost marshal of Washington, D.C., prohibited street serenading "because it

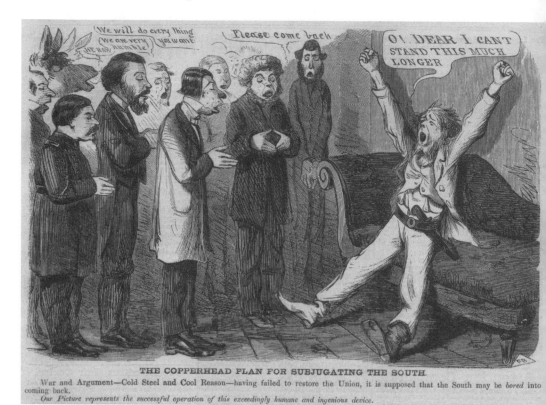

THE COPPERHEAD PLAN FOR SUBJUGATING THE SOUTH.

War and Argument—Cold Steel and Cool Reason—having failed to restore the Union, it is supposed that the South may be *bored* into coming back.
Our Picture represents the successful operation of this exceedingly humane and ingenious device.

The Copperhead Plan for Subjugating the South: The Republicans ridiculed the Peace Democratic notion that a truce could result in the South returning to the Union. McClellan and Pendleton are depicted on the left of the picture. (*Harper's Weekly*, October 22, 1864)

causes confusion, disorder, and annoyance to the sick."[38] Pendleton was counting the costs of war.

Almost immediately upon session opening, Pendleton addressed the House on the administration's aggrandizement of power. In the spring, Lincoln had suspended the writ of habeas corpus in Maryland because Baltimore authorities had proven unable to prevent rioters from destroying bridges and telegraph wires leading to Washington, D.C. In addition, some twenty thousand Marylanders had gone south to fight for the Confederacy. Many Maryland citizens who remained were arrested, and one of those, John Merryman, sought release from prison on a writ of habeas corpus. In May 1861, acting as a circuit judge, Chief Justice Roger B. Taney issued the writ in *Ex parte Merryman,* denying Lincoln's power to suspend the writ. Lincoln disregarded the ruling, and during the summer, Maj. Gen. Nathaniel P. Banks of the Department of Annapolis arrested the chief of police of Baltimore under suspicion of complicity with the Confederates. The mayor and board of police responded with outrage at this "arbitrary exercise of military power" and notified the federal government that they interpreted Banks's action to include the suspension of law enforcement by the entire police force.[39] Banks termed their acts as noncompliance with the federal government and arrested the entire board. He then ran the civil police headquarters himself, discovering what he believed to be a hidden arsenal intended for the Confederates. The House requested that the president provide more information on the matter but received no satisfaction.[40]

In a message to Congress, Lincoln justified his refusal to obey Taney's ruling as well as the actions of General Banks by referring to Section 9 of Article 1 of the Constitution. He claimed this clause applied to the executive branch of government and allowed the president to suspend the writ in case of rebellion or insurrection.[41] Pendleton bitterly attacked the president's actions in suspending the writ of habeas corpus. Representing the minority view of the Judiciary Committee, he contended that Section 9 included instructions aimed specifically at the Congress and enumerated eight specific restrictions on that body. The second restriction stated that *Congress* did not have the power to suspend the writ "unless, when in cases of rebellion or invasion, the public safety may require it."[42] If Section 9 applied to Congress, he argued, then the exception must apply to Congress as well, rather than to the president, as Lincoln contended.

For the better part of an hour, Pendleton put the House through a refresher course in the study of law. He based much of his argument on that of his wife's uncle, Chief Justice Taney, in *Ex parte Merryman*.[43] Citing legal texts and precedent-setting cases, he justified his stance. Most telling, he noted that when President Thomas Jefferson apprised Congress of an "alleged conspiracy for dismemberment of the Union," the Senate suspended the writ for three months.[44] While the House had refused to concur, the decision had fallen to the legislative body.

In conclusion, Pendleton examined a concern that motivated most of his political opposition to the president throughout the war—where did the powers gained in the exigencies of the Civil War end? If the president could suspend the writ of habeas corpus, Pendleton questioned, could he also negate the right to a "speedy trial" or a "trial by jury" that the Constitution also protected? Perhaps the condition of the country was so grave that he would have to ignore other portions of the Constitution as well. Once liberties were lost, Pendleton argued, there was no guarantee of their resumption outside of revolution. Pendleton saw Lincoln's actions as the thin section of the wedge that led to military despotism. Constitutional provisions could not be disregarded even in time of national emergency. "To suspend the Constitution in order to preserve the Government," he contended, "would be to stop the current of blood in the veins in order to preserve the life. To preserve the Government the Constitution must be preserved; its principles must be cherished; its limitations must be respected; its prohibitions must be obeyed."[45] To continually neglect the provisions of the Constitution eroded the value of personal liberties until the country would no longer sustain them. In spite of Pendleton's warnings, the House tabled his resolution that labeled Lincoln's action a usurpation of congressional power.[46]

Despite this setback, Pendleton's limited support of the administration's war effort continued as it had during the special session. Pendleton repeatedly voted in favor of resolutions upholding the war to maintain the Union under the Constitution. He supported bills enlarging the number of volunteer engineers, organizing staffs for army divisions, and establishing national foundries, armories, and arsenals. He also continued to express his concern for ensuring the timely and generous pay of troops. In all these measures, he carefully considered the effect such actions had on the presidency. In line with his fellow Extreme Peace Democrats, Pendleton was a member of the loyal opposition.[47]

When Republicans sought to prosecute the war through unconstitutional means, however, Pendleton balked. One of the policy areas that frequently elicited a response related to economics. Because of the economic importance of Cincinnati and Pendleton's ability to clearly articulate Jacksonian principles, he became a key Democratic spokesman on economic issues. He evaluated all financial questions using three criteria: constitutionality, equity, and expediency. Pendleton's midwestern Democratic ideology laid the foundation for this test. With each measure, he weighed whether the Constitution prohibited the proposed activity. The issuance of greenbacks was an example of an unconstitutional measure according to Pendleton. If a bill was constitutional, he then determined if it equitably distributed the burden to all sections of the country and to all income levels. He opposed certain aspects of the tax bill because he believed it did not meet these criteria. Finally, he queried if the proposed measure fulfilled the needs of the country in an efficient and expeditious manner. For example, he questioned Thaddeus Stevens on the Republican request to give the secretary of the treasury power to purchase coin. Pendleton acquiesced to the measure only after being convinced that it was necessary and expedient. During the war, Pendleton established a pattern of examining financial issues, which he maintained during the Reconstruction Era.

One of the first important economic battles involved providing for costs of the war through the issuance of treasury notes or "greenbacks." Pendleton argued that the federal government did not have the power to make treasury notes a legal tender and noted that the House had never even considered such an idea. As a Jacksonian, Pendleton found no power in the Constitution to permit this action. To strengthen his view, he cited Alexander Hamilton, who, he argued, had stressed that such powers were restricted to the states. Dredging up Daniel Webster, another spiritual forebearer of the Republican Party, Pendleton said Webster went even further by contending that neither the states nor the federal government could make anything but specie legal tender.[48]

With the support of one of his major hometown newspapers, Pendleton enumerated other objections beyond the important constitutional argument. He asserted, on very practical grounds, that this plan would inevitably lead to a depreciated currency and economic ruin, a greater threat to the Union than the Civil War itself. He questioned how Congress could make all contracts payable in these notes when some of them specifically called for repayment in specie. The notes were to be issued at an equivalent value to the twenty-year, 6 percent bonds, which were worth only ninety cents on the dollar. Immediately, Pendleton contended, the issuance of notes asked holders to forfeit 10 percent of their value. As time passed, depreciation would continue. Pendleton predicted apocalyptic consequences for issuing greenbacks, listing a litany of devastating outcomes including that "prices will be inflated; . . . incomes will be diminished; the savings of the poor will vanish. . . . Private ruin and public bankruptcy, either with or without repudiation, will inevitably follow."[49]

Vallandigham also opposed the bill, along with some Republicans and Unionists. This bipartisan group sponsored a substitute bill calling for the issuance of interest-bearing notes that were not legal tender. Pendleton backed the substitute, but it went down to defeat. Immediately the previous question was voted on and passed. Yet the question had a life of its own. Pendleton would return to the issue of greenbacks following the war.[50]

Another financial matter that better defined Pendleton's position on monetary questions was the authorization of Secretary Chase to purchase coin. Even though the bill to print paper money as legal tender for all government liabilities passed the House, the Senate amended the bill so that the federal government was required to pay interest on certain bonds in specie or gold coin. When the bill was returned to the House, Pendleton unsuccessfully attempted to amend the bill to pay military troops in coin as well. In an effort to obtain more specie by enticing buyers, however, Thaddeus Stevens moved to authorize Chase to sell seven and three-tenths percentage notes at market, rather than par, value as had been previously required. Pendleton immediately questioned Stevens regarding this bond issue, wondering why Chase needed this extra provision when less than a month earlier the Congress had allowed him to sell $500 million in bonds to purchase coin. The interest paid in coin now amounted to $40 million per year. While supporting the use of loans to pay the debt, Pendleton questioned why the secretary of the treasury should be authorized to sell more than ten times the amount needed, while gaining the additional right to issue notes at market value. Stevens explained that the public was unwilling to buy the bonds in coin when their interest would be paid in paper currency, except at a very reduced rate. But Chase was not allowed to offer the bonds so low. While they had not been purchased in sufficient quantities at par value, he was confident they would do better at market value and lose much less money for the government. After being appeased by this reasonable answer, Pendleton supported the bill. His opposition originated not out of simple partisan bitterness but out of financial and constitutional differences.[51]

A more acceptable means of raising revenue for Pendleton was increased taxation when it did not adversely affect his constituents. As the House grappled with many important national issues during the Civil War, Pendleton retained his concern for his district when dealing with the tax issue. The fact that 1862 was an election year no doubt brought his constituents to mind, but Pendleton's record of addressing their concerns had remained unfailing. He worked to lower the tax on four main industries prevalent in Cincinnati: breweries, tobacco processors, candle makers, and meat packers. First, he asked the House to reduce the assessment on lager beer from one dollar per barrel to one cent per gallon. In a humorous interlude, Pendleton called the attention of his fellow congressmen to the beneficial aspects of beer, a beverage he found pleasure in imbibing. A Republican from Missouri recalled that lager beer "did more to elect Mr. Lincoln President of the United States than any other drink." Pendleton responded, "Then it was diverted from its original use."[52] Amidst laughter, Stevens argued that the additional lager tax was still small enough to prevent any discomfort for those who preferred the beverage. Republican temperance advocates found little humor in the proceedings.

The bill also proposed taxes on tobacco products, candles, and slaughterhouses. Representatives of Cincinnati companies wrote to Pendleton to explain their predicaments and to request alternative taxes. Pendleton introduced their letters into the *Congressional Globe* but was unable to aid the firms significantly.[53]

In spite of these failures, Pendleton continued his efforts to shape the tax bill. In the spirit of Jacksonianism, he was afraid that the burden of the bill would fall on the lower classes, and instead he proposed a new license fee for professionals. Under his plan, lawyers, physicians, and preachers were required to obtain licenses to serve in each state.[54] After some amendments, the proposal was attached to the bill. Pendleton further sought to tax at one-fifth of 1 percent the "monies, credits, investments in bonds, notes, stocks, [and] joint stocks."[55] Pendleton argued that as money invested in agriculture and manufacturing was taxed, so should money invested in bonds or mortgages. There was no justifiable reason why certain investments should be tax exempt. Pendleton's proposal would have increased his own taxes. Once again Thaddeus Stevens opposed Pendleton's idea, saying that people who invested in bonds were taxed by the newly instituted income tax to help pay for the war, and he would not condone double taxation. Pendleton's plan failed in spite of his rebuttal that the income tax only affected those with investment incomes over six hundred dollars. His plan was for those whose income was less than that sum.[56]

Pendleton concluded his work on the bill by asking Congress to allow the states and their tax collectors to levy the new war tax. Because a system of collection existed in each state, he saw no reason for spending large amounts of money to establish an unnecessary federal bureaucracy. He reminded his colleagues that never before in the country's history had such a tax been assessed, and he believed that it should be as unobtrusive as possible. Behind this suggestion lay Pendleton's suspicion of a strong federal government, which he believed this act would create and which would intervene in the lives of Americans on a grand scale. As before, Stevens blocked Pendleton's suggestions. Because of the Republican reluctance to adopt his amendments, Pendleton voted against the tax bill. In spite of his belief that it was a constitutionally sanctioned method of raising funds, Pendleton reasoned that the tax burden was not distributed equitably.[57]

Pendleton's opposition to the Confiscation Act of 1862, however, was based on Jacksonian constitutional scruples alone. He had dealt with this issue briefly in the special session, and he called for restrictions to ensure that the process was judicious. The House Judiciary Committee reported a series of bills and resolutions concerning the confiscation of the real estate, personal property, and slaves of those involved in the Rebellion. Pendleton moved unsuccessfully to table each one.[58] Cox and Vallandigham joined Pendleton in fighting this measure because it dealt with a clearly definable constitutional issue and broached the matter of emancipation. Cox called this proposal a "bill of attainder," meaning it removed the civil rights of persons based on their alleged treasonous activities.[59] Confiscation also punished their children, he argued in somewhat of a legal stretch, for a crime in which they had no part. Concerning the confiscation of slaves, Peace men queried what agency, civil or military, would be in charge of the slaves and what policies would it adopt. Cox and Vallandigham opposed the extra expense of having the army take care of the freedmen, fearing that soldiers' supplies would be diminished. The idea of arming contrabands for combat duty struck fear in the hearts of House Democrats. Moreover, they were alarmed that Radical Republicans planned to use confiscation as a pretext to emancipate all slaves. Pendleton repudiated the idea as an unconstitutional extension of federal power. Most Democrats were simply unwilling to accept the notion that slavery was a moral evil.

While the government might exploit the seized properties to defray the costs of the war, Pendleton and his colleagues thought that this act was not warranted. The president expressed his own concerns about the bill, believing that the Constitution forbade the government from seizing property for longer than the lifetime of the offender. Lincoln's threatened veto prompted the Radicals to add an explanatory resolution to the bill limiting the term of confiscation. Pendleton opposed the measure in any form. He hoped for a quick national reconciliation, attainable only without such injurious legislation. Confiscation solidified opposition in the South, he believed, thus extending the war. In spite of his efforts, the bill passed.[60]

As Pendleton anticipated, Radical Republicans used the successful passage of the Confiscation Act in the House to push for further measures to free enslaved African Americans. Radicals sought a timely abolition, while other Republicans, including President Lincoln, advised a cautious and gradual program of compensated emancipation. These conflicting goals slowed the realization of abolition and allowed Pendleton and the Peace Democrats to oppose the Republicans in each legislative effort in this direction. Pendleton placed states' rights above most other principles and was unwilling to see the inequity in allowing African Americans to remain in bondage. In March 1862, the president requested Congress to supply financial aid to any state that began a policy of gradual emancipation. Roscoe Conkling of New York introduced the resolution, which passed by a partisan vote. Lincoln then met with representatives of the Border States and encouraged them to adopt such policies. In return, the president promised federal funds for compensated, voluntary emancipation, followed by congressionally approved colonization of both freedpersons and free Northern African Americans. Bills proposing such a plan for the District of Columbia and the federal territories soon came before Congress. Pendleton and the Peace Democrats worked unsuccessfully to table these measures. The bills had an unexpected consequence in the Democratic party ranks. Moderate and Extreme Peace Democrats, previously split over the extent of support due Lincoln's administration, temporarily allied against compensated emancipation.[61]

The Democratic party had long championed the right of states to decide the issue of slavery. Pendleton consistently upheld the party's principle of state sovereignty on domestic issues based on a strict constructionist view of the Constitution. At the outbreak of the Civil War, Pendleton and his partisan friends blamed the Republicans, a sectional party replete with ardent abolitionists, for scorning the possibility of compromise with the threatened slave owners. Pendleton's support of the federal war effort depended on Lincoln's adherence to certain conservative, Democratic war goals defined as maintaining "the Constitution as it is, and . . . restor[ing] the Union as it was."[62] These beliefs precluded any federal intervention on the issue of slavery. Echoing Pendleton's view, the Ohio Democratic Convention in 1862 attacked the Republicans for changing the war from preserving the Union into an abolitionist crusade.

Other reasons for Northern opposition to emancipation included a widespread belief in white supremacy and a fear that large numbers of freedmen would move to the Northern states. Pendleton's constituents expressed concern about job competition from newly freed slaves moving to Ohio. Reports of blacks working for twenty-five cents per day or less circulated around the state. The absence of legislation forbidding blacks to enter the state further exacerbated these fears, resulting in race riots in several cities including Cincinnati. Beyond worrying about job competition, Pendleton's constituents shuddered at the misguided thoughts of interracial marriages, black assaults on white women, and social and political equality, all of which Democratic newspapers predicted would occur after emancipation. The *Cincinnati Enquirer* saw financial ruin at the prospect of freeing the slaves. While suggesting the freedmen would undoubtedly become the burden of state taxpayers because of their alleged laziness, the paper stereotypically argued that the end of slavery would destroy the large Southern market for Ohio goods and create economic chaos in the city. At an ideological level, Democrats used the notion of "white unity and white entitlement" to unify Northern and Southern Democrats. It also enticed Irish and other Catholic immigrants to attach themselves to the Democracy where their "whiteness" afforded them instant status.[63] Even so, many of the fears expressed by Democratic Ohioans about emancipation resonated well beyond the party, illustrating the wide and ugly net cast by the ideology of white supremacy in the mid-nineteenth century.[64]

Ohio Democrats structured the 1862 election campaign around the banner of "negrophobia." A man of his party and in many respects his times, Pendleton joined this effort when he returned home seeking his reelection. Though he had fought prejudice in Cincinnati against European immigrants, he maintained his own when it related to the color barrier. In September, Lincoln issued his preliminary Emancipation Proclamation, using the exigency of war to right a longtime national wrong. In so doing, he revealed his hatred of the "peculiar institution" while ensuring that abolition would be the major question in the October election in Ohio.[65] But other emotional issues also existed. The loss of loved ones in battle and no end in sight to the conflict, combined with weeks of anxiety throughout the summer and early fall because of the threatened siege of Cincinnati by Confederate cavalry commander John Hunt Morgan, disillusioned many voters about an administration that promised so much and delivered so little.[66] It was no surprise that the surge of patriotism after the firing on Fort Sumter waned quickly when Lincoln requested an additional 74,000 Ohio troops.[67]

In preparing for the election, the Republican majority in the Ohio legislature gerrymandered the First District, taking the heavily Republican seventh ward of Cincinnati from the Second District and including it in Pendleton's reconfigured district. Because of Republican gains in 1861 and his district's new boundaries, Pendleton expressed serious concerns to a supporter: "My friends say I have a sure thing. . . . I am hopeful enough to make every exertion, but not confident enough to be very much disappointed at defeat."[68]

Pendleton's exertions commenced with his nomination at the Hamilton County Democratic Convention on October 3, 1862. He adopted as his platform the state convention's resolutions that mirrored his congressional record. The platform expressed devotion to the Constitution and the Union as they were, attacked abolitionists for igniting the war, and rejected the confiscation and emancipation acts. Furthermore, the party berated the Republican General Assembly for failing to pass laws forbidding freedmen entry into the state.[69] In his speech accepting nomination, Pendleton castigated the administration's disregard for the Constitution and the American people over three perceived atrocities: "Emancipation, taxation, and war." He asked his constituents to examine their principles, warning that if they were not applied to the government, "it will sink in the abyss of a military despotism or licentious anarchy so that neither you nor your children will live to see its resurrection."[70]

The *Cincinnati Commercial* responded quickly by endorsing Republican Party principles and Pendleton's opponent, Col. John Groesbeck. The newspaper ignored the substance of Pendleton's scruples and reduced the issues to questioning his loyalty to the Union. Falsely accusing him of sympathizing with the secessionists, the paper assailed his voting record as injurious to the war effort. Minimizing the emancipation efforts by the Republicans, the *Commercial* asserted that it was simply a war measure and pertained only to slaves in Confederate territories. The editors also sought to hurt Pendleton's reputation by associating him with Vallandigham. In some respects, that was correct. Pendleton had campaigned with the Dayton representative, but, while they were both Extreme Peace Democrats, Vallandigham had been far more militant in Congress. Notwithstanding repeated efforts to explain his position, Vallandigham's opponents grouped him with the secessionists because of his proposal to reorganize the Union into four districts. His scheme provided for equal representation of the four districts in the Senate, instead of two senators from each state, in an effort to address sectional concerns more effectively. Republicans construed the plan as an endorsement of secession. The *Commercial* even questioned Vallandigham's sources of campaign funds, tying the Daytonite to a conspiracy involving John Foster. Foster had been discovered corresponding with a secessionist about advancing the cause of the Democrats in Ohio.

The paper had no evidence of a tie between Foster and Vallandigham, much less Pendleton, so it simply leveled accusations. The paper charged that Foster had obtained Southern funds for Ohio Democratic campaigns. Regardless of the allegations, Pendleton's record was much less extreme than Vallandigham's. Pendleton had been more supportive of war measures than his colleague, gaining a favorable reputation among friends and even some foes.[71]

Pendleton responded to these allegations on the pages of the *Cincinnati Enquirer.* The newspaper accurately recounted his promotion of those war measures required by the president to conduct the war within the restraints of the Constitution. The editors reminded readers of Pendleton's support of generous reimbursement for volunteers and declared that inconsistency was really a trait of the Republican president, not Pendleton. The *Enquirer* noted the deleterious effects sure to be realized from emancipation, citing Lincoln's letter to a group of clergymen in Chicago in September 1862, where he rejected the notion of emancipation because of some of these very problems. Within two weeks, the president had recanted and had issued the preliminary Emancipation Proclamation.[72] In a letter to a New York Democratic meeting, Pendleton reiterated his position that emancipation was unconstitutional. He cited the need for adherence to the institutions of the Founding Fathers to restore the Union and questioned the effectiveness of coercion to reunite the country. "Whatever may be the success of our arms, how ever much they may be enabled to break the military power of the South, love for the Union and the Government, faith in their justice, beneficence, and virtue, appreciation of their value are essential to their restoration."[73]

In spite of a statewide Republican victory by 55,000 votes the year before, the gerrymandering of the First District, and the attacks on the loyalty of Democrats, Pendleton won reelection by 1,227 votes. In fact, the gerrymander hurt the Republicans. The Second District, from which they removed the seventh ward, fell into the hands of Democrat Alexander Long by a margin of 131 votes. If Republicans had left the districts alone, they could have prevented the lost seat. The Democratic campaign of raising racist fears and questioning the constitutionality of Lincoln's actions paid dividends in the state. The Democratic Party swept Ohio with a majority of 80,000 in 1862. Ohioans elected the entire Democratic state slate, and the party filled fourteen of the nineteen seats in Congress. The wave of Democracy did not help Vallandigham, however, who lost in yet another gerrymandered district in Dayton.[74]

Shortly after the election, Pendleton addressed an audience just outside of Cincinnati, restating his position on the war and announcing a new direction adopted by most Peace Democrats. While he believed the conflict could have been prevented through compromise, he had decided upon the outbreak of war to "maintain the Government and enforce obedience to the Constitution.

He was in favor of attaining the ends and purposes of the war in the shortest and speediest way. . . . The greatness and glory of the country depended upon the Union; it was worth every sacrifice—worth more than peace, desirable as peace might be."[75]

While Northerners took to the battlefields, Pendleton reminded his audience that he had endeavored to force the administration to act in a way conducive to future reunification. In practice, he had held the president firmly to traditional constitutional proscriptions because he believed they were as important during war as in peace. After defending his record on war measures, he turned to address the changing face of the administration. Lincoln's determination to seek compensated emancipation and his trampling of constitutional rights through unlawful arrests demanded a new approach by the minority party. While the Extreme Peace Democrats had provided only limited support of the president in conducting the war, even less than the Moderate Peace Democrats, that succor would now end. Moderates such as Samuel Cox were withdrawing their commitment as well. Their backing, which had been based on a war to restore the Union as it was under the Constitution, could no longer be extended to a war for emancipation. This shift had begun in the second session, and Pendleton informed his constituents that, following the break, he would stand firm against this new Republican crusade.[76]

Pendleton stood as a member of a legitimate opposition; he was no traitor. He never plotted a conspiracy with the Confederacy or expressed a desire for their success. He was a loyal unionist, and yet a confirmed racist. Continually declaring his support for Northern troops in word and deed, he voted for all appropriations and war measures that did not challenge his view of the Constitution. Pendleton maintained a hierarchy of principles. At the top, he upheld the Jacksonian strict constructionist view of the Constitution, which provided the foundation for several other key principles: states' rights, civil liberties, limited presidential power, and white supremacy. These were unalterable. Ranking somewhere below was his desire to see the North win the Civil War. Republicans equated winning the war with preserving the Union, but Pendleton did not. He believed that Lincoln's administration had hindered rather than fostered reconciliation. Reunion could be achieved much more quickly and easily through compromise, concession, and peace. While seeking to sustain his principles, he frequently opposed Republican actions in Congress. Yet he was no mere obstructionist. Pendleton often supported measures to supply the troops and conceded that war might be a necessary evil. He advocated many legitimate revenue-raising techniques, only to be forced to oppose them due to partisan amendments favoring Republican political cronies. His willingness to sustain the war effort was always tempered by his fierce defense of the Constitution.

Pendleton wanted a return to the America he had known before the war. That is why he clung so tenaciously to his hierarchy of principles. He did not fully recognize, however, that the maintenance of those principles inhibited the war effort. As the conflict limped into its third bloody year, and Lincoln adeptly made emancipation in the Confederacy a key goal, the character of the war changed. As it did, Pendleton refused to accept this new war aim. His resolve only intensified. The America he had once known and sought to preserve was fading with the emerging realities of the coming social and economic revolution. Though that revolution was the logical extension of many of his own political ideals, Pendleton never entertained the idea of applying Jacksonianism to Black America. As the twilight of the old America approached, Pendleton dug in his heels and became an obstructionist, a role he had carefully avoided in previous congressional sessions. He saw no other way to slow down the whirlwind of change he was so unwilling to accept.

Pendleton the Obstructionist

By the late summer of 1862, President Abraham Lincoln had forged a powerful, centralized government from a small, diffused antebellum system. Instituting the draft, an income tax, higher tariffs, and property confiscation and issuing a preliminary emancipation proclamation, even while circumventing civil liberties such as the writ of habeas corpus, Lincoln expanded the role and authority of the federal government to a position not previously imagined. Lincoln's use of the war to accomplish his longtime goal of destroying the slave system was shrewd and demonstrated his understanding of the inconsistency between the country's founding documents and ideals and the noxious institution. Most of these actions constituted necessary wartime acts. Some Democrats, however, viewed some of them as strictly partisan Republican endeavors. Yet, despite these policies, the Union forces had made few advances against the Confederacy.

George Hunt Pendleton used the military's poor showing to further repudiate what he viewed as Lincoln's aggrandizement of power. The executive not only had disregarded constitutional proscriptions and violated individual rights in the cause of the war, Pendleton charged, but also had failed to achieve any significant military gains. No matter how repetitive his appeals sounded in the halls of Congress, Pendleton resolved to reiterate Democratic principles and champion constitutional liberties for white Americans. Though Pendleton's opposition to the Republican administration made him appear to be a Southern sympathizer, the expanding government's inept war record seemed to legitimize his position. As long as Northern forces did poorly, his criticisms remained credible. The possibility of changing military fortunes clearly threatened his political agenda, because successes on the battlefield would justify Lincoln's policies. This prospect left Pendleton and all Peace men vulnerable.

As the conflict ground on, and when the president issued the official Emanci
pation Proclamation in January 1863, Pendleton renewed his determination to
thwart further government expansion.[1]

Early in the third session of the Thirty-seventh Congress, Pendleton led
the charge against Thaddeus Stevens and a bill he introduced, "An Act to Indemnify the President." Stevens endeavored to exempt the president, and any
member of the military involved in suspending the writ of habeas corpus, from
criminal or civil prosecution.[2] Pendleton immediately responded with a formal
protest to the Congress printed in the *Congressional Globe*. It was signed by
thirty-five other members, including notable Peace Democrats such as Clement Vallandigham, Samuel S. Cox, and Daniel W. Voorhees of Indiana. The
protest reiterated Pendleton's previous arguments against the alleged power of
the president to suspend the writ. The fact that such a bill was introduced, the
Peace Democrats contended, proved that they had been correct; the president
did not need the bill if he had acted legally. The protest further contended that
those who had been treated maliciously and illegally by military authorities,
only to be released upon recognition of their innocence, had no recourse in the
courts. "It could never be proper to indemnify the President and those acting
under his authority at the expense of the citizen whom they had injured."[3] By
removing the right of redress, by indemnifying the president, and by allowing
unlawful arrests to continue, Congress was acting unconstitutionally, the pro-
testers asserted. They also decried the tactics of Stevens, who pushed the bill
through in less than an hour with no debate.[4]

When the bill returned from the Senate for reconsideration in the House,
Pendleton again tried to halt its passage. Together with other House Democrats, he used dilatory tactics, delaying the proceedings and preventing a vote
on the bill. The Democrats delayed business for hours by calling for repeated
votes excusing members from being present. At one point, the proceedings became laughable as a member from Indiana rose to a question of order that was
rejected because the House had previously voted on excusing his absence. In
another instance, William Holman, a War Democrat from Indiana, said, "To
render the order of the House more effective, would it be in order to suspend
the writ of *habeas corpus?*" Bringing the laughter to an abrupt halt, Pendleton
responded, "That has already been suspended under the call of the President."[5]
Pendleton took these proceedings as anything but humorous and opposed all
efforts to pass the bill. It did pass, however and, even worse for him, was upheld
by the Supreme Court.[6]

A second major bill, which Pendleton deemed equally detrimental to all
American citizens, was a conscription bill, eventually known as the Enroll-
ment Act. The bill gave the federal government control over state militias and

their officers, which Democrats believed to be under the supervision of state governments alone. Peace men suggested a variety of possible abuses as logical ancillaries to such an act. If the draft passed, it left open the possibility of the government entering into a future war without the consent of the states. The Republic had been founded on a fear of standing armies in peacetime, which many Democrats believed would result from this bill. Speaking briefly, Pendleton emphasized his concern over further strengthening the executive office. Combined with the Indemnification Bill, this legislation went a long way toward military despotism. He could not help but see an inconsistency in using the army of a free republic, created by the power of a draft, to subdue a segment of the nation that had defied established laws.[7]

Through the collective efforts of Pendleton and his party, the Democrats managed to amend the bill. Specifically, they modified portions of the bill that called draft dodging a "treasonable practice" and allowed the military to arrest and hold those that did not report for duty when called. Their amendments eliminated the treason clause and allowed evaders trials in civil courts. In the end, Republicans pushed this bill through Congress as well, but it continued to meet opposition even outside of Congress.[8] In the eyes of many Jacksonians, the Conscription Act, "biased against the poor, magnifying white racial fears, and involving the federal government as never before in local affairs," represented everything they stood against.[9] In the wake of the Emancipation Proclamation, they asserted, it appeared the Republicans were willing to sacrifice the interests of the common white man for the benefit of the black man. When combined with other tensions in the bubbling cauldron of New York City, the draft resulted in mob violence.

Associated with the need for more Northern troops, a bill calling for the enlistment of African American troops elicited a similar response from Democratic critics. Congress had passed the Militia Act in July 1862, but many Radical Republicans were frustrated by Lincoln's unwillingness to implement it. The act allowed the president to form and use black regiments, but did not require it. Now seen as a means to implement Lincoln's recent Emancipation Proclamation, Stevens introduced a bill compelling the enlistment of 150,000 black troops. He later backed down, accepting a substitute giving the president the discretion of raising as many black troops as needed. The new bill added a provision to compensate unionist slave owners for slaves who left to join the military. As with previous legislation, Stevens tried to ram his bill through the House without committee consideration and without debate. Pendleton and the Democrats would not be excluded. As with the Indemnification Bill, Peace Democrats brought the legislative process to a halt using various dilatory rules. After a night of roll call votes and reconsiderations on adjournment, Republicans finally gave in and accepted a full-scale debate.[10]

Pendleton took advantage of this opportunity to speak before the House. He began by noting the failure of black recruitment in Kansas. Within two weeks of being sworn in, half of a black regiment had deserted with bounty in hand. He also cited a resolution by Justin S. Morrill, a Republican from Vermont, stating that the army had sufficient troops and abundant supplies to win the war. It had passed easily with the vote of every Republican present. Pendleton wondered how the situation could have changed so dramatically in the two months since that resolution passed. He further questioned the results of enlisting blacks. The number of white volunteers would dwindle, he predicted, and discipline among and between white and black regiments would be difficult to maintain. He astutely wondered what would happen with the black troops following the war. They could not be relegated to social and political inferiority after fighting for the Union and the Constitution. The Congress would have to award them political rights, an idea not readily accepted even in the free North. Tying this issue to military reverses the Union forces had recently suffered, as well as to the declining value of legal tender notes, Pendleton suggested that these were the bitter fruits of a new war policy. Lincoln had called northwesterners "into the Army under the pretense that the war was to be for the Union and the Constitution, when, in fact, it was to be an armed crusade for the abolition of slavery."[11] This deception was the root cause of declining volunteers, he argued, and thus the rising need for conscription and African American troops. The bill, Pendleton concluded, would not only lead to the defection of the loyal Border States but also strengthen Southern resolve to continue the fight.[12]

Pendleton's efforts and those of other Democrats led to several modifications in Stevens's bill. As passed by the House, it did not allow the enlistment of the slaves of loyal citizens, placing black officers in charge of white troops, or the recruitment of blacks in Border States. Nevertheless, the entire episode proved to be a study in futility. The bill never became law, as the Senate deemed previous measures sufficient. Perhaps of greater importance is the effect this debate had on the soldiers themselves. White soldiers began to defend the idea of raising more black soldiers because of their desire to see the war end. Pendleton had been right earlier when he suggested that many Union soldiers would resist fighting with blacks, but that opposition began to wither in the war weariness of 1863 and 1864.[13]

Pendleton's disagreements with the administration stopped short of supporting any action that would needlessly injure troops operating under Lincoln's command. Pendleton sought to provide for their needs and addressed a military problem he read about in the *Cincinnati Times*. A correspondent reported that medical facilities and standards were inadequate among Maj. Gen. Ulysses S. Grant's troops. Pendleton immediately introduced a resolution in Congress to investigate the allegations. The assistant surgeon general at St. Louis, Robert C. Wood, quickly asked Pendleton for the source of his information and interviewed General Grant and his men to clear up the matter. From his research, Wood concluded that the report was false. Pendleton assured him that he did not wish "to make groundless complaints," but rather to ensure good care for the troops.[14]

In February 1863, Congress passed the National Bank Act. It chartered banks authorized to issue national banknotes based on a percentage of the value of their holdings in U.S. bonds. These notes, then, were not backed by specie. Secretary of the Treasury Salmon P. Chase proposed the idea to encourage currency reform and to provide the government with more revenue. Although the act ultimately added little to the treasury, it did establish a uniform national banking system and forced hundreds of unstable state banks out of business. Democrats inevitably viewed this act as an attempt to resurrect the Second National Bank. Upholding his Jacksonian roots, Pendleton uniformly opposed this centralization of monetary power and movement away from hard currency. Midwestern Peace men especially loathed the plan, as they feared it would reestablish New England control of western banking.[15]

In a speech on the last day of the Thirty-seventh Congress, Pendleton addressed a constitutional question that had arisen earlier in the session but one for which he would gain no satisfactory answer. Earlier, Vallandigham had introduced a resolution to have the Committee of the Judiciary investigate the exclusion of certain newspapers from the mail.[16] As a member of the committee, Pendleton worked unsuccessfully to censure the president for his actions in authorizing the postmaster general to bar newspapers he believed to be perpetrating treason or causing insurrection. Citing congressional precedents from 1840, Pendleton argued that the postmaster general lacked constitutional authority to prohibit the circulation of the mail; only Congress could act in this area. The provision for the freedom of the press, he continued, inherently included the right to use the services of the Postal Department. Again, Pendleton noted several occasions where congressmen, including John C. Calhoun and Daniel Webster, agreed that only Congress could decide on appropriate restrictions. Knowing that the Republican defense relied on military exigency, Pendleton reiterated that the Constitution was equally valid in war and in peace.[17] Referring to their reasonings based on "military necessity" and "martial law" as "flimsy pretexts," he erupted, "they are the specious names under which cowardice seeks to skulk from observation while it gratifies its malignant rage. They are the inventions of despotic power, distorted from their original purpose by a party distressed and baffled by the humiliations of a war which it had not the virtue to prevent and has not the ability to manage."[18]

Pendleton must have breathed a sigh of relief as he left Washington on a cool spring day in March 1863. Though still feeling the stinging rebuke of Republicans whose large majority led to the ineffectiveness of his party, Pendleton believed his positions and actions were both justified and constitutional. As he looked forward to some time away from the political battlefield, hopes lingered in the back of his mind for the next Congress. Several leading Democrats had mentioned his name for Speaker of the House. It would take large Democratic gains in the midterm election to make that position attainable. The *Cincinnati Enquirer,* along with many other western papers, had already backed the idea, writing that Pendleton was above corruption and had faithfully stood by the Constitution. "The West," the *Enquirer* declared, "[was] entitled to the next Speaker on the ground of locality and political service."[19] Pendleton corresponded with party leaders seeking support for his bid, but Samuel Cox was also mentioned as a possible candidate, as he had received several votes in the previous Congress. In a letter to Alexander Long, a friend and supporter, Pendleton expressed his concerns about Cox: "The unreliability of my competitor increases every day. He shivers in every breeze."[20] Regardless of his inconsistent congressional record, Cox also busily drummed up support. Recognizing the dangers of their competing candidacies, the two met and decided to leave the nomination to the Ohio delegation caucus. They did not wish to divide the vote and weaken their party's chances. Pendleton failed to receive a majority of the Ohio caucus vote, and Cox made the run. At least one member of the delegation explained that he had committed his vote for Cox before knowing that Pendleton was a candidate. Yet a more plausible reason for Pendleton's defeat was apparent. James J. Faran, the previous editor of the *Cincinnati Enquirer,* told Long that Cox probably won due to the votes of the War Democrats in the caucus. Cox had a more moderate reputation, based on his congressional record, than did Pendleton.[21] The Democrats remained a deeply divided party.

Pendleton's break between sessions proved anything but uneventful. He traveled throughout the Buckeye state, speaking at Democratic conventions during the fall campaign. What would have been a relatively normal canvass in Ohio was shattered when the military arrested Clement Vallandigham. The newly assigned commander of the Department of the Ohio, Maj. Gen. Ambrose E. Burnside, feared the rise of the Sons of Liberty, a secret organization that allegedly supported the Confederate cause and was often associated with the Peace Democrats by the Republicans. On April 13, 1863, Burnside issued a series of general orders to Ohioans concerning bearing arms and uttering public statements sympathetic to the Confederacy. Vallandigham, Pendleton, and others were scheduled to speak to a rally of Knox County Democrats at Mount Vernon a couple of weeks after the order was announced. Burnside had thrown down the gauntlet, and Ohioans knew Vallandigham would run right into it. He saw arrest and the resulting political martyrdom as guaranteeing him the Democratic gubernatorial nomination for the fall election. The procession into Mount Vernon on May 1 was four to five miles long with some five hundred wagons. There were so many people that they would not all be able to hear the speeches. As a result, the town set up stages elsewhere and gathered impromptu speakers to discuss the issues of the election. When he got up to speak, Vallandigham noticed that there were two military men near the stage with pencil and paper in hand to take notes. These were Burnside's men, and Vallandigham did not want to disappoint them. He unloaded on Lincoln's administration of the war and Burnside's abuse of power by restricting free speech. Burnside rightly interpreted these comments as defiance of his order and had Vallandigham arrested at his Dayton home on May 4 at 2:30 A.M.[22]

Pendleton, George Pugh, and Alexander Ferguson acted as Vallandigham's counsels, though he conducted his own defense at the trial before a military commission. After Vallandigham failed to gain his own release, Pugh appealed to the circuit court for a writ of habeas corpus, but the judge stated that he had no authority over a military trial. The military tribunal feared that execution would make Vallandigham a martyr, so they sentenced him to prison for the duration of the war, but President Lincoln intervened and banished him to the Confederacy. Pendleton stayed with his friend throughout the trial and kept in close contact after he was expelled. The Confederates wanted nothing to do with him. With their help, Vallandigham quickly escaped to Canada on a blockade runner, and there Pendleton and Pugh often met with him. Many Buckeyes had spoken of Vallandigham as a possible candidate for governor, and his arrest indeed made him a martyr for the Democratic cause. The state convention acted on the sentiments of Ohio's Democrats, nominating Vallandigham with Pugh as his running mate.[23]

To Pendleton, Lincoln's support of Burnside vindicated his warnings about the administration's erosion and disregard of constitutional freedoms. In reality, Lincoln was upset with Burnside's actions, which he believed ultimately helped the Democrats and hampered the war effort by further disrupting Northern unity. Nonetheless, Pendleton, along with eighteen Ohio Democrats, wrote the president to lodge a complaint and requested the return of Vallandigham. Lincoln responded by accusing Vallandigham of encouraging resistance to the war effort, but said he would remove the sentence if the petitioners publicly signed a statement supporting the war effort. They declared that if Vallandigham was wrongly imprisoned, his release should not be contingent on such a demeaning arrangement.[24]

Democrats around the country responded in like fashion. A meeting in Albany, New York, crafted ten resolutions castigating the president's actions.

They echoed Pendleton's frequent assertions in Congress that military exigency did not mitigate the government's responsibility to preserve individual liberties. Democratic government, they argued, demanded their maintenance. Lincoln responded to the "Albany Resolves" with an open letter. The president justified his actions and launched an attack on those who hid behind the protections of the Constitution in their bid to destroy it and the nation. And indeed, Lincoln's position deserved consideration. The Constitution never anticipated a civil war and such an emergency demanded extreme measures. Lincoln took no pleasure in expanding the role of government and agonized over most every decision. In his mind, he stretched the Constitution for a short period of time to preserve the Union and end slavery. Lincoln's most decisive volley queried, "Must I shoot a simple-minded soldier boy who deserts, while I must not touch a hair of the wiley [*sic*] agitator who induces him to desert?"[25] Nonetheless, the Democrats were undeterred.

Meanwhile, Ohio Democrats continued to make the most of the situation, campaigning around the state and attacking the Republicans with a familiar litany against confiscation, conscription, emancipation, and the suspension of habeas corpus.[26] Pendleton, Pugh, and like-minded men took to the stump. Pendleton wrote to an Indiana Democratic meeting, as the excitement extended outside the state, that freedom of discussion was a constitutional right. "Living, I shall assert it; and should I leave no other inheritance to my children, by the blessing of God, I will leave them the inheritance of free principles and the example of a manly, independent and Constitutional defense of them."[27] Speaking at the Ohio state convention, Pugh said, "I may not agree with Mr. Vallandigham in all his opinions respecting the prosecution or the conclusion of this war . . . but I will maintain his right to express those opinions."[28] These men risked their liberty by speaking so freely against the arrest and the actions of the administration, but Pendleton believed that "Order 38 . . . [had] accomplished its purpose."[29]

The administration successfully removed Vallandigham from the political arena. Though physically absent, the arrest initially catapulted him into a competitive position. His prospects looked good at the outset, and Pendleton worked tirelessly for him, but Vallandigham fell to Union challenger John Brough by a huge margin. While Vallandigham ran significantly better than the Democratic vote the year before, the Republicans gained almost seventy thousand more votes than in the previous election. Some Democrats cried fraud, but there was little evidence to substantiate the allegation, at least in the home vote. In the soldier vote, there was coercion and, in at least one case, no Democratic ballots provided. Yet, even if all of the soldier votes cast had gone for Vallandigham, he still would not have won. The Union victories at the battles of Gettysburg and Vicksburg undoubtedly helped Lincoln's party. The Republicans made gains in the House of Representatives as well, eliminating Democratic chances for the speakership.[30]

Heedless of these losses, recently elected Congressman Alexander Long from Ohio, a peace-at-any-price man, rose before the newly seated Thirty-eighth Congress to propose an armistice. He suggested that Lincoln ask former presidents Franklin Pierce and Millard Fillmore, along with Thomas Ewing of Ohio and any others he might choose, as commissioners to meet at a peace conference with the Confederate leaders to restore the Southern states to the Union with their previous rights. The resolution failed. Though Pendleton supported it, most Democrats refused to go along. Pendleton further tested Democratic unity by introducing a resolution denouncing Vallandigham's arrest as unconstitutional. That resolution failed as well, though more Democrats supported it than had voted for Long's proposal.[31]

Long did not rest after his initial defeat, however, and shortly thereafter addressed Congress in a lengthy speech. He denounced the war and asserted that after three years the Union was not close to victory. In fact, he argued, the president's assault on the Constitution only made that prospect less likely. The Radical Republican legislative program left him cynical concerning reconciliation. "An acknowledgment of the independence of the South as an independent nation," he jabbed, "or their complete subjugation and extermination as a people" were the only two possible alternatives at this stage of the conflict.[32] Long preferred the former. The Republican response was vituperative. Schuyler Colfax, Speaker of the House, came down from his chair to fight for Long's expulsion. As he had done for Vallandigham, Pendleton led the defense of his friend.[33]

Pendleton prefaced his remarks by deliberately refusing to take a position on Long's statements. Rather, Pendleton based his views on constitutional principles and the history of the House, whose chief function, he recalled, was "discussion."[34] While the House had the right to decide on the form and process of debate, it could not regulate the expression of opinion. It could expel members for improper conduct, but not censure them for presenting the views of their constituents for the consideration of the Congress. Otherwise, Pendleton asserted, the minority party would forever be reliant on the majority opinion. Moreover, the right to state opinions was not dependent on the exigencies of the country. Great conflict did not prohibit the free discourse of ideas, as some Republicans had suggested. After enumerating several examples from English and American history concerning expulsion, Pendleton called on his colleagues to prevent the disfranchisement of Long's constituents and the destruction of the Constitution.[35]

Many other Peace Democrats followed Pendleton's lead in defending Long's right to speak. Benjamin G. Harris of Maryland went too far in his defense, however, when he said that he hoped the Union forces would fail to subjugate the South. Their failure, he opined, would prevent possible despotism. For his statements, Harris was censured by the House. Samuel Cox argued that Long had the right to express his opinions, citing remarks of several Republicans who had earlier suggested recognizing the Confederacy. The lengthy debate over Long's expulsion ended with mixed results. Although Pendleton and the Peace Democrats prevented his ouster, they could not avert a resolution of censure.[36]

After the initial partisan attacks calling for Long's ouster died down, the main issue of the first session became the federal government's position toward African Americans. Because the president's Emancipation Proclamation held no force of law, the congressional Republicans sought to bolster it by urging a new amendment to the Constitution. Pendleton was the obvious choice to lead the Democratic response. He had many times evidenced his commitment to white supremacy in previous battles against abolition. Even more, as the most prominent midwestern Democrat and one of the few to be in the House for four consecutive terms, he held a leadership role in the severely factionalized party. Among Peace men, there was no other midwesterner of his stature.[37]

The amendment passed the Senate with the support of Republicans and some War Democrats but met with stiff opposition in the House. Pendleton aggressively relied on time-tested Democratic principles to excoriate the amendment as inexpedient. First, he noted that an amendment could not possibly be ratified by the required twenty-seven states, as only nineteen remained in the Union. Even if the abolitionists gained the votes of four of the Border States, they would still be considerably short of the required number. If Southern states, under military rule, were forced to ratify the amendment, he feared that the Union would never last. Besides these problems, he argued, President Lincoln was already dealing with a backlash in response to the proclamation as indicated by lower volunteer rates. Northern states did not support such a proposition. Furthermore, he continued, the amendment was unconstitutional. His was a novel argument, but once the amendment was ratified, ending slavery could no longer be construed as unconstitutional. Recognizing this problem, he changed gears and came at the issue from yet another angle. The Constitution did not have jurisdiction over the internal affairs of the states. This was not an amendment, he asserted. It was a revolution and "another step toward consolidation, and consolidation is despotism; confederation is liberty."[38] After a historical discourse on the nature of government in America, Pendleton concluded, "I have desired to maintain that the States are sovereign; that their powers are inherent; that they comprise the undelegated mass; that the Federal Government is their agent, derives all its powers in their name; . . . and its powers are . . . limited to the grants declared in the Constitution."[39] On the strength of his arguments, enough House Democrats opposed the amendment to prevent the necessary two-thirds majority, and it died in the session.

Pendleton responded to the proposed Bureau of Refugees, Freedmen, and Abandoned Lands as he had abolition. Operating as part of the War Department, the bureau was designed to act as a relief agency for the freedmen, establishing an educational system and a labor contract system between planters and the African American laborers. On constitutional grounds, he considered freedmen under state control. Moreover, Pendleton believed an alternate system was already in place. The army had put freedmen to work, and the tax the army placed on black workers could care for women and children. Cox stigmatized the bill as too expensive, but for Pendleton the issue went far beyond finances. He concluded that federal interference in the form of centralized bureaus in the Southern states would inhibit reunification. That the War Department controlled the bureau suggested too great a role for the military in the postwar South, perhaps suggesting martial law. This idea was repugnant to Pendleton. The federal government's policies toward Native Americans served as his case in point. After years of military control and well-intentioned philanthropy, Native Americans were still not assimilated. Further, Pendleton predicted strong resistance by Southern whites. In short, Pendleton had no wish to tinker with the prevailing racial and social systems in the South. While he sympathized with the plight of newly freed African Americans living in limbo somewhere between citizenship and slavery, his compassion stopped short of federal intervention to provide a better life for them.[40]

Republican efforts to end slavery constitutionally stirred other controversies linked to their vision of the postwar United States. In a policy statement outlining his plan for reconstruction, Lincoln stated his willingness to recognize Southern state governments when one-tenth of the voters, as of 1860, took oaths of loyalty and accepted the Emancipation Proclamation. In August 1864, Radical Republicans took his plan a step further. Sen. Benjamin Wade of Ohio and Rep. Henry Winter Davis of Maryland introduced a bill requiring that 51 percent of the white male citizens in each reconstructed state create a new constitution abolishing slavery. These new constitutions would have other stipulations as well. They would prohibit those who served in the Confederate army or government from voting or holding office, and the states would be required to repudiate the Confederate war debts.[41]

During the debate on the Wade-Davis Bill, Pendleton rose to speak. His words dripped with exasperation. After mentioning the bill's provisions, Pendleton sighed that at last the truth was disclosed. Mounting taxes, unthinkable casualties, and illegal arrests had not been squandered to reunite the nation but to bring about a revolution. With growing outrage, Pendleton seethed, "If

revolt against constituted authority be a crime, if patriotism consist in uphold
ing in form and spirit the Government our fathers made, those in power here
today are as guilty as those who in the seceded States marshal armed men for
the contest."[42]

With even more indignation, Pendleton heaped scorn on the bill's constitutionality. He wondered where the authority was granted the federal government
to take over a state, appoint a governor, and force a new constitution on its
citizens. Republicans placed the bill under the umbrella clause that gave Congress the power to guarantee a republican form of government in each state.
Pendleton insisted that such governments had flourished in the South throughout the war. Even if they had not, he questioned how that clause could be construed to allow for abolition when the Founding Fathers had not prohibited the
institution. Pendleton feared that if the government intervened and legislated
domestic issues in the South, it could surely do so in Ohio or anywhere else.
Reiterating his states' rights position, he declared that "if this be the alternative
of secession, I should prefer that secession should succeed."[43] He favored living
in an autonomous state with a free government, rather than in the Union under
despotism. After these remarks, so reminiscent of those that secured Long's censure, Pendleton softened his final statements. The only road to reunion under
a true republic, he concluded, was if the American people returned the Democrats to power in the Northern states. While Pendleton failed to prevent the
passage of the bill, President Lincoln pocket vetoed it on the grounds that he
was unsure if Congress could constitutionally abolish the institution of slavery.
Indeed, Pendleton must have smiled at the President's reasoning.[44]

The rest of the first session of the Thirty-eighth Congress was just as turbulent. Pendleton continued to address the House on a variety of issues. As a
member of the Committee on Ways and Means, he focused much attention
on financial matters and maintained his earlier position on those issues. When
it came to the needs of the soldiers, he was happy to vote them supplies.[45] Yet
he used a litmus test concerning revenue raised for the war effort by evaluating
each measure against his constitutional beliefs and his midwestern convictions.
One example was a bill to allow the secretary of the treasury to sell gold coin
at his discretion. Pendleton opposed the bill as it enlarged the secretary's power
and put the government's financial stability at risk. Part of the proposal would
have allowed the government to exchange gold for greenbacks, which were
worth only fifty to sixty cents on the dollar. When the greenbacks were issued,
they were fiat bills of exchange, accepted by the public at face value backed by
faith in the government. Now, Pendleton argued, the government expected
citizens to take an even greater loss by making the greenbacks legal currency.
Private interests seeking private gain, he believed, precipitated the bill. The

aggrandizement of power by the secretary, who with just a few million dollars' worth of gold could manipulate the gold market dramatically, was too great.[46] Pendleton also worked his states' rights views into the financial debates by fighting for the right of states to tax the national banks as well as government bonds and notes.[47] On both issues, he was powerless to gain their enactment.

On other topics that surfaced during the session, such as confiscation, conscription, and freedom of the press, Pendleton remained consistent in his opposition to the enhancement of federal power.[48] When a bill to organize the territory of Montana was proposed, Pendleton objected on the grounds that the suffrage provision delineated requirements based only on age and gender, not race. Pendleton read this as an attempt to provide the vote for blacks, the next step in the Republican postwar plan after emancipation. Republicans repeatedly denied that their aim was political equality for the freedman, but they passed this bill over Democratic opposition and suspicion of their motives.[49]

By the close of the first session, Pendleton had grown weary of playing the obstructionist. Remaining loyal to the Union as it was, he opposed what he viewed to be Republican usurpations of power and unconstitutional restrictions on personal liberties. Maintaining Jacksonian principles, he set his own course. He did not blindly follow others such as Vallandigham, whose notorious reputation tainted future political endeavors for himself and his party. Nor did he consistently support moderates such as Cox, whom he felt conceded too much support to an unworthy administration. Pendleton's hierarchy of principles consistently guided his path. Though he clung to his racism—and his other views may have been too conservative for the realities of a changing America—he represented a large segment of the Midwest that was not ready for the changes ahead. In spite of the difficulties of his role, Pendleton's principles, combined with his reputation for hard work and excellent oratory, propelled him to the highest levels of national prominence in the Democratic Party.

Yet Pendleton's principles would also cost him. Not only would they cost him politically, but they would also take their toll personally. His family was shunned from formal engagements and social events in Washington. Nonetheless, when Alice bore a new baby girl, the family reflected George's political commitments by naming her Anna Peace Pendleton. But she was not a healthy child. While Pendleton was battling for peace in the halls of Congress, little Anna Peace was fighting for life at home. Like so many babies in the nineteenth century, she would not live through infancy.[50]

As the Democrats faced the 1864 presidential election, they had serious obstacles to surmount. Because the Civil War had torn away a sizable portion of their national party, Northern Democrats had to unite the various factions of those who remained loyal to the party. At the Democratic National Convention in Chicago, party leaders sought to nominate a ticket that would appeal to all ideological and geographical sectors of the Democracy. They desired to unite the East and West as well as the war and peace factions of their party. Of all the potential candidates who might unify the party, Pendleton epitomized the type of person the Democrats sought. The candidate could not be someone who appeared sympathetic to the Confederate cause, but had to represent those who opposed the administration of the war. Some began to think George Pendleton fit the bill.

From Victory Came Defeat

Returning home to Cincinnati in July 1864, George Pendleton anticipated the coming turbulent and trying times associated with the fall
elections. Though some Democrats around him wavered and bent
with the popular wind, Pendleton remained steadfast in his position. Peace-at-
any-price men (also called "ultras") and Extreme Peace Democrats maintained
their congressional unity and reflected the growing peace sentiment among war-
weary Northerners. Desiring the nomination of a Peace Democrat for president,
this group considered Horatio Seymour of New York, Thomas H. Seymour of
Connecticut, and possibly even Pendleton as the most likely prospects. Electing
a peace man, the ultras and extremists believed, would announce to the Confederates that the North sought true compromise and peace. Moderates such as
Samuel S. Cox ended their post-Emancipation Proclamation association with
the Extreme Peace Democrats, fearing a public perception of disloyalty. Under
Cox's leadership, Moderate Peace Democrats supported continuation of the war
for the Union but repudiated Lincoln's call for emancipation. Joining with War
Democrats, the moderates sought to nominate Gen. George B. McClellan at
the upcoming convention.[1]

Four months prior to Pendleton's trip home, Ohio Democrats gathered in
Columbus to elect delegates-at-large to the national convention. War Demo-
crats seized control of the gathering through adept maneuvering and elected
George Rex presiding officer. Rex organized the convention and the prowar
men elected the four delegates-at-large. Three favored the nomination of Mc-
Clellan, a War Democrat: William Allen, Allen Thurman, and Rufus Ranney.
Passing over more intractable Peace men, such as Vallandigham and Samuel
Medary of the *Crisis,* delegates chose one Peace Democrat: George H. Pend-
leton. Pendleton's early but limited support of the war effort and his tactful

opposition to Lincoln afforded him a reputation for moderation. Moreover, War Democrats sought to placate the strong peace element in Ohio with their choice of Pendleton and hoped that they could persuade him to support McClellan. For War Democrats, the chief aim was the defeat of Vallandigham. Gen. George W. Morgan of Licking County sacrificed his personal hopes for one of the four slots to prevent a split vote favoring Vallandigham. Dayton residents later ensured Vallandigham's presence at the national convention, however, when they elected him a district delegate.[2]

In spite of the divisions, Pendleton had some reasons for optimism about the upcoming election. His reelection bid in 1862 had resulted in substantial gains for the entire party, reflecting the successes of the Democrats outside of Ohio as well. Pendleton and his party pinned their hopes to defeat Lincoln on the downward curve of the war effort, leaving the party open to a flank attack. Republicans were relying on victories in the late spring and summer campaigns being waged by generals William Sherman and Ulysses S. Grant. By July, however, both men had fallen short of their goals. Mounting Union losses combined with Lincoln's disregard for civil liberties left many Northerners livid. Losing confidence in the president, Northerners tired of the war. With Lincoln's July call for more volunteers, peace sentiment exploded. Representing this cresting tide, Pendleton hoped either to ride to another term in Congress or to a bid for higher office. If Union war fortunes changed, however, Democratic chances of defeating the president would be seriously undermined. Even worse, Lincoln's conversion of the Republican Party into the National Union Party and the addition of former War Democrat Andrew Johnson to his ticket garnered support among wavering War Democrats.[3]

Although Lincoln's political fortunes depended on an improving war effort, the president also faced divisions within his party. Lincoln threw his support behind a constitutional amendment ending slavery, a move that undercut his Radical Republican opponents. Interestingly, the Radicals had done the spadework for what Lincoln had long desired. His support for the amendment was the logical progression from his earlier amendment proposals and the Emancipation Proclamation. Yet Radicals, such as Ohio's Benjamin F. Wade, lost confidence in the president's war leadership and questioned his Reconstruction plans, especially after he pocket-vetoed the radical Wade-Davis Bill. A Republican senator from Kansas, Samuel C. Pomeroy, shared this disillusion. As the head of an informal group dedicated to promoting the candidacy of Secretary of the Treasury Salmon P. Chase, Pomeroy issued a circular calling Lincoln's chances of reelection remote and urged his swift withdrawal. The effort failed.[4]

Another radical movement directly defied Lincoln. Meeting in Cleveland in May 1864, his opponents formed a new party, the Radical Democrats, and nominated a hybrid ticket. John C. Frémont, a radical Republican, ran for president; his running mate was John Cochrane, a War Democrat. Positioning themselves on a platform supporting a constitutional amendment to end slavery and endorsing the rights of free speech and habeas corpus, Radical Democrats sought wide bipartisan support. Frémont proved a reluctant nominee, however, and vowed to withdraw if Lincoln was not renominated. Most Republicans viewed this convention as an attempt to divide and conquer their party. Democrats were equally suspicious. While they publicized the effort as a means to split the Republicans, they had no intention of supporting the Radical Democrats. Even so, the movement further convinced many Democrats that Lincoln was vulnerable.[5]

It remained problematic, however, how Democrats would cope with their own handicaps. War Democrats favored General McClellan, who had served as a major general in Lincoln's army. While he favored vigorous prosecution of the war to restore the Union, McClellan balked at the president's disregard for civil liberties. In a letter to Lincoln in July 1862, McClellan had expressed his discomfiture at the confiscation of private property and warned against interference with slavery. McClellan's well-publicized differences with the president over these and military matters resulted in his dismissal. Leading Peace Democrats, such as Pendleton, Vallandigham, and Fernando Wood of New York, opposed the general. Not only did he accept the legitimacy of coercion, but also he had been responsible for the arrest of several members of the Maryland legislature who were allegedly acting in collusion with the Confederacy. McClellan carried out this injustice without allowance for a writ of habeas corpus. Peace Democrats equated this action with Burnside's arrest of Vallandigham.[6]

Pendleton and the Democratic congressional caucus met prior to the summer break and called for a peace platform at the upcoming Chicago convention. The strength of the peace sentiment in Congress, combined with the growing power of that element in the Midwest, persuaded many War Democrats to advise McClellan to appease the Peace Democrats through public support of an armistice. General Morgan wrote him repeatedly, emphasizing the growing numbers of Pendleton and Vallandigham followers in Ohio. Fearing a peace faction bolt at the convention, Morgan suggested that McClellan present the appearance of unanimity and subscribe to Medary's ultra peace paper, the *Crisis*. In response, McClellan complained to New York editor William C. Prime, "I receive so many suggestions that I have determined to follow my own judgment in these matters. Morgan is anxious that I should write a letter suggesting an *armistice*!!!! If these fools will ruin the country, I won't help them."[7]

The Peace Democrats vowed to fight McClellan's nomination. Vallandigham and Wood held public meetings in Dayton and New York in support of Gov. Horatio Seymour of New York. When Seymour declined to run, Vallandigham turned to Connecticut's governor, Thomas H. Seymour. Some of Ohio's Peace Democrats urged either Pendleton or Vallandigham to seek the nomination. Others found in Pendleton a possible vice-presidential candidate. Pendleton had no illusions about his chances for the presidential nomination and did not actively form an organization to that end. Some of his supporters in Ohio did work on his behalf, though their efforts were no match for the McClellan campaign machine. So strong was McClellan's name recognition and organization, now supported by wealthy New Yorkers August Belmont and Samuel L. M. Barlow, that any Peace Democratic candidate had little chance. As they could not select the nominee, the peace faction hoped to use its strength to secure a peace platform.[8]

Democratic national chairman August Belmont and members of the national committee postponed the Democratic convention from early June to late August to allow the party time to respond to any changes in Union military fortunes.[9] Days before the convention began on August 29, both factions labored to gain their immediate goals. Vallandigham's hotel room bustled with War and Peace Democrats coming and going, but Pendleton carefully stayed out of the frenzy, recognizing that while his presidential hopes were slight, his chances for the second slot on the ticket remained strong. He allowed Vallandigham to function as his surrogate in the political maelstrom of the convention. While the Daytonite fought hard for a Peace Democratic candidate, he quelled rumors of a bolt by vowing to support whomever the gathering chose. War Democrats feared that a peace candidate or platform would taint the ticket with treason, while Peace Democrats equated a war candidate with a forfeiture of principle. Both sides recognized, however, the need for harmony if they hoped to defeat Lincoln. There was no desire to repeat the fiasco of 1860. While both sides worked to bolster their strength, party leaders recognized that compromise was their only option.[10]

The first order of business upon the opening of the convention was to hammer out the party platform. The Committee on Resolutions began deliberations immediately. The committee elected James Guthrie of Kentucky as its chair, with twelve votes, defeating Vallandigham with eight. A McClellan supporter, Guthrie wanted to finish writing the platform as quickly as possible to enable the nomination of the general without delay. He feared that another night of deliberations would only work to the advantage of the general's opponents. Guthrie formed a subcommittee to expedite consideration of resolutions.[11] Most were accepted easily, but one offered by Vallandigham generated considerable opposition:

Resolved, That this Convention does explicitly declare, as the sense of the American people, that, after four years of failure to restore the Union by the experiment of war, during which, under the pretense of a military

necessity or war power higher than the Constitution, the Constitution itself has been disregarded in every part, and public liberty and private right
alike trodden down, and the material prosperity of the country essentially
impaired,—justice, humanity, liberty, and the public welfare demand that
immediate efforts be made for a cessation of hostilities, with a view to an
ultimate Convention of all the States, or other peaceable means, to the
end that at the earliest practicable moment peace may be restored on the
basis of the Federal Union of the States.[12]

While not a member of the committee, Pendleton supported Vallandigham's
efforts. William Cassidy, editor of the pro-McClellan *Albany Argus,* vociferously opposed the plank, as did August Belmont working through the McClellan
men on the committee. They were unsuccessful in defeating it in the subcommittee though, and the proposal went to the entire Committee on Resolutions.
Demonstrating the strength of the large peace contingent, Vallandigham beat
back various substitutions, and the peace plank became part of the platform.
While Belmont did not like the peace resolution, he grudgingly accepted it as
the price of party unity.[13]

As Guthrie read the resolutions to the full convention, a negative rumbling
arose after he presented the peace plank. Neither War Democrats nor the peace-
at-any-price faction was happy. The bitterest denunciation came from the leader
of the latter camp, Alexander Long. He assailed the plank as a sellout and called
for a more explicit statement demanding an armistice and the recognition of
Confederate independence. Long forced the War Democrats to defend Vallandigham's resolution in order to prevent acceptance of an even more drastic
position. Cox maneuvered to cut off debate, and the convention accepted the
platform with only four dissenting votes.[14]

The overriding desire for harmony on the platform stemmed from the need
for party unity. Peace Democrats recognized that McClellan had the strength
to win the nomination; they refused to let the war faction control the platform
as well. War Democrats disliked the peace resolution, but they realized that
as a minority party they could not afford the luxury of endemic factionalism. Moreover, they hoped that McClellan's nomination would make the peace
plank meaningless. Constant political maneuvering by both sides discredited
the rumor of a secret deal between the factions. Most likely, members on both
sides made the obvious concessions as compromise became inevitable.[15]

After the convention, Belmont explained to McClellan that Vallandigham's
resolution was a concession by Peace men to the War Democrats and could have
been even more egregious. Yet Vallandigham single-handedly pushed the plank
through in the face of stiff opposition. He later stated that he had repulsed any

suggestions for substitutions, many of which War Democrats would have considered even more disloyal. Belmont was mistaken. Like the Republicans, he misunderstood the Peace Democrats; Belmont viewed them as a homogeneous unit. Vallandigham and Pendleton stood apart from ultras such as Alexander Long or Benjamin Harris of Maryland because of their commitment to the Union. Belmont failed to realize that the plank was not really a compromise; it represented a centrist position while rebuffing Long's extremist followers.[16]

With the acceptance of the platform, the convention turned toward the nominations. John P. Stockton of New Jersey nominated General McClellan, seconded by Cox. Michael Stuart of Ohio nominated Thomas Seymour. The Ohio delegation decided not to nominate Pendleton due to McClellan's strength. Rather, they held him out for the vice presidency. Seven states had promised Pendleton all or part of their votes, but Belmont's organization and money proved too formidable. To further dampen Ohio's bid for Pendleton, some McClellan supporters offered to make him McClellan's running mate on the ticket. Pendleton's faction followed his lead and supported Thomas Seymour. On the first ballot, the general received 174 votes, well above the 151 needed. Thomas Seymour received 38 votes. Horatio Seymour collected 12 votes in spite of his official declination. The Ohio delegation withdrew momentarily after the initial balloting to reconsider its split vote: 8½ for McClellan, 10½ for Thomas Seymour, and 2 for Horatio Seymour. Vallandigham, Pendleton, and several others switched their votes to McClellan to show unanimity with the party. But Long and his backers continued to press for Thomas Seymour. The Ohio delegates returned to the convention and changed their vote to 15 for McClellan and 6 for Thomas Seymour. Other states recast their ballots, and McClellan won the nomination with 202½ votes; Thomas Seymour trailed badly with 28½. In a show of unity, Vallandigham moved that the delegates make the nomination unanimous; the motion carried amidst loud cheering.[17]

All that remained was to select McClellan's running mate. William Allen of Ohio nominated Pendleton, calling him a "man of honor, integrity, and a gentleman of truth."[18] James Guthrie, nominated by Asa M. Dickey of Vermont, received support from Belmont and the War Democrats. He had been working closely with the McClellan men at the convention. Hailing from a Border State, Guthrie offered a sectional balance to the ticket. Delegates from several states nominated leading Democrats, honoring favorite sons out of courtesy. With the exception of Pendleton and Guthrie, the other nominees received few votes outside their own delegations. The first ballot brought 65½ votes for Guthrie and 55½ for Pendleton, with the rest scattered among seven others. Though Guthrie led on the first ballot, he ultimately withdrew his name from consideration because War Democrats realized the need to reconcile with their peace brothers.

After all, peace leaders such as Vallandigham and Pendleton had accepted Mc-Clellan. For that reason, several states, including powerful New York and Pennsylvania, with large numbers of electoral votes at stake, committed their votes to Pendleton on the second ballot. Pendleton won the nomination unanimously at the end of the second ballot amid thunderous applause. Pendleton was not only a candidate who could garner the vote of the peace faction but also a midwesterner to balance the eastern orientation of McClellan.[19]

Because the delegates knew Pendleton was present, they clamored for him to speak. Traditionally, nominees stayed away from the conventions and only issued a statement after they received official notification of their nomination. In a highly unusual move, Pendleton approached the lectern and expressed his appreciation for this mark of approbation from the Democracy. Standing fast on the Jacksonian principles and positions he had upheld in Congress, he promised to proceed "in entire devotion to those principles which lie at the very foundation of our government and which are the basis of the Federal Constitution, and of the rights of the States and of the liberties of the individual citizens . . . [I] shall endeavor to be faithful to those principles which lie at the very bottom of the organization of the democratic party."[20] Pendleton concluded with his hope that the election of McClellan would again restore constitutional government to the country. After finishing the business of the convention, the delegates closed in raucous fashion with nine cheers for the ticket.[21]

Republicans viewed the dichotomy between the platform and the recognized position of the Democratic nominee with both disdain and optimism. During the Democratic convention, Gideon Welles, Lincoln's secretary of the navy, confided in his diary his uncertainty about the president's chances for reelection. He no doubt gained confidence for the campaign when he noted days later that the Democrats "have just committed a mistake in sending out a peace platform. . . . There is fatuity in nominating a general and warrior in time of war on a peace platform."[22] The *Cincinnati Commercial* emphasized the Republican position which asserted that productive negotiations required military successes. If the Democrats, who declared the war a costly failure, won the election and called for a negotiated peace, the Confederates would assume that they had won. They would, therefore, extract heavy concessions for returning to the Union. Republicans were unwilling to pay that price.[23]

Shortly after the convention disbanded, news reached the North of Gen. William T. Sherman's victory in Georgia and his occupation of Atlanta. This triumph, combined with Adm. David Farragut's earlier defeat of the Confederate fleet at Mobile Bay, influenced McClellan's wording of his acceptance letter and set the fortunes of the Democratic Party reeling. The party had just adopted as its standard a platform that called the war a dismal failure. With these military successes, Democratic chances for victory dramatically faltered, and McClellan fell under heavy pressure to repudiate the platform. His previously stated position did not coincide with the platform, because he had always supported coercion to restore the Union. A final blow faced by McClellan and the Democrats was the reunification of their opposition. Frémont withdrew from the race when his Republican supporters recognized their scant chances for success; they preferred to see Lincoln win rather than McClellan.[24]

Pendleton and his fellow Democrats anxiously awaited McClellan's official letter of acceptance. Pendleton stood on the platform, but he was unsure about his running mate. Because of this uncertainty, Pendleton did not write out his personal views on the issue until McClellan's position was clear. He probably feared that if his stance were made public, the perceived division would ruin their chances for victory. Instead, Vallandigham pressured McClellan on Pendleton's behalf. At a ratification meeting in Dayton with Pendleton present, Vallandigham reiterated that the platform, which the convention had endorsed, called for peace. Moreover, in a letter to the general, Vallandigham warned McClellan to avoid being swayed by eastern War Democrats who were encouraging him to repudiate the peace plank. If he did not reject the easterners, Vallandigham cautioned, he risked losing 200,000 western votes. Even Barlow suggested that McClellan handle delicately the concerns of Peace men. Anticipation mounted with the passing of each day. With the lines so tightly drawn, McClellan had to reunite a party that only days earlier had ostensibly accomplished harmony through compromise.[25]

McClellan wrote six drafts of his acceptance letter before making his views public. After grappling with the platform and attempting to reconcile it with his own views, the general repudiated Vallandigham's plank. McClellan's earlier drafts alluded to an armistice with the purpose of negotiations toward peace on the basis of Union. If the Confederates rejected the proposal, he insisted that the course of coercion be reinstated. His final draft changed the wording and emphasis. In his official reply to the Democratic Executive Committee, McClellan maintained that the war should be continued until the South repudiated secession. Confederate capitulation was the prerequisite to armistice and peace. The platform, however, called for immediate peace without reunification; there was no imperative for negotiations and no stated allowance for continuation of hostilities. The Peace Democrats hoped that an armistice would eventually result in the end of secession. McClellan decided to construct his own platform, leaving the Pendleton peace faction out in the cold.[26]

Response to the letter was predictable. War Democrats wrote McClellan with great relief, praising him for rewriting the party position. In their minds, his response signified the difference between union and disunion. One correspondent noted that his letter silenced Republican critics who accused the Democrats of being secessionists. It was apparent from these letters that even prowar Democrats viewed Pendleton's peace faction as disloyal.[27]

The letter did nothing to bring the party together, and Vallandigham, furious at this rebuff to his position and pride, vowed not to campaign for the general. Cox empathized with Vallandigham's anger and notified McClellan's New York friends that the letter had upset Ohio's Peace men. He tried to convince the general that there were only minor differences between him and the platform and continued to press McClellan to appease Peace Democrats. Rumors surfaced again that Vallandigham would lead a peace faction bolt from the party. Some War Democrats secretly hoped that he would, believing it would remove the stigma of disloyalty from the party. But Vallandigham's fury abated when he concluded that any such continued opposition would only work in Lincoln's favor. As a face-saving gesture, he did hold a meeting of the chieftains of the Sons of Liberty, but only to work hard to prevent a party split.[28]

Democratic fortunes depended on Pendleton's response to the letter. Barlow feared that if Pendleton did not accept it, the party would lose key midwestern votes. Peace men encouraged Pendleton to reject the letter because it effectively prevented him from playing a significant role on the ticket. As a peace man, Pendleton was nothing more than added weight on McClellan's presidential train. But in the interest of unity, he did not repudiate McClellan. Though upset at McClellan's resistance to the platform, Pendleton joined Washington McLean, chief owner of the *Cincinnati Enquirer,* in stroking Vallandigham's wounded ego and encouraging him to speak for the ticket. While their efforts were successful, McClellan's letter set the stage for further controversy.[29]

Much of that friction surrounded the nomination of George Pendleton for the vice presidency. Because of his running mate, McClellan encountered a backlash from some supporters despite his rejection of the peace plank. Some wrote letters commending the general's position of removing the "hard difficulties" of Pendleton and the Peace men from the campaign. Others suggested ways to keep Pendleton from being a problem, specifically limiting his public appearances.[30] So much concern surfaced that some began to talk about removing Pendelton from the ticket. One correspondent urged McClellan to have Pendleton write a public letter agreeing with the general's position on the war. "And if he will not do so immediately, let him resign as nominee. And let the Chicago Convention (it being in permanent session) . . . appoint a man . . . who will agree with the Principal Candidate."[31] Belmont received similar advice. Such a letter would have created a firestorm in the Midwest. Further demonstrating that some War Democrats considered the peace element disloyal, others expressed fear that McClellan might be assassinated if elected in order to put Pendleton in the White House.[32]

MARVELOUS EQUESTRIAN PERFORMANCE ON TWO ANIMALS,

By the celebrated Artist, PROFESSOR GEORGE B. MAC, assisted by the noted Bare-back Rider, GEORGE H. PENDLETON, on his Wonderful Disunion Steed, PEACEATANYPRICE.

N. B. *The beautiful creature*, PEACEATANYPRICE, *recently imported from Europe, was sired by* JOHN BULL, *and dam'd by* AMERICA.

Marvelous Equestrian Performance on Two Animals: Republicans made political hay of the Democratic ticket in 1864 and the obvious division within the party. McClellan's repudiation of the peace plank doomed the campaign and put Pendleton in an awkward position. (*Harper's Weekly*, October 8, 1864)

The Union Party pulled no punches in attacking Pendleton. Painting him as a Southern sympathizer, Lincoln's supporters printed a series of pamphlets detailing Pendleton's congressional career and that of other Peace men. These publications continued the misrepresentation of his record that Pendleton had faced in the 1862 election. Democrats rebutted the Union Party's slander with their own statement about Pendleton's congressional activities. In a counter pamphlet, they trumpeted the numerous times he had supported war measures and his careful attention to the needs of Union soldiers.[33]

The lack of an acceptance letter from Pendleton became a focal point of attack by the Union Party. The *New York Times* repeatedly requested a public statement of Pendleton's position in light of the McClellan letter and refused to let the issue die. Democrats wanted Pendleton to remain as invisible as possible because of the obvious differences with his running mate. Sensing that Pendleton needed to make some kind of a public statement, August Belmont sent him telegrams asking that he accept McClellan's letter.[34] In his response, Pendleton expressed dismay at the absence of an official notification of his nomination from the party's executive committee. He regretted that the committee had not made public its decision to forego a formal letter of notification as this would have prevented much slander in the papers.[35] Expressing what he knew Belmont already realized, Pendleton emphasized the strength of the Peace Democrats in the Old Northwest and their disappointment with McClellan's letter. He believed that they would support the ticket regardless, if there were no more pronouncements of support for continuing the war. Pendleton went on to vindicate the peace position and debunk the idea that Peace Democrats were unfaithful to the Union or the Constitution. "This is a mistake," he contended; "they love both. They would give up neither. The[y] believe both can be maintained through peaceful agencies and only through those agencies. And it is because they believe these agencies will be fairly tried that they give us any support at all."[36]

Pendleton also informed Belmont that he would not participate heavily in the campaign because the press would have misrepresented his position. Besides, he contended, "I could not be more emphatic in my expressions of attachment to the Union, than I have heretofore been or more ready to sacrifice every personal and party interest to maintain it.—and I cannot believe that more declarations now would convince anybody who will not take the trouble to know, or will disbelieve what I have said."[37] As for Belmont's request for a public expression of agreement with McClellan, Pendleton answered that he could not "take back or qualify" what he had said for years in Congress. McClellan's repudiation of the platform left Pendleton in a precarious position. To actively support his running mate, Pendleton had to disavow his own record. To publicly express his disapproval of McClellan's stand meant the end of party electoral hopes. Because of his commitment to principle and party, he could only hide from the public eye despite his expressed willingness to help in any other way that Belmont might suggest.[38]

With the national convention adjourning in early September, there was precious little time before the October Ohio state and congressional elections. Cox expressed his concerns to McClellan about his own chances. He thought that the Peace men were little threat to him, even though he had abandoned their cause after the convention. He was more concerned about the reviving Northern confidence in Lincoln due to the recent military successes. Such fears materialized in key states such as Ohio, Indiana, and Pennsylvania in the October elections. Republicans routed Democrats and viewed the results as precursors to the presidential contest. As such, hopes faded for McClellan and Pendleton. In Ohio alone, the Democrats lost twelve of the fourteen previously held congressional seats. Cox was one of the casualties. George E. Pugh, who ran for the First District seat Pendleton had relinquished, lost as well. Peace Democrats blamed McClellan's letter, and war men castigated the platform.[39]

The election results prompted Belmont to push Pendleton once more to become actively involved in the campaign. Belmont stopped short of recommending that Pendleton appear with McClellan in public, however, because a joint presentation would only accentuate the party division.[40] As an indirect response, Pendleton wrote public letters to John B. Haskin and C. L. Ward, members of the Democratic state committees of New York and Pennsylvania, respectively. Pendleton emphasized his devotion to the Union and said that he had supported appropriations bills in Congress unless they were "loaded down with fraudulent items for the benefit of contractors" or were "made a stalking-horse for some abolition scheme."[41] Forthrightly stating his position in contrast to McClellan's, he declared, "I am in favor of exacting no conditions, insisting upon no terms not prescribed in the Constitution, and I am opposed to any course of policy which will defeat the reestablishment of the Government upon its old foundations, and in its territorial integrity."[42] If Belmont wanted him to campaign, Pendleton would do so, but only on a limited basis. The October elections may have suggested to him that the campaign was futile. He was determined to go on the hustings on his own terms, however, in order to use the opportunity to salvage his credentials for future endeavors.

Because candidates normally did not campaign directly, Pendleton made only a few carefully choreographed public appearances. Arriving in New York on October 26, he was soon serenaded by the "McClellan Legion" and expressed deep gratitude for their greeting as military men determined to preserve the Union. But in a larger sense, Pendleton used the occasion to address the Union pamphlets that had attacked his congressional record. Pendleton noted that Congress was not even in session on one of the dates that he supposedly voted against an appropriation. After questioning the publication's credibility, Pendleton weaved a declaration of position on the war from three sources: the opinion of Ohioans, excerpts from two of McClellan's statements, and the party platform. The people of Ohio, he stated, demanded the restoration of the Union "by conciliation and peace if they can, by all the force and power which a teeming population and a fruitful soil can give them if they must."[43] The election of the Democratic ticket would produce restoration through the former means. Quoting from McClellan's military correspondence to the president, Pendleton vilified Lincoln's expansion of executive power. He also used part of McClellan's letter of acceptance that called for a spirit of compromise leading toward restoration of the Union. Finally, Pendleton noted that the Democratic platform committed the party to obtaining peace.[44]

In the short but astute speech, Pendleton combined elements of both party factions, made them appear harmonious, and cloaked his personal views by voicing the opinion of others. He did not compromise his principles; rather, he alluded to them by choosing select portions of McClellan's statements with which he agreed. In that sense, he emphasized the peace plank without offending McClellan's convictions.[45]

A week later, Pendleton made another public appearance in Philadelphia. After a customary serenade from a crowd of supporters, he referred to the historic events that had formed the United States of America in that city and praised the liberties handed down from the fathers of the nation. Specifically, Philadelphia was the birthplace of the basic American freedoms of speech and the press, the home of the writ of habeas corpus. In an even more vague discussion of how to save the Union than his New York speech, Pendleton spoke of his home: "We in the West love the Union. We believe it to be the guarantee of peace, prosperity and liberty."[46] Stressing the regional importance of his section, he concluded that westerners supported McClellan because they believed he could reunite the country. With these words, Pendleton closed his campaign.[47]

In his absence, Democratic papers across the country carried on the battle while party orators criss-crossed the nation on the stump.[48] The *Cincinnati Enquirer* and the *New York World* dismissed the errant claims of Union papers such as the *New York Tribune* that Pendleton preferred to see the nation divided rather than have slavery abolished.[49] In addition to responding to partisan attacks, Democratic papers noted that even the Union papers found it difficult to censure Pendleton's character. While they disagreed with his position on the war, they found him "courteous and dignified, statesmanlike and manly," a person of integrity above reproach.[50] He unquestionably lived up to his nickname "Gentleman George." Because of his consistency and adherence to principle, Union papers respected him more than other leading Democrats such as Samuel Cox. They viewed Cox as a wavering opportunist due to his frequent shifts of position after the Emancipation Proclamation. The *New York Times* asserted that this was the reason Pendleton was the vice-presidential candidate rather than Cox.[51]

Democrats continued the uphill battle into early November. Combined with the changing fortunes of the Union military forces and the poor Democratic showing in the October elections, party hopes plummeted even further on October 18 when the peace-at-any-price men under Alexander Long held a convention in Cincinnati. Their bolt from the party had been rumored since the Chicago convention, but it was incorrectly associated with Vallandigham. Long explained that he had felt bound to the party convention because he was a delegate but was released from that commitment by McClellan's repudiation of the platform. The meeting examined McClellan's war record thoroughly and

then denounced the general as an ally of the Republicans because of his rejection of Democratic principles. While Pendleton's name was not specifically
mentioned, probably due to Long's friendship, the vice-presidential candidate
was also guilty of disloyalty to the party by his association with McClellan. In
their resolutions, the peace-at-any-price men declared the war unconstitutional
and the administration the true enemy of the Union. The Democratic Party
was a "Peace and States Rights Democracy," they insisted. For all their fury, the
delegates remained negativists, and when Long refused a separate nomination,
the meeting adjourned with little to show for its work and a public impression that the Democracy was hopelessly divided. The only positive Democrats
could salvage from this debacle was that Long's bolt made the McClellan and
Pendleton ticket seem moderate by comparison.[52]

Nonetheless, on election day, Lincoln's victory was assured. Ohioans voted
overwhelmingly for Lincoln, with the president winning a majority of 60,055
votes in the state, including 31,389 from the soldiers.[53] Lincoln even carried
Pendleton's home county, Hamilton. Despite the loss of Ohio, McClellan ran
surprisingly well. For example, Lincoln received 23,186 fewer votes than had the
Union candidate for governor, John Brough, in the 1863 election. McClellan
garnered 10,537 more votes than did Vallandigham in that same election. Apparently, McClellan's strong showing demonstrated that some Ohio Democrats
disagreed with Vallandigham's peace philosophy.[54] Across the country, Lincoln's
popular majority was 406,815, and he swamped McClellan in the Electoral College, 212 to 21.[55]

Democrats wrote McClellan expressing condolences and providing excuses
for his failure. While some blamed Long for encouraging ultras not to vote,
one Ohioan condemned Pendleton and the Peace Democrats: "The Vice nomination was made to appease this class of men, and in the effort to draw them
to the support of the ticket a far greater number of patriotic voters were driven
off."[56] While Pendleton's position was contrary to McClellan's, the idea that he
would have fared better on a war platform with a like-minded running mate is
unfounded. The peace faction was simply too strong to be ignored.[57] The division between the War and Peace Democrats, frequently expressed by a division
between eastern and western Democrats, presaged the conflict between western and Bourbon Democrats following the war. Pendleton's response, as it had
been before and would be in the future, was to try to unite the party around a
common Jacksonian ideology. In 1864, he was unsuccessful.

Pendleton expressed deep disappointment in the election, though he had anticipated the results. He had wanted to return to Congress prior to his nomination for the vice presidency.[58] Now he would be out of public office for the first
time since 1854. As he returned to Washington for his final session in Congress,

Pendleton must have felt helpless against the sweeping tide of change in America. Yet for the moment at least, he joined in the battle to determine the face of the postwar nation.

Pendleton arrived in December to confront yet another Republican effort to pass a constitutional amendment abolishing slavery. Pendleton addressed the House to reiterate the points he had made in the previous session and clarify those that the Republicans had questioned. He stated that the power to amend the Constitution was limited by both the letter of that document and its spirit. Republicans, and some Democrats, had argued that the letter was the only proscription against amendment. In this debate, Pendleton faced an unlikely opponent, Samuel S. Cox. Having made a dramatic about-face on this issue, Cox declared in a rebuttal that if three-fourths of the states agreed, they could even abolish the republican form of government. Pendleton disagreed. He noted that such an act disturbed the "very foundation of our system of government, and to overthrow that idea is not to amend but to subvert the Constitution of the United States."[59] If only one state rejected the plan, it would have the right to resist. He cited several other examples of Cox's contention gone awry. He asked Congress if by an amendment to the United States Constitution, three-fourths of the states could dictate to Ohio that they could no longer have two houses in their legislature. He noted that it was not forbidden by the letter of the document. In each hypothetical situation, he suggested that while the actions were not expressly prohibited, they certainly went against the spirit of the Constitution.[60]

Cox reduced Pendleton's argument to a question of partisanship rather than constitutional legality. Pendleton contended that to abolish slavery by amendment was to subvert the spirit of the Constitution because it undermined the authority of the states. In that regard, Pendleton upheld states' rights. Cox quoted John C. Calhoun, a name synonymous with that doctrine, who had said that in accepting the United States Constitution, a state "modified its original right of sovereignty. . . . A portion of that sovereignty had been placed in the hands of three-fourths of the states."[61] As the ratification of the amendment was left to the states, Cox did not believe that the principle of states' rights was violated. Even so, he presented the Republican argument that denying enslaved African Americans freedom constituted the subversion of republicanism, the foundation of the Constitution. While Democrats generally disagreed, the whole argument boiled down to who determined what did or did not subvert the Constitution. Cox found his answer "in Congress by two-thirds of both houses, and in the states by three-fourths of the legislatures."[62]

Both Cox and Pendleton cared less about the slavery issue than the Union. Pendleton believed abolition prevented peace and restoration. Cox struggled with whether it precipitated or delayed reunion. In the end, and as evidence of his continual wavering, Cox decided an amendment might prohibit peace negotiations and voted against the amendment. But Cox's arguments for its constitutionality influenced some congressmen. While the Democrats had defeated the Thirteenth Amendment in the previous session, this time they did not have the numbers. Pendleton's argument did not convince enough members of his own party to remain opposed. The amendment passed with two votes to spare, 119 to 56. Sixteen Democrats voted for it, while eight abstained. Although some evidence suggests that money and patronage flowed freely to influence the outcome, it is inconclusive. Undoubtedly some Democrats were influenced by Belmont and Manton Marble's *New York World,* which supported the amendment, believing it would encourage Southern states to return to the Union quickly in order to prevent ratification. Undoubtedly for some Democrats, the changing war fortunes allowed them to see the writing on the wall. Perhaps a few finally realized that slavery did in fact subvert republicanism. Whatever the reasoning, the vote indicated divided leadership within the Democratic Party and indecision about the future once the war was over.[63]

As Pendleton neared the end of his congressional career, he had one more piece of legislation on his docket.[64] Consistent with his reform legislation efforts in the Ohio Senate and in his early years in Congress, Pendleton introduced legislation to expedite communication between the House and cabinet members.[65] The plan called for the presence of cabinet members in the House on Monday and Thursday mornings to answer questions regarding their duties and the effect of proposed legislation on their departments. They were to be allowed to participate in debates under the rules of the House but could not vote on legislation. On the session's last day, Pendleton received, by unanimous consent, an hour to discuss his bill as an honor for his years of service.[66]

Pendleton delivered his last speech to the House on May 3, 1865, on H.R. 214. When the bill had been reported two months earlier, James A. Garfield, Republican of Ohio, expressed his support for the idea. Cox, however, presented a lengthy speech in opposition.[67] He believed that the bill would lead to an increase in the power of the executive branch to the detriment of the Congress. In an ironic twist from their disagreement about the Thirteenth Amendment, Cox reversed his constitutional argument on this issue. While Cox had accepted the amendment on the basis that the letter of the Constitution did not forbid it, he now opposed Pendleton's reform bill because the spirit of the Constitution did not apply. In particular, he referred to the section that disallowed any executive officer from holding a seat in the House. While Pendleton's bill did not confer a seat with all its privileges, Cox maintained, it infringed on the spirit of the passage. Further, Cox feared that executive influence on the floor of the House would only increase, possibly interfering with the legislative process and escalating party conflict. With the expansion of presidential powers during the war, Cox shuddered at the prospect of adding to such aggrandizement.[68]

As a longtime opponent of expanding executive authority, Pendleton had no intention of allowing his bill to grant the president greater latitude. Seeking to allay Cox's fears, he portrayed the interaction between the cabinet and representatives as limiting executive influence. In his mind, the bill brought out in the open that influence, rather than leaving it in the dark, smoke-filled rooms of secret meetings and lobbying. Consistent with Jacksonian principle and similar to modern "sunshine laws," Pendleton believed the people had the right to know how and why government officials operated and passed laws. As a result, he hoped department heads would no longer be able to hide behind cleverly written letters or delayed responses to House inquiries, which only tended to subvert the legislative process. Under the bill's terms, these men would have to go before the House and answer questions from both sides of the aisle. Pendleton stressed that cabinet officers were already required to report to Congress. It was time, he proposed, that congressmen take full advantage of that provision and hold cabinet members accountable.[69]

Pendleton then addressed Cox's concern about the bill's constitutionality. He cited the House's right to open its doors to any person it wished to hear. In addition, Congress had the right to determine the duties of the cabinet as evidenced by precedents. When Congress created the Treasury Department, it conferred upon it certain duties that had to be fulfilled. Congress could constitutionally add to the duties of those officers.[70]

Pendleton's motivations for introducing and pushing the bill stemmed from multiple sources. His concern for government efficiency began very early in his political career and did not diminish over time. Then too he had experienced the frustration of seeking information from a cabinet officer, only to receive a delayed or insufficient response. Finally, by direct interaction and clearer knowledge of the activities of that government branch, he hoped Congress would keep the president from trampling on the Constitution as he believed Lincoln had done during the war.

Though Pendleton had maintained a reputation for consistency throughout the war and the election of 1864, he began to realize that his own political goals depended on the resolution of party divisions. Nevertheless, not until after the war had ended and he had suffered another electoral defeat did Pendleton begin to consider departing from traditional party positions to rebuild the factionalized Democratic party. As a result, Pendleton began to understand that the party must consign past positions to the past and move on to new issues in the future based on fundamental party principles. This move would require a reinterpretation of Jacksonian principles and result in a continued evolution of the midwestern Democratic ideology, but the task was imperative. He had to find new ground, founded in Jacksonian thought, or else be passed by as he continued to fight old battles now lost.

Pendleton and Party Unity

The Ohio Idea

George H. Pendleton faced a serious personal and political crisis during the spring of 1865. Shorn of public office for the first time in almost eleven years and suffering from the pangs of losing his bid for national office, Pendleton chafed at the prospect of enforced retirement. Yet he quickly responded to the new realities. Although making money was not his major concern, he returned to Cincinnati and resumed his law practice.[1] Politics remained his first love, however, and he immersed himself in the activities of Ohio's Democracy. Pendleton was in an ideal position as a party decision maker because he was now firmly entrenched among elite Democratic leaders.

Little came easily to his party, and the end of the war in April sent Democrats reeling. They lacked a clear sense of the future. War-related issues had eroded traditional principles and had split the party into competing factions. The war itself had discredited many prominent leaders. In strict political terms, Democrats lacked a firm perception of public opinion. Also, the party was rocked by the assassination of Abraham Lincoln in April 1865. Thrust into the uncomfortable position of having been the political opposition to a slain president, Democrats felt strangely out of place. Though they had opposed much of what Lincoln stood for, no member of the loyal opposition condoned this act of savagery. The difficulty now was distancing themselves from it. Uncertain about the propriety of restoring partisan ties with former Confederates, Democrats seemed totally confused about the sudden ascent of Andrew Johnson to the presidency. As a sign of national unity, they immediately pledged their support for the new president. While such promises were inevitable given the circumstances of Lincoln's assassination, Democratic forcefulness substantiated their proclamation of support and belief that Johnson would throw off the

Union mantle and reclaim his status as a Democrat. For the moment, then, the party gave him time to settle into office and develop his program.[2]

Until late spring, Johnson was evasive about his Reconstruction plans, but on May 29, 1865, he broke his silence and announced a program of presidential restoration rather than presidential Reconstruction. Instead of calling Congress into a special session, he issued two separate but related executive proclamations. The first offered amnesty and the return of property to former Confederates, with the exception of several groups, if they would take a simple oath of allegiance. The second applied to the process of restoration in North Carolina. Johnson named a provisional governor, limited voting rights to only white men who had undergone his process of amnesty, and authorized the election of delegates for a special state convention to draw up a new constitution. Over the summer, he issued similar orders for six other Southern states. Johnson went one step further by specifying requirements for readmission to the Union. He directed that each state must abolish slavery, repeal ordinances of secession, and invalidate the Confederate debt. But he implied that the status of freed African Americans was a matter falling within state jurisdiction. Most Democrats were thrilled. Under Johnson's formula, the party anticipated a rapid return to a states' rights federalism as existed before the war, with the abolition of slavery the only significant change.[3]

Pendleton signaled his support of presidential restoration in August when he made the keynote speech at the Ohio Democratic convention.[4] He called on his listeners to move past the conflict and acknowledge that postwar America would be different. In accord with the president's guidelines, he accepted the end of slavery while opposing a constitutional amendment granting citizenship to African Americans, an issue that he believed ought to be left to the states. Pendleton conveniently forgot his own comments during the war that allowing the African Americans to fight in the war would necessitate having to grapple with the issue of citizenship rights. He also recognized the right of the Southern states to be represented immediately in Congress and the Electoral College, pending their recognition of the supremacy of the Constitution.[5] Demonstrating how in tune Pendleton was with the party, Ohio Democrats adopted a lengthy list of resolutions after his speech, pledging support for Johnson's Restoration plan. Pendleton also took to the stump for the party cause, but Republicans so dominated the 1865 elections that the Democrats had little hope for the future. It was just too soon after the war, and Lincoln's assassination was too fresh in the minds of voters for the Democrats to defeat the "bloody shirt" tactics used by their opponents.[6]

Pendleton continued to address Reconstruction issues after the elections. He believed that bringing the Southern Democrats back into the party was essential. To that end, he supported Johnson's veto of the Freedmen's Bureau Bill, which he viewed as an imposition on the dominion of states and an attempt at the consolidation of federal power as well as a waste of money. Pendleton blamed the huge national debt on the Republicans, echoing the sentiments of many Americans who languished under oppressive taxation. He also praised Ohio for its treatment of blacks. African Americans had the right to pursue economic advancement free of restriction, he contended, and in some areas of the state had access to public schools. Pendleton acknowledged that he differed with some Americans regarding testimony by blacks in the courts, but he suggested that the juries should decide what witnesses were credible. Many Ohioans opposed giving blacks political freedoms or allowing them to move into the state, and Pendleton agreed with these racist principles as well, supporting the 1865 Democratic state platform, which sought to maintain white supremacy.[7]

The civil rights of the freedmen was a pivotal issue for Republicans. Radicals rejected Johnson's plan because of his wish to leave the issue to the states. Johnson's veto of the Freedman's Bureau Bill and the Civil Rights Bill in 1865 and 1866, respectively, sealed radical opposition to presidential restoration. Moderate and conservative Republicans wanted to work with Johnson, even after his vetoes, but when the president refused to support the proposed Fourteenth Amendment, they too parted company with him. These battle lines pitted Johnson against the majority in both houses of Congress. Democrats hoped to capitalize on the developing division between Republicans and the president. Though opposed to Johnson's wartime policies, Democrats such as Pendleton now joined him to fight further consolidation of federal power.[8] When the Ohio state Democratic Convention convened in May 1866, Vallandigham, Pendleton, and Allen G. Thurman dominated the meeting. The gathering resolved as their goals the implementation of Johnson's plan for restoration of the Southern states and the subsequent reestablishment of the national Democratic Party. In an effort to gain conservative Republican votes, Pendleton expressed his willingness in the keynote speech to associate with men of any partisan affiliation in support of Johnson's Reconstruction plan. In reality, Pendleton probably concluded that Johnson was a covert Democrat around whom the party could coalesce. Eastern Democratic newspapers agreed on the need to support Johnson but chided Ohio Democrats for not ousting leading Peace Democrats following the war. Easterners feared that Republicans would use the prominence of Peace Democrats to charge that the entire Democracy was disloyal.[9]

Johnson hoped to take advantage of Democratic support on these issues by grafting the party into the National Union movement. Johnson and his supporters envisioned the effort as a continuation of Lincoln's Union Party of 1864 and as a third party comprised of what the president considered a national consensus backing presidential restoration. Some conservative Republicans, such as Thurlow Weed, William H. Seward, and James R. Doolittle, feared that if they continued to oppose Johnson they would drive him into the Democratic camp. To prevent this, they proposed a somewhat different but similar third party along the lines Johnson wished, but a party composed of both conservative Republicans and Democrats. While Johnson viewed the movement as a personal organization, these conservative backers considered it a means to build a new national organization, tied to the president's fortunes for now but not so in the future. Conservatives then essentially duped moderate Republicans, such as Henry J. Raymond, chairman of the National Union Party, by arguing that the Union movement was merely a pro-Johnson vehicle, not intended as a third party. On the other side, some Democrats, such as Pendleton and Vallandigham, feared the organization would swallow their party. Still others believed that they would gain control of the Unionists and make it a Democratic auxiliary. Though they differed in their reasoning, all of these groups, except for Pendleton and his supporters, agreed that they had to exclude Peace Democrats to avoid the charge of coddling traitors.[10]

In response to the call for a national meeting, Ohio's Union and Democratic organizations convened to elect delegates for the convention. Pendleton's active canvassing and strong political positions in support of Johnson led to his election by the party as a delegate-at-large.[11]

Some of Johnson's Union supporters, both Republicans and eastern Democrats, feared that Copperhead involvement would lessen public support of the meeting, which convened on August 14 in Philadelphia.[12] They wanted to ensure that unblemished Union men controlled all the proceedings. Fernando Wood, Clement Vallandigham, and Pendleton were the leading Peace Democrat delegates at the convention. Wood and Vallandigham withdrew under pressure from the Unionists. Pendleton was the only leading Peace Democrat to face no overt opposition, possibly demonstrating that he was now considered more moderate. Pendleton's war record was not as odious as that of many other Peace men both inside and outside his own party because of his tact and congeniality. "Gentleman George" did not allow political differences to cross the line into personal differences. Also, he had worked hard for the Democracy in 1865 and 1866, espousing party ideology and meshing it with Johnson's restoration plans. Pendleton's position in the party, considering his national prominence as the 1864 vice-presidential candidate, made him far too influential to be barred ignominiously from the convention. If the Republicans wanted any sense of bipartisanship within the National Union movement, they had to allow Pendleton a seat at the convention. Yet the convention apparently only begrudgingly accepted his presence. Pendleton was not placed on any committees, and he made no comments during the proceedings. He lost nothing, however, in remaining largely invisible at the gathering. For him, it was a means of determining the public mood. If the movement did well, he was in on the ground floor. If it did not, he was not too deeply associated with it. In short, he could not lose.[13]

The National Union Convention at Philadelphia adjourned after three days, ending the first national political convention in six years. Union leaders maintained solidarity among the delegates of varying political positions by focusing on the Reconstruction issues upon which all agreed. The platform emphasized most of what Pendleton had articulated in 1865. No new political party was established, yet Democrats and Unionists recognized their dependence on each other. Unionists needed Democratic support to defeat the Radicals; Democrats needed Johnson's plan to succeed in order to regain Democratic strength in the South. It was an uneasy alliance of convenience, but Ohio Democrats such as Pendleton found very little to quibble over in the convention resolutions.[14]

The campaign of 1866 moved into full swing in Ohio, and Pendleton continued his canvassing.[15] The Hamilton County Democrats held their convention on September 4 and rewarded Pendleton's service to the party by nominating him for Congress from the First District. Incumbent Republican Ben Eggleston had defeated Pendleton's friend, George E. Pugh, two years earlier by more than two thousand votes, so Pendleton's task was daunting.[16] Pendleton addressed the convention and outlined the campaign strategy he had been developing since the end of the war. He first called on his listeners to put the past behind them and concentrate on the issues of the present. Peace Democrats needed their constituents to focus on the immediate issues because they could not appeal to voters outside the party if the Republicans used the bloody shirt tactic successfully. Pendleton accepted the results of the war, namely the defeat of the concept of secession and the end of slavery. He was unwilling to compromise his Jacksonian understanding of states' rights, however, including his belief in limited federal authority and a democratic system restricted to whites alone. He was only disposed to support fusion with the Johnsonites because the Philadelphia Convention endorsed that primary doctrine. But the National Union Convention had allowed Radical Republicans to establish the political agenda of the campaign. While the Radicals offered new proposals for the Reconstruction process, Johnson's supporters remained defensive and spent most of their political energy simply opposing Radical ideas. Pendleton, in endorsing the platform, limited his field of vision, presented himself once again as an obstructionist, and set the stage for failure.[17]

Pendleton's energetic labor on the hustings prior to his nomination continued throughout the ensuing campaign. He made more public appearances in

1866 than in any previous contest. As expected, Eggleston and the Republican press attacked Pendleton on his war record.[18] Pendleton reiterated his customary defense. He rebuked his opponent for his two-year congressional record in which he blindly followed the leadership of Radical Republicans, such as Thaddeus Stevens and Charles Sumner, contrary to the pro-Johnson sentiments of his constituents. Pendleton reversed Eggleston's charges and questioned the congressman's commitment to the Union in light of his opposition to a speedy process of Reconstruction. What his opponent sought, Pendleton argued, was not a Union under a federal government but the consolidation of states under despotism. That was not what Ohio soldiers had fought to achieve.[19]

Pendleton's campaign was victimized by events that occurred outside his state. Two major outbreaks of violence in Southern states led to public concern that Johnson's plan for restoration would not work. In Memphis, a white mob pillaged a black section of the city, killing more than forty people. Ex-Confederates in New Orleans used Johnson's restoration program to obtain control of Louisiana. Unionist whites and blacks disregarded the authority of the former Confederates and held a constitutional convention to provide freedmen with suffrage in order to weaken the power of their political opponents. The mayor of New Orleans obtained Johnson's approval to prevent the gathering. Using a white mob, the mayor broke up the convention with violence, resulting in many more deaths. Johnson's ties to this type of lawlessness hurt his chances for obtaining new supporters in Congress.[20]

Moreover, Johnson proved detrimental to his own cause when he hit the campaign trail on his controversial "swing 'round the circle." Gideon Welles counseled the president to exercise care, knowing that he was not adept at handling criticism. Johnson failed to heed that advice and responded extemporaneously to his hecklers. His frequently vulgar and acerbic rebuttals produced headlines across the nation—he even referred to Charles Sumner, Thaddeus Stevens, and Wendell Phillips as traitors—presenting an undignified portrait of the man in the White House. His trip proved a fiasco as conservative Republicans began to lose interest. Meanwhile, Johnson failed to gain moderate Republican support because of his public opposition to the Fourteenth Amendment. As Republicans began to turn away from the National Union movement, Democrats gradually gained control, further encouraging more conservative Republicans to abandon the cause. The snowball effect undermined the bipartisan appeal of Johnson to supporters throughout the North.[21]

Johnson's blunders combined with a number of factors to defeat Pendleton. The efficient use of the bloody shirt by Radical and Moderate Republicans kept war issues fresh in the minds of voters, hurting his chances for gaining bipartisan support. More importantly, Pendleton had not stepped beyond his party's platform. Perhaps he could not be expected to do so, but his unwillingness to stress other issues limited him to the questions that his opponent could use most effectively. However hard Pendleton fought to turn the mind of the electorate from the war, Reconstruction issues only forced him to reveal his earlier stance. Pendleton had taken up the Johnson banner, and when Ohioans began to have doubts about the president's plan, they turned on Pendleton. The result produced Pendleton's defeat by 926 votes. Trounced throughout the state, only three Democrats were elected to Congress out of nineteen seats. Pendleton was not satisfied with his results, even though they were much better than Pugh had managed in 1864. He had worked too hard to fail in this crusade. The election ended fusion with the Johnsonites, but of far greater significance, Pendleton now began to look for a new issue to strengthen the Democratic Party.[22]

The severe defeat of the Democrats in the 1866 election in Ohio and across the country left some of the party's political positions meaningless. With a Republican majority in Congress and Reconstruction issues under its control, Pendleton and his fellow partisans began to look to the financial question as a new issue upon which to rebuild the party. Repeated interregional conflicts between the midwestern and eastern wings of the party in 1864 and 1866 stemming from differing views on the war had taught Pendleton a lesson. The difficulty of gaining support for midwestern Democratic concerns in the East caused him to turn his eyes southward. During the 1866 campaign, he, along with many Democrats, saw the need to rebuild the Southern Democracy but had been unsuccessful with Reconstruction issues. Pendleton realized this approach, however much sense it made in the short run, was an expedient that failed to reestablish the Southern Democracy, did not restore the prewar party's sectional alignments, and lent credence to Republican attacks that the Democrats had flirted with treason during the war. Pendleton had the imagination and drive to propose a new direction through his sponsorship of the Ohio Plan, a path he hoped would settle lingering wartime issues and refashion the Democracy by reviving its Jacksonian heritage. He found in the monetary question a means to link two potentially strong elements of the party. He recognized the similarity between Southern and midwestern views on currency and financial policies, as opposed to positions of eastern Democrats. He believed that if the two sections could unify upon the foundation of midwestern Democratic ideology, he could pressure the East to recognize a new regional leadership in the party, move the Democracy away from a dead past, address new issues popular with voters, and gain the presidential nomination for himself in 1868.[23]

Pendleton adopted realistic goals. Both the South and the Midwest were undergoing severe financial collapse brought on partly by the devastation of the Civil War and two years of poor harvests, and partly by the Republican policy of deflationary contraction of the currency. Republicans had created a national bank system during the war to provide a mechanism for promoting uniformity of currency and for selling government bonds. National banks bought bonds and were granted the privilege of issuing a limited amount of banknotes in return. The government also began issuing greenbacks, based on the good faith and credit of the U.S. government, as an additional means of financing the war. By war's end, almost $450 million in greenbacks were in circulation. Following the war, Secretary of the Treasury Hugh McCulloch began rapidly removing those greenbacks from the currency in an effort to return to specie payments. He reduced the amount to $399 million by 1866 and, based on the authorization of the Contraction Act of 1866, increased the withdrawal by another $44 million until the act was repealed in 1868.[24]

Pendleton had opposed both of these initial measures. Consistent with his party's Jacksonian heritage, he neither wanted to see the national government gain greater power nor watch capital become increasingly concentrated in the northeast portion of the country. Traditionally, Jacksonian Democrats had opposed a national bank system on the basis of both these concerns and sought a more equitable distribution of capital throughout the country. In addition, they had opposed paper currency because of its propensity toward inflation and the possible creation of a system where the well-to-do held the specie while the common man had to rely on unstable currency. Both of these two key concerns of Jacksonians came to fruition during the Civil War in spite of opposition from Peace Democrats such as Pendleton. But times had changed. Pendleton had to weigh the impact of killing the national bank system and reducing the number of circulating greenbacks. Pendleton already had evidence of what would happen if the latter were pursued too aggressively because of McCulloch's plan. Then, too, Pendleton had to evaluate the respective needs of his beloved Midwest and the South, from which he hoped to rebuild the strength of his party.

To bring change, Pendleton needed to devise a means to make currency more accessible in the Southern and midwestern economies. While the initial legislation designated a share of the national bank charters for these regions, the Treasury Department, during the war years, allowed New England and New York City to claim most of the charters. It was convenient for Washington to have the system regionalized as the government sought funds for the war effort. In addition, the South forfeited potential branches during secession. Following the war, Southerners sought ways to keep currency in their section because Republican economic policies did not provide for their financial needs. Money that went south chasing cotton and other agricultural crops stayed there as Southern farmers diversified to meet their own needs for foodstuffs and economic recovery. There was too little currency coming in, however, and the result of the lack of capital and the Southern attempt at self-sufficiency was a declining demand for midwestern farm goods. Southern and midwestern farmers as well as small businessmen found it difficult to find loans due to the limited capital in their regions. Pendleton hoped to alleviate the plight of both sections while rebuilding his party.[25]

The money question raised a host of financial and political concerns. In their April 1867 convention, the State Sovereignty Democrats, an extreme states' rights group that later encouraged Kentucky to nullify congressional Reconstruction legislation, launched the debate. The organization, spearheaded by Henry Clay Dean and Alexander Long, believed that the Democratic Party had disowned its principles, and they threatened to form a movement calling for total repudiation of the national debt. In June, Washington McLean of the *Cincinnati Enquirer* tempered the proposal by suggesting that the United States pay the entire federal debt in greenbacks. Traditional hard-money Democrats rejected that sweeping proposal, believing that dramatic inflation would result. Long, Dean, and McLean, all former Peace Democrats, were responding to the cries of midwestern farmers who believed contraction of greenbacks would cause crop prices to fall, making it more difficult to pay off their debts.[26]

Hugh J. Jewett, a prominent Ohio Democrat, fearing the extreme nature of both plans, suggested a conservative alternative that offered bondholders the choice between repayment in greenbacks or an exchange of their bonds for taxable securities bearing lower interest rates. Jewett further suggested that greenbacks replace national banknotes that were secured by government bonds. The process included withdrawing the banknotes and buying the bonds back with greenbacks, which could then be put into circulation to replace the notes. The plan provided multiple blessings for midwestern Democrats. First, it would save the government millions in interest currently being paid on the bonds. Second, it would maintain currency levels in their section of the country, preventing crop prices from falling and interest rates from rising too steeply, they believed. The government could then put the income from taxes and savings from lower interest payments into a sinking fund to pay the outstanding bonds as they matured.[27]

McLean recognized that these conflicting and often confusing plans were beyond the understanding of most ordinary voters. Under these circumstances, he sought an articulate and recognizable spokesman; Pendleton seemed the logical choice. During his congressional terms, Pendleton had established a solid reputation on finance and financial matters. Equally vital, Pendleton continued at the forefront of Ohio Democratic politics despite his 1866 loss. Nothing better illustrated his position than his selection as president of the Democratic State Convention in January 1867, which he controlled along with

Vallandigham and Thurman. But Pendleton was not yet ready to assume the role McLean desired for him. Instead, Pendleton still hammered at congressional Reconstruction. His address to the convention stressed the necessity of continued opposition to Republican programs. Vallandigham was just as unimaginative. Repeating stale accusations, his committee on resolutions blamed Republicans for oppressive taxes and for needlessly expanding the national debt by the military occupation of the South under the spate of their recently passed Reconstruction laws. Just as predictable, his committee blasted Republicans for their continuance of high tariffs that accomplished nothing for midwesterners, but merely filled "the pockets of Eastern monopolists."[28] On that platform, the convention nominated Thurman for governor.

The campaign began with no references to debt payment, and Pendleton did not mention debt reduction in his public speeches as late as April 1867. Instead he continued to attack congressional Reconstruction and the Fourteenth Amendment, both of which trampled on state sovereignty, he contended. By the summer, however, Pendleton began to develop his own scheme for eradicating the public debt and the evils of the country's financial system. After some cajoling by McLean, Pendleton began to strike out alone, asking the party faithful to support him rather than letting others formulate a Democratic monetary policy. Yet the form his plan took was not as extreme as McLean had wanted. The issue on which Pendleton staked his political future was the payment of a portion of the Civil War debt in greenbacks.[29]

Pendleton used the 1867 campaign to initiate a year and a half of travel with the dual purposes of restructuring the Democratic Party and building support for his presidential bid in 1868. The public debt issue became the theme for this effort. He first addressed this topic in Minnesota on July 11, 1867. Jewett had unveiled his plan in a speech just six days before, but it was not printed in Cincinnati newspapers until after Pendleton returned from Minnesota. Whether he had knowledge of the Jewett plan is unclear, but what is clear is that Pendleton, a figure of national stature, thought along similar lines. Pendleton condemned the federal policy that allowed bondholders to purchase the securities in depreciated currency, receive 6 percent interest in gold, and pay no taxes on the income. Meanwhile, agrarian and trades workers, who could not afford such investment, struggled under the combined weight of heavy debt loads and high taxes to pay the excessive interest rate. National banks held a sizable portion of these bonds as collateral for the issuance of banknotes, thus enhancing their economic power. The Ohio legislature had expressed similar outrage in 1866 when it called for state taxation of national securities. Bank owners not only received 6 percent interest on the bonds but also gained the right to loan banknotes at rates of 6, 8, or even 15 percent. Pendleton decried this system:

"The manifest interest of the people is, that these bonds be redeemed in legal tender notes. The interest on these bonds would thus be saved, and the currency, if any be needed, would thus be furnished free of cost to the people."[30]

Pendleton began to specify the provisions of his plan in a speech in Lima, Ohio, while carefully dissociating himself from McLean's inflationary notions. The total national debt, Pendleton said, amounted to $2.2 billion, with $140 million in interest paid yearly. Half of the debt was in five- to twenty-year bonds, callable after five years, and yielding an interest rate of 6 percent yearly. Pendleton limited his proposal for paying the debt in greenbacks to these bonds, because purchasers bought them with legal tender, and no contractual stipulation existed regarding their redemption. In addition, Pendleton was no mere inflationist. Greenbacks were a means to an end for him, not an end in themselves. The national banks held $400 million of these bonds, which, Pendleton asserted, the government could call in at an annual savings of $24 million in interest payments without causing inflation. Pendleton understood that, without the interest from those bonds, the national bank system would collapse. He maintained that the interest saved could be added to a portion of existing tax revenues and be used to create a sinking fund to pay off the rest of the federal debt over a period of sixteen years. To succeed, the plan required not only the momentary continuation of high taxes but also the reduction of federal spending. The plan would not cause overt inflation of prices because, as banks redeemed their bonds, they would no longer have the required collateral to issue banknotes. In essence, the greenbacks would replace the banknotes. Nonetheless, Pendleton contended that some currency inflation was desirable to make capital more available for rebuilding the South, reviving an economy in recession, and making it easier for farmers to pay off their debt. He could assure the country an end to war taxes after a specified time period while providing the necessary capital for Southern agricultural needs and the nation's growing industrial concerns. After all, the gains of paying off the debt, he argued, outweighed any possible detriment caused by limited price inflation.[31] Ultimately Pendleton's plan called for an eventual and complete return to specie, a fact often neglected by critics.

Pendleton's plan sparked the criticism of many skeptics. At a gathering in Cleveland on September 18, he cited a *New York Herald* article questioning the legality of paying the "five-twenties" in greenbacks. Pendleton rebutted this attack by repeating Ohio Republican John Sherman's assertion that the proposal was legal. Pendleton also addressed the accusation that his plan would flood the economy with $2.2 billion in greenbacks, causing the national currency to drop in value and essentially repudiating the debt. His plan called for the payment of the five-twenties, which amounted to only half that figure, and then slowly redeemed the greenbacks already in circulation. The greenbacks would function as a replacement for the banknotes that could no longer be issued by banks based on those bonds. Attempting to put the plan in terms most voters could understand, Pendleton noted that the plan was not designed "to add one dollar to your taxes, or one dollar to the currency."[32]

In Milwaukee a few weeks later, Pendleton contended that his idea would limit inflation by stabilizing the greenback's value at approximately seventy-one cents in gold per dollar as legal tender. The gold in the sinking fund would be converted to greenbacks to redeem the five-twenties when they matured. After they were retired, the government could gradually lower taxes by $150 million and still have enough available in 1874 to pay off the gold bonds. Taxes could again be reduced after 1874, allowing for gradual withdrawal of the greenbacks. Pendleton estimated that by 1881 the nation could retire its debt and return to specie payments. Pendleton asserted that by the time his plan achieved its goals, the Republican method would have paid little more than the annual interest on the debt.[33] In fifteen years, accumulated interest would double the debt, while Republican contraction schemes reduced the economic base from which taxes were gathered.[34]

Pendleton also addressed questions of personal inconsistency because of his vote against the Legal Tender Act in 1862. Congressional Democrats, who had almost unanimously joined Pendleton, remained consistent on this issue through 1866 when they supported McCulloch's monetary contraction program. Within two years, however, most of them voted to end contraction. The explanation for this reversal, and Pendleton's apparent contradiction, supplies some insight into the party's postwar quest for unity. Pendleton initially deemed greenbacks an evil, but because the government considered fiat adequate for the soldier, he believed the same standard ought also to apply to the five-twenty bondholder. Moreover, manufacturers and laborers in the Midwest valued greenbacks as the key to prosperity in the postwar recession. Yet they also viewed bondholders and bankers as the reason for much of their financial trouble and saw no reason for them to have favored status in the eyes of the government. While Pendleton's goal was the resumption of specie, he could find no reason to scorn the utility of greenbacks to make that transition as painless as possible.[35]

There were several threads of continuity within his otherwise seemingly contradictory position. Pendleton had long opposed the national bank system. Based on his Jacksonian roots, he thought that the national banks prevented the Midwest from achieving its economic potential. Pendleton played on the midwestern complaint, latent since the days of Jackson's war on the Second Bank of the United States, that the East monopolized the country's capital. In addition, Pendleton tried to appeal to a broad constituency by using Jacksonian methods. His own support base, largely Ohio farmers and urban immigrants, traditionally voted Democratic and blamed Republican financial policies for their current financial woes. In addition, Pendleton attempted to appeal to eastern laborers, much the same way Andrew Jackson had, on the basis of class conflict. Pendleton railed against the privilege and special status Republicans afforded to bondholders, reminiscent of Jackson's attack on Nicholas Biddle and eastern banks. Pendleton capped his argument by returning to Jackson's governmental philosophy. Pendleton disdained the existing financial system as an auxiliary part of the plan of national consolidation that the Republican Leviathan state had created during the war. Through monetary contraction and the maintenance of the National Bank System, he further reasoned, eastern Republican financiers kept the Southern states under their thumb. Through a reinterpretation of Jacksonianism to address a new issue, Pendleton's goals remained the same even if his methods changed. His plan would destroy the National Bank System, squelch privilege and monopoly, benefit the Common Man, thwart the Republican power grab, and ultimately facilitate a relatively painless and prosperous return to specie.[36]

The fall elections gave Pendleton a boost in his marathon effort to employ the developing Pendleton Plan as the road to the White House. The results in Ohio, a pleasant surprise for the Democrats, came about only through strenuous efforts; Pendleton alone had visited thirty counties in fewer than two months. The Republicans did poorly. Rutherford B. Hayes won a closely contested gubernatorial contest by three thousand votes, a victory that can only be explained by the strength of his personal popularity and Civil War service. The Democrats gained a majority in the Ohio legislature, which meant that Benjamin Wade, a leading Radical Republican, forfeited his seat in the United States Senate. In addition, Ohio voters overwhelmingly rejected a proposal to amend the state constitution and allow black suffrage. While Democratic gains in Ohio resulted largely from the widespread use of pure racism and the opposition to black suffrage, rising support for Pendleton's debt payment plan played a role as well.[37] In the long run, opposition to black suffrage simply would not sustain party strength, and Ohio later did ratify the Fifteenth Amendment. The 1867 election represented an early success in the process of educating the party on Pendleton's financial ideas, a program focused on tomorrow rather than yesterday. Writing of the party's bright future to New Yorker Horatio Seymour, Pendleton said, "Our labor will just have begun for there comes the question of administering the power which will be confided to our hands."[38]

Pendleton's plan engendered considerable debate throughout the nation. At first, both major parties in Cincinnati, represented by the *Commercial* and the *Enquirer,* endorsed the payment of five-twenties in greenbacks. Ohio Republican

John Sherman asserted that the idea was legal.[39] Some leading Radical Republicans such as Thaddeus Stevens and Benjamin Bannan proposed similar ideas. The Radical *Daily Gazette* supported the idea for a time. The Democratic *Enquirer,* however, advocated an increase in the number of greenbacks in circulation to accomplish the goal. Yet the 1867 election results and the growing midwestern support for Pendleton and his plan caused the Republicans great consternation and forced them to reassess their initial approval. Some began to counsel adoption of the payment plan, while others suggested initiating a federal tax on the bonds to placate those who thought bondholders had become a privileged class. Joseph Medill, editor of the Republican *Chicago Tribune,* warned John Sherman that the Republican Party could no longer rely on Reconstruction to win elections. In order to maintain power, Medill suggested, the Republicans needed to placate midwesterners on financial issues.[40]

Eastern Republicans, far more fiscally conservative, continued to label Pendleton a repudiationist. The *Nation* argued that the country's reputation with European investors was at stake.[41] Jay Cooke, a leading eastern financier who had overseen the wartime sale of the five-twenties, also attacked Pendleton's ideas. The custom had always existed, he argued, for the government to pay bonds in specie, and Secretary of the Treasury McCulloch had pronounced them payable in that manner. Cooke's agents, authorized by the government, had sold the bonds with that understanding. Pendleton was not swayed. According to him, each bondholder could have read the law authorizing the bonds and found that only the interest was promised in coin. Though the custom had been to pay bonds in gold, the Legal Tender Act, which provided for the five-twenties, broke that precedent. Cooke's arguments nonetheless influenced Sherman, who came to believe that, as the public, including foreign investors, bought the bonds with the understanding that they would be paid in gold, the government must honor that implied agreement.[42]

Some Republicans may have seen in the currency issue a repose from the dangerous issues associated with congressional Reconstruction. Indeed, they viewed this popular midwestern question as a means to deflate a Democracy swelling from their successes in blocking black suffrage. Yet the Republicans had their own divisions, as Radicals attempted to maintain their power in the party. Conservative Republicans in the Midwest slowly withdrew their support from the greenback scheme, associating it with the Radicals. Many eastern Republicans had never supported the idea. Southern Republicans desperately wanted currency expansion of some kind in their region for the purposes of rebuilding their economy. Because of their lack of consistency on the issue and Pendleton's willingness to make greenbacks his calling card, Pendleton quickly assumed leadership of the issue. The 1867 election returns were in part a result of its growing importance. Instead of deflecting interest from Reconstruction and strengthening Republican power in the Midwest, support for the Ohio Idea coalesced around Pendleton.[43]

The Pendleton Plan, or the Ohio Idea as it became known, coupled with the resounding Democratic victory in the October 1867 election, elevated Pendleton to leading midwestern contender for the presidential nomination. The *Enquirer* boosted him regularly over the following months. His candidacy picked up momentum, the paper noted, when approximately twenty major newspapers around the nation endorsed Pendleton's bid.[44] With increasing confidence, Pendleton undertook a substantial correspondence to bolster his ranks. His strategy was to correspond regularly with a leading Democrat in each state to keep up on affairs and to build momentum for his nomination. As such, he wrote to friends in various parts of the country urging them to push for state platforms that supported the payment of the debt in greenbacks. Moreover, he contacted leading party newspapers and supervised the circulation of eighty thousand copies of his Milwaukee speech.[45] Ever the prudent politician, he tactfully advised state organizations to instruct their delegates for the national convention to vote for him and his plan. He left no opportunity unexplored, requesting from the Democratic National Committee a list of new appointees from states, presumably Southern, who were not represented at the last convention. He undoubtedly wished to ensure they understood that the Ohio Idea was aimed at improving their devastated economy as much as paying the national debt.[46]

With the new year came another state convention. The Ohio gathering was so anxious to become the first state to endorse Pendleton for the presidency that it set aside the rules and adopted such a resolution at the outset of the proceedings. The Columbus convention then sent for the awaiting Pendleton, who addressed them briefly on the key issues.[47] Before adjourning, delegates adopted a series of resolutions that reflected Pendleton's ideas. They praised the party for its victories in 1867 and vowed to continue to oppose Republican attempts to consolidate federal power through congressional Reconstruction. They also decried Republican efforts to force African American suffrage on the states and the resultant political control of Southern states by freedmen. After reaffirming support for abolition and lauding the gallantry of the Union soldiers, the concluding resolutions on financial questions echoed the major features of the Ohio Idea. The *Enquirer,* though supportive of more inflation, eventually concurred.[48]

The Pendleton movement swept much of the Midwest and gained enough support to influence congressional activity. In January 1868, Republicans in both houses launched a counterattack by voting to repeal the Contraction Act of 1866, ending the reduction of greenbacks.[49] More to the point, they also considered Sherman's Funding Bill, which formed the foundation of the Republican plan for handling the public debt. The bill called for the issuance of thirty-year bonds at 4.5 percent interest and forty-year bonds at 4 percent interest in exchange for five-twenty bonds, with the interest and principle of the new bonds paid in coin. Pendleton rejected the proposal because it thwarted the payment of the five-twenties with greenbacks and failed to tax bondholders. Moreover, it preserved the National Bank System, because it continued the system of issuing banknotes based on bonds held as security by each branch. Finally, Pendleton feared that the resulting delay in paying the debt would make it a permanent fixture on America's economic landscape.[50]

For the time being, congressional Republicans failed to pass the Funding Bill, giving added impetus to Pendleton's candidacy. Democrats in Nebraska, West Virginia, Indiana, Missouri, Kentucky, and Minnesota joined with Ohio in declaring their support for him.[51] Fueled by this groundswell, Pendleton tried to influence the Democratic National Committee in its decision regarding the location and date for the national convention. He hoped for an early meeting in a midwestern city. He obtained neither objective. National Chairman August Belmont, the leader of the eastern Democratic banking interests known as "swallow-tails," blocked these attempts and convinced the committee to accept the bid of New York City.[52] Belmont's strong-arm tactics indicated the strength of the hard-money wing of the party, but the selection did not dampen Pendleton's spirits. Members of his organization in New York had been working hard and remained optimistic. By March, Pendleton could see his support coalescing. The Midwest was firm, largely due to its agrarian composition, and he was confident of carrying Oregon, California, and Nevada and hopeful about Pennsylvania, Connecticut, and Indiana. A group of supporters in Oregon, where Pendleton owned a large tract of land, named their town in his honor. County Judge George W. Bailey recommended the name because of his support of Pendleton's politics, especially during the Civil War, and favor for the Ohioan continued to abound.[53] By April all the midwestern states backed his candidacy except Missouri, but the *Enquirer* was sure of its support as well. Based on his experience in 1864, Pendleton believed that these states could create a surge in the early balloting and stampede hesitant delegates. But he did not delude himself and recognized that the battle would not be easy.[54]

In an odd twist, the group that had briefly comprised the State Sovereignty Democrats supported chief justice and former Republican Salmon P. Chase for the presidency, despite his long advocacy of universal suffrage, universal amnesty for Southerners, and the National Bank System. Chase strongly opposed the Ohio Idea. While remaining anathema to Pendleton and his supporters, Chase toned down his more prickly positions by arguing that the suffrage issue should be left to state legislatures. He also expressed his opposition to the special tax status of bondholders despite his hard-money stance. Alexander Long, one-time friend of Pendleton, now viewed him as a political rival and opposed the Ohio Idea. Long was bitter about Pendleton's rising political fortunes on an issue Long believed was his own. As a result, he began a petty and personal crusade to take back control of the Ohio Democracy by insidiously suggesting that Pendleton could help his future political prospects by withdrawing as a candidate and leading the Chase movement at the convention. Unwilling to betray his political philosophy or his supporters and doggedly determined to maintain control of the Ohio Democratic machinery, Pendleton refused.[55]

In this mixture of politics and personality, Vallandigham joined Long in letting personal concerns interfere with party considerations. Vallandigham remained upset over his 1867 Senate seat defeat by Thurman, whom Pendleton had eventually supported. Pendleton may have believed that Thurman was a better leader for a party trying to move beyond the war. Thurman's early acceptance of the Ohio Idea played a role too. The fact that delegates to the Ohio convention supported Thurman over Vallandigham undoubtedly influenced Pendleton as well, as he was seeking the support of those same people for the presidential nomination. More importantly, although he had originally endorsed Vallandigham for the seat at the 1867 state convention, Pendleton realized that public support for him now would create too close an association with a man many eastern Democrats considered a political pariah. Such a mistake would affect his chances for nomination. Vallandigham remained a nominal advocate of Pendleton, but, joining Long and Belmont, he made Chase his second choice. Belmont saw his opposition to the Ohio Idea as more important than the need to aid the party in developing its Southern strength. Challenged by Tammany Hall and the New Albany Regency, two competing interests within the New York Democracy, Belmont and the swallow-tails sought to gain control of the party in their home state. Perhaps Chase was just a diversion who would draw attention away from the Pendleton Plan and open the door for another candidate more to the liking of Belmont. Whatever his intent, Belmont was cautious and did not wish to open the party up to new potent leaders.[56]

Pendleton also faced several other serious contenders for the presidential nomination. Some Indiana Democrats pushed Thomas Hendricks, even though he had publicly stated he preferred the Senate. Hendricks was connected to the National Bank System, having sat on the board of directors of a branch in his home state. Gen. Francis P. Blair Jr., of Missouri, who had previously been a Republican, was also supported by some Democrats, but Chase seemed the more obvious choice should the convention decide to go outside the party. Many Southerners favored Gen. Winfield S. Hancock because of his friendly administration of Louisiana and Texas following the war. Gov. Horatio Seymour of New York was the strongest possibility for the hard-money men. Seymour opposed the Ohio Idea but was conservative on Reconstruction and had a war record that attracted former Peace Democrats. As in 1864, he repeatedly declined to have his named used, but left the door open just enough to keep his supporters interested. Pendleton respected Seymour as a politician and as an administrator, but did not agree with his financial policies. In Seymour eastern Democrats found a logical compromise candidate, though no single strong alternative surfaced against Pendleton. The Ohioan's prospects looked good.[57]

But appearances were deceiving, and the forces arrayed against Pendleton within the party became more aggressive as the convention loomed. Manton Marble received much correspondence urging him to ignore the pleadings of McLean, who lobbied him for Pendleton. Belmont encouraged Marble to discount the financial question and focus his editorials on the issues of Reconstruction and African American suffrage. Tammany's *New York Leader* blasted Pendleton's plan as revolutionary and utopian. There were more pressing issues, it argued, that needed immediate attention. In short, fiscally conservative Democrats believed that Pendleton could not garner the support needed to win the election. The Ohio Idea was, in the minds of these men, repudiation at worst and highly inflationary at best. With the nomination of Gen. Ulysses S. Grant by the Republicans, some Democrats worried that Pendleton's peace background would work against the party.[58]

Newspapers were rife with rumors about various machinations before the convention. The *Enquirer* warned Ohio's delegates to be wary of eastern Democrats who were involved in a conspiracy to woo them away from Pendleton. Several days before the opening gossip surfaced that Hendricks had withdrawn his name from consideration. A day later, Hendricks announced that he was not out, but refused to head the opposition against Pendleton. Amidst all of the hearsay, the party remained deeply divided. Ultrainflationists and Belmont's swallow-tails comprised opposite ends of the spectrum, with Pendleton in the middle. While those who favored extreme inflation probably could ultimately support Pendleton, the eastern hard-money advocates, with money and influence to employ against him, could not. Though Pendleton entered the convention with 149 convention votes in his pocket, more than any other candidate but not enough to win, his organization suffered from an absence of efficient leadership because of the struggle between Pendleton, Vallandigham, and Long. As one Chase booster noted, these personality differences enhanced the chief justice's prospects, as the divisions prevented Pendleton from trading and bartering with other delegates. In spite of decided opposition, his supporters, in the form of the "Pendleton escort," were ready to take New York by storm.[59]

The weakness of the Ohio delegation was quickly revealed. Saturday, July 4, marked the first day of the convention. Only the sweltering heat of the city dampened the excitement of opening ceremonies. The delegates met briefly and determined to abide temporarily by the rules of the last convention. Gen. George W. McCook, the head of the Ohio delegation, pleaded against the old rules, hoping to change the convention's traditional two-thirds vote for nomination to a simple majority. Ohio's Pendleton men believed that they had a majority already committed. McCook failed, however, and the convention adjourned until Monday, giving the anti-Pendleton groups time to marshal their forces. McCook's lack of success led to several new spokesmen in the Ohio delegation. George E. Pugh, Gen. George Morgan, Hugh J. Jewett, and Washington McLean stepped in to reinforce Pendleton's chances.[60]

The following Monday, the convention met again and elected Horatio Seymour as the presiding officer. Ohioans supported his selection, hoping it would remove him as a candidate. The next order of business concerned the platform. A floor vote decided to hammer out the planks before the nomination, which some considered a favorable move for Pendleton. If a greenback plank were adopted, his chances for nomination would look positive, though there were no guarantees. If not, the Democrats were doomed to repeat their debacles of 1860 and 1864 when the process of forming a platform had so polarized sectional grievances that the party could not present a united front. Ironically, the same proved true in 1868.[61]

In spite of Belmont's influence and Seymour's early convention speech blasting paper currency, soft-money men controlled the platform committee. On older issues, the party acknowledged that slavery and secession were casualties of the war, pleaded for the immediate restoration of the Southern states, and asked for amnesty for the former Confederates. The platform also railed against the congressional Republican plans for Reconstruction while reiterating the partisan position on states' rights and African American suffrage. Turning to the new and important issues of national finance, the members of the committee espoused four separate resolutions. First, they called for the rapid payment of the national debt with the "lawful money of the United States," unless specifically designated in coin.[62] Second, they demanded equal taxation of all types of property, including government bonds. In the third resolution the delegates advocated one currency for all Americans, further solidifying the party's stance in support of paying the five-twenty bonds in greenbacks. Finally, they insisted that the government stop the high expenditures presently being committed to support the armed forces still active in Southern states and through appropriations for the administration of the Freedmen's Bureau. Economy in government, Democrats believed, was the quickest route to debt payment and lower taxes. The platform did not directly call for the destruction of the National Bank System, nor did it include a provision to return the country to specie payments within fifteen years. Still, the planks could best be associated with Pendleton.[63]

The platform was a clear victory for Pendleton and illustrated the strength of his support base.[64] As a midwesterner, Pendleton represented many farmers who saw in the Ohio Idea a means to easier debt repayment through an expanded currency. Yet Pendleton undoubtedly hoped to appeal to another growing group of voters—labor. The platform echoed Pendleton's often repeated sentiments for "one currency for the government and the people, the laborer and the office-holder, the pensioner and the soldier, the producer and the bond-holder."[65] Edward Kellogg, a merchant turned author and economist of radical leanings after the Panic of 1837 ruined his business, had begun the process of influencing trade unionists to support greenbacks as early as 1848.[66] Moreover, Pendleton realized the practical necessity of recognizing the growing laboring element in his hometown of Cincinnati, and perhaps more importantly in New York City, where much of his strongest political opposition resided. Representing an early response by labor, the fledging National Labor Union supported many of the principles on currency delineated in the Democratic platform of 1868. Though Tammany Hall needed to maintain the support of tens of thousands of immigrant workers, the political machine was still too powerful to be forced to capitulate to labor demands. The other powerful factions within the eastern Democracy had economic interests that ran contrary to those of labor and farmers. In the end, the Ohio Idea was ahead of its time politically and economically. Labor was not yet organized enough to exert the pressure necessary to overcome the competing political elements in New York that controlled so much of the Democracy. Bringing laborers and farmers together in political concert would have to wait for another day and another platform.[67]

Yet Pendleton's appeal to labor went well beyond the confines of his own party. Indeed, Radical Republican leaders such as Thaddeus Stevens had sought to tap into a traditional support base, the trade unionists, by proposing the end of the National Bank System and the redeeming of five-twenties in greenbacks. Conservatives within the Republican Party, however, were no longer willing to subject themselves to Stevens's Radical leadership. The National Bank System represented the successful war effort against the secessionist South. To disband it would be to turn their backs on one of their greatest achievements. Moreover, many Republicans viewed the bank as a necessary component in postwar economic development. As a result, they rejected Stevens's ideas and stood for the National Bank System and hard currency. For labor, this party position was the last straw. Not only had they been forgotten in the Republican scramble for African American political equality, but also, in the waning years of Reconstruction as the political system began to focus on other issues, the Republicans dismissed out of hand labor currency concerns. Disillusioned, trade unionists sought to foster an independent party movement (Labor Reform Party) as an offshoot of the National Labor Union.[68]

The question facing the convention now was whether the party would learn from the mistakes of 1860 and 1864, or split its platform and nominee again. Illinois and Iowa, when called on for their choice, deferred to the Ohio delegation to name its favorite son. Maine, however, was too anxious and could not wait. Stealing Ohio's thunder, Marcellus Emory of Maine moved, amidst great clamor, "in behalf of the laboring masses of Maine," to nominate Pendleton for president.[69] Gen. George W. McCook of Ohio was left to second the motion. The nominations of President Andrew Johnson, Asa Packer of Pennsylvania, General Hancock, and Hendricks quickly followed.

The first ballot gave Pendleton 105 votes and 65 to Johnson, his nearest competitor, but far short of the needed two-thirds majority. Over the next series of ballots, Pendleton expanded his vote total to a high of 156½, but his hopes plunged when Indiana, which had supported him to that point, split between him and Hendricks. As weary delegates caucused, Pendleton knew his time had passed. Prepared for this contingency, he had written a letter of withdrawal to McLean in the spirit of party unity to be used if McLean felt Pendleton's candidacy was doomed. McLean thought the moment had arrived after the fourth ballot, but the Ohio delegation wished to press ahead. On the fifth day, Pendleton's total dropped by one hundred, and Vallandigham presented the letter. The Daytonite then worked unsuccessfully to get the New York delegation to change its vote to Chase. On the twenty-second ballot, McCook, representing Ohio, nominated Horatio Seymour. He said that Pendleton supported the idea and that Seymour was a man who could unite the divided party. Seymour won the nomination unanimously.[70]

From the outset, two major factors impaired Pendleton's efforts. With Grant's selection by the Republicans, Pendleton's association with the Peace Democrats stirred harmful wartime memories. Nevertheless, Seymour shared a similar liability. Of greater significance was the Pendleton Plan. The two largest eastern states worked hard to prevent his nomination. When Indiana's support wavered, angry Ohio Pendletonians vowed to prevent Hendricks from winning because some blamed Pendleton's demise on Indiana's defection. At the same time, most Ohioans, except Vallandigham, refused to support Chase. He was too identified with the Republicans during the war and did not represent the views of midwestern Democrats on most important political issues. With Pendleton's support, Ohio led the charge for Seymour. An eastern nomination for the second consecutive convention might open the door for a midwestern candidate in

1872. Though Seymour did not accept the Ohio Idea, he was more sound than Chase on the other aspects of the platform that concerned Ohioans.[71]

The party had learned very little from the 1864 campaign. Though the midwestern Democracy, with support from the South, had gained strength, it could not totally direct the convention. Too many Southern delegates had favored candidates to whom they had closer ties, such as Johnson and Hancock. Southerners had long held to a hard-money position, based on old-style Jacksonianism and did not wish to compromise their system of trade in which world markets paid gold for their crops. At the same time, they needed more currency in circulation to recover from the devastation of the war. They failed to realize that the Pendleton Plan provided that currency in the interim with the promise of a return to specie payments in a reasonable amount of time, all the while maintaining a very Jacksonian attack on the National Bank System.[72]

Pendleton's plan also tried to appeal to Northern laborers, some of whom still distrusted him because of his position on the Civil War. Perhaps the five-twenties represented the Union war effort, and the Pendleton Plan reignited Northern labor nationalism. Maybe Jay Cooke had been correct when he argued that millions of the five-twenty bondholders were in fact laborers. Regardless, when combined with the unwillingness of conservative eastern Democrats to support the evolving midwestern Democratic ideology, Pendleton's bid fell short.[73]

Because of regional divisions, economic diversity, and intrastate power struggles, the party once again failed to produce harmony. In short, the party did not understand how to proceed as a minority. Pendleton had hoped that by winning Southern support he could pull eastern Democrats along kicking and screaming, and he almost succeeded. The end result, however, was a ticket and platform representative of a divided and floundering party.

Though disappointed, Pendleton did not sulk about his defeat. Instead, he began to campaign extensively for the party and Seymour. When rumors surfaced that his friends intended to nominate him in the First District for another race for Congress, he respectfully declined in order to serve the party in the canvass. Over the following months, Pendleton traversed Ohio, Indiana, Illinois, and most of the Midwest. He also traveled east, speaking on the merits of the platform and of Seymour. He did not mince words regarding the currency issue; rather, he continued to espouse his Ohio Idea. Long did not respond as well to his setback, however, and he tried to convince Seymour to decline the nomination by announcing that the strife between the supporters of Pendleton and Hendricks was so great that they were not going to support the ticket. Pendleton's involvement quickly dispelled Long's credibility.[74]

Other innuendoes were focused more directly at Pendleton. The *Cincinnati Gazette* accused him of inconsistency regarding his relations as a stockholder of the Commercial National Bank of Cincinnati. The paper alleged that when Ohio placed a tax on national banks within its borders, the Cincinnati bank refused to pay and encouraged other national banks to protest the law. Pendleton, as a stockholder and member of its board of directors, the paper argued, was a party to this action. Charles Foote, president of the bank, responded that the Supreme Court of Ohio struck the law from the books as unconstitutional, the position argued by the bank. Regardless, the tax was not on the bank itself but on its stockholders. Pendleton had paid the tax with no complaint even though its legality was in litigation. The bank had become a "free state" bank sometime before May 1868 anyway, so Pendleton could not be accused of being a stockholder in the very institution he sought to destroy. As for himself, Pendleton wrote a letter to J. Sterling Morton of Nebraska noting that he held $5,000 worth of stock in the bank, which was no longer a national bank, and held stock in no other national banks. A thorough investigation of his personal investments revealed that he did not hold government bonds either, which many midwestern Democrats would have viewed as hypocritical.[75]

Pendleton's probity in his personal investments was not the only focus of scrutiny. Once again, the *Gazette* published a letter Pendleton reportedly wrote to Somers Kinney in Houston, Texas, encouraging Kinney to resist the Radical Republican government that was placed in charge of Texas during Reconstruction. Both the *Gazette* and the *New York Times* published the letter to make it appear that Pendleton was advocating further rebellion. Pendleton immediately wrote a public letter denouncing the Kinney correspondence as a forgery, but the *Times* professed not to believe the denial.[76]

The opposition aggressively attacked Seymour through Pendleton. Republican newspapers blasted Pendleton's influence on the platform as repudiation and the road to excessive inflation. Eastern Democrats feared Seymour would hold too closely to the platform if elected. Reports continued to circulate that Pendleton had supported Seymour only to defeat Hendricks. The goal of the scheme was for Seymour to lose so that in 1872 the party would choose a midwestern candidate, ostensibly Pendleton. Pendleton's Herculean efforts on Seymour's behalf belied this charge, but his canvass apparently went unnoticed.[77]

Long had not lessened his resistance to Seymour, however, and when the October state elections in Maine, Ohio, and Pennsylvania went against the Democracy, he attempted a desperate last-minute charge to convince Seymour to withdraw in favor of Chase. The *New York World* approved of the plan, fearing that Grant's prestigious war record hurt Seymour and kept the focus off important issues. Moreover, vice-presidential candidate Francis Blair had been so outspoken against congressional Reconstruction that he had given some Americans the impression that he advocated overthrowing the reconstructed

Southern state governments by force. The solution, Long and Marble asserted, lay in a new ticket. Though Blair appeared willing to step down, Seymour hesitated, fearing that escaping a sinking ship without a battle to save it was irresponsible. The effort to dislodge Seymour further illustrated party divisions. Belmont, speaking for most Democrats, issued a letter from the Democratic Executive Committee calling for party unity and sustaining Seymour as the standard-bearer. But the dissension within the party continued.[78]

Democratic losses in October elections in Maine, Ohio, and Pennsylvania foreshadowed defeat in November when Grant beat Seymour. The result was particularly bitter to Pendleton when Seymour lost in Ohio by a margin of more than forty thousand votes. Intraparty recriminations filled the air immediately. The *Enquirer* tried to soften the loss by unearthing the standard Democratic explanation that Republicans stole the election through fraud. As the editor of the *New York World* and spokesman for eastern Democrats, Manton Marble disagreed. While he acknowledged that congressional Reconstruction programs harmed Seymour in the South, the greater fault rested with the Ohio Idea. In retrospect, each interpretation contained an element of truth. Federal troops stationed in several unreconstructed states had indeed interfered with the voting process. Eastern hard-money Democrats either had shunned Seymour because of the party platform or had not voted in silent protest. They simply were unwilling to accept Pendleton's reinterpreted Jacksonianism, turning a blind eye to their own inconsistency with party ideology. Moreover, the contrast between Seymour's vacillating wartime record and Grant's heroism posed an almost insurmountable barrier to any possible Democratic victory. Even so, neither McLean nor Marble gave the Ohio Idea its just due. To have ignored the financial issues would have cost Democrats valuable support in the Midwest. But Pendleton's innovative program had even larger dimensions. When the Republicans concentrated on Reconstruction issues and waved the bloody shirt, the Democrats were placed on the defensive. In that sense, the Ohio Idea implicitly accepted the results of the Civil War, neutralized any lingering issues connected to Reconstruction, created the means for Democrats to forge sectional reconciliation, and provided them with the possibility of formulating fresh programs more in tune with the future than the past. Yet Pendleton buttressed all of this progress on a new interpretation of the well-worn Jacksonian principle. Pendleton willingly took on new positions and allowed the midwestern Democratic ideology to evolve in an effort to unite party factions. Yet not all Democrats were willing to go along. Indeed, some voters probably could not grasp the complexity of the plan. Whatever the reasons for failure in 1868, Pendleton understood that both he and his party stood on the threshold of a new political era. In a letter to Seymour after the election, Pendleton called for an end to the finger-pointing.

Optimistically he wrote, "The tone and organization and discipline of the party in Ohio is entirely unbroken."[79]

Returning to private life in Clifton, Pendleton took a well-deserved break from politics. Living at the Bowler estate, the home of his widowed sister who was traveling in Europe, Pendleton was surrounded by luxury. The mansion decor must have reminded him of the palatial homes he had seen in Europe. Pendleton often opened the residence to visitors to walk with him through the greenhouses and across the expansive lawn.[80] Settling back into private pursuits, Pendleton returned to his law practice as well as his interest in organizing a railroad south from Cincinnati.[81] Pendleton was not long back at work when calamity struck. Early in the summer of 1869, children playing on a canal boat spooked his horse as he crossed a bridge in his carriage. The frightened animal almost overturned the vehicle, and Pendleton jumped out of the carriage. He dislocated his right ankle so badly that a bone nearly penetrated the skin. The injury confined him to bed for months and restricted his activity for more than six months. His recovery was extremely slow, and the long confinement to his home left him susceptible to illness. As the time approached for the Democratic State Convention, Pendleton's poor health prevented him from playing any role at the gathering.[82]

The party floundered in the wake of the 1868 defeat. Though Pendleton and his backers had accepted the results of the Civil War, attempted to unite the party around new issues, and sought conservative Republican support, some Democrats wanted even more change. Believing that the party leadership in Ohio, mainly Pendleton, McLean, and Thurman, had relegated him to insignificance, Vallandigham introduced a scheme to develop an even more diverse political alliance. In an unsuccessful bid for power within the party, he had struck out on his own when he supported Chase for the presidency. At the same time, he ran unsuccessfully for a seat in Congress. Though his new purpose had not yet been revealed, Vallandigham and his supporters called for the acceptance of congressional measures, including the Reconstruction amendments, in an attempt to gain greater support in the North. At the same time, the "New Departure," as Vallandigham's idea eventually became known, called for a "hands-off" policy in the South, or a nonenforcement position that would not violate the Democracy's states' rights position. This early form of the New Departure did not include any portion of Pendleton's debt payment plan.[83]

Vallandigham's motivation to father a program that repudiated much of what he had supported for the last decade lay in personal ambition. After the end of the Civil War and Pendleton's nomination for the vice presidency in 1864, Vallandigham realized that the reputation he had forged as an obstreperous Extreme Peace Democrat during the conflict had left him unelectable.

Just as discouraging, he had alienated Pendleton, who recognized that Vallandigham was a liability in the revitalization of the Democratic Party during the postwar years. These factors developed into a full-fledged schism between the two when Pendleton supported Thurman in his successful bid for a Senate seat in 1867. In the 1868 campaign, therefore, Vallandigham sought to supersede Pendleton's leadership and his allies by creating a new party platform under his own direction. Over the next year, the *Enquirer* gave Vallandigham's developing movement lip service, but had for months been rehashing the party's opposition to Reconstruction efforts. Pendleton and like-minded Democrats could not stomach the proposal because on the surface it forced the party to compromise long-held principles. Beyond principle, Pendleton's personal ambitions prevented him from letting the Daytonite gain the upper hand within the party. While Pendleton too sought to revitalize the party with new issues, he was unwilling to play the hypocrite to do so. Moreover, he certainly was not about to let another midwesterner challenge his leadership position in the party. Though he could claim to stand on principle, Pendleton's growth and willingness to take the party in new directions were stunted in large part due to personal considerations. He was now multiplying the party divisions he had tried to reduce. Due to his influence and that of his friends, the Democratic-dominated Ohio legislature rejected Vallandigham's ideas. In April 1869, it voted against ratifying the Fifteenth Amendment.[84]

Republicans held their state convention in June 1869 and renominated Rutherford B. Hayes for governor on a platform committed to ratification of the Fifteenth Amendment. Seeking to make a mockery of the Democratic focus on economy in government, they faulted the Ohio legislature for its excessive expenditures and misuse of funds. In that vein, they charged that the Democrats had prolonged the session unnecessarily and cost the taxpayers even more money. The Republicans made no mention, however, of the financial issues relating to either greenbacks or the tariff.[85]

When the Democrats met in July 1869, they addressed a much broader spectrum of issues, although they continued to support the Ohio Idea. After the Supreme Court ruled that the government could legally refund the five-twenty bonds in the currency in which they were purchased, Congress passed the Public Credit Act requiring their payment in coin. In their platform, the delegates criticized the law and the failure to tax interest paid on government bonds. To attract the support of laborers and consumers, other planks endorsed "a limited number of hours in all manufacturing workshops" and "liberal grants of land from the public domain to the actual settlers" rather than to the "swindling railroad corporations."[86] Delegates also condemned high tariffs for favoring New England manufacturers and bankers at the expense of midwestern farmers and merchants.

POLITICAL BODIES EMBALMED

DEMOCRATIC CONVENTION

DEMOCRATIC PARTY DIED

Mrs. MacRightwing. "Och! Sorrer, thin, and is the poor crayter jist dead?"
Undertaker Belmont. "Oh no, he's been dead this long time, but his friends couldn't bear the notion of his being buried; so we embalmed him and kept him in sight till—well, till we couldn't keep him any longer."

Political Bodies Embalmed: August Belmont, chairman of the Democratic party, is depicted as the undertaker in the death of the party. Pendleton is pictured just to the right of his hand on the casket. (*Harper's Weekly,* August 8, 1868)

Another plank exonerated the Democratic legislature of misusing government funds and turned the tables on Republicans by charging that President Grant was the real culprit. His administration needlessly squandered taxpayers' money by unconstitutionally keeping troops in the South. Above all, the platform directed its major attack on the proposed Fifteenth Amendment, maintaining that suffrage was a matter of states' rights. The delegates stopped short of a major political breakthrough. While they called on conservatives to join with them and address new concerns, the platform did not mention the New Departure.[87]

The gubernatorial nomination contest revealed some support for the idea of making the Democracy more appealing to conservatives outside the party. Samuel F. Cary of Hamilton County, a possible candidate who had previously been a Republican, favored labor and supported Pendleton's Ohio Idea. He represented a group of like-minded Republicans in Hamilton County that supported reforms in favor of labor and fused with the Democrats in this election.

Gen. William S. Rosecrans was another candidate. Although a Democrat, he remained an unknown commodity beyond his war record. Frank Hurd of Knox County offered Pendleton's name, and the response was so favorable that supporters sought to nominate him by acclamation. Amidst the great applause a delegate said that Pendleton had not consented to the use of his name. In fact, he had written the convention a letter unequivocally rejecting any possibility of running for office because of his injury. His supporters refused to relent until Pendleton dispatched a telegram specifically declining consideration. With that, the convention settled on General Rosecrans.[88]

Ohio's Democracy had a difficult time locating Rosecrans, who had been serving as minister to Mexico; for an embarrassing month the party was in limbo. When Rosecrans did receive the notification, he declined due to pressing personal and business affairs. Of more significance, he did not agree with the party's platform, and he called on Democrats who were unwilling to change their principles to withdraw from leadership positions. Specifically, Rosecrans opposed the Ohio Idea and advocated a more liberal approach to African American suffrage. Rosecrans's rejection of the nomination and lecture to the party astonished the state central committee. Meeting in haste in Columbus on August 11, the committeemen disregarded Rosecrans's advice and unanimously chose to impose upon Pendleton in their hour of need.[89] No one else, they said, "could receive so earnest and cordial an indorsement [sic] from the Democratic and Conservative people of this State."[90]

On the surface, Democratic prospects appeared bright. Across the state, party workers wheeled into action, and a Cincinnati ratification meeting led by George Pugh and Samuel F. Cary endorsed Pendleton for his unsullied personal reputation and indefatigable service in addition to the Ohio Idea. Furthermore, McLean spurred his readers to support Pendleton as a prelude to his next bid for the presidency in 1872 and reprinted laudatory articles from other Ohio newspapers. Even Marble was helpful and published an editorial backing Pendleton.[91] But beneath this facade, Pendleton hardly helped himself in his letter of acceptance when he reminded the party that he did not want this nomination due to his health and other personal matters. In typical Pendleton style, he spoke of his willingness to support Rosecrans when he was nominated and mentioned the names of others who could have ably replaced him after his declination. He admitted that he had only entered the campaign because of his sense of duty to the party: "I would consider their request as an imperative command to make the canvass, and I would do so to the best of my ability."[92]

Pendleton had been overly optimistic with regard to his recovery from the accident when he accepted the nomination. The hot weather of summer made his confinement unbearable and added to his slow recuperation. Unable to travel, Pendleton relied on surrogates. To begin with, he asked friends to organize the campaign with meetings at the township level throughout the state. Such meetings, he believed, were more effective earlier in the campaign than mass political rallies because they touched people at the grassroots level through a discussion of key issues. The last month of the campaign Pendleton reserved for the emotional appeals generated by larger gatherings. Pendleton's direct involvement would have to wait until then because of his indisposition. McLean again proved integral to this approach. The *Enquirer* consistently reported Pendleton's views and responded directly to Republican attacks.[93]

As Pendleton could not travel on his own behalf, voters came to him. One such impromptu crowd serenaded him at his house in Clifton, requesting an address. Taking advantage of the opportunity, he questioned Hayes's opinion that the difficult matters of the postwar era were solved. Republicans were increasing the national debt, he argued, because the secretary of the treasury redeemed the five-twenty bonds in coin instead of greenbacks. Using the *Commercial* as his source, Pendleton recounted the economic uncertainty that Ohio was experiencing, blaming it on unfair Republican taxes that burdened labor. He decried their onerous high tariffs, monetary contraction, and the National Bank System. He opposed Hayes's solution to the suffrage question even more because the Fifteenth Amendment nullified the Jacksonian doctrine of states' rights.[94]

Pendleton's health remained so perilous that he made just one more public appearance before the election. A nonpartisan group called a meeting to raise funds for building a home for Ohio's widows and orphans of Union troops and invited both candidates to attend. Pendleton could not refuse. Ohio Republicans had inserted a plan in their platform calling for the establishment of such an institution. Although still incapacitated and visibly shaking, he gave a short speech. The effort was worth the cost. Hayes, detained by a previous engagement, could not attend, which cast doubt on his commitment to that needy group.[95]

Despite this oversight, Hayes was optimistic but not cocky. Democratic fumbling over choosing a candidate elated him, yet he did not discount Pendleton's formidable strength. The Republicans waved the bloody shirt, portraying Pendleton as a reactionary seeking to undo the fruits of war. Rehashing settled issues such as African American suffrage and Reconstruction could not be allowed to engender further conflict with the South, Republicans argued. As for financial questions, Republicans contended that Pendleton was no more trustworthy than his colleagues in the Ohio legislature.[96]

Pendleton struggled valiantly against these odds but never recuperated enough to generate his hoped-for surge in the final days. He lost by just over 7,500 votes out of a total of 465,000, although to his credit he reduced the Republican majority from 1868 by 11,000 votes. The *Enquirer* blamed the loss entirely on Pendleton's inability to campaign. It was remarkable, McLean rationalized, that the infirm Pendleton was able to run such a close race, as Hayes had been very active throughout the state. Yet there were other factors. The poor organization of the party hurt Pendleton in some central counties. In addition, the issues Pendleton focused on were weakened by previous events. The Public Credit Act, though not to Pendleton's liking, resolved for the present the payment of the bonds. Though Ohio refused to ratify the Fifteenth Amendment, most of the other states had done so. The resolution of both matters may have caused some Ohioans to believe they were helpless to bring about change. If that were the case, it was not evident in the state legislative elections, where the Democrats did very well. Had not the Hamilton County Democrats fused with reform-minded Republicans, they probably would have maintained control of the state legislature. Instead, the balance of power lay in the hands of these reformers. On a strictly partisan basis, the Republicans had a majority. The *Commercial* interpreted the results as the end of Pendleton's chances for the presidency while the *Enquirer* believed they were still intact. Time would prove the *Commercial* correct. Pendleton's inability to win a majority in Ohio did not bode well for his hopes for higher office.[97]

Pendleton had tried to put the war questions behind him after his defeat in 1866. He had attempted to unify the party by rebuilding the Southern Democracy through the Ohio Idea. Though party divisions caused his plans to fail in 1868, Pendleton stopped short of adopting the New Departure. Though his hostility toward Vallandigham's idea was based on personal principle and ambition, Ohio's Democrats supported his decision for the time being. Any attempt at building Democratic power, he believed, had to be true to Jacksonian principles. The election of 1869 demonstrated that Reconstruction was still important to many Ohio voters, but the introduction of the New Departure and the fusion of the Hamilton County Democrats with reform-minded Republicans were precursors to party policies in the 1870s. As these forces gained momentum, Pendleton would have to decide to continue the process of reconciling new issues with old ideology or be left behind. In the meantime, he accepted an offer from the board of directors of the Kentucky Central Railroad to serve as president of that line. Pendleton entered a decade of private business endeavors, but never strayed far from the political arena.[98]

The Great Railroad Case and
the Road to the Senate

F our years prior to George Hunt Pendleton's ascendancy to the presidency of the Kentucky Central Railroad, the company became embroiled in what became the Midwest's "Great Railroad Case." Though not a participant in any of the incidents under litigation, Pendleton could not avoid involvement due to his positions as trustee of the estate of Robert Bowler and president of the railway. These events had the potential of discrediting Pendleton's carefully crafted image as a contemporary Jacksonian. The allegations he faced in this case and in the subsequent Belknap scandal seemed to suggest he was just as much a benefactor of privilege and influence as the political opponents he had fought against for years. As a result, in the 1870s, Pendleton faced a fight for his political life and for the political ideals he had dedicated his life to advance.

The Great Railroad Case involved Robert Bowler, Pendleton's brother-in-law, a director of the Covington and Lexington Railroad, the predecessor of the Kentucky Central Railroad. The former was a relatively short carrier running between the Kentucky cities of Covington, on the Ohio River, and Lexington, just southeast of the state capital. The plaintiffs accused Bowler of fraudulent management to facilitate his own takeover of the line. During the 1850s, local municipalities and county governments partially financed the railroad through bond subscriptions while the public sale of first and second mortgage bonds provided the rest of the massive amount of needed capital. Though the Covington and Lexington increased its income year after year, its high debt load required more income than it generated to cover the interest due on bonds. As a result, in 1857, its directors suspended the payment of interest on its first and second bonds and issued third mortgage bonds at a heavy discount. Bowler, who owned $200,000 of the second bonds, purchased an additional $100,000 of the third issue. With much of his fortune at stake, he determined to protect his investments by taking control of the company.[1]

In 1858, other investors had recognized Bowler's substantial interest in the line by electing him a director. He immediately sought to address the suspension of interest payments. In a surprising move, Bowler suggested to the board that they pay the interest due on the inferior third mortgage bonds while continuing the suspension of the interest on the first and second mortgage bonds. First bond holders, having substantial investments at stake, accepted the plan hoping that a sacrifice of interest in the short term might protect their capital in the long run. The second bond holders, however, generally had less invested and decided to challenge the proposal. They threatened to sue the company if it did not pay the interest due.[2]

Undaunted, Bowler floated yet another suggestion, ostensibly to secure the railroad's future stability. In May 1858, he proposed that the company issue a circular publicizing the need for an additional $800,000, to be raised from the sale of bonds, to put the line in "first-class" condition. He maintained his intent to delay interest payments on the first and second bonds, but not the third. He assured the first and second bond holders that paying the interest on the third mortgage bonds was vital to maintaining the railroad's credit rating.[3]

The following November, a group of second-issue bond holders, led by James Winslow, made good on their earlier threat and filed suit in Lexington. The court sustained them and ordered the line sold to satisfy their demands for payment. Although Bowler had undervalued the line when he reported it not worth more than $1.5 million, two bidders appeared who saw through the subterfuge. The first, a group known as the Harrison County Investors, offered $2 million but were outbid by a second group that paid $2.25 million for the carrier. This price was a bargain, as the railroad was actually worth more than $4 million.[4]

During these developments, Bowler followed his own interests and expanded his role from director to manager. He managed the company's daily operations, supervised improvements, and continued his policy of avoiding interest payments. Moreover, his public statements undervaluing the line proved to be a ploy that caused many third bondholders to sell their holdings at greatly reduced prices. Bowler exploited this situation. By the time the court rendered its decision, Bowler owned more than 50 percent of the third mortgage bonds and a sizable portion of the second mortgage bonds.[5] But Bowler went even further. Using a third party, William H. Gedge, as his front man, Bowler actually headed the investment group that purchased the railroad, using less than $70,000 of his own money. The sale left Bowler the largest bondholder and chairman of the board of directors.[6]

In 1861, Bowler and his junior partners reorganized the property as the Kentucky Central Railroad Company. Upon discovery of Bowler's duplicity, disgruntled board members of the old Covington and Lexington began to investigate the possibility of another suit. After uncovering information suggesting that Bowler had purposefully devalued the railroad in an attempt to assume control, and finding witnesses who were willing to testify to that effect, these former board members hired a Cincinnati lawyer. Peter Zinn accepted the case on a contingency basis, but the prospects were not good for a successful suit. Even before Zinn filed the court papers in 1870, Bowler, several of the potential witnesses, and a few of the old Covington and Lexington board members had died.[7]

By the time Zinn took his case to the Kenton County Circuit Court, Pendleton had become enmeshed in the litigation. He had been involved with the Kentucky Central as a member of the board of directors and as vice president prior to 1870, when he assumed the presidency.[8] Pendleton's company lawyers argued that Zinn had filed his case after the statute of limitations had expired. They also suggested that Zinn filed in the wrong court, as the original case had been examined in the Fayette County Circuit Court, which still had jurisdiction. In 1871, the Kenton County Circuit Court justified the pessimism of the old Covington and Lexington board members when it ruled against them. Undaunted, Zinn and his legal team filed an appeal.[9]

In the meantime, Pendleton and the Kentucky Central exploited the favorable court ruling. After the controversy over the sale of the Covington and Lexington in 1859, the Kentucky legislature had been unwilling to grant the company a new charter. Until 1871, the Kentucky Central operated under the old Covington and Lexington charter, but the court decision removed any lingering obstacles, and the legislature issued a new one. In February, Pendleton reorganized the firm under the new charter as the Kentucky Central Railroad Association.[10]

The railway immediately faced a conflict that would determine its future viability. Investors in Cincinnati hoped to build a line south from the Queen City through Kentucky to Chattanooga. Unless the proposed Cincinnati Southern Railroad, which the city of Cincinnati spearheaded, incorporated the disputed line into its route, the results for the Kentucky Central would be devastating. If the Kentucky Central were not included, the competition could force the Kentucky Central into bankruptcy, as the majority of the Southern-bound passengers and freight would take the through-route Cincinnati Southern rather than a series of short lines. Another problem soon surfaced. The court of appeals, which had pondered Zinn's motion for eighteen months, reversed the decision of the circuit court and ruled in favor of the Covington and Lexington investors.[11]

In 1873, both sides petitioned the court for specific details on how the ruling affected the Kentucky Central. The railroad also filed for a rehearing of the case. If allowed to stand, the decision would force the Kentucky Central into receivership. Nearly a year later, the court of appeals handed down another ruling that was more favorable to the Kentucky Central.[12] The old company board decided that its best route was a negotiated compromise with the Kentucky Central. By this time, both sides were ready to end the lengthy legal ordeal. The City of Covington, which held $300,000 in Covington and Lexington bonds, delayed matters further, however, as it attempted to construct a compromise that the city council would accept.[13]

In the midst of those negotiations, Pendleton's role became more controversial. Zinn informed the Covington council that Pendleton had orchestrated a meeting of Covington and Lexington stockholders. Pendleton's goal, Zinn alleged, was to buy the old company stock to eliminate the grounds for the case. Undoubtedly this out-of-court action would have left Zinn with no reward for his years of labor. Pendleton immediately responded, "The managers of the 'Bowler Interest' . . . have not attempted . . . to buy the stock of the Covington and Lexington R. R. Company for the purpose of 'settling' with themselves, or any other purpose."[14] Yet he made it clear that they had the legal right to do so should they deem it in their interest. Pendleton also denied a published financial statement of the Bowler interest as Zinn's fabrication. Zinn defended himself, but the event did little toward solidifying a compromise.[15]

The negotiation process was fraught with other conflicts as well. Proposed compromises were negotiated, rejected, and renegotiated; the process was tedious and time-consuming. In the meantime, the Kentucky Central continued the appeals process as efforts to compromise faltered. By now, the case had become so publicized that Pendleton felt compelled to issue a public letter when he rejected a proposed settlement from the Covington City Council. That body responded by threatening to continue the court battle. But both sides apparently had had enough. Within a week of Pendleton's rejection of the proposal, they reached an accommodation. In May 1875, ten years after Bowler's death and the early rumblings of a lawsuit, the Great Railroad Case came to an end.[16]

The compromise led to the formation of still another company. The Kentucky Central Railroad Association transferred its assets to a new Kentucky Central Railroad Company that issued $5 million in stock. The settlement gave the municipalities and counties with investments in the Covington and Lexington stock in the new company equal to the principle of the bonds they held. It did not, however, pay the interest due on their bonds. Covington and Lexington stockholders acquired stock in the new company worth 75 percent of their original investment. Zinn and his associates received $1 million in stock for their fees and as payment for the advances in prosecuting the case. The compromise granted the remaining $2.4 million in stock to Bowler's heirs, represented by Pendleton, as majority owners of the Kentucky Central's bonds. The Bowler estate became the largest stockholder, but it did not own a majority of the stock. The compromise also forced the Bowler estate to forfeit all claims to the third mortgage and income bonds it had held from the old line. In May 1875, the settlement was finalized.[17]

In accepting this arrangement, Pendleton succeeded in preserving the Kentucky Central Railroad and protecting the financial standing of the Bowler estate. In the process, however, he had been dragged through almost a decade of unfavorable press coverage. Although journalists usually referred to the "Bowler heirs" or the "Kentucky Central" rather than using Pendleton's name, he was guilty by association. Throughout the controversy, journalists had constantly reminded Cincinnatians of Pendleton's wealth and his connections with big business. Pendleton, the Democrat who had always appealed to the working men in Cincinnati, was now linked with the "moneyed interests." In spite of that stigma, the railroad case did not damage Pendleton's reputation as badly as it might have. The 1875 solution was a true compromise. Pendleton had not been forced by the courts to reconcile with the old line stockholders; he had accepted a proposal that protected the interests of the investors and the municipalities involved. Those cities represented working-class people. In their eyes, Pendleton's acceptance of the compromise was a signal of his desire to be upright and honest. Jacksonians had long come from all classes, even in the Midwest. More importantly, midwesterners, especially those who were upland Southerners, had no qualms about well-to-do men like Pendleton who pursued personal benefit as long as it also advanced the public interest. The public continued to regard him as a man of high standing as evidenced by the continued call for his political activity.[18] The question of Pendleton's integrity would be challenged again, however, in his capacity as president of the new Kentucky Central.

Pendleton's supervision of the Bowler estate certainly played the key role in his selection as president of the Kentucky Central, but his public prominence was seen as a boon for the railroad as well. He made it clear from the start, however, that he was not simply a figurehead president. The successes of the Kentucky Central demonstrate his active management and desire to update and improve the line. During his tenure, the railroad built a new station in its northern terminus at Covington. The company improved the roadbed and eventually replaced iron rails with steel. The *Covington Journal* reported that major accidents on the Kentucky Central were fewer than most lines due to the fastidious care given to the rails by management. Expansion of the line toward Knoxville, Tennessee, began under Pendleton's leadership, and the line leased various portions of nearby roads to improve service. Pendleton actively pursued the building of a bridge between Covington and Cincinnati and sought to make the Kentucky Central a key portion of the future Cincinnati Southern Railroad route connecting the Ohio River Valley with the South. Pendleton's political experience was vital to the success of the line, and he became quite adept at lobbying the Kentucky State Assembly for permission to expand. Even with the improvements, competition and the high costs of updating the line took their toll. The company continued to show profits, though not as high as previous years. While the Kentucky Central developed a solid reputation, Pendleton renewed the personal battle for maintaining his own standing.[19]

A year after the Great Railroad Case settlement, Pendleton once again fell under press scrutiny. In early 1876, rumors began to connect him with the fraud and corruption of the Ulysses S. Grant administration. One casualty of these inquiries and investigations was Secretary of War Maj. Gen. William W. Belknap. He resigned amid speculation that he had accepted bribes in licensing sutlers at army and Indian posts in the West. One sutler, Caleb P. Marsh, allegedly made a deal with Belknap's wife to pay her a portion of the profits if she influenced her husband on his behalf. After Mrs. Belknap's death, the rumor continued, Marsh made a similar arrangement with Belknap's fiancée, Mrs. Amanda Bower, who was the former Mrs. Belknap's sister. When Grant got wind of the scandal, he demanded Belknap's resignation. In the melee that followed the removal, or resignation, of Belknap and other key administration personnel, journalistic appetite for further scandal grew more ravenous. Pendleton's name was dragged into the affair by Charles Nordhoff, a reporter for the *New York Herald,* and by other Republican papers.[20] Pendleton's connection to Belknap had begun when Pendleton requested that the War Department pay for services the Kentucky Central had rendered during the Civil War. Although Secretary of War Edwin M. Stanton earlier rejected the claim, Pendleton secured remuneration through Belknap. Using secondhand information, Nordhoff accused Pendleton of bribing Belknap through his new wife, Amanda Bower, to obtain payment of the railroad's claim.[21] Having finally settled the court battle in Kentucky, Pendleton now faced a scandal of national proportion and possible political repercussions of significantly greater magnitude.[22]

Grant's diminishing hopes for a third term and the newly elected Democratic majority in the House of Representatives encouraged the investigative reporters. Sometimes described as "mugwumps," these journalists had two goals. First, they sought to bring an end to administrative corruption in the Grant administration. Second, they wanted to suggest that Democrats were involved in the misdeeds as well as the already implicated Republicans. Pendleton was a prime target because of his national stature and his principled attacks on the Republicans. Nordhoff and others accused Pendleton of paying Mrs. Bower, soon to be Mrs. Belknap, a figure ranging from $10,000 to $70,000, to influence her husband-to-be regarding payment of the Kentucky Central claim. Bower was a resident of Cincinnati; since being widowed, her husband's estate was in the hands of Mr. Bower's partner, Ezra Leonard. Bower was due some $15,000 from her husband's portion of the firm and another $15,000 from a life insurance policy. She hired Pendleton and his brother Elliot as attorneys to manage her estate. Rumors suggested that the Pendletons were suing Leonard for payment of money owed Bower. In the event that he could not secure payment, Pendleton allegedly promised to pay Bower the $30,000 himself if she could help him obtain the Kentucky Central claim.[23]

The accusations did not stop there. One rumor suggested that Pendleton paid Bower by covering the expenses of a lavish trip to Europe. Giving credence to this innuendo, Pendleton, whose family was vacationing in Europe, spent most of the year in the United States attending to the Kentucky Central, but did travel to Europe during the summer of 1872. In that period, so the allegations went, he journeyed with Mrs. Bower and Mrs. Caleb Marsh to Liverpool.[24] Pendleton allegedly took care of Mrs. Bower's every need. One newspaperman was even more salacious. He insinuated that the two carried on an illicit affair, traveling together in Spain while Mrs. Pendleton stayed in France. The rumor suggested that this affair continued until Mrs. Pendleton ordered her husband to meet her and the rest of the family in Paris.[25]

Upon reading the *Washington Capital* story in the *Cincinnati Enquirer,* Pendleton immediately responded with unqualified denials and denunciations of those who perpetrated the untruths. Although refusing to acknowledge the talk of an affair with so much as a public statement, he wrote Hiester Clymer, chairman of the Committee on the Expenditures of the War Department, "I pronounce the story in every respect absolutely false, and I request the Committee to investigate the case immediately."[26] Pendleton also offered to testify before the committee as soon as possible. Demonstrating his outrage, he sent another letter to Milton M. Sayler and Henry B. Banning of the House of Representatives requesting that his appeal to Clymer be honored. Finally, Pendleton wrote to Sen. Allen G. Thurman, an Ohio Democrat, and Sen. John W. Stevenson of Kentucky, a partner in the Kentucky Central, seeking redress. Four days after the letters were written, investigations began.[27]

Hiester Clymer had a dual reason to resolve this case. First, he did not want the public to view him as too partisan a Democrat in his quest to root out corruption in government. The attack on a major Democratic figure such as Pendleton was clearly designed to embarrass the party and Clymer, who had been investigating the Grant administration scandals. Second, and perhaps more important to Clymer, Nordhoff suggested that he had traveled with Pendleton and Bower to Europe in 1872 and was a party to Pendleton's alleged corruption. Not surprisingly, Nordhoff was the first to be questioned as the investigation opened. He testified that he had no personal knowledge of the case but had received his information from Henry V. Boynton of the *Cincinnati Gazette.* Boynton left Washington, D.C., on prearranged business and was unavailable for questioning until March 14, the day Pendleton arrived and spoke before the committee. Alice Key Pendleton rushed to the capital to be with her husband.[28]

Pendleton testified at length before the House committee regarding his association with the railroad and his pursuit of the Kentucky Central claim, especially in response to Clymer's question about the status of the claim when Pendleton became company president. Pendleton gave a brief history of the railroad since its formation in 1858, when Robert B. Bowler bought the company. Bowler formed a copartnership, Pendleton noted, which continued even after his death. In 1869, Pendleton told the committee, "I became president of the road, chiefly because I represented the estate of Mr. Bowler, who was my brother-in-law, and who had a large interest in it at that time."[29] In this new position, Pendleton explained that he spent most of his time grappling with the case brought against the railroad by former interests. As the litigation drew to a close, Pendleton continued, he focused on day-to-day operations. It was at that time that he learned about the existing claim. In speaking to one of the company partners, John W. Stevenson, Pendleton discovered that the company still sought the claim and was willing to pay up to 50 percent of the amount to whomever could obtain payment. That percentage worked out to a potential finder's fee approaching $80,000. After receiving the sanction of each partner, Pendleton commenced investigation of the claim.[30]

In the process of this investigation, Pendleton learned the claim's basis. Northern railroads had cooperated with the government during the Civil War by forming a convention. Under its terms, they settled on a set rate for transporting soldiers, supplies, and other freight. For those railroads in areas susceptible to Confederate attack, the federal government agreed to pay higher rates. The Kentucky Central was one of those eligible for this higher compensation. In fact, it had been occupied on four or five occasions by the Rebels and sabotaged several times. The government paid the railroad the higher rate for services rendered from August 1864 until the end of the conflict. Prior to August 1864, however, payment was based on the agreed upon railroad convention rate. The pending claim, then, was for the difference between the higher rate for railroads in danger of Confederate occupation and the regular convention rate during the earlier months of the war.[31]

Upon further questioning, Pendleton revealed the names of those officials with whom he had spoken throughout the claims process. In November 1870,

Pendleton had a meeting with Secretary Belknap for about a half-hour. Belknap referred the claim to Assistant Judge Advocate General William M. Dunn, who was responsible for rendering a decision. Pendleton freely admitted during testimony that he had known Dunn previously as a colleague in the House. Moreover, Pendleton conceded that he had met with Dunn on more than one occasion in regard to the claim.

As Dunn examined the case, he read over the report of the quartermaster-general of the United States, Gen. Montgomery C. Meigs, who disallowed the claim in 1864, and sent Pendleton a copy in order to write a response. Pendleton complied, and Dunn took his reply under consideration. Pendleton also met with Meigs to discuss his reasoning for rejecting the initial claim. Meigs enumerated two reasons. First, the War Department under Secretary Stanton did not believe the Kentucky Central deserved the higher rate. Second, Meigs suggested that the government had paid to have the railroad change its gauge during the war and therefore considered those costs additional payment. Pendleton, replying to Meigs's statements, produced documents showing that the road had not changed its gauge during the conflict. Meigs had confused the Kentucky Central, then the Covington and Lexington, with the Louisville and Lexington. In addition, Pendleton showed that railroads such as the Baltimore and Ohio and the Louisville and Nashville, which suffered similar difficulties from the Confederates, had received even higher rates than the Kentucky Central requested. After several months of consideration and examination of this evidence, Dunn decided in favor of the railroad on the merits of Pendleton's presentation.[32]

The committee did not end its inquiry with the decision-making process in the War Department. The line of questioning changed course and began to focus on the propriety of the railroad's remuneration of Pendleton. One member insinuated that as the representative of the Bowler estate, which now owned three-fifths of the company's stock, Pendleton in essence made a contract with himself to realize 50 percent of the claim if he obtained payment. Pendleton protested that he had consulted with each of the partners, his nephew who was an heir of the estate and of age, and Mrs. Bowler (Pendleton's sister), both of whom consented to the arrangement. Pendleton remarked that to the best of his recollection, he received about $80,000 and the company about $68,000 from the claim. The company representative, A. H. Ransom, who had placed the original petition, had a right to some of the money, which both parties paid. As for his purported bribery of Mrs. Bower and through her, Secretary Belknap, Pendleton denied having paid anyone connected with the War Department to expedite the claim. Finally, Clymer, once again trying to exonerate himself, asked if Pendleton had ever met him in Europe. Pendleton could not recollect any meeting.[33]

After Pendleton left, the committee interviewed a number of people who were intimately associated with the claim, and even some who were at best tangentially involved. Senator Stevenson corroborated Pendleton's statement that the partners and Mrs. Bowler had consented to his proposal. Boynton, of the *Cincinnati Gazette* and one of the originators of the accusations against Pendleton, also testified and divulged his sources. Discrediting himself, Boynton cited a lengthy list of individuals who had heard rumors and stories from others. One source was Gen. J. B. Kiddoo who implicated Mrs. Caleb Marsh.[34] Mrs. Marsh was summoned and testified that Mrs. Belknap had denied in a discussion receiving $70,000 for the Kentucky Central claim but that had ended their conversation on the matter. Marsh was also questioned regarding the trip to Europe. She confirmed that Pendleton had traveled with her and Mrs. Belknap to Europe, but said no impropriety took place, as Pendleton was Mrs. Belknap's attorney and in charge of her estate. Ezra Leonard, Mr. Bower's business partner, was called and denied the existence of any lawsuit between the then Mrs. Bower and himself over her deceased husband's estate. In fact, Leonard believed Pendleton to be a "mutual friend" of both himself and Mrs. Bower and Leonard thought of the widow as a "sister."[35] The inquiry ended with concluding remarks from Gen. William Dunn, who confirmed every aspect of Pendleton's story regarding the process of requesting the claim. He actually downplayed the relationship between himself and Pendleton, picturing their connection as little more than a casual acquaintance. Dunn swore that at no time had he been paid or even pressured to permit the claim. In the final analysis, Dunn believed it was a just claim and had requested the treasurer to pay on that basis.[36]

Though the House committee completely exonerated Pendleton from any wrongdoing, Republican newspapers continued their attacks. Rejecting the committee's legal findings as the consequence of a Democratic majority, they assailed Pendleton on ethical grounds.[37] The *New York Tribune* suggested that Pendleton, as guardian of the two minor Bowler heirs, had an obligation to obtain the claim for them. In accepting such a large fee, they argued, he was stealing from the children. The *Cincinnati Enquirer* was quick to defend Pendleton. It pointed to the finding of the House committee that Pendleton was not and never had been guardian of the Bowler heirs. Mrs. Bowler was the guardian, and "if she found no grounds for complaint, the Government certainly has none."[38] In addition, George P. Bowler, the only Bowler heir of age, publicly expressed his appreciation to his uncle and believed that the money could never pay for all that Pendleton had done for him in the past. In reality, the money was going to the company, not the family directly. One could argue that the $68,000 was better than nothing, which was what the line had received until Pendleton got involved. Nonetheless, there certainly is a question of propriety here. This may very well be a story of relationship and influence, which some viewed as inconsistent with Pendleton's Jacksonianism—yet he still carried a bit of his father's Whig paternalism with him. In addition, this was the way the government operated, though Pendleton later realized that the system allowed too much room for corruption. The allegations of bribery and adultery against him, however, were nothing more than unfounded partisan attacks. Pendleton lived with the nagging question of who was responsible for the rumor about the affair until the death of his sister. When Mrs. Bowler was on her deathbed, she sent for the Pendletons, who were vacationing in Florida. When they arrived, she pleaded with them, "Can you forgive me?" She went on to tell them that she had been jealous of Mrs. Belknap, her longtime friend, and started the rumor to hurt her, not Pendleton.[39]

The political nature of the allegations against Pendleton was undeniable. Although the evidence of corruption within the Grant administration fouled Republican prospects for winning the presidency in 1876, the allegations about Pendleton led to a public backlash that similarly tarnished the Democrats. Sensing this opportunity, Republicans argued that Pendleton, though innocent in the eyes of the law, was guilty in the court of public opinion. For years he had based his political identity as the champion of the agrarian and working classes in Cincinnati and Ohio. His accusers now suggested that the improprieties in obtaining such a large fee had revealed self-serving motives that alienated his constituents. Indeed, in some ways, Pendleton's actions smacked of the very privilege he had long opposed. Yet Pendleton's career was far from over. Midwesterners did not forget what he had done for them in the past. As the party developed new factions in the 1870s, Pendleton continued to remember the Common Man and thereby maintain his support base. His vociferous and immediate response to the allegations against him, his constant and unwavering position regarding the appropriateness of his actions, and the obviously partisan nature of the charges resulted in Pendleton maintaining much of his support in Ohio. In fact, some Democrats viewed him as a victim of Republican malice. The more important issue for labor and farmers in Ohio became federal monetary policies in the 1870s, not the personal accusations against Pendleton.[40]

Though embroiled in the day-to-day duties of the Kentucky Central and seeking to clear his name of any wrongdoing in the Great Railroad Case, as well as the Belknap improprieties, Pendleton was able to remain actively involved in the leadership of the Democratic Party, not only in Ohio but also nationally. Aside from his personal difficulties, Pendleton's struggles in the face of a divided party well represented the political milieu of Gilded Age America.

During the 1870s, both Republicans and Democrats sought party cohesion and unity in the midst of a sectionalized country. With the war over and many of the primary Reconstruction issues resolved, both parties struggled in the wake of losing the foundation of their identities for the previous twenty years. They sought to justify their existence to the voters. The tragedy that had befallen the country a decade earlier had not vanished from the political realm with the surrender at Appomattox Court House. In fact, with the end of the war and the lack of a common enemy in the South to unify the North, the sectional divisions between East and West became even more prominent. The struggle facing the parties was to gather enough support among the country's various sections to control the government, thus preventing the all-too-prevalent political deadlock. As a result, both major parties in this era sought to develop divergent stands on questions such as the refunding of Civil War bonds, the currency issue, tariffs, labor issues, and agrarian concerns, but they continued to be deeply split internally. Parties were caught between what had worked for them in the past and the need to find new strategies for a changing political milieu without fracturing their supporters. For much of the decade then and even beyond, the Democrats moved from one issue to the next in the search for elusive unity.[41]

The Democracy faced divisions geographically and ideologically. In the East and South, and to a lesser degree in the Midwest, a new faction of Democrats known as the Bourbons was emerging. These men were conservatives who discounted the concerns of farmers or laborers and favored a probusiness government posture. They believed in limited government, used racism as an issue, advocated the gold standard, favored low taxation, and opposed corrupt officeholders and the protective tariff. While most of these positions were seemingly in line with traditional Jacksonianism, Bourbons were inconsistent, Pendleton argued. They believed the government should foster economic growth, accepted the National Bank System, and ignored the plight of the Common Man. As a result, they consciously fought against Pendleton and those Democrats who accepted his midwestern Democratic ideology. Bourbons held so strongly to their antipathy toward ordinary voters that they bypassed opportunities to defeat the Republicans in order to prevent "the masses" from influencing the government. Bourbons did differ from their Republican adversaries on the role of the federal government. Yet, because they often supported Republican economic proposals, the Bourbons felt the need to distinguish themselves from their political opposition. Their means of doing this was to focus on organizational and administrative reform within their party. To demonstrate this new emphasis, Bourbons especially opposed the growing strength of political machines such as Tammany Hall in New York.[42]

Most midwestern Democrats did not accept the Bourbon position. Party leaders such as Pendleton were unwilling to neglect the party's midwestern constituency, which was largely labor and agrarian. Pendleton differed from the

HARD OR SOFT MONEY?
Does Mr. GEORGE H. PENDLETON think "*the War was a Failure?*"

Hard or Soft Money?: Thomas Nast attacks Pendleton's fee from the Kentucky Central Railroad war claim against the federal government. Nast put the incorrect date on Pendleton's bid for the vice presidency, however. (*Harper's Weekly*, April 1, 1876)

Bourbons on such important issues as payment of the five-twenty Civil War bonds, issuance of greenbacks, and labor and farm concerns, yet he supported their commitment to many other traditional Democratic principles. Pendleton believed that the party had to remain consistent with its heritage. He was unwilling to break with the past ideologically as he believed the Bourbons had done. He was willing, however, to develop new issues based on those same principles. A dyed-in-the-wool Democrat, Pendleton could not stomach the Bourbon willingness to see Republicans win rather than support issues favored by the lower classes. Yet he did not consider organizational reform as sufficient and focused on maintaining an ideological distance from the Republicans to give voters a choice. He desired to see the party truly distinguish itself from its opposition, as the Peace Democrats had done throughout the war, believing that it was the only way to coalesce the party and return it to prominence. This was how a minority party was supposed to function.[43]

After Pendleton's close defeat in 1869, the party faired poorly in the 1870 Ohio campaign, electing only four out of nineteen seats in Congress. By contrast, the Republicans elected their entire state ticket. Pendleton did not withdrawal from public view after his loss. Considering his physical condition, he had done surprisingly well. Instead, he continued to make public appearances throughout Ohio and outside the state when he was available.[44] Pendleton did not attend the 1870 Democratic State Convention due to the demands of continued recuperation and his new position with the Kentucky Central. The lack of older Democratic leaders in attendance left the convention duties in the hands of younger, less experienced Democrats. With no leader rising to take the lead and push the party in a new direction, Ohio Democrats simply drifted.[45] Hoping to put an end to the Democratic skid, Clement Vallandigham reintroduced his suggestion for a "New Departure" following the election. The program was adopted at a Montgomery County party meeting in 1871 and presented to the state convention. Now that the battle over the Fifteenth Amendment was over, Pendleton acquiesced to Vallandigham's proposal from his familiar position as president of the meeting. New Departure supporters waged a fierce and ultimately successful battle to have their platform plank adopted.[46]

The New Departure called on the party to accept the Thirteenth, Fourteenth, and Fifteenth Amendments as "accomplished facts," no longer legitimate political issues.[47] What was at stake was their enforcement. As a result, Democrats now demanded that the government interpret the Constitution from the perspective of strict constructionism, preserving the power and rights of the states. In addition, other planks sought universal amnesty for former Confederates, a tariff for revenue only, the end of land grants to large corporations, civil service reform, and just taxation. For much of the 1870s, these planks formed the platform of the party. They were acceptable to Bourbon Democrats as well, and the midwestern Democrats under Pendleton sought to entice their support. Yet the platform also contained a key midwestern position, which Bourbons chose not to accept, as demonstrated by several planks that called for enacting the old Ohio Idea: interconvertable bonds (payable in greenbacks), banking reform, economy in government, and the return to specie payments in a just fashion.[48] Pendleton did not see his support of the New Departure as inconsistent with his ideology. Rather, it was a simple acknowledgment of what was reality in postwar America.

The convention nominated Gen. George W. McCook, who had unsuccessfully led the Ohio bid for Pendleton's presidential nomination at the 1868 Democratic National Convention as their candidate for governor in 1871. Having fully recovered from his incapacitating ankle injury in 1869, Pendleton canvassed extensively for McCook and the party. In his speeches, Pendleton focused primarily on currency issues. His goal was to reach Ohio's sizable agrarian and labor constituency. Censuring Republican policies regarding currency and tariffs, he said, both placed unnecessary burdens on the poor and laborers and lined the pockets of bondholders with gold. Undoubtedly, Pendleton had some difficulty swallowing the New Departure. As a trade-off, he emphasized the platform's consistency with his own monetary position. The fresh perspective allowed the Ohio Democrats to focus on a set of issues long neglected by the party while continuing its emphasis on financial concerns.[49]

The New Departure's biggest proponent would not live long enough to see its impact. Vallandigham accidentally shot himself during a court case while he was demonstrating that the victim could have shot himself. Undoubtedly, his dramatization was convincing. He did not know the gun he was using as a prop was loaded.[50] Yet Vallandigham remained as contentious in death as in life, especially among Southerners, who despised the New Departure. Pendleton was the recipient of some of this loathing in spite of Southern support for his stand on currency. The editor of the *Columbus Mississippi Dispatch,* William H. Worthington, wrote to William Allen, who had been unwilling to associate with the new doctrine, "Mr. Pendleton was a favorite with us Southern Democrats, but his yielding to Vallandigham's daring movement, utterly destroyed his popularity. This defection in leadership is the main cause of our present weakness and demoralization."[51] Southerners were not ready to concede the Fourteenth and Fifteenth Amendments as necessary results of the war. In Ohio, the New Departure's impact was unclear. The Democrats did fare better than in 1870, gaining enough seats to split the Ohio Senate, but they failed to elect General McCook, who had to stop campaigning due to poor health. Midwestern Bourbons had not supported the party platform because of the Ohio Idea, and the resulting division undoubtedly aided the Republicans in maintaining their Ohio Assembly majority. As a result, the legislature selected Republican senator John Sherman for another term in Washington.[52]

Disillusioned by the Bourbon opposition within the party, some Democratic laborers sought to form a third party. These men detested the contraction policies of the Republicans. Thomas Ewing attempted to lure these workers back into the Democratic fold by emphasizing the Ohio Idea but eventually involved himself in the National Labor Reform Convention. He attempted to persuade the Democratic leadership to consider a coalition with a third party that grew out of that convention known as the "People's Party," but was unable to obtain their support. That would not be the case with a different third party, however.[53]

The Republicans faced threats from third-party movements as well. They had rejected Pendleton's idea to pay the five-twenty bonds in greenbacks and passed legislation in 1869 making them payable in gold. Eventually, they refunded the five-twenties and other bonds fundable at 6 percent interest with lower interest bonds that were specifically designated to be paid in gold coin. These policies alienated midwestern Republicans who had supported payment of the five-twenties in greenbacks. Republicans suffered from the same malady as the Democrats—endemic internal factionalism over how to modernize the party. As a result, another third-party movement emerged known as the Liberal Republican Party. These men focused primarily on such issues as civil service reform, the corruption in Grant's administration, and tariff reform.[54]

Liberal Republicans held a national convention in Cincinnati and, after much deliberation, nominated Horace Greeley to run against Grant in 1872. Greeley's political positions had often been controversial and even contradictory. Greeley supported the protective tariff and forced the convention to leave out of the platform the plank on tariff reform. He was no civil service reformer either, but had supported a one-term presidency amendment to the Constitution, something Ohio's Democrats would call for in 1874. Greeley picked up Vallandigham's New Departure ideas seeking recognition of the changed role of the black man in American society but took that position to its logical conclusion seeking enforcement of the Fourteenth and Fifteenth Amendments. As a result, Ohio's Democrats found him hard to swallow. His paper, the *New York Tribune,* had long attacked the Democracy, particularly Northern Peace Democrats during the war. Yet, lacking a better option and seeking a coalition, Democrats held their collective nose and chose Greeley as their standard-bearer as well.[55]

Before any of the conventions met, Pendleton focused on one of the key issues that united this unlikely coalition: civil service reform. In sending his regrets for being unable to attend the annual January 8, 1872, Jackson Day celebration, Pendleton wrote at length about the need for such a reform. He attacked the corruption among many of the Republican appointees in federal offices. Placing his party squarely in opposition to that practice, he denounced the Republican perception of public positions as political prizes to be used for personal and partisan gain, in both money and power. Federal employment was a public trust, he believed, and not designed for an elite group of partisans whose only qualifications for office were party service. Pendleton was only beginning to define his position with regard to civil service reform, but he based his support of it on the Jacksonian principles of democracy and opportunity. Pendleton's concerns later formed the foundation of his call for a civil service that was predicated on merit and could not be used to raise funds for a political party. Aware of the growing split among Republicans on this issue, he called for cooperation between the disgruntled Liberal Republicans and the Democratic Party. Pendleton managed to alleviate some of the Southern pressure on him for his acquiescence to the New Departure by focusing their attention elsewhere. More importantly, he demonstrated his ability to take the pulse of the nation. He had hit upon one of the most important political issues of the era as well as predicted the coalition of Liberal Republicans and Democrats. In addition, he continued the process of reinterpreting Jacksonianism to address these new issues.[56]

Although Pendleton supported the necessity of fusion, he rejected the prospect of supporting Horace Greeley, a longtime enemy of Democrats, because he and the Liberal Republicans advocated a quick return to specie payments. But Pendleton was in Europe when the Democratic National Convention nominated Greeley and missed the opportunity to emphasize his misgivings. On his return, Pendleton proved an organizational loyalist and sought to convince fellow Democrats that support for the national ticket did not amount to betraying their party. In that regard, Pendleton limited his public statements to criticism of the Grant administration and only commented about issues he supported such as universal amnesty for former Confederates, limited executive power, the end of martial law in the South, termination of land grants to railroads, fair federal taxation, and civil service reform. Yet deep down, Pendleton must have realized that he had shelved party principle for expediency in order to revive the Democracy. The Liberal Republican position on currency was particularly hard to accept. Apparently, other midwestern Democrats shared his foreboding. On election day, many Ohio Democrats stayed home, and Grant carried the state. But the contest was a catharsis for the Democrats. While the Liberal Republican Party disappeared, Pendleton and his supporters now understood that temporizing was self-defeating. While they had gained Bourbon support, they had lost labor voters, who felt alienated by both parties. In addition, the Democrats had failed to decide on what issues they intended to champion in the future.[57]

The Democracy's main priorities in 1873 lay in reorganizing and in finding winning issues from the debris of the Liberal Republican fusion fiasco. One key event, the failure of Philadelphia banker Jay Cooke's investment schemes, which sparked the Panic of 1873, solved the problem by dramatically shifting the entire texture of national politics. Sensing that they were on the threshold of a new era, Democrats blamed Republican currency contraction for the financial collapse. As their remedy for recovery, midwestern Democrats resurrected the greenback issue and in the process revived Pendleton's career. He found other issues that seemed just as promising. Farmers, joined by an unlikely ally in certain railroad interests, redoubled their efforts at currency inflation through greenbacks. Some railroads favored inflation because they believed it would make it easier for them to pay off their considerable debt. Recognizing his own railroad interests, Pendleton joined them, further enhancing his stature as a greenbacker. Moreover, Republican mistakes encouraged Pendleton. The litany of their foibles grew in volume, ranging from the notorious attempt of the Republican-controlled Congress to raise its remuneration through the "Salary Grab," a serious disregard of public sensibilities during the growing recession, to their connection to the Crédit Mobilier scandal, which implicated many prominent Republicans who took bribes in the form of securities linked to Crédit Mobilier and the Union Pacific Railroad. In return, the railroad had received land grants and federal loans, much of which had lined the pockets of key investors. As Democrats faced the fall elections of 1873, both Pendleton and his party had every reason to expect a triumphal return to power. As an advocate of limited currency expansion and a critic of Republican corruption, Pendleton seemed the prophet redeemed.[58]

Recognizing the opportunity that 1873 afforded them, Ohio Democrats returned to an old party favorite as their gubernatorial standard-bearer, as some of the "best and brightest" were not available. Pendleton had run and lost in 1869, and General McCook had fallen to a similar fate in 1871. Vallandigham was dead, and Gen. George W. Morgan had voted for the Salary Grab. In this impasse, the party asked William Allen to return to the Ohio political scene after twenty-five years of retirement from public service. His nephew, Allen G. Thurman, who was up for reelection to the Senate, no doubt had some influence in the decision.[59]

William Allen ran his campaign as if he had never left politics. Concentrating on Republican weaknesses, Allen condemned their financial policies for causing the Panic and criticized the corruption that abounded in the Grant administration. The state party platform was just as censorious and contained a lengthy denunciation of the Crédit Mobilier scandal as well as the Salary Grab.[60]

Pendleton was heavily involved in the canvass, supporting Allen throughout the state. With renewed vigor and excitement about the party's positions and his own linkage to them, he was able to campaign without hesitation. He had known Allen for many years, and they shared a similar Democratic philosophy. Pendleton did not worry about compromising his principles or supporting the party candidate this year. Thomas Ewing and other Democrats who advocated the maintenance of fusion with the moribund Liberals went unheeded. For Pendleton, it was time for the older generation of Democratic leaders to redirect the party.[61] In a typical speech in Greenville, Pendleton addressed the scandals that gave the Democrats a head start into the campaign. He criticized the inappropriate, if not illegal, manipulation of the civil service as a source of campaign funds by the Republican Party. Much of what he said that night and throughout the campaign, however, reiterated his previous financial views. Pendleton launched volley after volley at the Republican's currency contraction schemes, the privileges they afforded to bondholders, and the unfair National Bank System.[62] Unlike the responses of the late 1860s, Pendleton's message this time proved popular among Ohioans, both Democrats and Republicans, who believed greenbacks could relieve the distress caused by the recession. Pendleton's efforts, combined with that of other party leaders and the favorable political winds of 1873, gave Allen a victory. In congratulating him, Pendleton wrote, "The people of Ohio . . . feel the utmost confidence that your wisdom and fairness combined will put the party on such sound and honest foundations that your election is the inauguration of a new era in our political history."[63]

Allen's triumph sent a message to members of both parties in Ohio and across the nation. Pendleton put the Bourbons on notice that he would remain firm on financial issues and that a sizable portion of the party concurred. Allen's success also encouraged Congress to reconsider its position on currency issues. Congress passed the Inflation Bill in 1874, which proposed an increase in both greenbacks and banknotes. James A. Garfield was one of only a handful of Republicans in Congress opposed to the plan, once again demonstrating the division between eastern and midwestern Republicans. The bill also split the Democrats, with Bourbons opposing it and most midwestern Democrats favoring it. Grant vetoed the proposal in a move some—but not Pendleton—viewed as Jacksonian. While Jackson opposed greenbacks, he also opposed the National Bank System and privilege. Pendleton's approach accepted greenbacks or even inflation as a necessary, but temporary, evil to achieve all objectives. The Inflation Bill did not meet his stipulations, but it was a step in the right direction. Nonetheless, Congress could not override Grant's veto.[64] Yet the issue was far from dead. The Democracy in Ohio had succeeded in enticing the support of farmers, laborers, some railroad security owners, and even some industrial groups.[65] From that foundation, the Democracy moved into the 1874 contest. The revival of the Ohio Idea thrust Pendleton back into a leadership position. Friends and foes alike referred to Ohio Democrats as "Pendletonians" because of their currency position. As a result, Pendleton stepped up his involvement in the campaign.[66]

Pendleton's increased participation resulted in numerous partisan attacks from Republicans. In 1873, Pendleton invited the state constitutional convention and members of the General Assembly to his estate for a social gathering. Republican papers suggested that he was attempting to set himself up for the presidency. If the convention succeeded in creating a new state constitution, they argued, a new General Assembly would be seated and he could be chosen as one of Ohio's senators. From there, he would launch his bid for the presidency. Pendleton had held such bipartisan gatherings on previous occasions. The *Enquirer* succinctly responded by calling those editors "stupid."[67]

Moving further away from the 1872 efforts at compromise with the Bourbons, the Ohio state Democratic Convention accepted Pendletonianism even more than it had in 1873. The assembly chose Thomas Ewing, a strong supporter of greenbacks, as president of the convention. He had wanted a much more specific statement on currency than that the Democrats had adopted in 1873 and got his wish. Of the fourteen resolutions in the revised state platform, nine dealt with economic issues. The first five reiterated the principles of the old Ohio Idea, reminding the state that the five-twenty bonds had originally been payable in greenbacks and criticizing the law passed in 1869 making them payable only in coin. The other planks dealt with the familiar issues of reduced taxes, a lower tariff, and reforms in land grants and civil service. Accentuating the centrality of the currency issue, Pendleton kicked off the campaign with the opening speech on the hustings.[68]

As he had in 1868, Pendleton sounded the old refrain against Republican policies. He blamed the Republicans for the Panic of 1873 and suggested that continued contraction would cripple business and cause further unemployment. He clearly stated, however, much as he had in the 1860s, that he favored an eventual return to specie payments. He believed that if greenbacks replaced the national banknote system, sufficient currency existed to sustain business growth. With this growth and the resultant increase in demand for capital, he maintained, greenbacks would slowly and painlessly rise in value until they were at par with gold. Then, he argued, the country could return to specie payments. He concluded with an explanation of the five-twenty resolution in the party platform. The document did not call for payment of the bonds in greenbacks, he insisted, because most of the owners were not those who had originally purchased them. Most of those were speculators who had bought them after the 1869 law required payment in gold. The law ought to be upheld, he stressed, but he would resist too quick of a return to specie payments.[69]

Republicans responded with the same attacks they had leveled in the 1860s but with little success. Their claims that Pendleton sought repudiation of the federal debt made few converts. Even a quick perusal of Pendleton's position disproved that assertion. Yet the attacks poured in from eastern Republicans and Bourbon Democrats, who insisted on portraying him as a demagogue. Pendleton traveled extensively throughout the state, refuting these misrepresentations and benefiting the party immensely. The Bourbon Democrats still did not support the midwestern perspective on currency, however, and rumblings against Pendletonianism continued. Horatio Seymour called for a "good currency" and a quick return to specie payments.[70] Yet the result was another triumph at the polls. The Democracy won thirteen of the twenty congressional seats in Ohio, and nationally the party regained control of the United States House of Representatives.[71]

Before the newly elected Democratic House could be seated, Republicans acted while they still had a majority and passed the Resumption Act of 1875. In this legislation, Republicans, along with Bourbon Democrats, attempted to settle the question concerning resumption. The Republicans desperately hoped to unite their party around this bill because of the divisions over the issuance of greenbacks. For Pendleton, it was a double-edged sword. Although the issue encouraged division among the Republicans, it was no less divisive in his own party.[72]

The Resumption Act called for free banking by granting national banks the right to expand the issuance of banknotes with the limitation that for every $100 in new banknotes, $80 of greenbacks be removed from circulation. A limit was set on greenback contraction, forbidding the total circulation from falling below $300 million, a drop of about $82 million from existing balances. The expansion of banknotes was designed to entice Southern support because it would ostensibly rectify the imbalance of currency in the South as compared to the Northeast. The act also allowed the treasury to acquire gold by selling bonds. Republicans contended that gold was needed to redeem greenbacks on the day resumption of specie payments was to occur, January 1, 1879. The bill satisfied Bourbon Democrats who favored a quick return to specie payments as well as western railroad and industrial leaders who endorsed the increase in banknotes. Most midwestern and southern Democrats were displeased, however. Many of them, like Pendleton, accepted some of the principles in the bill, but they could not stomach increasing the power of the national banks.[73]

The Republicans rammed the bill through Congress in an attempt to foster party unity prior to the 1876 election. The hopes of western railroad and industrial leaders that the bill would ease currency restrictions were not realized. With Americans depositing more savings in banks as a hedge against the lingering depression following the Panic of 1873, banks had no need to print more notes, as they had sufficient funds for loans. The effect of the act, therefore, reduced the amount of currency in circulation—be it banknotes or greenbacks—and accelerated the economic downturn.[74]

In Ohio, a divided Democratic state convention agreed on a gubernatorial platform opposed to the Resumption Act and renominated the immensely popular William Allen. But endemic divisions, separating midwestern Bourbons from Pendletonians, ensnared the platform committee, resulting in two reports. A majority leaned toward hard money and acceptance of the Resumption Act, but a minority upheld the party's previous position. In a floor fight, the Pendletonians demonstrated their power when the delegates adopted the minority report. The well-organized campaign of the Republicans termed Allen's platform a "rag baby" and exploited this Democratic split, noting the public statements of Allen's Bourbon nephew, Allen Thurman, in opposition to the platform. In addition, the Republicans attempted to deflect harmful economic issues by focusing attention during the canvass away from national issues. Instead, they stimulated xenophobia and disdain for Catholicism by accentuating the issue of perceived Roman Catholic influence in the public schools.[75]

Despite these divisions and Republican attempts at diversion, Pendleton stressed the currency issue throughout the campaign. The nation focused its attention on Ohio because it was the most populous of the midwestern states. Either of the two men running for governor, Rutherford B. Hayes or William Allen, was a potential presidential candidate if he won. Eastern interests emphasized the currency issue and watched Pendleton's words closely. He held to his position as before, and the Republicans leveled their standard charge of inflationism at him. The presence of the inflationary enthusiast Samuel F. Cary on the Democratic ticket for lieutenant governor gave credence to Republican tactics. Moreover, the Resumption Act hurt the Democrats in two ways. It united the opposition for the first time in several years, and it caused the Democracy to lose much of the manufacturing and industrial support the party had gained as a result of the Panic of 1873. These groups believed the act would increase the circulation of banknotes and alleviate capital shortages in the Midwest. While midwestern Democrats, under Pendleton's lead, agreed with the principle of short-term currency expansion, they could only accept it in greenbacks, not banknotes. They viewed the Resumption Act as giving the national banks a privileged position, a monopoly as it were, from which they could control currency levels. As a Jacksonian, Pendleton had always sought the destruction of the National Bank and an eventual return to specie payments. He usually disagreed with the Republicans on how the return to specie could be achieved and how quickly such a plan ought to be implemented. The Panic of 1873 demonstrated to him that the Republicans were moving too quickly. But Pendleton now realized that his hope of finding a compromise currency position for the Democrats that would unite both the midwestern and Bourbon elements was a fading dream. Most eastern and even some midwestern Democrats, all Bourbons, placed the issue above party unity and supported the Republican Resumption Act. As the country approached the 1879 deadline for resumption, the issue was becoming a moot point.[76]

In the end, the campaign revolved around other issues. Leaving the currency question to Pendleton, Allen focused on the Republican-contrived issue of the influence of Catholicism in the public school system and whether public funds should go to Catholic schools. This old issue resurfaced when the Democratic state assembly passed a measure ensuring that Catholic prison inmates had ac-cess to priests and religious worship of their choice. Although the Democrats had a plank in their platform that called for a strict separation between church and state, the Republicans relied on latent anti-Catholicism, which had fueled the Know-Nothings before the war, to paint Allen as a supporter of Catholic attempts to exert inordinate influence on the schools. The tactic succeeded, as Allen lost to Hayes by a narrow margin—about 5,500 votes. The campaign identified Hayes as a rising political star as well as the Democracy's continuing struggle with factionalism.[77]

Although losing the key Ohio battle in 1875, Democrats were optimistic about presidential prospects for the following year. A group of laborers and farmers did not share this feeling. With the continuing division in the Demo-cratic Party over greenbacks, some voters in Ohio left the Democracy due to frustrations with the Bourbons and joined the National Independent Party. This new organization met in Cincinnati and subsequently participated in a national convention that nominated Peter Cooper for the presidency and adopted a plat-form supporting an inflationary greenback policy. Ohio Democrats addressed this defection during their convention, but once again, Bourbons dominated the platform committee. And once again, the delegates adopted a soft-money minority report. Remaining consistent with their past position, Democrats sought to retain their labor and farm voter base, some of which had joined the third-party movement, by compromising between ultrainflationists and Bour-bons. The platform called for the repeal of the Resumption Act, flexible cur-rency based on the interconvertable bond, and the substitution of greenbacks for national banknotes. Perhaps a greater question before the delegates than the platform was which Ohioan to support in the presidential race. One *Cincinnati Enquirer* survey of forty-five leading Democrats found four-fifths in favor of Pendleton as their first choice. He was unwilling, however, to allow his name to be forwarded. The scandals revolving around the Great Railroad Case and the Kentucky Central claim no doubt influenced his decision. Beyond that, he had made few inroads in bridging the chasm between midwestern and eastern Democrats, which had thwarted his 1868 bid. Republicans were delighted to have him out of the race. As a result, former governor Allen, representing the soft-money men, became Ohio's favorite son nominee.[78]

Pendleton was undoubtedly happy to see the results of the convention. Al-though he had served as chairman of the meeting many times before, the de-cision by the delegates to again honor him held new meaning. Although the Great Railroad Case was settled and the House investigation had exonerated Pendleton of any link to Belknap's corruption, Republicans still intended to smear his reputation. To Pendleton, the chairmanship signaled the regard his fellow Democrats held in his probity. Furthermore, they rewarded his loyalty by selecting him as a delegate-at-large to the national convention in St. Louis. Coming on top of the party's endorsement of his financial plans and Allen's selection as a presidential nominee, these events indicated that the supposed sunset of Pendleton's political career would yet be delayed.[79]

The national convention did not proceed as either Allen or Pendleton preferred. Democrats chose a Bourbon, New York governor Samuel J. Tilden, as their standard-bearer, with running mate Thomas A. Hendricks of Indiana, who sympathized with the general midwestern preference for soft money. The platform attacked the Resumption Act, but primarily supported the eastern Democratic hard-money position. To prevent further division in the party, Tilden did not take a strong stand on either side of the issue. Rather, the platform focused on the theme of reform initiated in the 1872 party plank. The Democracy still favored revamping the civil service and sought to make government jobs "posts of honor assigned for approved competency and held for fidelity in the public employ," the end of corruption in the government, and a change in federal policy toward the Southern states.[80] As usual, Pendleton campaigned heavily for the party in Ohio.

He was outraged after the election results failed to give Tilden the victory. The votes of three unreconstructed southern states, Florida, Louisiana, and South Carolina, plus one Oregon vote, were disputed. The twenty electoral votes in question, if credited to Hayes, would give him a victory. Democrats assailed the returns that came back in his favor, suggesting Republican fraud. Convinced that Tilden had won, Pendleton and other Ohio Democrats held a meeting in Columbus to discuss the political crisis. Pendleton was one of seven men chosen to draw up resolutions. The committee demanded that Congress address the situation and rebuked Grant for calling up large numbers of troops to protect the disputed ballots, which to committee members symbolized Republican martial law in the South. Speaking later, Pendleton said that "this is the crucial test of the capacity of our people for free government."[81]

Congress ultimately settled the issue through an electoral commission, but many Democrats believed that the Republicans had "stolen" the election. The *Enquirer* stood amazed that the incoming president, Rutherford B. Hayes, could speak of civil service reform after the purported corrupt deal Republicans had struck to get him in office. Democrats had been decrying the corruption of the Grant administration, and Hayes appeared to be its embodiment. Civil service reform meant the cleanup of corruption in the bureaucracy for Democrats, but just as importantly, it demanded the eradication of fraud and misconduct among elected officials. Yet for all of their incredulity, the Democrats obtained some of the changes that they wanted. As a result of earlier negotiations, Hayes removed federal troops from the South, and the process of restoring white Southerners to leadership began. Pendleton, who had spent an extended period of time in the warmer climate of the South in late 1875 due to the illness of his daughter, recognized that these men were far more concerned about Reconstruction issues than they were about currency. In Hayes's defense, he hoped to encourage white southern politicians to vie for black votes within the political system, thereby ensuring the freedmen political influence. But his hopes for viable southern Democratic and Republican parties failed. Though the Republicans gained the White House, the Democrats gained strength, however limited, in the southern half of the country. But it would be a long time before they effectively unified their ranks. In the meantime, the election also had the effect of keeping government—and perhaps more correctly, Republican—corruption before the American people. With Pendleton's plans for a party compromise over the financial issue an apparent failure, it was civil service reform upon which the Democracy began to make strides toward party cohesion. It was this issue that would thrust Pendleton once again into the center ring of national politics as the 1880s began.[82]

"Kicking Against the Goads"

Pendleton and Civil Service Reform

Though defeated in the presidential contest of 1876, Democrats, particularly in Ohio, were optimistic about 1877. Pendleton and fellow party leaders believed that large segments of the electorate agreed with them that Republicans had stolen the presidency through chicanery. Democrats also blamed the widespread labor unrest in the summer of 1877 on the contraction of the currency by the Republicans, who were moving toward Resumption in 1879, as well as on the failure of the government to coin silver. President Rutherford B. Hayes called on federal troops to put down numerous strikes and uprisings in Pennsylvania, Ohio, West Virginia, and Maryland. Moreover, Republicans faced internal fragmentation due to disagreements over President Hayes's Southern policy and his commitment to civil service reform. The combination of dissatisfaction with the economy and divisions within the Republican Party led Pendleton to believe that, in spite of his past inability to reunite the Democratic Party, he had new opportunities provided by the onset of the 1877 campaign. Thus he set his sights on a seat in the United States Senate.[1]

In Columbus, Pendleton joined Sen. Allen Thurman, Thomas Ewing, Gen. George Morgan, and other leaders in planning for the state convention to be held in July 1877. The result was a foundation for a state platform that would include, according to Pendleton, demands for the remonetization of silver, "the maintenance of the greenbacks . . . , the gradual extinction of the National banking system and the repeal of the Resumption Act."[2]

After denying various rumors about political machinations to secure a Senate seat, Pendleton opted not to attend the convention that met in Columbus on July 25. The *New York Times* predicted a division in Ohio between the forces supporting Pendleton and Thomas Ewing's greenback laborers.[3] That there was a conflict at all suggests that Pendleton was not the inflationist Bourbons and

Republicans painted him. Ewing's plan was long term and far more inflationary. The convention nominated Richard M. Bishop for governor on a platform that echoed Pendleton's prescriptions. Though he personally would not have chosen Bishop, Pendleton opened the campaign on a muggy August day in Columbus with a speech concentrating on labor issues in an increasingly industrialized economy. "My Fellow-Citizens," he began, "I speak to you to night because our country suffers; because honest, industrious men seek employment in vain, and their families want food."[4] He directed his entire message to the struggling laboring class. They should not seek special arbitrators and protective legislation, he argued, because then capitalists would just seek and gain control of the government and subvert such efforts. Rather, he argued, laborers should support the Democratic Party, which was attacking the root of their problems—bad Republican policies. Pendleton embarked on his familiar refrain regarding the Resumption Act, high taxes and tariffs, greenbacks, and coinage of silver. Ewing followed Pendleton in a much longer speech that covered the same topics and continued the assault on Republicans. Pendleton trumpeted these themes throughout the campaign as he traveled extensively for the canvass.[5]

Pendleton also participated in two public debates with James A. Garfield, one of the leading Republicans in Ohio. In preparing for these meetings, Garfield wrote his wife that "Pendleton is a gentleman—we shall have a courteous debate."[6] Once engaged, Garfield attacked the positions of the Democratic Party, suggesting that during the previous twenty years it had been an obstructionist element in national politics. Pendleton focused on Garfield's Achilles' heel, Republican financial programs with which many Ohio Republicans disagreed. Pendleton, according to the *Cincinnati Enquirer,* won the debates. Garfield believed that whoever spoke last won, splitting the debates between them. Regardless, Pendleton's strong showing enhanced his popularity and bolstered his Senate bid.[7]

The divisions within the Republican Party hurt the chances of their candidate for governor, William H. West. While Democrats such as Pendleton applauded Hayes's policies in the South and his attempts at civil service reform, such actions split the Republicans and opened the door for Bishop's victory. So divisive was the civil service reform issue that Garfield credited it as an important factor in the Democratic win. Democrats gained a 25 to 10 majority in the Ohio Senate and a 66 to 41 edge in the state assembly. As a result, civil service reform played a vital role in shaping the first item of business for the newly elected General Assembly, the selection of a new senator.[8]

Pendleton, Thomas Ewing, and Gen. George Morgan were the leading contestants for the seat that would be vacated by Republican Stanley Matthews. The *Cincinnati Enquirer,* now edited by James J. Faran and John R. McLean, maintaining its extreme inflationist position, advocated Ewing.[9] Pendleton began an active letter-writing campaign.[10] As Pendleton and Ewing were the most recognizable soft-money candidates for the seat, their battle was perhaps the most heated. Ewing men denounced Pendleton as being too "aristocratic" and not having enough "sympathy with the suffering millions" to be an effective senator.[11] This was an easy means of attack in light of the railroad scandals in Pendleton's past, but it demonstrated more accurately, perhaps, Republican attacks notwithstanding, that Ewing and Pendleton had real differences on currency issues. The contest intensified when a Democratic legislative caucus was scheduled for January 10, 1878, in Columbus. The caucus choice would become senator after a rather perfunctory vote by the Democratically controlled Ohio General Assembly. The Chicago *Inter-Ocean, Philadelphia Times, Lexington Press,* and other papers predicted a Pendleton victory. The first ballot placed him ahead of the pack, with forty votes to Morgan's twenty-two and Ewing's seventeen. The second ballot gave Pendleton forty-six, just one short of the total needed. In spite of considerable efforts by the supporters of Morgan and Ewing, Pendleton was able to use his experience, service, popularity, and faithful support of the Ohio Idea and civil service reform to win the seat on the third ballot.[12]

The Democratic competitors quickly put the contest behind them, and state party unity largely remained intact.[13] Because Democratic assembly leaders placed the Senate seat decision at the top of their agenda, the question was settled early in the session. As a result, Pendleton had more than a year before he would leave the Queen City to begin his work as a U.S. senator. During that time, he continued to maintain his private law practice and his involvement with the Kentucky Central Railroad. The Great Railroad Case had caused the Cincinnati Southern Railroad to find an alternative route through Kentucky, leaving the Kentucky Central with stiff competition by the late 1870s. After stepping down from the presidency in 1880, Pendleton served the company one more year as a director. The railroad was preparing for new extensions into Kentucky in an effort to increase revenue. Two years later it was purchased by Collis P. Huntington, president of the Chesapeake and Ohio, who combined several lines to create the Chesapeake, Ohio, and Southwestern Railroad. He placed the line under the control of his nephew, Henry E. Huntington, who continued to improve the road and brought it through some difficult times in the mid-1880s. The railroad bridge between Covington and Cincinnati was finally completed in 1888, allowing the carrier direct access to the Queen City. In 1890, the line was sold to the Louisville and Nashville, a road with which it had cooperated for several years. The sale allowed Pendleton's short line, a Bluegrass "Thoroughbred," to become a vital part of a new main line running from Cincinnati to Atlanta.[14]

Though business kept him away from the State Democratic Convention in June 1878, Pendleton was still involved in the inner workings of the state party. The 1878 campaign was the high-water mark of the currency issue, as Democrats won eleven of the twenty congressional seats in the election but lost most of the key state offices.[15] Although the results did not indicate a discernible trend, events in 1878 diminished the Democrats' hopes of exploiting the currency question. That year Congress passed the Bland-Allison Silver Act, which allowed for limited coinage of silver. Though the act had little impact on the amount of floating currency, Ohio's economy entered an upswing, reducing pressure on Congress with regard to the silver issue. In addition, the date for greenbacks to achieve par with gold was January 1879. As that time neared, greenbacks rose in value because economic growth had increased the demand on currency, and contraction by the Republicans had reduced the amount of paper money in circulation. As a result, when Pendleton entered the Senate in March 1879, he faced a dilemma. An important issue upon which he had been elected was quickly evaporating. It was by no means dead, however, and Pendleton had begun to put more emphasis on silver. Nonetheless, before he left for Washington, Pendleton began to focus his attention on a new position on a separate but increasingly important political issue from which to launch yet another attempt to unite his party.[16]

Pendleton wasted little time before involving himself in the legislative process. He supported his party in its attempt to limit the presence of federal troops and officials at polling places in the South and in Northern urban areas.[17] He asked the Senate to request that the secretary of war grant worn, condemned, or outdated military ordnance to be displayed in Cincinnati as a part of a monument to Col. Robert L. McCook of the 9th Ohio Volunteers. The Senate concurred. Pendleton also voted in support of the Warner Silver Bill, which would have begun a movement toward the remonetization of silver. Sen. Thomas F. Bayard of Delaware, chairman of the Finance Committee, resigned his position in opposition of the bill. Members of the Democratic caucus immediately began to circulate a resolution among its members asking Bayard not to resign and vowing to let the bill go for the session. Pendleton refused to sign the resolution, remaining steadfast in his support of silver inflation.[18]

Pendleton also had little time before he was immersed in the accoutrements of a Senate seat. He found a place to live and participated in his first caucus of Democratic senators. He was assigned to committees dealing with the 1880 census and Indian affairs. He and his wife entered into the elegant world of Washington social events as well, which included a visit with President Hayes at the White House. And Pendleton was inundated with visitors from Ohio seeking government offices. As the Washington *Evening Star* reported, "Being

'Gentleman George,' he went without any [breakfast], and made himself hungry rather than offend any of the hungry office seekers."[19] Yet the scene disturbed Pendleton and refocused his attention on civil service.[20]

Demonstrating his continued interest in the machinery of government, on March 26, Pendleton introduced a bill similar to the one he had introduced in the House during the latter stages of the Civil War. Harkening back to his father's Whig roots, Pendleton saw value in strengthening the role of Congress with respect to the executive. He was also influenced by his respect for the British parliamentary system. Pendleton's Senate Bill No. 227 proposed that the heads of cabinet departments hold seats in both houses of Congress. In a speech a month later, Pendleton defended this innovation as he had before, emphasizing the need to improve communication between the executive and legislative branches and to eliminate governmental inefficiency. The bill was printed and given a hearing, with the Senate creating a committee to look into the merits of the idea. The committee included Pendleton and Thomas Bayard of the Democrats and Roscoe Conkling and James G. Blaine of the Republicans along with other notables. Even so, the idea died.[21]

Pendleton returned to Ohio following his first Senate session to look after one of his investments, a dairy farm, and to participate in the election of 1879. The state convention nominated Thomas Ewing for governor on a platform that demonstrated the changing political winds. Ewing unquestionably represented the ultra-soft-money position, and the platform continued the assault on the use of federal troops at polling places in the South. Pendleton believed that this was another means of trampling states' rights and maintaining Republican control of those states. Yet on the campaign stump, Democrats moved beyond the old issues and began a new focus. They criticized Hayes's administration for its inability to produce effective civil service reform, a topic of increasing interest for Pendleton and Ohio Democrats.[22] To his credit, however, Hayes had made some strides in that direction. He named prominent reformer Carl Schurz as his secretary of the interior, and he established a merit system within that department. Hayes deprecated the running of the New York Customs House by Chester A. Arthur, a Stalwart or spoilsman associated with Sen. Roscoe Conkling, who ran the state Republican Party machine. In 1877, Hayes issued an executive order prohibiting government employees from participating in political campaigns in any fashion. This was an attempt to prevent Arthur from assessing "contributions" for the party from customs house employees, a practice Hayes found unethical. The president removed Arthur as customs collector in New York, a position noted for its control over about seven hundred government positions and a large percentage of government revenue, and had reformer Dorman B. Eaton write a report on the English system of civil service.

Hayes later backed away from his executive order as it related to political assess ments and left undecided the decision regarding who should be the permanent replacement for Arthur.[23]

In Ohio the campaign was not solely focused on reform. Gubernatorial candidate Thomas Ewing did not represent the platform well. The platform called for the free coinage of silver, the replacement of banknotes with greenbacks, and the destruction of the National Bank System—positions more akin to Pendleton's Ohio Idea than Ewing's ultra-soft-money position. As a result, Pendleton, not wishing to be too closely associated with Ewing, played a limited role in the canvass and only gave attention to issues he supported. As Ewing represented an issue that was losing viability by 1879, he did not prove a successful candidate.[24]

The second session of the Democratically controlled Forty-sixth Congress opened in December 1879. In his capacity as chairman of the Committee to Make Provision for Taking the Tenth Census, Pendleton tried to shepherd the necessary bills through the Senate while battling with Hayes over the appointment of census supervisors. As president, Hayes was responsible for nominating the supervisors who would begin their duties upon confirmation by the Senate. Hayes submitted a list of Republicans to be Ohio's census supervisors even though the census legislation clearly stipulated that the supervisors were to be chosen on the basis of fitness and not partisan affiliation. Pendleton recommended that the Senate reject the list, and its members concurred. The two sides eventually agreed on a compromise list of supervisors, but Pendleton worked to limit Hayes's future interference in the census process by sponsoring a Senate resolution calling for the president to account for the removal and replacement of supervisors.[25]

Pendleton also immersed himself in the government's dealings with Native Americans, not only due to his position on the Committee on Indian Affairs but also because of his private affinities. While traveling the United States in 1876 for the Democratic Party, Pendleton and his wife, Alice, met a Cheyenne named Making Medicine interned at Fort Marion, Florida. Moved by the spartan nature of his life, the Pendletons decided to sponsor Making Medicine's education and spiritual formation.[26] As a result of his personal experience, Pendleton supported a bill that would grant individual tracts of land to Native Americans. The bill also called for the appropriation of federal funds to support schools in the East designed to educate Native Americans so that they could succeed in American society. Pendleton and the committee sought to destroy some aspects of Indian culture, motivated partially by a belief that it was savage and partially by a conviction that "Americanizing" the Indians would reduce the incidences of bloodshed on the Great Plains. Even so, Pendleton defied expectations once again. His largely humanitarian efforts in this case demonstrated significant growth from his disparaging comments of 1858 about the "Digger Indians." The principles discussed by Pendleton and Congress were largely implemented by Secretary of the Interior Carl Schurz during the Hayes administration and laid the foundation for the Dawes Act of 1887.[27]

The third committee on which Pendleton served grappled with foreign relations. In this committee Pendleton raised concerns regarding the power of consular courts in Japan, China, Egypt, Madagascar, and elsewhere. The consuls in these regions had the authority to hear cases related to American citizens abroad and mete out punishment in spite of the fact that the Constitution prescribed different guidelines for these proceedings in the United States. In the consular courts, no provision existed for indictment proceedings, grand juries, or jury trials. Pendleton proposed that the Judiciary Committee investigate this issue, and the Senate concurred. It did not act on this recommendation, however, during this session.[28]

Amidst his Senate responsibilities, Pendleton and his family enjoyed life in the nation's capital. They purchased a home on K Street, an expense many senators could not afford. In fact, some could not even afford to bring their families with them to the capital. The *Evening Star* aptly described Pendleton when it quoted the Dayton *Journal,* "[Pendleton] may be democratic in politics, but he is not so in his personal habits, for he is as hard to reach as an oyster in the soup-bowl of a charity entertainment."[29] Not only did he own a home in Washington, but also he had a fine home overlooking a cliff at Newport, Rhode Island. He built "Cave Cliff" in 1877 for his wife, whose name appeared on the deed. The *Newport Journal* described it as "literally a cottage," meaning that the euphemism often used to apply to the large mansions built there did not apply in this case. While it lauded the view from the house, the structure itself was described as "very plain."[30] Here he and his family could escape the oppressive heat of summer in the Chesapeake Bay area and hobnob with neighbors such as noted American historian George Bancroft. Newport was a resort community for the wealthy, described by one author as "quiet enough to be restful, bohemian enough to be interesting, ostentatious enough to be stimulating."[31] It attracted both the rich and the intellectual. Bancroft was also a neighbor in Washington, living just a few blocks away on H Street. Bancroft was an old Jacksonian who had joined with the Union Party during the war, supported an abolition amendment as an issue around which to refashion the Democratic Party, held to a hard-money position he believed was Jacksonian, opposed Pendleton's (and any Democrat's) bid for the presidency in 1868, but noted, "In my old age I continue as in my youth to trust the people."[32] Pendleton and Bancroft shared an interest in German history, politics, and language. Bancroft once held a reception at his home for presidential aspirants at the whimsical suggestion of a friend. The party included John Sherman, Thomas F. Bayard, James G. Blaine, and of course, Pendleton.[33]

While Congress was in session, the Pendletons frequently attended gatherings at the White House, as well as receptions at the homes of other congressmen and senators. Alice Pendleton and daughters Mary Lloyd and Jane Frances regularly received guests in their home, usually on Monday evenings. As accomplished harpists, Alice and Jane entertained guests, frequently accompanied by the likes of Secretary of the Interior Carl Schurz. Pendleton's interaction with Schurz and others from the opposite side of the aisle added to the mystique of "Gentleman George." Yet he was not the typical aristocrat. Pendleton made the most of his associations, to be sure. His interaction with Schurz undoubtedly influenced his growing interest in civil service reform. At the same time, through this relationship, he was able to influence Schurz's Indian policy. Part of the "Gentleman George" image went beyond dealings with the powerful and the aloofness he generally displayed to reporters. He never lost touch with the common Ohioan, as evidenced by the internal consistency of his political career. When the Democratic Party announced Cincinnati as the site of its 1880 convention, he graciously received Ohio serenaders at his home. The importance he placed on currency and civil service reform evidenced his concern for his constituents. Even his relationship with Making Medicine demonstrated his ability and desire to step outside the confines of class and position. Part of his gentlemanliness was his Jacksonian concern for men of all stations. Yet he was never able to apply that equality to men across all races. Even so, Pendleton quickly grew fond of the lifestyle he maintained in Washington.[34]

Pendleton returned to Cincinnati in June, while his family traveled to Lennox, Massachusetts, for the summer. Earlier in the year he had convinced Democratic leaders to hold the national convention in Cincinnati, yet Ohio's influence at these proceedings was minimal. The delegates bypassed two leading Ohio hopefuls, Henry B. Payne and Allen Thurman, in favor of Gen. Winfield S. Hancock of New York.[35] The national platform did reflect Ohio's position on a variety of issues ranging from bimetallism to the tariff, however. It also demanded "a genuine and thorough reform of the civil service."[36] The Democrats decried what was called the "great fraud of 1876–77" and demanded a law prohibiting the use of civil service positions as political payoffs. Although "Pendleton did not take an active part in the proceedings of the convention," he did perform his usual duties in the fall campaign.[37]

Democrats hoped to take advantage of the split within the Republican Party among the Stalwarts, or spoilsmen, led by Roscoe Conkling, the half-breeds such as Garfield and James G. Blaine who were divided on the issue of spoils, and the mugwumps, the advocates of civil service reform. The Democrats were divided as well, and Hancock could not solve a raging internecine conflict in the key electoral state of New York. He also failed to find a midwestern issue that was of the same magnetism of past financial questions. Further confusing the campaign was the civil service reform issue. Both parties claimed to support the concept in somewhat vague platform statements, but the Republicans had included the issue in their platform only after much debate. Following Garfield's close victory that fall, it remained to be seen whether the Republicans would make good on their promise of reform. The Democrats, particularly Ohio newspaper editors Faran and McLean, had been quick to point out Hayes's failings in this area.[38]

The *Enquirer* promptly reinvigorated its attack on the sham of Republican civil service reform following Garfield's election. Within days, office seekers had begun their lobbying for Garfield's political "plums."[39] Pendleton joined in the newspaper's offensive. Shortly after the final session of the Forty-sixth Congress opened, he reintroduced his bill to provide seats for cabinet members in Congress. Two days later, on December 15, Pendleton introduced two more bills. He designed the first to create a reformed civil service. His goal was to find and place qualified people in government positions rather than continue the spoils system whereby the winning party used government offices as political payoffs. He also called the Senate's attention to a second bill that would prohibit political assessments. The Republicans, who had controlled federal patronage for two decades, used these assessments on the salaries of government workers to help fund presidential campaigns and party advancement. After Ulysses S. Grant failed to make such reforms a part of his administrative program, and the much more committed and persistent Hayes had been unable to install a permanent system of reform, Pendleton believed it was time for the Democrats to seize upon this political issue.[40]

Pendleton's motivations for supporting these reforms encompassed both civic and partisan rationales. Pendleton had been interested in "good government" since his days in the Ohio Senate. He consistently pursued governmental efficiency throughout his terms in the House of Representatives. There he first offered the idea of granting cabinet members seats in the House for the purpose of accountability and encouraged the use of merit for advancement in the military. Pendleton's father's Whig influence and his own short-lived fusion with the Liberal Republicans encouraged his interest in improving the government bureaucracy. Just as Pendleton's Ohio Idea had sought to destroy the power and privilege of the National Bank, his civil service reform bill would seek to limit the unfair advantage the patronage system gave to the party in power and the wealthy few that dominated it.[41] Pendleton's strict constructionism of the Constitution fostered these reform ideas as well. The system of spoils no longer functioned in the manner for which it was designed. It granted too much power to a few individuals and encouraged corruption. The Crédit Mobilier and Star Route scandals, in addition to the other frauds associated with the Grant administration, had enhanced public awareness and concern for reform. Both Grant and Hayes had made attempts to improve the civil service but in each case had fallen short of lasting change.

After Garfield's assassination, Pendleton believed the very future of the government depended on reform. "I believe the duration of our government in its present popular form depends upon a return to the good old practices which prevailed so universally during the administrations of our three early Democratic Presidents—Jefferson, Madison and Monroe—Offices are public trusts, not spoils, and as such they must be recognized and treated as such."[42] Also, Pendleton had great respect for the British governmental system and believed it provided a helpful model for the United States to emulate. He had studied that structure as a student traveling in Europe years earlier. His admiration for the British parliamentary and civil service systems pushed him in the direction of reform and provided its theoretical foundation.[43]

Although he did have many civic motivations to support reform, Pendleton was also influenced by partisan concerns. Since the end of the Civil War, Pendleton had been attempting to unite the Democracy around certain key issues founded upon Jacksonian principles. Each time he had met with failure because of an unwillingness among his fellow Democrats to put party ahead of sectional or individual aspirations. Considering Pendleton's past conflicts with eastern Democratic political machines, he undoubtedly believed that the patronage system endowed urban machine bosses with far too much influence within his party. Civil service reform had served as a unifying principle in the 1872 election and had brought together diverse Democratic elements that were previously divided over issues such as the currency question. Consequently, this was an issue that could be used as a weapon against the Republicans throughout the country. The corruption of Grant's administration, the numerous scandals emanating from Congress, and the lingering questions surrounding Hayes's election left many Americans disgusted with politics and the federal government. Though publicly calling for reform, the Republican Party had been impotent to produce meaningful change. In addition, eliminating assessments of federal employees could financially cripple Republican campaign efforts. Reform, then, would benefit the Democratic Party. It would also profit Pendleton. He was a political animal. The *New York Times* noted his ambitions for the presidential nomination in 1884 shortly after the 1880 election.[44] His personal ambitions cannot be separated from his partisan goals. Just as with the Ohio Idea, if reform succeeded, he might be able to use it as a springboard for making another run at the presidency. In any event, Pendleton couched his justification for reform in terms of the need to eliminate corruption, the public demand for government efficiency, and the exigency within the party that required unification on a specific issue.[45]

Yet Pendleton was a member of the party of Jackson. Each January 8, his fellow Democrats assembled to celebrate their political father and to discuss the party and its prospects. But Jackson had initiated the spoils system. He had expanded the use of patronage with the defense that the bureaucracy had become too aristocratic. The spoils system, or "rotation" as he called it, was more democratic. Pendleton had been a consistent Jacksonian. Once challenged on his consistency when he inaugurated the Ohio Idea because of its short-term reliance on paper money, Pendleton proved those accusations false. Once again he faced charges of inconsistency in advocating the overthrow of Jackson's patronage system, but Pendleton was a man motivated by principle. He was also a politician who recognized the absolute necessity for change and adaptation. Perhaps Pendleton harkened back to Jefferson here more than to Jackson, but he defended his position in Jacksonian terms. He reinterpreted Jacksonianism to address the issues of the day. Earlier he had been invited to speak at a January 8 celebration in Pittsburgh. Unable to attend, he wrote a lengthy letter stating his views on Jackson. Pendleton admired Jackson's character traits of "firmness, honesty, independence, love of liberty, an exalted patriotism, an abiding trust in the integrity and wisdom of the people." After a lengthy discourse on the issues of the day, he concluded by suggesting what had made the Democratic Party successful in the past: "Fixed in its principles, it adapts their expression to the changing condition of human society—constant in its aims and purposes it seeks to attain them by the means best adapted to the exigencies of public opinion and the shifting phases of affairs."[46] In civil service reform, Pendleton was attempting to maintain his principles in the face of a rapidly changing world. The system that Jackson had created was failing to promote democracy. Indeed, one historian has suggested that politics in this era was simply a competition for political office.[47] The spoils system no longer provided equal access to government jobs, Pendleton argued. Politicians did not seek out men of ability for governmental offices, but rather, they sought men of party loyalty. Power devolved into the hands of a few powerful men. Jackson had fought against the formation of such an aristocracy in decrying the power of the Second Bank of the United States; Pendleton did so in attacking the abuse of the civil service. Although Pendleton's plan might limit Jackson's notion of rotation in office, he could argue that Jackson's goals for rotation, that of providing more opportunity for more Americans in government jobs and squelching privilege, had been lost in the system he had created. Reform would benefit the party, Pendleton argued, by giving access to positions without regard to political affiliation. As long as the Democrats were unable to win the White House, they would be locked out of most federal government jobs. Reform would open up offices to all. A person of any background, any partisan belief, could compete for a position. Ability would dictate the results, not whom one knew or how much money one could contribute to a political cause. The existing aristocratic system would be replaced by a democratic system of filling government offices. In a society in which education was becoming increasingly available, Pendleton believed reform could continue Jackson's democratic principle, if not his means.[48]

Pendleton's bill ending political assessments was fairly straightforward; it called for eliminating that corrupt practice. Pendleton's other bill, which called for reforming the civil service, was based on a proposal introduced by Congressman Thomas Jenckes in 1868, three years after Pendleton lost his seat in the House. It called for a civil service commission comprised of five members appointed by the president and confirmed by the Senate who would oversee a new procedure for placing individuals in federal positions on the basis of ability. The bill only included a small percentage of government jobs, so Pendleton could not rightly be accused of replacing one elite group with a meritocracy. The proposal would give the president little involvement in deciding how the civil service commission would operate. Its responsibilities included deciding on qualifications for various positions, creating and administering examinations, and establishing guidelines for dismissals. Admission to the civil service would be at the lowest levels, with promotions based solely on merit for upper level positions. Grant had appointed such a civil service commission, but Congress had failed to maintain its funding. Hayes had the commission do research and implemented some of its rules in the New York Customs House and Post Office while Secretary Schurz used its system in the Department of the Interior. Hayes even issued an executive order forbidding political assessments but rescinded it in the face of Republican opposition. Pendleton praised Hayes's successes, as far as they went, as examples to follow, while referring to British examples as well. These formed the basis of his bill, yet he understood it was not perfect. It was, however, a start.[49]

Dorman B. Eaton, chairman of Hayes's Civil Service Commission and chairman of the executive committee of the New York Civil Service Reform Association, was a long-standing advocate of reform, but he believed that Pendleton's bill had some significant flaws. Two key facets of the bill were of dubious constitutionality. Pendleton's bill required dismissal of government officers by the commission, giving it judicial powers. The bill also gave the commission authority to execute the law, a power the Constitution assigned only to the president. Congress did not have the authority to delegate that power.

Beyond the constitutional issues, Eaton believed the bill was unworkable. It placed too much responsibility in the hands of the commission. It could not practically hold hearings on all the removals as required by the bill. In addition, the system of promotion was nebulous. As a result, the New York organization drafted another proposal, largely Eaton's own work, and sent him to present it to Pendleton.[50]

After listening to the proposal, Pendleton set his bill aside and replaced it with Eaton's version. The New York Civil Service Reform Association pledged its support in return for this decision. Pendleton's original initiative won him a place on a select committee to conduct hearings on the merits of the issue.[51]

The new Pendleton bill retained the fundamental concepts of the first proposal but attempted to correct some of the defects. It created a five-member commission chosen by the president without the consent of the Senate of which no more than three members could be from the same party. The commission would work with the president in formulating regulations and administering civil service examinations. The bill allowed the commission to select a chief examiner and numerous subordinate examiners to lighten the load. The examinations were to be competitive, and entrance into the service was kept at the lowest levels following a probationary term. Promotions were to be based on merit. Removals had to be filed with the commission, though hearings were not required. The act applied to Washington departments and any customs houses or post offices with more than fifty employees. The Senate committee reported the bill on February 16, 1881, but the Democratically controlled Senate did not act upon it during the Forty-sixth Congress. This delay, coupled with the knowledge that the next session would bring an evenly divided Senate, suggested a lack of unanimity in Pendleton's party.[52] It remained to be seen what an incoming Republican-dominated House and a divided Senate would do with the issue. In the meantime, President-elect Garfield grew tired of the endless line of office seekers waiting outside his door.[53]

In the midst of the debate over the bill that would crown Pendleton's political career, he was growing in stature and reputation among his peers. He received invitations to speak on civil service reform outside of Washington, D.C. He regularly attended receptions and dinners with Alice at homes ranging from those of fellow senators and the attorney general to the Hayes White House. Pendleton and Hayes had been political foes in the 1869 gubernatorial campaign in Ohio, but Pendleton was not one to let political disagreement affect personal relationships. Too, both men found that their affinity for civil service reform allowed them to find common ground on the political battlefield. Pendleton found his responsibilities as senator leading toward bipartisan interaction as well. When a delegation from Ohio arrived in Washington for the inauguration of James A. Garfield, Pendleton set up a reception for the entire group. Pendleton introduced a resolution in the Senate calling for a temporary committee to prepare for the inauguration of James A. Garfield and Chester A. Arthur. He was immediately appointed to serve on the three-man committee and accompanied Vice-President-elect Arthur in a carriage to the inaugural festivities. Though always cordial, "Gentleman George" must have found it a bit awkward to sit with the Stalwart Arthur after having recently introduced bills to outlaw many of the practices Arthur had used in the New York Customs House. Nonetheless, Pendleton fulfilled his responsibilities without regard for partisanship or ideological differences. Yet he was always the Democrat. His peers in the Senate selected him to chair the party caucus after only two years of service. He was also selected to chair two committees—the census committee and a new committee created in the wake of his proposal to give cabinet members seats in Congress. In addition, he presided over the body for most of the session because no president pro tempore was elected. He would quickly take on the mantle of leadership and be forced to defend his party. With the incoming Senate divided very closely, the battle was on to gain control of the major committees.[54]

As was customary, President Hayes had called a special session of the Senate to consider the appointments of the new president prior to his leaving office. A divided Senate found it difficult, however, to decide who should fill its leadership positions.[55] The Republicans determined to leave such questions, as well as major committee assignments, until after the new Senate convened. Pendleton rose to challenge the delay. He and Sen. Henry L. Dawes of Massachusetts got into some "good-natured sparring" over the swing vote of Sen. William Mahone, a Readjuster-Democrat from Virginia, who was one of two deciding votes in the evenly divided Senate.[56] The other was David Davis, an Independent from Illinois, who decided to work with the Democrats, giving them a 38 to 37 advantage. The jocularity ended after the lunch break. Dawes charged that the Democratic caucus, in the process of arranging committees, approached Mahone and offered him the position of sergeant-at-arms for his disposal if he would vote Democratic. Pendleton became angry at the allegation and demanded that Dawes reveal who had approached Mahone. When he demurred, Pendleton stiffened his resolve, "name him, name him," he intoned.[57] Other Democratic senators joined the fray, wanting to call Dawes's bluff. Others jumped in to quell the rancor, but it was far from over. The next time Dawes rose to speak before the Senate, Democratic members hissed, "name the man, name the man." Ironically, it was the Republicans who had made a deal. Mahone ended up siding with them, throwing the Senate to the Republicans with Arthur's deciding vote. In return, the Republicans gave him control over a portion of his state's patronage and allowed Mahone to name two Senate officers, the secretary and the sergeant-at-arms. The lack of good faith among the parties resulted in obstruction on both sides and only highlighted the importance of civil service reform.[58]

Most notable for this session, however, was the conflict among Republicans. The party had matched President-elect Garfield with Chester Arthur as his vice-presidential running mate as a means of unifying the party between East and West and as a sop to the Stalwarts. Garfield was a half-breed, and civil service reformers were not pleased with the selection of his running mate. Arthur had a notorious past, and many believed he was nothing more than the minion of Sen. Roscoe Conkling, in spite of his nomination acceptance letter that some reformers saw as more supportive of reform than Garfield's. Garfield sought to mollify his opponents and gave the Stalwarts a number of important government offices. When it came to the crown jewel of such positions, the New York Customs House, he nominated William H. Robertson, a half-breed. Senators Conkling, who referred to reformers like Pendleton as "Snivel Service Reformers," and Thomas Platt of New York joined with Chester Alan Arthur to write a letter of protest to Garfield. When the president-elect did not retract his choice, Conkling and Platt decided to resign from the Senate fearing that the Senate might ratify the appointment. The session adjourned with Garfield having dealt a decisive blow against Conkling and "Me Too" Platt, when they failed to garner reelection by the New York legislature as they had planned. The Senate confirmed Robertson.[59]

A mentally unstable and disgruntled Stalwart named Charles Guiteau added an important chapter to the saga of civil service reform. On July 2, 1881, as President Garfield was about to embark on a summer vacation, Guiteau shot him in the back at the Baltimore and Potomac Railroad station in Washington, D.C. Guiteau, who had repeatedly and unsuccessfully sought a diplomatic post from Garfield, later said that he shot the president for the benefit of the party and exalted, "I am a Stalwart of the Stalwarts."[60] Garfield lingered for eighty days, wavering between signs of improvement and decline. Guiteau, and perhaps most congressional leaders as well, assumed that the Stalwart vice president would change Garfield's policy upon his ascension to the office. That was not to be. Guiteau's bullets ended not only Garfield's life but also much of the opposition to civil service reform.[61]

Just after the assassination and during a congressional break, Ohio held a gubernatorial election. Pendleton did not participate in the state party convention, though he was involved in planning the canvass. He spoke infrequently, but when he did, civil service reform was first on his lips. Reform, he announced, would lift the party out of its morass. The incumbent Republican governor, Charles Foster, won reelection, however, and the Republicans regained control of the state assembly. As a result, Democratic support for Pendleton as a presidential candidate in 1884 surfaced, because a Republican assembly certainly would not retain him in the Senate. Pendleton's congressional break ended abruptly, cut short because of Garfield's death, and he returned to Washington for a brief session in October.[62]

In December 1881, President Arthur's first message to Congress announced his support of civil service reform and inaugurated a significant break with his Stalwart allies. In a lengthy passage, Arthur, a close friend of Conkling and a long-time Stalwart, called for a system that produced able and talented government officials, provided stability in federal offices, and encouraged promotions based on merit. Although many feared he might be a Conkling sycophant as president, Arthur quickly asserted his independence by leaving Robertson in office. The paucity of appointments for his longtime associates in New York caused disgruntlement among many Stalwarts. Arthur's cabinet selections received mixed reviews from reformers, but they did solidify his independence from Conkling. In addressing Pendleton's bill directly, the new president expressed reservation about one facet—calling for entrance into the civil service only at the lowest grade. He also cautioned against some features of the British system that had never gained acceptance in the United States and expressed the fear that certain types of examinations would lead to an exclusively young, college-educated civil service. Though reserved in his support, Arthur stated his concurrence with the competitive system and asked for an appropriation to enforce previous civil service laws if Congress failed to pass new legislation.[63]

Pendleton wasted no time in reintroducing his reform measure. The second day of the session, December 6, 1881, he brought his civil service reform bill before the Senate. The following week, he defended it and answered criticisms and questions. In particular, Pendleton addressed the spoils system, examining its propensity for corruption and its burden on those elected officials who had to make patronage decisions. He also took a few moments to point out that Garfield's assassination made reform imperative. The spoils system, Pendleton said, "made Guiteau a possible aspirant for office, and assassination a possible vengeance for his disappointment."[64] The merit system, Pendleton continued, encouraged a skilled service and prevented removals for purely political reasons, impeding this type of criminal endeavor for office. The bill did not restrict removals, Pendleton assured his Democratic colleagues, except to protect officials from political assessments. He also responded to the president's message, saying that the examinations would be created to test for proficiency for each position. They would not be tests of a classical education. Pendleton concluded his statements with an appeal to his side of the aisle, arguing that this measure was in the best interest not only of his party but also of the country.[65]

In this speech and in another two months later, Pendleton addressed the concerns of a fellow member of the Committee on Civil Service and Retrenchment, Republican senator Henry L. Dawes. Dawes presented the Senate with a rival measure that retained competitive examinations but eliminated the Civil Service Commission. Instead, he suggested that each executive department take responsibility for giving the examinations and making the appointments. Dawes also specified that appointments be made from the applicants with the three highest scores, while Pendleton had not stipulated a specific number. Dawes believed that his system clearly focused responsibility for appointments and cleansed the old system. Pendleton addressed Dawes's concerns regarding the constitutionality of the commission and its powers. More important, he highlighted the two key features of his reform: uniformity and the separation of those who appointed from those appointed. The Civil Service Commission would "secure uniformity of examination" and a "standard of excellence."[66] Of equal and perhaps greater importance for reform, the commission stood between the office seeker and the officials endowed with the power to appoint. Dawes's system allowed the two sides too much interaction. With separation, Pendleton argued, the twin evils of corruption and inefficiency were eradicated. Although Pendleton felt assured that the differences separating the two men were not significant, their bills contained other variances. Dawes included no restrictions on political assessments, nor did he make provision for the president to expand the coverage of the reform as necessary, whereas the Pendleton bill did. Dorman Eaton of the New York Civil Service Reform Association was alarmed. He quickly provided a public rebuttal to the Dawes bill and urged adoption of Pendleton's proposal. The civil service committee continued its hearings on these and related matters.[67]

The hearings called on men such as Dorman Eaton and George William Curtis, editorialist for *Harper's Weekly,* who had devoted many years to the pursuit of reform. The committee also heard from Henry G. Pearson, postmaster of New York, regarding successful reforms implemented there. Pendleton listened to recommendations for further improvements, such as expanding the president's authority to remove civil service commissioners and instituting apportionment guidelines to establish geographically balanced appointments. The committee reported the bill to the Senate favorably, but no action was taken during the session.[68]

Opponents were not cowed by the demands for reform. Sen. Benjamin Hill, a Democrat from Georgia, was most vociferous in his defense of patronage. Hill advocated frequent changes in the executive branch. Rotation, he believed, would do away with the evils of the system. He found no solace in the legislation and assailed those who publicly supported reform, but who voted for Arthur in the 1880 election. Other members of the Senate echoed Hill's sentiments, believing that they largely owed their seats to the influence they gained through the use of spoils. As a result, neither house considered the bill before the end of the first session.[69]

Debate at this session of Congress was not limited solely to the Pendleton Bill. Indeed, Pendleton had numerous other issues with which to grapple, and he often voiced his opinion on them. While once again engaging Dawes in debate, Pendleton tackled a matter dealing with polygamy and the Mormons in Utah. A bill sponsored by the Republicans would have punished Mormons who practiced bigamy or polygamy by removing their right to vote. Pendleton did not believe that the Congress had the authority to legislate on an election issue within a crime bill. More important, he recognized not only that most Mormons were Democrats but also that they practiced polygamy. The result of this legislation would "transfer the political power of the Territory to the Republican Party—a party which had 1,500 votes out of 15,000."[70] Pendleton perceived that the bill was politically motivated, and while he opposed this Mormon practice, he resented Republican attempts to make political gains from it.[71]

Pendleton also reiterated his position on national banks when he addressed a bill proposing to issue 3 percent federal bonds. Pendleton supported an amendment to make the 3 percent bonds the basis for currency in circulation. Some members opposed this amendment because it would result in lower interest rate bonds, meaning that the national banks would earn less money, and perhaps some might be forced into bankruptcy. Pendleton saw no loss in this prospect. Higher rates unfairly hurt laborers, he maintained, and they shouldered the tax burden.[72]

Continuing that line of argument, Pendleton protested against the high and unevenly levied tariff schedules. Pendleton described tariffs as "bounties" that in essence gave manufacturers a grant of money for articles they sold.[73] High tariffs caused prices to rise, he contended, causing the laboring class greater hardships in obtaining the goods they needed to survive. Pendleton did not oppose tariffs; in fact, he supported them as a source of revenue. He simply called for revisions to prevent foreign tariff barriers and to keep prices down.[74]

The session also dealt with the issue of Chinese labor in the United States. Both major parties had planks in their 1880 platforms calling for limitations on the large numbers of Chinese who were flooding America's Pacific shore in search of work. They took jobs paying very low wages and generally earned the scorn of American labor. Pendleton supported the ban on immigration: "We cannot bring in upon our civilization on the Pacific coast the hordes of Chinese, devoted to everything which is repugnant to our religion, to our morals, to our habits, to our civilization, and expect it to increase in purity and power there."[75] Pendleton could justify his position as a Jacksonian concern for the lower class. Part of Pendleton's support was undoubtedly rooted in his objectionable belief in white supremacy.[76]

Shortly before the session ended, Pendleton rose to urge an investigation into Republican political assessments for the coming election. Pendleton secured a copy of a letter sent to Republicans holding federal offices that requested an assessment. He presented it to the Senate. Both the National Civil Service Reform League and the Civil Service Reform Association of New York sent a letter to each of the officeholders informing them that it was illegal to contribute in this manner. George William Curtis, president of the league, wrote to Jay A. Hubbell, chairman of the Republican Congressional Committee and a Representative from Michigan who had sent the assessment letter, threatening to bring the issue to court. Hubbell refused to change his tactics, saying that the contributions were voluntary. Arthur's attorney general, Benjamin Brewster, did not aid the reformers when he issued an opinion that the 1876 law forbidding assessment requests did not apply to congressmen. Pendleton and the reformers met with little legislative success, but they had scored a decisive blow in the court of public opinion. Pendleton's timing was important because he once more brought the issue of reform to the forefront. The Hubbell assessment circular angered Americans for its audacity. Public opinion, building up pressure, neared irresistible force as a result of the Grant administration corruption, Belknap's fraud (which ironically had sullied Pendleton's name), congressional missteps such as the Crédit Mobilier and the Star Route scandals, and finally Garfield's assassination. The fall elections would serve as a referendum on civil service reform.[77]

It had been a busy, eventful, and tragic six months. Garfield's assassination, congressional infighting, and the battle for civil service reform had taken its toll on Pendleton. During the same time period he had suffered a loss within his extended family and personal illness, but he had not slowed down. His wife and daughters continued to receive guests on Monday evenings in their Washington home. When the session ended, Pendleton took his family to their Newport residence for a much needed reprieve. The respite did not last long. He was shortly needed in Ohio for the upcoming campaign.[78]

Though not solely focused on the reform issue, Ohio's election displayed the divisions within Ohio's Democracy on civil service reform. John R. McLean, editor of the *Cincinnati Enquirer* and an associate of Cleveland's Henry B. Payne, though previously tolerant and at times supportive of reform when he could use the issue to attack Republicans, came out against it. He used every avenue open to him to marshal forces against the newly formed alliance between Pendleton and Democrat John G. Thompson. Pendleton men were working in conjunction with Thompson, chairman of the State Central Committee, more out of political convenience than commonality of convictions. The Pendleton-Thompson faction was derisively labeled "mossbacks" because of their association with the older Democratic leadership. McLean's "Young Democrats" predicted the election of a Democratic president in 1884.[79] While arguing that the civil service reform bill would ruin the national Republican Party by drying up its source of money, McLean inexplicably disowned reform in search of political power at home in Ohio. Disregarding that the Pendleton bill would only apply to 10 percent of the government jobs, McLean charged that the bill would force Democrats to sacrifice the opportunity to employ the spoils system for the benefit of themselves. The conflict came to a head at the 1882 state convention in Columbus. McLean had used his paper to blast the reform ideas of Pendleton during the weeks prior to the gathering. Early in the convention, McLean scored a victory when Thompson was not elected to the state central committee. But McLean's success was short lived, as the delegates elected Thompson to chair the state executive committee and named Pendleton chairman of the convention. Somewhat surprised by his selection, Pendleton had to be located to accept the honor. Of greater importance, the platform contained a plank stating,

> *Resolved,* That we favor an honest reform in the Civil Service, and denounce the extortion of money from office-holders to corrupt the ballot and control elections as a most threatening, as it is the most insidious, danger that besets free government; and the shameless resort to such methods by the party in power, to carry its ends, evidences the utter abandonment of principle for place and spoils, under "Boss" rule.[80]

Considering the efforts against him, Pendleton came out of the convention a victor. The extent of his win was not clear, however.[81]

While the platform endorsed civil service reform, it did not specifically call for enactment of Pendleton's bill or his particular type of reform that included competitive examinations and the merit system. In fact, Pendleton appeared to be bending slightly under the pressure of Ohio Democrats who opposed reform. He was not outspoken on behalf of his bill during the debate over the platform. He gave no speech at the convention and only mentioned the issue in passing at a subsequent ratification meeting. Though he returned to his reform theme at Mount Gilead during the canvass, criticizing political assessments, he tempered it with the resurrection of an idea he had expressed in the Senate when faced with stiff opposition to the Pendleton Bill. Perhaps realizing that such a proposal was not feasible, he suggested the direct election of federal officials outside of Washington, such as postal and customs workers. He maintained his commitment to competitive examinations for officials working in the capital, but this retreat clearly appeared to be a sop to the opposition. Nonetheless, it was a reform that empowered the people and was not inconsistent with his principle. Although he remained a staunch advocate of reform, he was aware of the pressure of the McLean faction in Ohio. To remain in the Senate or to gain a nomination for president he would need the support of all Ohio Democrats.[82]

That support was not forthcoming. The *Enquirer* interpreted the convention results as a defeat for Pendleton and civil service reform. McLean commentated, "He was completely stripped of all consequence, save that which merely attaches to the fact that he is a United States Senator, and ran naked among his masters—the people—a public man without an approved public record; a man bearing the burden of rebuke."[83] McLean saw reform only as the complete removal of all Republicans from office upon the ascension of Democrats. Other papers around the state did not reach the same conclusion. The *Cincinnati Gazette* suggested that "Pendleton's civil service ideas . . . received a reasonably satisfactory indorsement [*sic*]." The *Plain Dealer* noted, "The Ohio Democracy have put themselves upon record in favor of *honest* Civil Service reform." The *Penny Paper* rebuked McLean's interpretation saying, "The *Enquirer* is not the Democracy of Ohio, by a long shot. It believes in Grant and Grantism."[84] These various views make it evident that the vague wording of the platform was deliberate: the Ohio Democracy was not unified on this issue.

The election also centered on other issues. On these matters, Pendleton was quite candid. While the party hit the usual refrain of tariff reform and anti-monopoly sentiment, it emphasized a local issue. The Republican majority in the Ohio Assembly had passed the Pond Law, which taxed those involved in liquor sales and forced those in that business to purchase and file a bond with the state government. German American Ohioans, especially in Cincinnati, believed that this legislation unfairly penalized them. Governor Foster gave them good reason to believe this when he connected alcohol with the allegedly inappropriate Sunday activities of German Americans. These Buckeyes had consistently voted Republican in Ohio since the Civil War, but they did not support Foster and the legislature on this issue. The Democrats appealed to this voting bloc for two years with planks aimed at ending the sumptuary laws. Because of the passage of the Pond Law and Foster's inflexibility on the matter, many German Americans voted Democratic in the fall elections.[85]

This state concern, however, did not supplant the debate on improving the national civil service. A leading Republican German American, Carl Schurz, showed the limited impact of the Pond Law issue by noting that the Republicans had lost votes in areas deemed to support such laws as well as in German

American precincts. The election results indicated that the Republicans had not addressed civil service reform to the satisfaction of many Americans. The dramatic trial and hanging of presidential assassin Charles Guiteau in late June, coupled with the political assessment scandal broken by Pendleton and the Democrats in Congress, caused many Ohioans to demand reform.[86]

The October election results clearly conveyed this message. Democrats won a resounding victory, not only in Ohio but also in Indiana, Pennsylvania, Connecticut, New Jersey, and New York. Civil service reform was a key plank in virtually every state party platform in 1882. Interpreting the election results as a mandate for his bill, Pendleton was reinvigorated to pursue civil service reform. The election results also predicted quite accurately what would occur in the November elections around the country. The Democrats made significant gains, beginning a return to power in Congress that would culminate with control of the House at the start of the Forty-eighth Congress. Pendleton faced a difficult decision, however. Newspapers had commented on his aspirations for the White House. He also heard the pleas of Democrats to go slow on reform until a member of their party was in the White House. In spite of the possible personal loss, Pendleton refused to wait. He believed the civil service bill would bring about a Democratic victory in 1884. If the 1882 elections could be interpreted as his mandate, then he believed he had to achieve reform, or by 1884 the party would once again be lagging behind.[87]

The second session of the Forty-seventh Congress began on December 4, 1882, and Pendleton had much on his mind. His initial concerns were familial. First, he and his family had moved into a stately mansion on 16th Street, NW. Second, his daughter Jane was quite ill and would be weeks in recovery before she could resume normal activity.[88] In the political realm, the third concern dealt with the issue that had been before Congress for more than a year. Inspired by President Arthur's second annual message to Congress in which he supported passage of Pendleton's proposal and the results of the election, Pendleton once again wasted no time in having his bill brought up for debate. On December 12, Pendleton again spoke on the subject. Reminding the Senate of the corruption in the civil service, much of which had been perpetrated under Republican administrations, Pendleton reviewed the report from the civil service reform hearings made during the prior session. In one division of the Treasury Department that employed more than nine hundred workers, some five hundred of the positions were considered superfluous. Almost $400,000 could be saved yearly, he argued, with the elimination of those unneeded employees. These positions had been maintained simply to add to the Republican patronage rolls. Pendleton tied the election successes of the Democrats in 1882 to the "acts of the Republican Party" that maintained this kind of inefficiency and

THE OUT-DEMOCRATS.

TAMMANY HALL. "Shake hands, that's the kind of Civil Service Reform I believe in."

Senator PENDLETON, in his speech delivered at Mount Gilead, Ohio, remarked: "It has been said that the abandonment of the spoils system will exclude Democrats from office when the day of our victory shall come. Not at all. On the contrary, I believe that the adoption of this policy as our party creed will hasten the day of the victory of our party, and its adoption as a law will, under any administration, fill many offices with Democrats. I believe Democrats will stand any test of examination, and in a fair field will not come out second best. Who shall do them the discredit to say that in any of the essential elements of character, or capacity, or fitness, they are inferior?"

The Out-Democrats: Pendleton argued that his civil service reform bill would put more Democrats in government office, regardless of the party's success or lack of success in elections. (*Harper's Weekly*, September 16, 1882)

fraud.[89] Turning from this censure, Pendleton addressed his own party. If the Democrats did not adopt reform, he suggested, they would face defeat themselves. He alluded to Jefferson's commitment to appointing only men who were fit. So important was the maintenance of this principle, according to Pendleton, that if the spoils system was not destroyed, "it will kill the Republic."[90]

Pendleton focused much of the rest of his lengthy commentary on objec
tions to the bill presented by his own party during the previous campaign
and in his consultations within the Democratic congressional caucus. First
he detailed the application of the bill: "The bill simply applies to the Executive Departments of the Government here in Washington and to those offices
throughout the country, post-offices and custom-houses, which employ more
than fifty persons."[91] The total number of offices affected did not exceed ten
thousand by his estimation.[92] How, he wondered, could this bring about the
demise of the Democratic Party as some feared?

In addition, Pendleton touched on the common complaint that the competitive examinations gave an unfair advantage to the college educated and would
produce a civil service of young individuals filled with book training who had no
practical skills or experience. Pendleton responded that the examinations were to
be tailored for each office and not based on a standard designed to test general
knowledge. He cited the report from the New York Post Office during the Grant
administration that had used competitive examinations until funding ran out.
Of those who competed and gained a position, 60 percent had only a common
school education, 33.5 percent had some high school education, and only 6.5
percent had a college education. Clearly, Pendleton argued, these results did not
suggest the creation of an academic civil service such as that in England. Pendleton wanted a system open to all Americans and believed the system his bill would
create would, in the final analysis, be more democratic than the spoils system.
This was a key aspect of his philosophical justification for supporting reform.[93]

Pendleton then dealt with the charge that his proposal would result in an
aristocratic civil service installed for life, or a meritocracy. Pendleton noted
that the bill placed few restrictions on removals, and thus it did not abridge
the president's power. It did not create lifetime tenure either. The proposal
would not lock Republicans into office, he continued, because the examination system would put Democrats into office during the last half of the Arthur
administration. Pendleton expressed optimism that his party was not simply
a party of spoilsmen. Whether the Democrats won or lost in 1884, under the
reform system, they would gain public offices. In addition, the results of the
test case in New York suggested that the civil service would not be restricted to
only the intellectual elite.[94]

Pendleton concluded his responses to critics with a word directed at those
who wanted a delay until after the Democrats gained the White House. Sen.
Joseph E. Brown of Georgia believed that the party would win the 1884 election, and then, "Everybody that is worthy and qualified shall have a chance for
the offices. Why will Democrats take a position to proscribe men of their own
party and to keep in power men of another party?"[95] To Brown and others,

Pendleton responded that the victory in 1884 was by no means assured. Without the proper response to public pressure for reform, he implored, the Democrats could not count on a victory. In addition, if they did not act now, the Republicans would have all of the power and money available to them through the corrupt spoils system as they entered the 1884 campaign. The combination of American public opinion and the threat of Republican political assessments and patronage made Pendleton believe that the time was ripe for action.[96]

Pendleton closed by proposing two amendments to his bill. In response to one of President Arthur's concerns, he suggested that the Senate remove the provision that limited entry into the civil service to the lowest grade. This had been included largely in response to those who believed that the bill would create a bureaucratic aristocracy such as in Great Britain. In addition, Pendleton accepted the suggestion of fellow Democrat James L. Pugh of Alabama to apportion offices among the states. The language of the amendment did not require this distribution but, rather, encouraged it. Pugh represented many senators from the South and Midwest who feared that the Pendleton Bill would act to limit government jobs to New Englanders and those from Atlantic states who had access to better education. With those proposed amendments, Pendleton finished his speech. For the next two weeks, the Senate debated the issue.[97]

Numerous amendments were introduced, and Pendleton was willing in most cases to see the bill altered. Sen. John T. Morgan, another Alabama Democrat, proposed that the restrictions imposed on the president in removing a commissioner of the Civil Service Commission be eliminated. The commission was originally planned to be comprised of five members, no more than three from any one party. Three of the members would work full time for the commission, while the other two were to divide their time between their governmental positions and the work of examining prospective officials. An amendment reduced the commission to three full-time members, allowing them to focus on their work unencumbered by the affairs of other departments. Ohio Republican John Sherman added an amendment that did away with the permanent appropriation for the board. Republican John A. Logan of Illinois made sure that the examinations administered by the board were related to the office being applied for, putting in writing what Pendleton had promised. Various other amendments limited the influence of congressmen in favor of any one applicant, prevented more than two members of one family from working in the civil service, and denied alcoholics the right to work for the government. All of these amendments strengthened the bill except perhaps that of Senator Sherman. The requirement that Congress pass yearly appropriations bills for the commission and its work placed the body on a weak foundation. Hayes's original civil service board had died because of a lack of funding.[98]

Perhaps the most important amendment came from Republican Joseph R. Hawley of Connecticut. Hawley proposed prohibiting political assessments and political removals. Democrats attempted to strengthen this provision by outlawing even voluntary contributions, but they failed. With the support of the judiciary committee, Hawley's amendment passed after some debate. As a result, this amendment allowed the bill to encompass both of Pendleton's original reform proposals.[99]

These deliberations divided the Senate along partisan and sectional lines. When Zebulan B. Vance of North Carolina moved to place large internal revenue offices under the scope of the bill, the parties divided. Republicans opposed the idea because these offices, which were generally outside of Washington, played an important role in the party machines. Though the Democrats supported it, Vance's amendment failed.[100] Logan decided to take Pendleton's amendment to apportion offices to the states "as nearly as practicable" and make it stronger. He moved to strike that phrase, making apportionment mandatory and reducing the role of merit to some degree in the bill. Western and southern senators tended to support this idea, and it eventually passed.[101]

Various other proposals surfaced but failed. One such amendment called for a six-year term for government officials. Another would have removed all officials and forced them to compete for the positions under the new system. As each new amendment arose, Pendleton reread portions of the original bill, explained passages, justified wording, and often proposed changes. Throughout the debate, he was constantly involved in the bill's progress and made sure that it was before the Senate continuously.[102]

The Senate voted on the Pendleton Bill on December 27, 1882. It passed by a vote of thirty-eight to five, with thirty-three members not voting. All five of the "no" votes were from Democrats. Only fourteen of the supporting ballots were cast by Democrats; thirteen were southerners while the other was Pendleton himself. More than half of the absent senators were Democrats, further demonstrating Democratic divisions. John Sherman voted with Pendleton. What at times had been a very partisan debate led to a fairly bipartisan vote in the affirmative, perhaps best explained by public pressure. In the House, the vote was much like the Senate tally. Forty-nine Democrats supported it, while thirty-nine were opposed. All but one Democratic member from Ohio voted nay, but an overwhelming majority of Republicans voted in favor. On January 16, 1883, President Arthur, the former Stalwart, signed the Pendleton Act into law. He appointed Dorman B. Eaton to be chairman of the new Civil Service Commission and consulted with Pendleton on a recommendation for a Democratic appointee, both actions demonstrating a serious attempt to implement the law. Pendleton suggested a young judge from Youngstown named Leroy D. Thoman, who quickly consented. Unlike Pendleton's many efforts in the past, this time he was successful in dramatically affecting the policy of the U.S. government. As in the past, however, he had failed to unite his party.[103]

Pendleton finished the second session of the Forty-seventh Congress with a major win and a minor loss. He had won a victory with the Pendleton Act, but he could not marshal the forces necessary to prevent the Republicans from passing a high protective tariff. The Senate adjourned on March 4, 1883, and Pendleton spent the next week working on behalf of his recommendation for the Civil Service Commission. Leroy Thoman arrived in Washington on the closing day of the session. Pendleton and Thoman met with Arthur on the sixth, after which Thoman accepted the position on the commission. Within the week, the new commissioners had found office space in the capital. Pendleton then returned to Cincinnati. The coming months would see him in a fight for his political life. The election of 1883 would determine the makeup of the Ohio legislature and therefore whether or not Pendleton would gain a second term in the Senate.[104]

Pendleton's triumph in Washington did not make him the toast of the Ohio state Democratic Convention, which met in June 1883. Pendleton arrived in Columbus on June 19, hoping to be chosen permanent chairman. More important, Pendleton sought endorsement for his civil service accomplishments. The divisions in the Ohio Democracy dating from the 1880 campaign still remained, however, and would only worsen as the convention proceeded. The "Young Democracy" had supported Henry Payne's bid for the presidential nomination in 1880, and this group largely opposed the Pendleton Act. The "mossbacks" were the old-line or traditional Democrats such as Allen Thurman and Pendleton. They tended to be more sympathetic to Pendleton personally, if not always to his civil service ideas.[105] When the convention opened, delegates focused on two key men as possible gubernatorial candidates: Durbin Ward and George Hoadly. The former was associated with the mossbacks, the latter with the Young Democrats. Hoadly gained the nomination, but on a platform that specifically endorsed the platforms of the state party for the previous three years and the national party for the last three presidential elections. One plank specifically demanded a "thorough reform and purification of the civil service."[106] The platform said nothing about Pendleton and did not specifically mention his act, but this was at the very least an endorsement. Pendleton's supporter on the Executive Committee, John G. Thompson, lost his seat. Pendleton spent most of his time in Columbus seeking to regain some semblance of strength within the state party. Instead, the forces of both Pendleton and Thurman, men who had virtually dictated party organization in the past, were substantially reduced. The Young Democrats got their man nominated.[107]

Henry Payne marshaled his considerable support against Pendleton. His son, Oliver, was treasurer of the Standard Oil Company and one of the original Cleveland oil refiners who joined with Rockefeller to form the nucleus of the Standard Oil trust. Oliver used his money and influence to further his father's career.[108] McLean continued a vigorous campaign against Pendleton's interests, attempting to enhance his control of the party machinery. His editorial page expressed continuous opposition to reform. One such column presented the views of Gen. James R. Steedman, a Democrat from Toledo and a member of the Democratic State Committee who had been a longtime Pendleton supporter. "It is hard to break politically with a man to whom I have been so long attached, but Pendleton has wronged the Democratic Party, and when it comes to a question between Pendleton and the Democratic Party, of course I am for the Democracy."[109]

At the Hamilton County Convention, Pendleton met more opposition. The meeting at the Highland House failed to result in nominations for the legislature that would secure Pendleton's return to the Senate. After the convention, Pendleton did not attend a ratification meeting for Hoadly or another gathering, although he was scheduled to speak at both. In Pendleton's eyes, the party was shattering. McLean used these absences to attack him. "Mr. Pendleton is not a Democrat. He has not a sentiment in sympathy with the masses of toiling people who compose the great majority of the Democratic Party."[110] McLean further suggested that Pendleton leave the Democracy and join with his supporters in the Republican Party. Growing more acerbic, McLean charged that the aristocratic Pendleton had spent $10,000 in a campaign to secure favorable nominations at the Highland House convention. When that failed, he bankrolled the bolt of a group of county Democrats who held their own convention at College Hall. These accusations were hypocritical in light of McLean's own inconsistency on civil service reform and later willingness to work with the Standard Oil monopoly. McLean had supported reform when it was politically expedient, and now conveniently forgot that this very issue played a key role in propelling Pendleton into the Senate in the first place. The "Reform Democrats," as the College Hall congregants were labeled, reportedly had a pledge of support signed by some six thousand Cincinnatians. In the end, they capitulated and resolved to support the state platform, to work for reform in local governments, and most important, to labor within the Democratic organization. They did not believe that the county convention demonstrated the will of the people of Hamilton County. When questioned on this split, Pendleton was noncommittal. He eventually canvassed the state, however, in favor of Hoadly and the Highland House ticket.[111]

The Democrats won a comfortable victory on October 9, after many defectors in the College Hall movement returned to the fold. Ohioans who supported civil service reform as well as those who did not could support the Democratic ticket. Pendleton represented reform to supporters. To the opposition, the convention was less than exuberant in its praise of reform. The continued opposition to the Republicans and their sumptuary laws worked in favor of the Democrats. The Democratic Party easily won control of the Ohio Assembly and they would soon decide the fate of Pendleton, who, in spite of his somewhat tenuous position in the party, celebrated the victory. The result of the state elections around the nation would be a slight Republican majority in the next Senate.[112]

As soon as the votes were counted, the bugle sounded for the battle ahead. McLean and the Young Democrats, having been successful in the first battle, now moved to win the war. They launched volleys at Pendleton from the comfort of McLean's editorial chair. McLean leveled abuse on the "sham" of civil service reform throughout December and January, while defending Payne against the attacks of Pendleton supporters.[113] Oblivious to his own inconsistency on the reform issue, McLean complained about the "greed" of the Democratic office seekers after the election, yet frequently blasted Pendleton for fathering an act that would only work against this group.[114] When the *Enquirer* was not criticizing reform or Pendleton's association with Republican reformers, it distanced Payne from his association with Standard Oil. Pendleton men wasted little time in exposing Payne's connection to this trust and his obvious inconsistency with the party's stand against privilege and monopoly found in such businesses. McLean reminded his readers that Payne did not own and never had owned stock in Standard Oil. The statement was accurate as far as it went, but Payne's relationship to the corporation was evident. Throughout the journalistic jockeying, McLean remained confident. So apparent was Pendleton's demise, the paper reported, that another senator had requested to have Pendleton's seat in the Senate chamber because it was in a better location than his own.[115]

Pendleton did not despair. He launched his campaign, beginning with letters to members of the Ohio Assembly. Pendleton's experiences in Ohio's politics had taught him the importance of strong organization and careful use of the press. In an attempt to steamroll assembly members, Pendleton men announced that they already had thirty-two votes committed to their man. Also, the whiskey distillers of Ohio worked hard for Pendleton because of his opposition to sumptuary laws. Just as important, Thurman suggested that the Pendleton group caucus with supporters of Durbin Ward, who also sought the seat, in an effort to defeat Payne. Though at first hesitant, Pendleton's handlers did meet with the Ward force when it became apparent that Payne's supporters had gained control of the assembly's administrative positions. In spite of these efforts, and Pendleton's trip to Columbus days before the Democratic caucus to lobby on his own behalf, his hopes were not high.[116]

On Jackson Day, the Ohio Democratic caucus met to vote on their candidate for the United States Senate. Once again, the vote in the assembly would be perfunctory because of the Democratic majority. The real battle ensued in caucus. While Pendleton paced outside his conference room, the Democracy's state representatives and senators easily nominated Payne. Payne gained forty-eight votes; he needed only forty-two. Pendleton came in a humiliating third, two votes behind Ward with only fifteen.[117] The vote meant political retirement for Pendleton. Though mentioned as a likely presidential candidate throughout much of his term in the Senate, he was no longer the "available" man.[118] It must have been a bitter pill for Pendleton, whose only significant mistake was implementing party policy based on Jacksonian principle. Judge Thoman, now a member of the Civil Service Commission, asserted that the Payne nomination would not "kill George H. Pendleton. He is not a man of mere local reputation." He even suggested, perhaps more as a compliment than as a realistic assessment, that Pendleton might now be in line for a presidential nomination.[119]

Pendleton was a victim of corruption and those who opposed civil service reform. The Democratic members of the Ohio House, when the Pendleton Act passed, were unanimous in their opposition. McLean and Payne built their campaign on that discontent. Even Allen Thurman publicly stated his repugnance toward the act but did not consider it a reason to replace Pendleton in the Senate.[120] But there were other factors involved in the caucus vote. If reform was the only issue, Thurman asked, "why can not they support Ward?"[121] His conclusion was that certain Ohio Democrats sought to create a political machine. Though he mentioned no names, he was referring to McLean and Payne as would-be bosses. McLean would be the political boss backed by Payne's financial resources. The *New York Times* declared that the decision was clearly one between reform and monopoly. "Mr. Pendleton stands for the former and Mr. Payne for the latter."[122] The paper was not alone in its perception that the Ohio Senate seat had been auctioned off to the highest bidder. Supported by Standard Oil, Payne could pay the highest price. Payne's name had not even been mentioned in fifty-four of eighty-eight Democratic county conventions according to one newspaper reporter. There was such an unpredicted move for Payne among Democratic members of the state legislature that many began to make allegations of payments from officers of Standard Oil to influence the vote. There was such uproar about the events that the legislature eventually instituted an investigation which found that upward of $100,000 was spread among its members in Columbus. The search found that a $65,000 check had been cashed in a bank used by Standard Oil in Cleveland and the money transported to Columbus. Eventually, the investigation resulted in substantial evidence of bribery, and the state assembly forwarded it to the

United States Senate with a request to further the investigation in 1886. The Senate debated the matter for three days with Payne's Ohio colleague, John Sherman, asking him to respond to the allegations. Payne would not speak. In the end, the Senate decided not to further the investigation, but not without a vocal minority lamenting the majority decision. The following year, Senator Payne voted against the Interstate Commerce Act. Many opponents believed that legislation like this regulation was the very reason Payne was supported by Standard Oil. His voting record in the House suggested he would be a force to prevent it. A political cartoon published shortly after the caucus depicted Pendleton bowing to McLean. The caption said, "Monopoly has been made king."[123] The *Times* noted the willingness of Payne to support protective tariffs that would benefit companies such as Standard Oil. Those who voted for Payne demonstrated a decided indifference to Pendleton's revised form of, and even more traditionally held, Jacksonianism. They contradicted the Ohio party platform that supported civil service reform and opposed the strengthening of monopolies and protective tariffs. Power politics clearly dictated the outcome. As a senator, Pendleton had tried to be consistent and judicious with the patronage available to him. As a result, he did not placate interests such as McLean back home. This caused McLean to bid for more influence in the party. It became a contest for control of the party, with Pendleton the victim. For McLean, he could easily ride the coattails of the powerful Standard Oil, but not without swallowing the bitter pill of hypocrisy and turning his back on much of what he had found repugnant in his political opponents throughout his long career. For Standard Oil, the goal was greater influence in government to foster its business interests. The combination of these factors spelled disaster for Pendleton's political career and, ironically, comprised the type of influence his reform bill sought to eradicate.[124]

Pendleton was also a victim of the transitional era in which he lived. At a time when businesses, fledgling unions, and farmer's organizations were centralizing, political parties were resisting that transformation. Pendleton tried to unify his party, in essence centralize its structure, but most politicos were not interested in that goal. Political parties remained hopelessly divided as state party chieftains sought to maintain local power and control. Much of that power was achieved through the use of the patronage system. Pendleton refused to use that system, as it was contrary to the reform he had proposed. As a result, Pendleton was swimming upstream. Rising business influence in politics and the continuing battle for local political power worked against him. He was ahead of his time in this respect, and gradually the civil service reform he fostered and the resulting bureaucratic change that took place in the national government forced change upon the parties. That change, however, would come too slowly to save Pendleton's political career.[125]

Though he had lost his Senate seat, Pendleton still had to finish out the term As a member of the Committee on Foreign Relations, he pushed again for determining the jurisdiction of consular courts. Pendleton believed that the system did not provide the necessary constitutional protections granted to residents of the United States when tried in consular courts outside the country. He participated in numerous discussions during the session and persuaded his colleagues of the need for and the constitutionality of the proposed changes. On March 6, Pendleton called for a vote on the bill, which the Senate passed.[126]

Pendleton never changed his perspective on the Constitution. Indeed, he valued principle even more highly than his own career, and it had cost him personally. He was a strict constructionist and even in his final days in the Senate frequently reminded his colleagues of that standard. For example, during an earlier debate on a bill to appropriate federal funds to foster education, Pendleton had expressed reservations about the use of federal monies by the states. When the issue arose in this session, he attacked the heart of it; he could find no constitutional provision for the federal government raising revenue for the purpose of giving it to the states for educational pursuits. He would rather the federal government reduce its obligations, lower its taxes, and allow the states to raise their own revenues for such purposes. He had no opposition to the ends, just the means. Nonetheless, the Senate passed the bill, but it died in the House.[127]

The Pendletons concluded the social season in early 1884 with a round of receptions. Well liked among Washington socialites, Alice and her daughters frequently helped other women with their own gatherings. The *Evening Star* reported that the second to last Pendleton reception was "attended by an assemblage representing the most exclusive element of Washington society."[128] The following week, Alice held her last reception. It was a bittersweet affair for her and her husband, who knew that their time in Washington would soon come to an end. But the Pendletons would not yet be done with public service.[129]

The first session of the Forty-eighth Congress did not adjourn until early July 1884. That gave Pendleton a convenient excuse for missing the state Democratic convention held on June 24. He was relatively pleased with the results of the meeting, though. The state organization maintained its position with reference to civil service reform. Of greater interest to Pendleton was the delegates-at-large slate to the national convention. The McLean-Payne organization had chosen four men to fill the positions, including McLean and W. P. Thompson, secretary of the Ohio subsidiary of the Standard Oil Company. The choice of Thompson, who was so closely associated with the monopoly, suggested that Payne and McLean felt confident of their control of the state party. But the convention was not in a mood to be dictated to by the Young Democrats. Instead, someone offered the name of mossback Durbin Ward as a delegate-at-large, and he was chosen immediately. Then John McLean was nominated,

OHIO.
The "Standard" of Democratic Civil Service Reform.

Ohio: Pendleton's defeat and removal from the U.S. Senate was the result of the type of privileged influence that the Pendleton Civil Service Act of 1883 sought to reduce. The irony is that it came from within his own party. (*Harper's Weekly,* January 26, 1884)

but another delegate proposed Thurman in his place. The resulting uproar at the convention was quieted only when it was decided to vote on both men together, rather than one or the other. Both were accepted. The slate was now half mossback. The fourth slot went to a Payne man from Cuyahoga County, Jacob W. Mueller. The delegation going to Chicago was by no means committed to one candidate. Payne's hopes of having Ohio's support for a presidential bid died as a result of these proceedings, and McLean's designs on forming a political machine were weakened. Though considered part of a mossback slate for delegates, Pendleton was not nominated as a delegate-at-large.[130]

Pendleton attended the national convention, although he did not participate. With regard to civil service reform, he was pleased with both the nomination of Grover Cleveland of New York and the platform. Some Democrats viewed Cleveland as a man who could garner the votes of the disaffected mugwumps of the Republican Party, who could not abide the corruption in Republican candidate James G. Blaine's past. In light of Cleveland's selection, Pendleton's stance on civil service reform seemed vindicated. Though the platform was vague on the topic, Cleveland's letter of acceptance was a stronger endorsement. While governor of New York, Cleveland had fought against the influence and power of Tammany Hall and supported civil service reform. So angry was the political machine that it sent John Kelly and a delegation of six hundred to represent its interests to the national convention. The New York Democratic Convention had voted to force the state's delegates to the national convention to cast all of its ballots for the candidate that received a majority vote among the state's delegates. Kelly did not have enough support to thwart Cleveland, who overcame a late surge for Hendricks led by Kelly to win nomination. Pendleton felt confident that Cleveland would use the Pendleton Act to create a viable bureaucracy, based on the New Yorker's history as a "good government" mayor and governor. When asked to divulge who he thought would win the election, Pendleton responded, "I believe that the public temper is such that the voters of the land are prepared to support the party which gives the best promise of administrating the Government in the honest, simple, and plain manner which is consistent with its character and purposes."[131] Pendleton defiantly refused to back away from reform, and he believed his congressional efforts had influenced Cleveland's nomination. What he had told his Democratic colleagues was true: they could not win if they did not espouse reform.[132]

Yet Pendleton could not claim complete victory. Cleveland was an unknown quantity when it came to most political issues. On others, he was anathema from Pendleton's perspective. Cleveland was a Bourbon and as such favored business interests over those of farmers and laborers, Pendleton's longtime concerns. Eastern Bourbons had come to accept Cleveland, in spite of his position on civil service reform, because of his strong probusiness leanings. Cleveland opposed greenbacks and free silver and wrote a public letter stating his support of maintaining the gold standard. Foreshadowing the Progressivism of the next century, Pendleton could not help but see an inconsistency in allowing big business to operate freely while fighting political corruption at the same time. In Pendleton's mind, the two went hand in hand, as was evidenced in his failed bid to retain his Senate seat. Cleveland managed to marry two seemingly disparate facets of the Democratic Party. Pendleton had been able to reconcile reform with Jacksonianism; monopoly and influence he could not. While Cleveland was stronger on reform than the platform had been, no one really knew what he would do as president.[133]

Pendleton immersed himself in the campaign. Ridiculing McLean's prediction that he would support the Republican candidate, Pendleton spoke at Democratic rallies around the state. In spite of his efforts, the state elections in October gave the Republicans a slight edge, foreshadowing the outcome of the presidential race in Ohio. Cleveland won the election, however, and Pendleton returned to the Senate to finish his term.[134]

Pendleton was not heavily involved in this last session. He attended regularly and participated in voting and debates, but he did not make any formal speeches of note. Arthur's administration had considered him for a position on the Civil Service Commission, but he declined. Pendleton looked on with interest as Cleveland entered office to see how he would administer the Pendleton Act. The National Civil Service Reform League sent Cleveland a letter expressing their concerns about the coming administration. He responded in a public letter reiterating his commitment to implementing the act. Further, Cleveland promised to retain certain Republican officials in office to complete their four-year terms if they had not participated in partisanship while in the federal service. If the reformers were pleased with Cleveland's statements, they were especially enthusiastic about most of his choices for the cabinet. Several cabinet members were supporters of the merit system. There was talk of Pendleton for a cabinet position, but it was not forthcoming. One cabinet selection did cause the reformers, particularly Pendleton, alarm. Cleveland chose William C. Whitney as secretary of the navy. Whitney was married to the daughter of Henry B. Payne and was viewed by most as a force working on behalf of big business. Though tainted by his association with the corruption and influence-peddling of Payne, Whitney represented Cleveland's probusiness stance.[135]

On March 5, 1885, Pendleton's final Senate session closed. Once again, he was ignominiously retired from public office, this time at the hand of his own party. Nonetheless, he would return home with some vindication due to the results of the 1884 election and the first days of Cleveland's administration. His work in the Senate had produced the federal civil service merit system, an enduring legacy, but even in his last great effort, Pendleton had failed to unify his party.

Minister Plenipotentiary and Envoy Extraordinary of the United States to Germany

The coming of the New Year in 1885 did not auger well for Pendleton. Not only had he lost his seat in the United States Senate, but also President-elect Grover Cleveland ignored him in selecting the cabinet. While he could rightly emphasize his service to the party and his instrumental role in securing Cleveland's election as reasons for obtaining such an appointment, Pendleton neither wallowed in self-pity nor publicly complained about the lack of an immediate sign of the administration's favor. Rather, he depended on his numerous political associates in Congress who bombarded Cleveland with suggestions that he name Pendleton to a foreign post. In particular, they maintained that he was exceptionally qualified to become minister to the Court of St. James because his six years on the Senate Foreign Affairs Committee had made him an expert on relations with Great Britain. He had spent considerable time in England over the years, studying and evaluating the British government and civil service system. Moreover, Pendleton had exerted much energy as a senator seeking to improve the consular court system, which was critical in defending American business interests abroad. Even more, his friends stressed, Pendleton's bearing and reputation as a gentleman would be most welcome in the upper ranks of English society. When Cleveland selected Pendleton's friend, Thomas F. Bayard of Maryland, as secretary of state, the Buckeye's supporters wrote to Bayard as well. William S. Groesbeck took a different tact with Bayard; he focused on Pendleton's service. "The spoilsmen," he argued, "should not be allowed to triumph over the most conspicuous civil service reformer in the democratic party."[1]

Bayard and Pendleton knew each other well. Both had been Peace men during the Civil War. In the Senate, they had nominated one another for president pro tempore of that body and supported civil service reform together.

They split over currency issues, though. Bayard had someone else in mind for minister to Great Britain, Edward J. Phelps. Instead, Bayard persuaded Cleveland to name Pendleton Minister Plenipotentiary and Envoy Extraordinary of the United States to Germany, a position Pendleton's friend and neighbor George Bancroft had held under Johnson and Grant during the time when Otto Von Bismarck unified Germany. Relations with Germany were strained prior to 1885, and Chester Arthur had removed the previous minister to Berlin due to conflicts stemming from trade disputes as well as the most pressing issue between the countries: dominance in the Samoan Islands. Bayard believed Pendleton had the character and comportment to reestablish good relations. In addition, Pendleton had studied at the University of Heidelberg when he was young and had visited Germany frequently on his many trips to Europe. The thought of serving in an official capacity in Berlin must have been enticing for Pendleton. The Senate quickly confirmed him with general public approval, and he prepared to leave at once.[2]

Cincinnatians threw their favorite son a going away party in late April 1885. More than 150 notables attended to honor Pendleton and to express appreciation for his service to the community and to the country. Departing shortly after this fete, Pendleton traveled to New York where civil service reformers greeted him with even more hubbub. George William Curtis presided over the gathering, which, while it applauded Pendleton's efforts, was aimed at continuing the process of educating the public on reform. Pendleton then left for Berlin with his wife and two daughters, Mary and Jane.[3]

They arrived in Berlin with much less fanfare than when leaving America. On May 21, he wrote to Bayard announcing that he had reached his destination. Pendleton was consumed over the next few weeks in seeking appropriate offices for the legation and getting settled. He requested extra money from the State Department to bring the legation's accommodations up to the standard maintained by France and Britain, but the money was not forthcoming. For his family, Pendleton found a small but comfortable cottage on a lake two miles outside of Berlin. He began to feel at home, but lamented the lack of good wine or whiskey. Though he had studied German as a youth, he had forgotten much of it and now had to review four hours daily. In spite of his busy schedule, Pendleton found time to keep up with events back home. He wrote to Bayard that he should not be concerned about the continued harangues of newspapers regarding civil service reform. They just showed "how deep seated was the evil," he suggested, and that when the anger died down, he knew Bayard would be glad to be a part of "this great thing."[4] Writing later he said, "I congratulate you on the success of the administration. The grumblers and spoilsmen have had their say, and now the honest voice of the country will be heard."[5] Both Bayard and Pendleton continued to take their lumps in the press regarding their support of reform, but neither backed down. Bayard wrote frequently to Pendleton, noting the opposition of some amidst the progress being made by the civil service commission.[6]

While enhancing his German skills, Pendleton assumed the daily responsibilities of his new position. He often acted as an information gatherer for the secretary of state. As such, he frequently sent newspaper articles to Bayard about German public opinion and political issues. Pendleton noted with pride the general approbation his Pendleton Act had generated among Germans. Yet, in spite of all his activities, Pendleton could not have any official interaction with the German government until he had gained an audience with Kaiser Wilhelm I. The German government delayed this meeting for some time without explanation.[7]

When Pendleton finally met with the Kaiser, he discovered the reason for the delay; Kaiser Wilhelm had been quite ill and unable to receive visitors. The encounter, however, opened the door for Pendleton to have formal interaction with the German government. Pendleton's daughters, Mary and Jane, marveled at the splendor of the German court. During their father's years in Berlin, they would be privileged to meet three successive rulers of the young German confederation, as well as their wives. Jane wrote an article about the exquisite etiquette and formality that surrounded her frequent interviews and receptions with members of the royal family. During her first Schleppen-court, the opening ball of the 1886 season, she recalled how bitterly cold it was. Even the large stoves were insufficient to heat the rooms adequately before the guests arrived, so a regiment of soldiers was ordered to march through the Alte Schloss, pausing long enough in each room to warm it. Jane remembered the earthy and heavy air they left behind. The opening ball was always a dazzling affair where diplomats from every country were formally presented, and all German women of noble birth who had reached the age of seventeen the previous year made their court debut. The women wore dresses with heavy satin trains three yards in length or longer. Jane was impressed with the courteousness of the elderly kaiser who greeted each of the diplomats in their native language. The Pendletons were used to formal receptions in America, but nothing could prepare them for the grandeur of a European court.[8]

Pendleton spent much of his first year attempting to reestablish good relations between the two countries. He corresponded with and met the German Empress; accepted pictures of the German Chancellor, Prince Otto Von Bismarck, and his son, Count Herbert Von Bismarck, to send to President Cleveland and Bayard; and presented pictures of the president to Bismarck.[9] Pendleton's reception in Berlin was testament to his ability to rebuild previously burned bridges, but his talents would be greatly tested in dealing with the Samoan situation. Bayard warned him that Germany had "given evidence of disposition to cherish schemes of distant annexation and colonization in many corners of the globe" and that he needed to bear this in mind as he conversed with the German chancellor.[10] Pendleton's first encounter with Bismarck led to a discussion about the recent German acquisition of the Caroline Islands in the South Pacific. The United States had few interests there but hoped to prevent conflict between Germany and Spain, which also had expressed a desire to acquire the islands. A more pressing issue forced Pendleton to be in frequent communication with Count Bismarck, the question of naturalized United States citizens originally from Germany and their right to return to their home country.[11]

German men of military age in the relatively young nation were required to enlist in the army for a term of service. Some who did not wish to comply chose to immigrate to the United States. After they acquired U.S. citizenship, a few of these men returned to Germany. Some came just to visit; others missed their home and families so much that they returned to stay indefinitely. These former Germans, now American citizens, were being arrested by German authorities and deported for evading military service and returning to live in Germany without permission. Under their new status as citizens of the United States, they appealed to Pendleton through the American Legation in Berlin.[12]

According to the Bancroft Treaty of 1868, Germans who immigrated to the United States and obtained citizenship could return to Germany for up to two years. After that time, they either had to leave or renew their German citizenship. Because there were more than ten thousand German Americans in Germany in 1885, the actions of Count Bismarck in expelling a few of them threatened many. Secretary of State Bayard instructed Pendleton on cases brought directly to him and provided information needed by Pendleton with regard to certain others. German newspapers followed the cases closely, pushing the issue into the spotlight. Pendleton corresponded frequently with Count Bismarck on this matter, using his legal background to argue on behalf of the German Americans and seeking to hold Bismarck to the letter of the treaty. Bismarck's concern was the impact that leniency on these individuals would have on future compulsory military service. He did not wish to provide an easy way out for Germans who sought to evade their obligations. As a result, Bismarck and German officials involved in these cases frequently used technicalities to sidestep the Bancroft Treaty. Pendleton did achieve minor successes on behalf of some German Americans, but the large number of similar cases suggested limited victories.[13]

Though saddled with frequent appeals from these German Americans throughout his tenure, no issue consumed more of Pendleton's time and energy than the question of who would control the Samoan Islands. Located in the

South Pacific, the islands produced coconuts and pearl shell as major commercial exports. More important was their strategic location as coaling stations and naval bases. The British established relations with the area in the early 1830s, bringing Christianity as well as inaugurating commercial interests in the islands. New Zealand authorities pressured Great Britain to annex the Samoan Islands, but without success. The United States had contact with the islands as early as 1839. American interest in the area initially involved whaling but soon extended to trade and strategic considerations with the development of the transcontinental railroad and the prospect of an interocean canal located in Central America. In expanding its role in the South Pacific, the United States created a set of rules governing conduct between its sailors and the Samoan people, gave the islanders gifts, and sent a commercial agent to establish its interests. Attempts on the part of the U.S. Navy commander Richard W. Meade to establish Samoa as a protectorate in 1872 failed when the Senate, in response to the American isolationist mood, did not ratify the treaty. Germany was the latecomer to the South Pacific, but quickly caught up with the other powers by establishing a trading company, Godeffrey and Son, at the port of Apia in the late 1850s.[14]

Each of the major powers recognized the strategic and commercial benefits of having a stake in Samoa. Britain was not anxious to invest much money in the islands and chose rather to use them as a bargaining chip in negotiations with Germany over other imperial concerns. The United States wished to maintain its interest primarily for strategic reasons, especially by obtaining the right to build a naval coaling and supply station at Pago Pago. The United States Senate did accept the 1878 treaty granting the United States this station, and in return, the United States agreed to use its "good offices" to mediate in any disagreement between an outside nation and Samoa. The ratification represented a changing American mood and the realization among some that Samoa was important for future American commerce in the South Pacific, even if that amounted to very little in the late 1870s. Just as they had in Hawaii, American secretaries of state cloaked most of these ambitions behind the language of democracy and the right of Samoans to maintain their independence. Though the United States was reluctant to annex Samoa, on the one hand, it did not wish to see any other power seize control. On the other hand, Germany was on a mission; the Germans had imperial aspirations, just as other major European powers, and under the leadership of Bismarck, Samoa fit this design.[15]

In many of the negotiations between the United States and Germany regarding Samoa, Britain either remained silent or favored German demands. But Britain had other and more pressing diplomatic concerns. The British sought greater influence in Egypt in conflict with the French and, even more, opposed German expansion in southwest Africa. To prevent treaties between France and

Germany supporting their positions in Africa, Britain decided to give Bismarck the freedom to colonize in the South Pacific. It was unlikely that Germany would ally with France, given their constant disputes, but Count Bismarck used British fears to gain their support in dealing with Samoan issues.[16]

German aggressiveness shortly before Pendleton's arrival in Berlin led to tensions with the United States. Increasing competition between American farmers who sold foodstuffs in Germany and German farmers resulted in a tariff war. Increasing assertiveness by Germans in Samoa in 1884 exacerbated the tension. The German consul in Samoa forced King Malietoa Laupepa to sign a treaty that created a German-Samoa Council of State consisting of three Germans and two Samoans and made a German officer advisor to him. When Malietoa requested support from other nations, the Germans instigated a rebellion that ended with the ascension of the German-supported candidate, Tamasese, to the throne with control over a portion of Samoa. As a result of these conflicts and the trade war, the United States had suspended diplomatic relations with Berlin in 1884. The following year, the burden of opposing the growing German thirst for colonial acquisitions dropped squarely in the lap of incoming Secretary of State Bayard. Much of Bayard's communication with Bismarck and the Kaiser was conducted through Pendleton.[17]

In late December 1885, King Malietoa entered the district of Apia, which the German consul had effectively taken over and raised his Samoan flag. When Malietoa refused to remove the standard, ten soldiers and an officer from a German warship stationed off the coast landed and removed the flag. Reports to Bayard suggested that the German consul had taken possession of the islands. Because the German minister to the United States, H. von Alvensleben, had earlier proposed a German protectorate over Samoa, Bayard was understandably alarmed. He wired Pendleton to speak directly with Count Bismarck for an explanation and to tell him that American interests must be protected. Pendleton complied and received Bismarck's conciliatory response. According to Bismarck, the German consul had acted without official sanction. In addition, reports to Washington were not entirely accurate, and the consul's actions had not been violent. When the American consul made a similar play and claimed Samoa as an American protectorate without orders from Washington, Bayard also had to backpedal. As a result of the continued tensions and lack of understanding regarding the authority structure in the islands, Bayard called for a conference in Washington to discuss the situation.[18]

Before the convening of these meetings, Pendleton suffered a tremendous personal loss. In May 1886, his daughter-in-law, Marie, who was married to Francis Key Pendleton and was expecting their first child, became quite ill. Mrs. Pendleton and her daughter Jane sailed to New York to help. In spite of their encouragement and comfort, Marie and the baby died during labor. The Pendleton women remained in New York to comfort their son and brother, Frank, following his loss. Shortly after this heartbreak, the Pendletons again faced tragedy. While riding in a carriage through Central Park, Mrs. Pendleton and Jane were in a terrible accident. Their horse spooked and began to run uncontrollably. Alice and Jane jumped from the carriage in an effort to save their lives. Jane survived the ordeal, but Alice did not. The news hit Pendleton like a shot. Bayard, who had watched his own wife suffer from prolonged terminal illness, expressed his heartfelt condolences. The German court gave Pendleton its sympathies as well.[19] But it was a loss from which Pendleton would not recover, especially as he could not return home in time for the funeral. Alice was buried in New York. When Jane recovered from her injuries, she returned to her father's side. Pendleton spoke freely of his sorrow to his friend Bayard, "I was greatly touched by your attendance at the funeral, and your loving tenderness to my poor little daughter." Knowing he had suffered the loss of his own wife, Pendleton commiserated, "In truth we have a brotherhood of sorrow. Berlin seems to me an exile now. . . . If I were not afraid to trust myself without work, I would feel greatly inclined to retire to my own home, but I have the greatest confidence in labor and time to cure the bruised and broken heart."[20] Frank traveled with his sister to Berlin and stayed with his father for a short time before returning to New York and his law practice. Mary and Jane stayed behind to console their father. While Pendleton remained minister, he obtained leave from Bayard and spent two months away from Berlin. Even after he officially returned to duty, Pendleton remained in Bad Homburg, hoping that its mineral spas would hasten his recovery. He only came to the legation infrequently during the summer.[21]

When Pendleton returned and was once again immersing himself in the work of the legation, Bayard planned to convene the Washington Conferences on Samoa the following summer. The conferences began in June 1887 with preliminary meetings between Bayard, Alvensleben, and British minister Sir Lionel Sackville-West. Bayard found the Germans obdurate, and the meetings did not commence as he hoped. Bayard noted that, based on the recorded land claims in the islands, more land was claimed by the three powers than existed. To rectify this situation, he called for a land commission composed of a representative from each of the three powers plus two Samoans. He also suggested a Samoan assembly and the maintenance of the king, vice king, and the traditions of the Samoan culture. To maintain influence in the island government, Bayard advocated that the three powers suggest nominees to the king from which he could choose ministers of foreign relations, interior, and treasury. When Alvensleben recommended a German prime minister because the Germans had the largest commercial interest in Samoa, Bayard balked. The goal, Bayard concluded, was not a protectorate but native autonomy. He clearly stated that the U.S. interest in Samoa would only increase in the future because of the transcontinental railroad and the prospect of a trans-isthmus canal in Central America. The conflict simmered between the United States and Germany. Sackville-West deferred to Alvensleben in the lesser matters, and when the Germans became more aggressive, he simply remained quiet, leaving Bayard to defend himself. Sackville-West privately thought that the three powers ought to divide up the South Pacific, leaving Samoa to the Germans, while the United States could claim the Sandwich Islands (Hawaii) and Britain the Tonga Islands. This position was naive, for the United States already had a clear association with Hawaii due to an 1878 reciprocity treaty. By the time of the meetings, Britain controlled Fiji and divided New Guinea with Germany. Germany also claimed the Solomon and Marshall Islands and was on a quest for more insular holdings. Bayard was under pressure at home to keep the Samoan Islands independent. More and more Americans, including key members of Congress, were beginning to see Samoa as vital to future American interests, especially after the construction of the long hoped-for Central American isthmian canal. They believed Samoa to be the logical supply and strategic base for American commercial and naval vessels when the canal was completed. The issues introduced in the preliminary meetings remained the sticking points throughout the negotiations, and many of the disputes were not resolved.[22]

After the meetings concluded, Germany quickly demonstrated its intractability with regard to Samoa. Based on an obviously contrived issue, German forces demanded $13,000 in reparations from Malietoa for insults and injustices allegedly perpetrated against Germans residing in Samoa. Germany backed this threat by sending four warships to Samoan waters. When Malietoa requested time, Germany declared war and replaced him with Tamasese—this time to rule over all of Samoa. Bayard was furious. Acting for the secretary, Pendleton lashed out at the German government during a dinner at the American legation in Berlin in the presence of a British official. The British minister outwardly agreed with Pendleton in their discussions, but his country failed to act in concert with Bayard's wishes. Again at Bayard's request, Pendleton suggested to Count Bismarck that an election for a Samoan vice king should take place as agreed to at the Washington Conference. Bismarck tended to view those conferences as an ongoing dialogue with few, if any, definite conclusions reached. Bayard rejected this interpretation. He feared that German control of Samoa could interfere with the interests of the United States in the South Pacific. Moreover, Bayard began to receive pressure from various influential Americans to act.[23]

Bayard's consul general in Apia called for military action against the German aggression. The secretary of the navy, William C. Whitney, also believed there should be a military response. President Cleveland pushed Bayard to be more vociferous in his protests. He consented to sending a second U.S. naval vessel to Samoa and called on Germany to accept a king chosen by the Samoans. The American Congress wanted more and appropriated $500,000 to protect American interests in the islands and another $100,000 to improve the harbor at Pago Pago. Nevertheless, Bayard was no imperialist, and he did not believe it proper for the United States to annex Samoa. Further, though beginning to build its new steel navy, American naval power in the South Pacific was no match for Germany's fleet. Cleveland sent the protocols of the Washington Conference to Congress, exposing to them for the first time the manner in which Bayard had stood up to Alvensleben. This information quieted congressional critics for the moment. Count Bismarck, recognizing the American furor over his actions and wanting to prevent a military conflict, called for yet another conference on Samoa, this time in Berlin. Bayard consented.[24]

The issue remained unresolved, however, during Bayard's tenure. The major reason Bayard later cited was that Pendleton suffered a stroke in April 1888, severing an important link between the United States and the German government. Bayard had no one to represent the United States at the impending conference. Pendleton had left Berlin for a brief respite to recover his health after he had experienced what appeared to be a minor illness. Doctors in Wiesbaden, where Pendleton was at the time of the attack, diagnosed it as a non-life-threatening stroke. He did suffer paralysis on his left side, however. Pendleton was strong enough to wire an associate at the legation to take over matters until Chapman Coleman could be appointed chargé d'affaires. Bayard granted Pendleton a leave of absence to recuperate. The doctors urged a three-month recovery period to allow for all of Pendleton's mental abilities to return. They did not think, however, that he would ever regain the use of his left leg. Pendleton was not yet ready to return to work after his sixty days of official leave, so Bayard wrote to Coleman concerning how to handle matters. Coleman was to continue to act as chargé d'affaires. Pendleton had to "be at his post—i.e.—so long as he is at Berlin, or some neighboring part of Germany, 'on summer leave,' as I think the phrase goes."[25] Bayard gave his old friend every possible benefit, but at the sacrifice of making strides toward a resolution of the Samoan question. Bismarck promised no German military action in Samoa until the Berlin conference could meet. Bayard would later lament that Pendleton's ill health had delayed the meeting and prevented him from resolving the matter prior to leaving office.[26]

Pendleton's health did not improve over the summer. By December 1888, though technically in charge of the legation at Berlin, Pendleton was still severely debilitated. One visitor remarked to Bayard on Pendleton's condition, "There is no disposition to converse on any subject, and apparently a general lack of interest in anything. While his mind seemed to act correctly, it was sluggish and he confined himself generally to answering very briefly, questions which might be put to him, and I observed a decided loss of memory as to dates and events."[27] While he resumed limited activity in Berlin, Pendleton was never to return to full health. He maintained his interest in politics back home and watched with dismay as Cleveland lost his reelection bid. With the American delegate to the Berlin conference still undecided, Cleveland thought it better to wait and let the incoming president, Benjamin Harrison, decide who should represent the United States at the meeting. Cleveland's defeat did provide Pendleton a graceful exit from office, and he officially resigned in April 1889. Though counseled to keep Pendleton in office, Harrison accepted his resignation and replaced him with William Walter Phelps of New Jersey.[28] When the Berlin Conference convened later in 1889, Britain, Germany, and the United States agreed to a tripartite protectorate over Samoa. Before the end of the century, the Samoan Islands were divided between the United States and Germany.[29]

Pendleton returned to Bad Homburg during the summer of 1889, continuing his recuperation with his daughters at his side. In the fall, they began to travel west, with the goal of eventually returning to Cincinnati. It was not to be. In Brussels, Belgium, Pendleton once again fell gravely ill and took a room at the Hotel Bellevue to rest and recuperate. Frank, his son, went to visit him along with his sisters, but promptly returned, optimistically reporting on November 23 that his father was doing better. Frank denied a rumor that his father had an abscess and noted that he was only suffering from some stomach trouble and would soon follow him home. However, his father continued to decline and on November 24 took a turn for the worse and passed on into eternity.[30]

Cincinnati's foremost son did not depart without the well-deserved praise of eulogizers. He was mourned and remembered in newspapers across the country. The government he had helped to shape throughout much of the nineteenth century brought his remains back to the United States on a military vessel. The Pennsylvania Railroad conveyed the casket to Cincinnati where Pendleton's body lay in state in Christ Church. He was buried in Spring Grove Cemetery in Cincinnati next to other family members. A host of dignitaries attended the services, including former president Rutherford B. Hayes and the governors of Ohio and Kentucky. Isaac Jordan, a Cincinnati attorney, gave a memorial address to a large gathering.[31] Jordan referred to Pendleton as a politician who viewed his role as that of a "trustee of the power entrusted to him" by Ohioans.[32] He spoke of Pendleton's beliefs, both the personal and the political: "Pendleton, in all his relations in life, was guided by deep and profound convictions. His mind was naturally strongly imbued with a moral and religious element."[33] Expressing his thoughts on Pendleton's belief in things beyond finite man, he noted that Pendleton "believed in God, and in an overruling Providence which governs the affairs of nations and in the lives of men. He believed in the divinity of Christ, his intercession for men, and the resurrection and the life to come."[34] In the end, Jordan suggested that Pendleton's epitaph should read, "Citizen of Cincinnati; United States Senator from Ohio; Author of the Bill to Regulate and Reform the Civil Service of the United States."[35] The Washington *Evening Star* focused on civil service reform in its tribute to the fallen statesman. "The benefit to the country of having such a character in politics, as a counterbalance to the sordid motives and petty aims of so large a multitude of the men who make a trade of public service, is beyond question." Pendleton's legacy went beyond party lines, the editor concluded, because he "surrendered his career as a sacrifice to a principle in which he firmly believed."[36] With all of the stirring scenes and kind words seen in newspapers and heard at the funeral, the *Cincinnati Commercial Gazette* best encapsulated Pendleton's life and political philosophy by quoting from his own farewell speech prior to leaving for Berlin:

> I have always been a Democrat, a partisan Democrat if you please, because I believe that the principles and methods of that party would conduce to the welfare of the country. But I have always held that parties were useful only when they served the highest interests of the country, and that he who served his country most faithfully served also his party most effectively. . . . I have, therefore, sedulously, steadfastly, endeavored to put our party on the highest plane of purity and honor, and to stimulate it to pursue lofty aims and honest methods. . . . I have trusted in the people, and found inspiration in the assured confidence that with them the right would vindicate the act.[37]

Conclusion

George Hunt Pendleton labored his entire political career to achieve three inseparable goals. In an era of intense Democratic factionalism stretching from the 1850s to the 1880s, he sought to unite his divided party around its traditional Jacksonian principles. Such an effort, Pendleton thought, was vital because the Democratic Party, far more than the Republican Party, provided ordinary Americans with a mechanism to shape government operations and implement sound public policies. In that sense, preserving the Democratic Party based on Jacksonianism became an end in itself. Moreover, on a personal level, Pendleton was extraordinarily ambitious. He recognized the rewards the party would bestow on a leader who could achieve those goals.

Yet though these goals do not seem particularly novel or set him apart from the hundreds of other politicos of the nineteenth century, Pendleton was a man who consistently defied expectation. In his commitment to principle, he did not hide his head in the sand and assume that today's problems could be addressed by yesterday's solutions. While he still held on to the principle, he recognized the need to reinterpret it and refashion it to meet new needs. In the process, he helped shape the midwestern Democratic ideology that maintained the party's traditional philosophies while proposing new methods of addressing contemporary issues. In his attempt to reunite his party, Pendleton refused to move toward the moderate middle of the political spectrum as most opponents assumed he would do and as many of his fellow Democrats believed the party had to do following the Civil War. Pendleton understood that the two-party system functioned best when it offered the American people choices—choices that empowered the voter to impact governance on issues of importance to them. And finally, in his quest for personal political success, particularly in the Gilded Age in which many historians see nothing but partisans grasping for power, Pendleton sacrificed his success on the altar of principle. At the moment of his greatest political achievement, the Pendleton Act of 1883, he met his greatest personal defeat. In each of these instances, Pendleton defied contemporary and even historical expectation, in pursuit of the America he idealized.

Influenced by his father's states' rights position, Pendleton adopted Jacksonian principles during the formative years of his career. Only occasionally during those early years did Pendleton waver in his devotion to Jacksonianism out of desperation or a lack of alternatives, such as when he entered the House of Representatives in 1857. Despite Pendleton's momentary wavering, he learned a harsh lesson. Consistency, based on Jacksonianism, was the best method to use in pursuit of his three goals. He utilized this education in practical politics during the events leading up to the Civil War. In the hectic months prior to the secession of the Southern states, Pendleton supported the Jacksonian principle of states' rights and limited government. Based on that premise, he opposed coercion. As an Extreme Peace Democrat, Pendleton achieved national prominence and upheld his philosophical position. While he gained one of his major goals in becoming Gen. George B. McClellan's vice-presidential running mate in the 1864 election, Pendleton failed to unify the Democracy around traditional principles.

After 1865, Pendleton, seeing the dramatic economic repercussions resulting from the war, began an effort to reunite his party, an effort that would continue the rest of his life. He formulated the Ohio Idea to pay off the war debt as painlessly as possible while working to return the country to the specie system so valued by Jacksonians. That commitment had additional dimensions. Pendleton transformed Jackson's hostility toward centralized banking into an effort to lessen the power of the national banking system and to improve the economic position of the common laborer. Pendleton worked against great odds. While most midwestern Democrats lauded his Ohio Idea, conservative probank forces, largely consisting of eastern bankers and Bourbon Democrats, were unsympathetic. Although Pendleton believed that his position was sound and could reunite his divided party, perhaps even securing his presidential nomination in 1868, he underestimated the strength of the Bourbons. They blocked his candidacy at the national convention, choosing Horatio Seymour, who rejected the Ohio Idea. Pendleton experienced an even more bitter defeat the following year when he failed in his campaign to become governor of Ohio. Unable to achieve any of his goals by 1869, Pendleton seemed to have reached the end of a political career notable only for its futility and failure.

That fate was far removed from his course of action. Pendleton was a political creature, and politics was never far from his mind. While he spent much of the early 1870s fighting off personal attacks on his integrity in the wake of the Great Railroad Case and the Kentucky Central Claim, Pendleton never lost sight of his three goals. In 1872, he emerged as an important Democratic powerbroker. In an apparent compromise of party and principle, Pendleton supported fusion with the Liberal Republicans, but fusion was an expedient, not a long-term policy. In particular, Liberal Republicans espoused certain reforms, especially good government through civil service reform, that Pendleton believed could bridge the gap between the Bourbon Democrats and the party's midwestern supporters. In essence, Pendleton took his father's Whig reformism and refashioned it for achieving Jacksonian objectives. Although the combination with Liberal Republicans failed, Pendleton believed that he found the means to secure his long-sought goals.

This episode paid another vital dividend for Pendleton, one more personal in nature. Although he had remained out of office for almost a decade, Pendleton continued to be a force in Ohio politics, often influencing the selection of candidates and the drafting of platforms. For that reason, Ohio Democrats, who controlled the legislature in 1879, returned Pendleton to active public service as a United States senator.

Gaining a national forum to advance his threefold agenda, Pendleton identified himself with civil service reform. To justify his desire to implement a merit system, Pendleton argued that Jackson had sought to provide equal opportunity through the use of the patronage system. In that vein, Jackson attempted to open government jobs to the average man, rather than turn them over to a wealthy party elite. Jackson built his administration on the principle of creating a more democratic government. While some aspects of Jacksonian Democracy were largely illusions, Pendleton sought to turn the rhetoric into reality. Pendleton asserted that the patronage system no longer achieved Jackson's goals and that the merit system was better equipped to do so in America's changing political milieu. Though the means had changed, the principle had not. And Pendleton was not alone in attempting to accomplish this type of adaptation. Stephen Skowronek has argued that presidents Polk and Pierce tried to do something very similar with Jacksonianism during their presidencies.[1] Pendleton truly believed that he could develop party strength and win the next presidential election for the Democrats by fostering civil service reform. In 1883, in the face of intense opposition from his own constituents, Pendleton pushed through the Pendleton Act, his most significant achievement.

Throughout the course of his career, Pendleton demonstrated the supremacy of Jacksonian principles in his political positions. Though at times he appeared willing to seek compromises within his party, and ultimately he had to sacrifice his own political ambitions, he remained faithful to this philosophy. Jacksonian principles dominated Pendleton's beliefs because he was convinced that his other two goals—party advancement and personal achievement—could be attained with faithfulness to principle. In the end, he was wrong. Civil service reform brought neither party unity nor personal success. Yet his consistency provided the party with stability throughout much of the nineteenth century and played a key role in maintaining its viability. Indeed, even though some of his principles were flawed, he left room in his political system for change and adaptation that could address those wrongs in the future. Pendleton stepped forward to lead when some were beginning to believe the party was no longer worth saving. He believed that for the party to remain solvent it had to offer Americans a distinct alternative. Even some who disagreed with Pendleton coalesced around his ideas. He was a focal point for the party, a controversial leader earning both criticism and praise. Whether they agreed with him or not, Pendleton kept members focused on the party and on moving ahead in a political system that at times appeared barely adequate to handle the strains the nation faced.

Ultimately, George Hunt Pendleton's principle was faulty and doomed to failure within the American system. The single greatest flaw was his racism. He is a poignant reminder that while ideology is important in partisanship and effective democracy, it must reflect sound principle to provide lasting benefit and success. A man's approach to politics reveals something significant about him. One's highest goals and aspirations for himself and his society are revealed in political activity, be they crass money grabbing or principled activism. Like the nation's founders, Pendleton understood that the democratic republic required virtuous men to succeed. While he recognized the role of ideology in virtue, his ideology failed to recognize how it limited democracy. In part, sound principle is defined by a proper understanding of democracy, something Pendleton limited only to whites. But even in his failings, Pendleton demonstrates that principle has the capacity to push leaders beyond their personal desires and their limitations toward the betterment of society.

The story of Pendleton's career amply illustrates this. Political scientists have much to offer historians here. Five years before Pendleton's death, a young political science graduate student at Johns Hopkins named Woodrow Wilson completed a manuscript that would become an influential book within the field.[2] Wilson, like Pendleton, had been heavily influenced by the parliamentary system of Britain. Similar to Pendleton's plan to introduce cabinet members into the House and Senate with nonvoting seats to encourage better communication between the branches, Wilson argued for the presidential cabinet to be comprised of senators. He lamented the dearth of communication between the branches of government, within the Congress, and between government and the public. Wilson critiqued the confusing and complex system of committees within Congress that resulted in a lack of accountability. Representatives and senators were seldom heard by the public. Their comments and even their speeches in Congress could be lost in actions of committee chairs or filtered through an unreceptive press. Congressmen spent little time communicating with the president, even when he was a member of their party. While not as concerned about the Common Man as Pendleton, Wilson recognized that the institutions and methods of Congress prevented the public from having a clear understanding of how it operated. In comparison, Britain's Parliament, where people spoke publicly and on the record, created an atmosphere where uninformed or self-serving actions were discredited immediately and parties had to have a coherent philosophy and implementation plan. The public demanded it because individual members could not hide behind the actions of the whole. The American Congress, he argued, dispersed responsibility so much that the public was incapable of holding any individual responsible. This was bad government.

Though couched in varying interpretations, political scientists of the twentieth century have argued on behalf of similar accountability structures. Pendleton's approach to politics left him open to the accountability his constituents might provide. Morris Fiorina in his well-known essay "The Decline of Collective Responsibility in American Politics" provides a pessimistic critique of the American governing system similar to Wilson's.[3] Fiorina notes that responsibility for actions by the government is diffused, and Americans, having little knowledge or understanding of the workings of government, cannot provide the needed accountability. For Fiorina, the solution is to develop well-defined party organizations with clearly demarcated political agendas, easily identifiable by the American public. More recently and more optimistically, John Aldrich notes that individual government officials can be held responsible for their actions at election time. Collective action in Congress can only be assessed through the mechanism of cohesive political parties.[4] Both men highlighted the importance of the role of voters in the accountability structure.

George Hunt Pendleton's career and political philosophy provide a great case study in evaluating these arguments. His attempts at uniting his divided party behind him, based on a strong ideological commitment, allowed for accountability. His midwestern Jacksonian democratic ideals were clearly identifiable. His position on the Ohio Idea and civil service reform were defining, giving voters a clear choice. As a result, he opened himself and his party to the corrective influence of the public. Where ideology was sound, it could be reinforced. Where it was unsound, it could be corrected. While this process takes time, it does provide the system of accountability that political scientists from Wilson to Aldrich have been seeking. Partisan ideology can provide clarity in an otherwise ambiguous governmental process, clarity that voters can see and respond to at the voting booth. Even Pendleton's ignominious removal from the Senate does not undermine this assertion. While the electorate will not always do the right thing, politicians have the responsibility to provide voters with a clear and honest choice. Perhaps what this incident shows is that the founders were right when they suggested the Republic would only last if it had a principled and virtuous citizenry. The next great question, which goes well beyond the scope of this work, is how such an electorate is established.

Pendleton's consistency also sheds light on the nineteenth-century political system in America. While most historians suggest that the Civil War destroyed the "second political party system" and ushered in a period of political equilibrium, Pendleton's career does not support that view.[5] Though the Civil War was a watershed event in many ways, particularly socially and economically, it was much less so politically. The Democratic Party, as viewed from Pendleton's perspective, went through relatively little change after the conflict. The issues shifted, but not much else did. The party divisions before the war still existed after 1865. Party leaders struggled for unity during Reconstruction much as they had during the Kansas crisis. Pendleton and other antebellum party leaders remained influential following the war. Most importantly, in the case of Pendleton, key factions within the party remained committed to the principles that had driven their political activity before secession. But Pendleton's is not a story of stasis alone, for he reinterpreted traditional ideology to meet the changing political needs of postwar America.

As Pendleton faced new issues and challenges for the party during Reconstruction and beyond, he considered them in the same framework and from the same philosophical foundation that he had laid prior to the firing on Fort Sumter. In a political system in which both parties had factional divisions on certain key issues, it was absolutely essential that an ideological demarcation between the parties be maintained. Otherwise, partisan lines would blur. Critics might suggest that Pendleton's conservatism in holding on to Jacksonianism prevented a true unification of the party and a speedy return to power. Pendleton's life seems to indicate a different interpretation. When he tried to bend to accommodate other factions, the party failed miserably at the polls. The resistance by those not committed to principle led to his failure. Rather, Pendleton's lasting heritage is found in his tenacious defense of principle, which acted to preserve the party during the second half of the nineteenth century. Pendleton sustained a party split by civil war and divided in its aftermath as a "respectable minority."[6] He was a force in refashioning it into a party that was clearly distinct from its opponent and founded upon reinterpreted Jacksonian principle. If the Democrats had floundered without any philosophical compass, the party and the two-party system itself might not have lasted at all. That they did is due, in part, to George Hunt Pendleton's lasting, if perhaps unexpected, legacy.

Notes

Introduction

1. John Joline to Thomas Mach, May 6, 1993, Mach personal correspondence.
2. Richard L. McCormick, "The Party Period and Public Policy: An Exploratory Hypothesis," *Journal of American History* 66 (Sept. 1976): 279–98; Joel H. Silbey, *The American Political Nation, 1838–1893,* Stanford Studies in the New Political History (Stanford, Calif.: Stanford Univ. Press, 1991).
3. Michael F. Holt, "Change and Continuity in the Party Period: The Substance and Structure of American Politics, 1835–1885," in *Contesting Democracy: Substance and Structure in American Political History, 1775–2000,* ed. by Byron E. Shafer and Anthony J. Badger (Lawrence: Univ. Press of Kansas, 2001), 93–116.
4. Clifford H. Moore, "Ohio in National Politics, 1865–1896," *Ohio Archaeological and Historical Society Publications* 37 (Apr.–June 1928): 251.

The Early Years

1. Henry A. Ford and Kate B. Ford, *History of Cincinnati, Ohio, With Illustrations and Biographical Sketches* (Cleveland, Ohio: L. A. Williams and Co., 1881), 73–84. A portion of this chapter was previously published as "Family Ties, Party Realities, and Political Ideology: George Hunt Pendleton and Partisanship in Antebellum Cincinnati," *Ohio Valley History* 3, no. 2 (Summer 2003): 17–30, and is reproduced here by permission of the publisher.
2. G. M. D. Bloss, *Life and Speeches of George Hunt Pendleton* (Cincinnati, Ohio: Miami, 1868), 7–8; *Cincinnati Enquirer,* Sept. 21, 1924; *The National Cyclopaedia of American Biography* . . . (New York: James T. White and Co., 1931), 3:273, 10:240; *Biographical Directory of the American Congress, 1774–1949* (Washington, D.C.: GPO, 1950), 1666.
3. Bloss, *Life of Pendleton,* 8; *Biographical Directory,* 1666.

4. Clara Longworth DeChambrun, *Cincinnati. Story of the Queen City* (New York: Charles Scribner's Sons, 1939), 160; "Woodward High School in Cincinnati," *American Journal of Education* 4 (Sept. 1957): 520.

5. "Ormsby Macknight Mitchel," *Dictionary of American Biography* Base Set, American Council of Learned Societies, 1928–1936, reproduced in *Biography Resource Center* (Farmington Hills, Mich.: Thomson Gale, 2005), http://galenet.galegroup.com/servlet/BioRC; Edward Deering Mansfield, *Personal Memories, Social, Political, and Literary, 1803–1843* (1879; repr., New York: Arno and *New York Times,* 1970), 277; DeChambrun, *Cincinnati,* 165; Francis P. Weisenburger, *The Passing of the Frontier, 1825–1850,* vol. 3 of *The History of the State of Ohio* (Columbus: Ohio State Archaeological and Historical Society, 1941), 206.

6. Bloss, *Life of Pendleton,* 11.

7. Dr. Renger to Thomas Mach, Oct. 26, 1992, Mach personal correspondence. Dr. Renger transcribed the Heidelberg records on George H. Pendleton by letter. Unfortunately, the university archives had no further information on his scholastic endeavors or achievement.

8. Bloss, *Life of Pendleton,* 11–16.

9. Notes of Julia Frances Brice, Misc. Personal Papers of Julia Frances Cox, San Jose, California. Julia Frances Brice was the daughter of Pendleton's daughter Jane. Miscellaneous clippings from the *Cincinnati Enquirer,* George H. Pendleton Papers, Ohio Historical Society, Columbus.

10. *New York Times,* Sept. 4, 1864.

11. Pugh and Pendleton were schoolmates at Woodward High and Cincinnati College. Bloss, *Life of Pendleton,* 16; Dumas Malone, ed., *Directory of American Biography* (New York: Charles Scribner's Sons, 1934), 14:419–20.

12. Court records for Cincinnati are currently housed in the Archives and Rare Books Department of the Blegen Library at the University of Cincinnati. Records are very scarce, if available at all, before 1857. Apparently, a courthouse fire destroyed most of them. There was nothing available on Pendleton or Pugh other than a case in which Pendleton himself was the plaintiff.

13. Evidence of Pendleton's involvement in real estate claims is found in the following: George H. Pendleton to A. M. Scarles, July 2, 1850, Eben Lane Papers, Chicago Historical Society, Chicago; George H. Pendleton to Samuel Bispham, May 17, 1854, Gunther Collections, Chicago Historical Society, Chicago; *Williams Cincinnati Directory and Business Advertiser,* vols. 1–37 (Cincinnati, Ohio: C. S. Williams, 1849–1887); Carrington T. Marshall, *A History of the Courts and Lawyers of Ohio* (New York: American Historical Society, 1934), 4:281. Pendleton's practice of the law continued after he entered public office. George H. Pendleton to Samuel Bispham, Esq., Dec. 2, 1858, Pendleton Papers, The Morgan Library, New York.

14. "Edward Deering Mansfield," *Dictionary of American Biography* Base Set, American Council of Learned Societies, 1928–1936, reproduced in *Biography Resource Center;* Mansfield, *Personal Memories,* 235.

15. Arthur M. Schlesinger Jr., *The Age of Jackson* (Boston: Little, Brown and Co., 1945).

16. The Market Revolution refers to the changing economic practices of Americans after 1815. Farmers began to specialize, focusing on one or two crops to sell for a profit

rather than on subsistence farming. Manufacturers began to find better, more efficient ways to produce and sell goods. All of these changes were taking place in an economic milieu rife with advances in communications and transportation capabilities. Harry L. Watson, *Liberty and Power: The Politics of Jacksonian America,* American Century Series, ed. Eric Foner (New York: Hill and Wang, 1990), 28–29.

17. William A. Sullivan, "Did Labor Support Andrew Jackson?" *Political Science Quarterly* 62 (Dec. 1947): 569–80; Edward Pessen, "Did Labor Support Jackson?" *Political Science Quarterly* 64 (June 1949): 262–74; Walter Hugins, *Jacksonian Democracy in the Working Class: A Study of the Workingmen's Movement, 1829–1837* (Stanford, Calif.: Stanford Univ. Press, 1960); Stephen E. Maizlish, *The Triumph of Sectionalism: The Transformation of Ohio Politics, 1844–1856* (Kent, Ohio: Kent State Univ. Press, 1983), 1–20; Watson, *Liberty and Power;* Charles Sellers, *The Market Revolution: Jacksonian America, 1815–1846* (New York: Oxford Univ. Press, 1991); Donald J. Ratcliffe, "The Market Revolution and Party Alignments in Ohio, 1828–1840," in *The Pursuit of Public Power: Political Culture in Ohio, 1787–1861,* ed. Jeffrey P. Brown and Andrew R. L. Cayton (Kent, Ohio: Kent State Univ. Press, 1994), 99–116. David Brown finds the Market Revolution interpretation lacking when applied to the South. David Brown, "Slavery and the Market Revolution: The South's Place in Jacksonian Historiography," *Southern Studies* 4 (1993): 189–207.

18. Lee Benson, *The Concept of Jacksonian Democracy: New York as a Test Case* (Princeton, N.J.: Princeton Univ. Press, 1961), 288–328; Ronald P. Formisano, *The Birth of Mass Political Parties: Michigan, 1827–1861* (Princeton, N.J.: Princeton Univ. Press, 1972); Stephen C. Fox, *The Group Bases of Ohio Political Behavior, 1803–1848* (New York: Garland, 1989), 119–40.

19. See also Daniel Walker Howe, *The Political Culture of the American Whigs* (Chicago: Univ. of Chicago Press, 1979); Michael F. Holt, *The Rise and Fall of the American Whig Party* (New York: Oxford Univ. Press, 1999).

20. Howe, *American Whigs,* 250.

21. Ibid., 302.

22. Lawrence Frederick Kohl, review of *The Rise and Fall of the American Whig Party: Jacksonian Politics and the Onset of the Civil War,* by Michael F. Holt, *American Historical Review* 105 (Dec. 2000): 1744.

23. *Population Schedules of the Seventh Census of the United States, 1850,* roll 687 (Washington, D.C.: National Archives Microfilm Publications, 1964), 41; *Population Schedules of the Eighth Census of the United States, 1860,* roll 973 (Washington, D.C.: National Archives Microfilm Publications, 1967), 477; *Population Schedules of the Ninth Census of the United States, 1870,* roll 1209 (Washington, D.C.: National Archives Microfilm Publications, 1965), 247.

24. *Cleave's Biographical Cyclopaedia of the State of Ohio: City of Cincinnati and Hamilton County* (Philadelphia: J. B. Lippincott and Co., 1873), 20; Benson, *Concept of Jacksonian Democracy,* 288–328; Fox, *Group Bases,* 119–40.

25. Garland A. Haas, *The Politics of Disintegration: Political Party Decay in the United States, 1840–1900* (Jefferson, N.C.: McFarland and Co., 1994), 1–51.

26. Bloss, *Life of Pendleton,* 9; Weisenburger, *Passing of the Frontier,* 215, 396; Norma Lois Peterson, *The Presidencies of William Henry Harrison and John Tyler,* American Presidency Series (Lawrence: Univ. Press of Kansas, 1989), 31–35.

27. Howe, *American Whigs,* 250.

28. Neomercantilism was a political philosophy calling for the government to promote economic growth through its policies. Political piety was another Whig belief that impacted the role of government. Whigs wanted to use legislation to promote their system of morality.

29. Clement Eaton, *Henry Clay and the Art of American Politics,* Library of American Biography (Boston: Little, Brown and Co., 1957), 87–88, 113–14, 171–76; Peterson, *Presidencies of Harrison and Tyler,* 1–15.

30. Richard N. Current, *Daniel Webster and the Rise of National Conservatism,* Library of American Biography (Boston: Little, Brown and Co., 1955), 115–18, 130–31; Eaton, *Henry Clay,* 146–52, 172–78; Eric Foner, *Free Soil, Free Labor, Free Men: The Ideology of the Republican Party before the Civil War* (Oxford: Oxford Univ. Press, 1970; repr., Oxford: Oxford Univ. Press, 1995), vii–xxxix; Peterson, *The Presidencies of Harrison and Tyler,* 66–72, 190–97; Haas, *Politics of Disintegration,* 1–51. For an emphasis on the "other issues," see Michael F. Holt, *The Political Crisis of the 1850s,* Critical Episodes in American Politics Series, ed. Robert A. Divine (New York: John Wiley and Sons, 1978); Michael F. Holt, *Political Parties and American Political Development from the Age of Jackson to the Age of Lincoln* (Baton Rouge: Louisiana State Univ. Press, 1992), 237–64; and Holt, *American Whig Party.*

31. Mark Voss-Hubbard, *Beyond Party: Cultures of Antipartyism in Northern Politics before the Civil War* (Baltimore, Md.: Johns Hopkins Univ. Press, 2002), 14.

32. John Ashworth, "The Sectionalization of Politics, 1845–1860," in *A Companion to Nineteenth-Century America,* ed. William L. Barney (Oxford: Blackwell, 2001), 41.

33. Current, *Daniel Webster,* 177–80; Avery Craven, *The Coming of the Civil War,* 2d ed. (Chicago: Univ. of Chicago Press, 1957), 346; Holt, *Political Crisis,* 102–12, 155–63; Joel Silbey, *The Partisan Imperative: The Dynamics of American Politics before the Civil War* (New York: Oxford Univ. Press, 1985), 166–89; Tyler Anbinder, *Nativism and Slavery: The Northern Know Nothings and the Politics of the 1850s* (New York: Oxford Univ. Press, 1992), 18–19; Voss-Hubbard, *Beyond Party,* 35–36, 107, 214–16.

34. Isaac M. Jordan, in a eulogy to George Hunt Pendleton, stated that the chaos of the Whig Party at this time caused Pendleton to choose the Democratic Party. *George Hunt Pendleton* (Cincinnati, Ohio: n.p., 1890), 25; Stephen Maizlish argues that the second-party system had already dissolved in Ohio by 1849, perhaps justifying the assertion that Pendleton could see the Whig demise coming. Maizlish, *Triumph of Sectionalism,* xiii. Holt sees a decline in the Whig Party during the early to mid-1840s, a revival by the end of the decade, and the eventual destruction of the party by the mid-1850s in *American Whig Party,* 208–11.

35. J. D. B. DeBow, *Statistical View of the United States, 1850* (Washington, D.C.: n.p., 1854), 399, as cited in Francis P. Weisenburger, "A Brief History of the Immigrant Groups in Ohio," in *In the Trek of the Immigrants: Essays Presented to Carl Wittke* (Rock Island, Ill.: Augustana College Library, 1964), 83–84; Weisenburger, *Passing of the Frontier,* 324; Alvin F. Harlow, *The Serene Cincinnatians* (n.p., 1950), 36; Clifford Neal Smith, *Early Nineteenth-Century German Settlers in Ohio (Mainly Cincinnati and Environs), Kentucky, and Other States . . .* (McNeal, Ariz.: Westland, 1984), 50.

36. Weisenburger, "Immigrant Groups in Ohio," 84; Charles Reemelin was the German statesman.

37. William E. Gienapp, *The Origins of the Republican Party, 1852–1856* (New York: Oxford Univ. Press, 1987), 60–64.

38. Ibid.

39. Holt, *Political Parties,* 75–80.

40. There is no major collection of Pendleton papers at any institution or in private collections. I located the living relatives of Pendleton to inquire as to the whereabouts of any extant papers outside of the miscellaneous letters scattered in various collections. Pendleton's great-grandson, John Joline, wrote on May 6, 1993, that any papers kept in the family were probably burned in a fire at his grandparent's house on Long Island in 1926. He was not certain if there had been any papers, but his cousin, Frances C. Cox, agreed that if there had been any in the family, they were probably lost in the fire. The fate of the Pendleton papers remains a mystery, as Pendleton's will also has not been located. The will of his son, Francis Key Pendleton, mentioned no papers, and his son, George Pendleton, died with no heirs. Mr. Joline and Mrs. Cox represent the only other family line, as the third Pendleton child who reached adulthood had no children. Frances C. Cox to Thomas Mach, Nov. 6, 1992, John Joline to Thomas Mach, May 6, 1993, Mach personal correspondence.

41. "George Ellis Pugh," *Dictionary of American Biography* Base Set, American Council of Learned Societies, 1928–1936, Reproduced in *Biography Resource Center* (Farmington Hills, Mich.: Thomson Gale, 2005), http://galenet.galegroup.com/servlet/BioRC.

42. *Cincinnati Commercial,* Sept. 18, 1856.

43. Pugh expressed his opposition to Know-Nothingism often but explicitly in the following letter: "Pleased to make some inquiries about these two cases—and keeps [*sic*] all Abolitionists and Know Nothings out of our Hamilton County post-offices. That one at Newtown is enough for the whole county." George E. Pugh to Alexander Long, May 27, 1856, Alexander Long Papers, Mss fL848, Cincinnati Historical Society, Cincinnati; Newspaper Clipping, n.d., Long Papers; Obituary of George Ellis Pugh, n.d., Rufus King Papers, Mss K54c, Cincinnati Historical Society, Cincinnati; *Cincinnati Enquirer,* May 21, 1847; Owen M. Peterson, "Ohio Leaders in the Democratic Convention of 1860," *Historical and Philosophical Society of Ohio Bulletin* 13 (Apr. 1955): 107.

44. John Ashworth, *"Agrarians" and "Aristocrats": Party Political Ideology in the United States, 1837–1846* (Cambridge: Cambridge Univ. Press, 1983), 178.

45. Ibid., 51, 199–215; Joel Silbey, *The American Political Nation, 1838–1893* (Stanford, Calif.: Stanford Univ. Press, 1991), 171–75; Nicole Etcheson, *The Emerging Midwest: Upland Southerners and the Political Culture of the Old Northwest, 1787–1861* (Bloomington: Indiana Univ. Press, 1996), 142.

46. Etcheson, *The Emerging Midwest,* 94.

47. Nathaniel Greene Pendleton, *Letter on Our Political Troubles* (Washington, D.C.: H. Polkinhorn, 1861), 1–8; Nathaniel Greene Pendleton held that the Southern states had the right to maintain slavery and suggested that the Missouri Compromise be reinstated as the formula for admitting future states. He sought compromise to prevent war, even proposing the formation of a central confederacy made up of border states between the North and the South to prevent bloodshed. While slightly later than the time period being discussed, this letter expressed the principle of states' rights that Nathaniel Greene passed on to his son, George.

48. Marvin Meyers, *The Jacksonian Persuasion: Politics and Belief* (Stanford, Calif.:

Stanford Univ. Press, 1957), 31; Robert V. Remini, *The Life of Andrew Jackson* (New York. Penguin Books, 1988), 305; Holt, *Political Parties,* 54.

49. Lawrence Frederick Kohl, *The Politics of Individualism: Parties and the American Character in the Jacksonian Era* (New York: Oxford Univ. Press, 1989), 5.

50. Ibid., 92.

51. Ashworth, *"Agrarians" and "Aristocrats,"* 19–21, 51, 131; Kohl, *Politics of Individualism,* 5, 6, 26, 58, 61; Silbey, *American Political Nation,* 79–88.

52. Nicole Etcheson, "Private Interest and Public Good: Upland Southerners and Antebellum Midwestern Political Culture," in *The Pursuit of Public Power: Political Culture in Ohio, 1787–1861,* ed. Brown and Cayton, 89; Etcheson, *The Emerging Midwest,* 28–39.

53. Howe, *American Whigs,* 302.

54. Ibid., 303–5.

55. *Ohio Statesman,* Sept. 14, 26, Oct. 6, 19, 1853; Bloss, *Life of Pendleton,* 17.

56. *Ohio Statesman,* Oct. 19, 1853; Bloss, *Life of Pendleton,* 17; Eugene H. Roseboom, *The Civil War Era, 1850–1873,* vol. 4 of *The History of the State of Ohio,* ed. Carl Wittke (Columbus: Ohio State Archaeological and Historical Society, 1944), 272–76.

57. *Ohio Statesman,* Sept. 14, 26, Oct. 6, 1853; Roseboom, *Civil War Era,* 124–36; Ashworth, *"Agrarians" and "Aristocrats,"* 233.

58. Bloss, *Life of Pendleton,* 18; Roseboom, *Civil War Era,* 279.

59. *Journal of the Senate of the State of Ohio,* 51st General Assembly, 1st sess., 1854, 3–4; Bloss, *Life of Pendleton,* 18.

60. *Journal of the Senate of the State of Ohio,* 51st General Assembly, 1st sess., 1854, 53–54.

61. Ibid., 152, 560–63.

62. Ibid., 152–53.

63. Ibid., 257 59, 489, 151.

64. One petition presented by Pendleton for the people of Cincinnati requested that the watchmen be elected by the people. *Journal of the Senate,* 51st General Assembly, 1st sess., 1854, 256.

65. The following provides several examples of Pendleton's compromise position. *Journal of the Senate,* 51st General Assembly, 1st sess., 1854, 490–93, 536–37.

66. *Ohio Statesman,* Sept. 14, 1854; *Cincinnati Commercial,* Sept. 18, 19, 1854.

67. Philip Shriver Klein, *President James Buchanan: A Biography* (University Park: Pennsylvania State Univ. Press, 1962), 286–87; Robert W. Johannsen, *Stephen A. Douglas* (New York: Oxford Univ. Press, 1973; repr., Urbana: Univ. of Illinois Press, 1997), 304–17, 335–37, 342, 435–36; Haas, *Politics of Disintegration,* 45–49.

68. *Cincinnati Commercial,* Sept. 26, 1854; Roseboom, *Civil War Era,* 279–93.

69. *Cincinnati Commercial,* Sept. 28, 29, 1854.

70. Gienapp, *Origins of the Republican Party,* 121.

71. The Buntline Tribe was a secret organization dedicated to placing a $250 tax on every immigrant coming into the country, thereby prohibiting entry to most. *Cincinnati Enquirer,* Oct. 1, 6, 1854.

72. Ibid., Aug. 13, Oct. 1, 3, 1854; *Ohio Statesman,* Sept. 29, 1854; *Cincinnati Commercial,* Oct. 10, 1854. The election results were as follows: Day, 7,716; Pendleton, 4,442. *Ohio Statesman,* Oct. 27, 1854.

73. *Cincinnati Commercial,* Sept. 13, 1855; *Ohio Statesman,* Sept. 16, 1855; *Cincinnati Enquirer,* Oct. 10, 11, 1855.

74. *Cincinnati Enquirer,* June 22, 1855.

75. Roseboom, *Civil War Era,* 298–310.

76. *Cincinnati Enquirer,* Aug. 14, 1856.

77. Ibid., Aug. 21, 1856; Jan. 12, 1855; Jan. 13, 1856.

78. T. C. Day to Fred. Hassaurek, June 29, 1856, Frederick Hassaurek Papers, Ohio Historical Society, Columbus.

79. *Cincinnati Enquirer,* Aug. 21, 1856. From a series of letters by Day to Hassaurek, it appears that Day did indeed have a heart ailment. T. C. Day to Fred. Hassaurek, June 29, Mar. 25, 1856, Hassaurek Papers. See also T. C. Day to Fred. Hassaurek, Mar. 10, May 30, June 24, July 27, 1856, Hassaurek Papers.

80. T. C. Day to Fred. Hassaurek, June 29, Mar. 25, 1856, Hassaurek Papers.

81. *Cincinnati Enquirer,* Aug. 15, 26, Sept. 7, 1856; *Cincinnati Commercial,* Sept. 15, 23, Oct. 7, 1856.

82. *Cincinnati Enquirer,* Aug. 14, 1856.

83. Ibid., Oct. 17, Nov. 7, Dec. 5, 1856.

The Young Politician from Cincinnati

1. *Cincinnati Enquirer,* Jan. 12, 1855.

2. Ibid., Jan. 13, 1856.

3. Roy F. Nichols, *The Disruption of American Democracy* (New York: MacMillan, 1948), 156; Philip Shriver Klein, *President James Buchanan: A Biography* (University Park: Pennsylvania State Univ. Press, 1962), 289–90.

4. Alice Nichols, *Bleeding Kansas* (New York: Oxford Univ. Press, 1954), 46–47, 94; Klein, *James Buchanan,* 300–301; Nicole Etcheson, *Bleeding Kansas: Contested Liberty in the Civil War Era* (Lawrence: Univ. of Kansas Press, 2004), 50–88, 139–168.

5. Robert W. Johannsen, *Stephen A. Douglas* (New York: Oxford Univ. Press, 1973; repr., Urbana: Univ. of Illinois Press, 1997), 553, 564; Etcheson, *Bleeding Kansas,* 146–47.

6. Johannsen, *Stephen A. Douglas,* 286–96; Nichols, *Bleeding Kansas,* 191–93.

7. Klein, *James Buchanan,* 296–97; Damon Wells, *Stephen Douglas: The Last Years, 1857–1861* (Austin: Univ. of Texas Press, 1971), 22–23.

8. Nichols, *Disruption of American Democracy,* 124–25; Wells, *Stephen Douglas,* 22–23.

9. Nichols, *Disruption of American Democracy,* 150–51.

10. *Congressional Globe,* 35th Cong., 1st sess., 1857, 3, Inter-University Consortium for Political and Social Research (ICPSR); G. M. D. Bloss, *Life and Speeches of George Hunt Pendleton* (Cincinnati, Ohio: Miami, 1868), 23; Nichols, *Disruption of American Democracy,* 150–52; Johannsen, *Stephen A. Douglas,* 589.

11. James A. Rawley, *Race and Politics: "Bleeding Kansas" and the Coming of the Civil War* (Philadelphia: J. B. Lippincott, 1969), 232–34; Gunja SenGupta, *For God and Mammon: Evangelicals and Entrepreneurs, Masters and Slaves in Territorial Kansas, 1854–1860* (Athens: Univ. of Georgia Press, 1996), 135. The results of the January 4, 1858, election showed 10,226 opposed to the Lecompton constitution, 138 for the constitution with slavery, and 24 for the constitution without slavery.

12. Klein, *James Buchanan,* 300–303, 310.

13. Kenneth M. Stampp, *And the War Came: The North and the Secession Crisis, 1860–1861* (Binghamton, N.Y.: Vail-Ballou Press, 1950), 47; Avery Craven, *The Coming of the Civil War,* 2d ed. (Chicago: Univ. of Chicago Press, 1957), 387–89; Klein, *James Buchanan,* 300–303, 310; Rawley, *Race and Politics,* 228; SenGupta, *For God and Mammon,* 133; Etcheson, *Bleeding Kansas,* 143.

14. Nichols, *Disruption of American Democracy,* 156; Rawley, *Race and Politics,* 246; Wells, *Stephen Douglas,* 30–42; Robert W. Johannsen, *The Frontier, the Union, and Stephen A. Douglas* (Urbana: Univ. of Illinois Press, 1989), 114.

15. *Congressional Globe,* 35th Cong., 1st sess., 1858, 12, ICPSR; Nichols, *Disruption of American Democracy,* 158–59.

16. *Cincinnati Commercial,* Sept. 16 to Oct. 12, 1858. The *Commercial* published a series of letters from Timothy C. Day containing these charges.

17. Nichols, *Disruption of American Democracy,* 160–67, 209–10.

18. *Congressional Globe,* 35th Cong., 1st sess., 1858, 18, ICPSR; Rawley, *Race and Politics,* 247; Wells, *Stephen Douglas,* 43–44.

19. *Cincinnati Enquirer,* Apr. 2, 1858; Nichols, *Disruption of American Democracy,* 209–10; Johannsen, *Stephen A. Douglas,* 610–11.

20. Nichols, *Disruption of American Democracy,* 169–70; Donald R. Moorman with Gene A. Sessions, *Camp Floyd and the Mormons: The Utah War* (Salt Lake City: Univ. of Utah Press, 1992), 10–20.

21. *Congressional Globe,* 35th Cong., 1st sess., 1858, 20, ICPSR; Nichols, *Disruption of American Democracy,* 168–69; Rawley, *Race and Politics,* 248; Johannsen, *Stephen A. Douglas,* 610.

22. Wells, *Stephen Douglas,* 44; Johannsen, *Stephen A. Douglas,* 609–10; Johannsen, *Frontier,* 240.

23. Floyd Oliver Rittenhouse, "George Hunt Pendleton: With Special Reference to His Congressional Career" (M.A. thesis, Ohio State University, 1932), 10; Nichols, *Disruption of American Democracy,* 171–72; Rawley, *Race and Politics,* 248–50; SenGupta, *For God and Mammon,* 136.

24. Rawley, *Race and Politics,* 250; Wells, *Stephen Douglas,* 44–48; Johannsen, *Stephen A. Douglas,* 610–16.

25. *Cincinnati Enquirer,* May 1, 1858; *Congressional Globe,* 35th Cong., 1st sess., 1858, 24, ICPSR; Rawley, *Race and Politics,* 250; Wells, *Stephen Douglas,* 46.

26. George H. Pendleton, *Letter of George H. Pendleton, of Ohio, to His Constituents* (Washington, D.C.: n.p., 1858), 2.

27. Ibid., 5–6.

28. Ibid., 5.

29. George H. Pendleton, *Speech of Hon. George H. Pendleton, of Ohio, on The Admission of Kansas; Delivered in the House of Representatives, June 9, 1858* (Washington, D.C.: Congressional Globe Office, 1858), 5.

30. *Cincinnati Enquirer,* May 1, 1858.

31. *Congressional Globe,* 35th Cong., 1st sess., 1858, 327; *Cincinnati Enquirer,* Jan. 29, 1858.

32. *Congressional Globe,* 35th Cong., 1st sess., 1858, 16, ICPSR.

33. *Congressional Globe,* 35th Cong., 1st sess., 1858, 327.

34. *Journal of the Senate of the State of Ohio,* 51st General Assembly, 1st sess., 1854, 73–74; *Ohio Statesman,* Jan. 13, 1854.

35. *Congressional Globe,* 35th Cong., 1st sess., 1858, 33, 43, ICPSR.

36. George H. Pendleton, *Speech of Hon. George H. Pendleton, of Ohio, on the Bill to Increase the Army; Delivered in the House of Representatives, March 17, 1858* (Washington, D.C.: Congressional Globe Office, 1858), 5.

37. *Congressional Globe,* 35th Cong., 1st sess., 1858, 1166–69; Pendleton, *Speech on the Bill to Increase the Army,* 3–5; Rittenhouse, "George Hunt Pendleton," 8.

38. Pendleton, *Speech on the Bill to Increase the Army,* 4.

39. Moorman, *Camp Floyd,* 10–21.

40. Pendleton, *Speech on the Bill to Increase the Army,* 4.

41. Ibid.

42. Ibid., 5.

43. Moorman, *Camp Floyd,* 41–42.

44. Robert J. Rayback, *Millard Fillmore: Biography of a President* (New York: Henry Stewart, 1959), 297–99.

45. Pendleton, *Speech on the Bill to Increase the Army,* 7.

46. *Congressional Globe,* 35th Cong., 2d sess., 1859, 51–53, ICPSR; Klein, *James Buchanan,* 325.

47. *New York Times,* Oct. 4, 1859; Bloss, *Life of Pendleton,* 25.

48. Rittenhouse, "George Hunt Pendleton," 11; Roseboom, *Civil War Era,* Eugene H. Roseboom, *The Civil War Era, 1850–1873,* vol. 4 of *The History of the State of Ohio,* ed. Carl Wittke (Columbus: Ohio State Archaeological and Historical Society, 1944), 336–39; Nichols, *Disruption of American Democracy,* 209–10.

49. *Cincinnati Commercial,* Sept. 16 to Oct. 12, 1858. This source material consisted of a series of open letters by T. C. Day printed in the editorial column.

50. Rutherford B. Hayes to Guy M. Bryan, Oct. 11, 1858, Rutherford B. Hayes Papers, Rutherford B. Hayes Presidential Library, Fremont, Ohio.

51. *Cincinnati Enquirer,* Sept. 23, Oct. 9, 12, 1858.

52. Pendleton showed growing strength among the electorate. In 1856, he had only won by a plurality. The combined number of votes of his two competitors would have defeated him. In 1858, Pendleton gained a majority victory. *Cincinnati Commercial,* Oct. 14, 1858.

53. *Cincinnati Enquirer,* May 29, 1858; Rittenhouse, "George Hunt Pendleton," 13.

54. *Cincinnati Enquirer,* Oct. 19, 1859; Stephen B. Oates, *To Purge This Land with Blood: A Biography of John Brown* (New York: Harper and Row, 1970), 274–302, 351–52; see also Hinton R. Helper, *Compendium of The Impending Crisis of the South* (1860; repr., Miami, Fla.: Mnemosyne, 1969).

55. Nichols, *Disruption of American Democracy,* 270–72.

56. *Congressional Globe,* 36th Cong., 1st sess., 1860, 533, 617–18; Nichols, *Disruption of American Democracy,* 272–75.

57. *Congressional Globe,* 36th Cong., 1st sess., 1860, 1193. Pendleton pursued the port of entry bill in the second session of the 36th Congress as well. Ibid., 36th Cong., 2d sess., 1861, 363. Pendleton's petition on the tariff came in the first session. Ibid., 36th Cong., 1st sess., 1860, 1984.

58. Ibid., 36th Cong., 1st sess., 1860, 2122–23; Bloss, *Life of Pendleton,* 23–25.

59. *Congressional Globe,* 36th Cong., 1st sess., 1860, 2123.

60. Ibid., 1095–96, 1202, 3085–86. Pendleton voted to table the Republican plan. Ibid., 8–10, 12–13, ICPSR; Nichols, *Disruption of American Democracy,* 151–53, 275–76.

61. *Congressional Globe,* 36th Cong., 1st sess., 1860, 1206–8; Ibid., 14, ICPSR.

62. *Congressional Globe,* 36th Cong., 1st sess., 1860, 1640 and 1645; Rawley, *Race and Politics,* 251.

63. *Congressional Globe,* 36th Cong., 1st sess., 1860, 1645.

64. Ibid., 1640–46; *Cincinnati Enquirer,* Apr. 17, 1860; *Congressional Globe,* 36th Cong., 1st sess., 1860, 17, ICPSR, and 36th Cong., 2d sess., 1861, 45, ICPSR.

65. *Congressional Globe,* 36th Cong., 1st sess., 1860, 1802–4.

66. George E. Pugh to Thos. C. Reynolds, Apr. 5, 1860, Charles E. Rice Collection, Ohio Historical Society, Columbus; *Cincinnati Enquirer,* Sept. 10, Dec. 1, 1859; Jan. 5, 1860; *New York Times,* Jan. 10, 1860.

67. George E. Pugh, *Speech of George E. Pugh, of Ohio, in the Democratic National Convention at Charleston, Friday, April 27, 1860* (n.p.: Lemuel Towers, 1860), 1–7, 11; *Official Proceedings of the Democratic National Convention, held in 1860, at Charleston and Baltimore* (Cleveland, Ohio: Nevins' Print, Plain Dealer Job Office, 1860), 37–38; Owen M. Peterson, "Ohio Leaders in the Democratic Convention," *Historical and Philosophical Society of Ohio Bulletin* 13 (Apr. 1955): 108–13; William B. Hesseltine, ed., *Three against Lincoln: Murat Halstead Reports the Caucuses of 1860* (Baton Rouge: Louisiana State Univ. Press, 1960), 51–57, 68–74; Joseph John Hemmer Jr., "The Democratic National Conventions of 1860: Discourse of Disruption in Rhetorical-Historical Perspective" (Ph.D. diss., University of Wisconsin, 1969), 156–59.

68. *Democratic Official Proceedings, 1860,* 182; *Cincinnati Enquirer,* May 18, 1860; Hesseltine, *Three against Lincoln,* 185–207, 232–40, 250–59, 271–78; Wells, *Stephen Douglas,* 235–36; Johannsen, *Stephen A. Douglas,* 764, 769–70. Douglas's proposals for withdrawal were less than magnanimous, according to Wells, because he knew that the conditions he placed on the withdrawal would not be accepted by Southerners.

69. S. S. Cox to Gen. Cass, July 15, 1860, Samuel S. Cox Papers, Ohio Historical Society, Columbus; Bloss, *Life of Pendleton,* 26; *Cincinnati Enquirer,* July 11, 1860; *Cincinnati Commercial,* Sept. 5, 12, 25, Oct. 3, 1860.

70. Bloss, *Life of Pendleton,* 26; Rittenhouse, "George Hunt Pendleton," 15–16. For further information on the 1860 elections and the Democratic response to Abolitionist Republicans, see John T. Hubbell, "Politics as Usual: The Northern Democracy and Party Survival, 1860–61," *Illinois Quarterly* 36 (1973): 27–28; Eric J. Cardinal, "The Ohio Democracy and the Crisis of Disunion, 1860–1861," *Ohio History* 86 (Winter 1977): 24–25.

71. *Cincinnati Enquirer,* Oct. 16, 1860.

72. Ibid., Oct. 11, Nov. 8, 30, 1860; Rittenhouse, "George Hunt Pendleton," 16.

73. *Cincinnati Enquirer,* Dec. 20, 1860. The paper expressed similar opinions earlier as well. Ibid., Oct. 31, 1860.

74. George H. Pendleton to Rufus King, Dec. 25, 1860, Rufus King Papers, Mss K54c, Cincinnati Historical Society, Cincinnati.

75. Hubbell, "Politics as Usual," 22–31; John T. Hubbell, "The Douglas Democrats and the Election of 1860," *Mid-America* 54 (1973): 126–29; Cardinal, "Ohio Democracy and the Crisis of Disunion," 21–27, 38–39.

76. Edward McPherson, *The Political History of the United States during the Great Rebellion . . .* (Washington, D.C.: Philip and Solomons, 1865), 64–65; Bloss, *Life of Pendleton,* 29–31.

77. Pendleton's petition, given to him by Cincinnati businessmen, was deemed by the *Cincinnati Commercial* to be a fraud. The paper first discounted the number and then claimed that many of the signatures represented men who denied signing the petition. Pendleton acknowledged the possibility of fraud because he had not researched the document. A municipal election in Cincinnati two months later, however, reinforced the assertion that most Cincinnatians supported the compromise. The Democratic ticket ran in support of the proposal and won a majority of four thousand votes. *Congressional Globe,* 36th Cong., 2d sess., 1861, 691; Bloss, *Life of Pendleton,* 27.

78. Stampp, *And The War Came,* 40–45; Craven, *Coming of the Civil War,* 433–36; James M. McPherson, *Ordeal by Fire: The Civil War and Reconstruction* (New York: Alfred A. Knopf, 1982), 139–40.

79. George H. Pendleton, *Speech of Hon. George H. Pendleton, of Ohio, on the State of the Union; Delivered in the House of Representatives, January 18, 1861* (n.p.: Lemuel Towers, 1861), 4.

80. Ibid., 5.

81. Ibid., 7.

82. Ibid.

83. Ibid., 8.

84. John Sherman, *John Sherman's Recollections of Forty Years in the House, Senate and Cabinet: An Autobiography* (Chicago: Werner, 1895), 174.

85. Ibid.

86. *Cincinnati Commercial,* clipping, n.d., 1861, found in Alexander Long Papers, Mss fL848, Cincinnati Historical Society, Cincinnati.

87. George L. Converse to S. S. Cox, n.d., 1861, Jan. 9, 1861, Cox Papers.

88. *Congressional Globe,* 36th Cong., 2d sess., 1860, 41–42, ICPSR; McPherson, *History of the Rebellion,* 76–77.

89. Ibid., 67–69. For members of the Committee of Thirty-three, see *Congressional Globe,* 36th Cong., 2d sess., 1860, 22. For a detailed examination of the Peace Conference, see Robert Gray Gunderson, *Old Gentlemen's Convention: The Washington Peace Conference of 1861* (Madison: Univ. of Wisconsin Press, 1961).

90. McPherson, *History of the Rebellion,* 67–80; *Congressional Globe,* 36th Cong., 2d sess., 1861, 45, ICPSR.

91. *Congressional Globe,* 36th Cong., 2d sess., 1861, 47–55, ICPSR; Nichols, *Disruption of American Democracy,* 453, 485–91.

92. Nathaniel Greene Pendleton, *Letter on Our Political Troubles* (Washington, D.C.: H. Polkinhorn, 1861), 1–8.

93. John C. Calhoun, *"A Disquisition on Government" and Selections from the "Discourse,"* The American Heritage Series, ed. C. Gordon Post, vol. 10 (New York: Liberal Arts Press, 1953), 19–31, 100–104. Calhoun suggested that the numerical majority system in America be replaced by a "concurrent" majority system. In so doing, he argued, each interest or section of the country could have a voice in legislation, protecting each from deleterious bills supported by a numerical majority. Margaret L. Coit, *John C. Calhoun:*

American Portrait (Boston: Houghton Mifflin, 1930), 231, 528–29; John Niven, *John C. Calhoun and the Price of Union: A Biography* (Baton Rouge: Louisiana State Univ. Press, 1988), 328–33.

94. *The Record of Hon. Clement L. Vallandigham on Abolition, the Union, and the Civil War* (Columbus, Ohio: J. Walter and Co., 1863), 73–93.

95. *Congressional Globe,* 35th Cong., 2d sess., 1861, 43, ICPSR.

96. William Catton and Bruce Catton, *Two Roads to Sumter* (New York: McGraw-Hill, 1963), 275–80; McPherson, *Ordeal by Fire,* 140–45; Stampp, *And The War Came,* 271–86.

97. *Cincinnati Enquirer,* Apr. 18, 1861.

98. Bloss, *Life of Pendleton,* 34.

The Tortuous Course: Pendleton and the Peace Democrats

1. Elbert J. Benton, Daniel J. Ryan, and Wood Gray are among those historians guilty of mischaracterizing the Peace Democrats. Henry Clyde Hubbart and Eugene H. Roseboom began the revision of this interpretation of Peace Democrats by noting that while there were some pro-Southern Copperheads, they were the exception. Most were Peace Democrats who reacted conservatively to Republican radicalism. Roseboom recognized that there were distinct factions within the Peace Democracy. Elbert J. Benton, *The Movement for Peace without Victory during the Civil War* (Cleveland, Ohio: Western Reserve Historical Society, 1918); Daniel J. Ryan, *Lincoln and Ohio* (Cleveland, Ohio: Ohio State Archaeological and Historical Society, 1923); Henry Clyde Hubbart, *The Older Middle West, 1840–1880: Its Social, Economic, and Political Life and Sectional Tendencies Before, During, and After the Civil War* (New York: D. Appleton-Century, 1936), 186; Wood Gray, *The Hidden Civil War: The Story of the Copperheads* (New York: Viking Press, 1942); Eugene H. Roseboom, *The Civil War Era, 1850–1873,* vol. 4 of *The History of the State of Ohio,* ed. Carl Wittke (Columbus: Ohio State Archaeological and Historical Society, 1944). Roseboom continued his revisionist writing in an article. Eugene H. Roseboom, "Southern Ohio and the Union in 1863," *Mississippi Valley Historical Review* 39 (1952): 29–44. See also George Fort Milton, *Abraham Lincoln and the Fifth Column* (New York: Vanguard Press, 1942); Richard O. Curry, "The Union As It Was: A Critique of Recent Interpretations of the 'Copperheads,'" *Civil War History* 13 (Mar. 1967): 25–39; and Eric John Cardinal, "The Democratic Party of Ohio and the Civil War: An Analysis of a Wartime Political Minority" (Ph.D. diss., Kent State University, 1981).

2. Frank L. Klement, *Lincoln's Critics: The Copperheads of the North,* ed. with introduction by Steven K. Rogstad (Shippensburg, Pa.: White Maine Books, 1999).

3. Vallandigham's brother previously attempted to exonerate him of treason. James L. Vallandigham, *A Life of Clement L. Vallandigham* (Baltimore, Md.: Turnbull Brothers, 1872), 369–85. The most prolific writer in the field, Frank L. Klement, was a revisionist. He viewed the Peace Democracy as the conservatives of the era. He debunked the accusation that the Sons of Liberty were disloyal and showed Vallandigham's involvement in the organization to be minimal. He found the Sons to be little more than a political fraternity obsessed with personal liberties and Democratic success. Some of Klement's works

include *The Copperheads in the Middle West* (Chicago: Univ. of Chicago Press, 1960); *The Limits of Dissent* (Lexington: Univ. Press of Kentucky, 1970); "Sound and Fury: Civil War Dissent in the Cincinnati Area," *Cincinnati Historical Society Bulletin* 35 (1977): 99–114.

4. John T. Hubbell, "Politics as Usual: The Northern Democracy and Party Survival, 1860–61," *Illinois Quarterly* 36 (1973): 22–35; Joel H. Silbey, *A Respectable Minority: The Democratic Party in the Civil War Era, 1860–1868* (New York: W. W. Norton and Co., 1977), 28–38. See also Leonard P. Curry, "Congressional Democrats: 1861–1863," *Civil War History* 12 (Sept. 1966): 213–29; Jean H. Baker, "A Loyal Opposition: Northern Democrats in the Thirty-seventh Congress," *Civil War History* 25 (June 1979): 139–55. David E. Long disagreed with both Klement and Silbey, seeking to extol Lincoln by denigrating the Peace Men, much as contemporary Republicans had. David E. Long, *The Jewel of Liberty: Abraham Lincoln's Re-Election and the End of Slavery* (Mechanicsburg, Pa.: Stackpole Books, 1994).

5. Silbey identified two main groups of Peace men utilizing Michael Les Benedict's significant new interpretation. Benedict named the Extreme and Moderate Peace groups. Silbey used different titles but a similar breakdown. A third grouping, the peace-at-any-price men, is essential, however, for a complete picture of the Peace factions. Michael Les Benedict, *A Compromise of Principle: Congressional Republicans and Reconstruction, 1863–1869* (New York: W. W. Norton and Co., 1974); Silbey, *Respectable Minority*, 92. For a more recent work, but one that returns to the more traditional and unsophisticated approach to Peace Men, see Joanna Cowden, *"Heaven Will Frown on Such a Cause As This": Six Democrats Who Opposed Lincoln's War* (Lanham, Md.: Univ. Press of America, 2001).

6. *Congressional Globe,* 38th Cong., 1st sess., 1864, 1517–19; Gray, *Hidden Civil War,* 160; Klement, *Copperheads in the Middle West,* 229–30; H. H. Wubben, "Copperhead Charles Mason: A Question of Loyalty," *Civil War History* 24 (Mar. 1978): 56.

7. Christopher Dell's work covered a longer period of time and attempted to delineate more precisely the different kinds of Democrats. He also chronicled the changes made over time by certain Democrats. Dell's work is helpful in analyzing specific individuals, but his criteria for categorization led him to few conclusions. For example, Samuel S. Cox was placed in four different groups at various times throughout his career. Dell's results leave the reader with only a blurred perspective of each Democrat due to constant category hopping. The information on Pendleton was sketchy, and Dell fell into the trap of lumping him with men like Vallandigham without qualification. Benedict's categorizations are more helpful for examining larger group trends within the party. Christopher Dell, *Lincoln and the War Democrats: The Grand Erosion of Conservative Tradition* (London: Associated Univ. Press, 1975).

8. Benedict labeled them Extreme Peace Democrats because they refused to compromise their position through unlimited support of the Republican war policies. Benedict, *Compromise of Principle*, 339–41, 344–45, 391–92.

9. Gray, *Hidden Civil War,* 43; Klement, *Copperheads in the Middle West,* 112–18; Frank L. Klement, "The Democrats as Sectionalists," in *Lincoln and Civil War Politics,* ed. James A. Rawley (Huntington, N.Y.: Robert E. Krieger, 1977), 97–102; Silbey, *Respectable Minority,* 100–105.

10. "George Hunt Pendleton," *Encyclopedia of World Biography*, 2d ed., 17 vols. (Gale Research, 1998), reproduced in *Biography Resource Center* (Farmington Hills, Mich.: Thomson Gale, 2005), http://galenet.galegroup.com/servlet/BioRC.

11. Nicole Etcheson, *The Emerging Midwest: Upland Southerners and the Political Culture of the Old Northwest, 1787–1861* (Bloomington: Indiana Univ. Press, 1996), 39.

12. *Evening Star,* Feb. 16, 1880; Edward McPherson, *The Political History of the United States during the Great Rebellion . . .* (Washington, D.C.: Philip and Solomons, 1865): The following votes exemplify the differences between Pendleton and Vallandigham. Pendleton was less radical in his voting. To table a resolution stating that suppression was impractical—Pendleton: yea, Vallandigham: nay, p. 76; Naval Appropriations Bill, 1861—Pendleton: dodged, Vallandigham: nay, p. 89; Resolution blaming war on disunionists in the South—Pendleton: yea, Vallandigham: dodged, p. 285; Resolution supporting Maj. Anderson and the president's action to aid him—Pendleton: dodged, Vallandigham: nay, p. 76. Klement, "Democrats as Sectionalists," 102.

13. Eugene H. Roseboom, *The Civil War Era, 1850–1873,* vol. 4 of *The History of the State of Ohio,* ed. Carl Wittke (Columbus: Ohio State Archaeological and Historical Society, 1944), 433; Klement, *Limits of Dissent,* 309–13.

14. Benedict, *Compromise of Principle,* 339–41, 344–45, 391–92.

15. David Lindsey, *"Sunset" Cox: Irrepressible Democrat* (Detroit: Wayne State Univ. Press, 1959), 54, 57; Silbey, *Respectable Minority,* 111.

16. Lindsey, *"Sunset" Cox,* 70, 90–95.

17. The lack of Pendleton's personal correspondence resulted in a scarcity of information for balancing the Republican press and campaign literature.

18. Charles Mason, a prominent Iowa Peace Democrat, provides another comparison to further explain Pendleton's political position. Mason drew a line between himself and the peace-at-any-price men but privately expressed his desire to see the Confederates win the war. Publicly, he only thinly veiled this view. He was so fearful that a Northern victory would mean the end of civil liberties that he did not want to see the Union forces prevail. Conversely, there is no evidence that Pendleton ever expressed a desire to see the Confederates win in battle. While he feared the erosion of liberties, he was willing to give limited support to the Northern war effort. Both men technically fit into the Extreme Peace category, but there were obvious differences. Wubben, "Copperhead Charles Mason," 52–65.

19. Kenneth M. Stampp, *And the War Came: The North and the Secession Crisis, 1860–1861* (Binghamton, N.Y.: Vail-Ballou Press, 1950), 288.

20. McPherson, *History of the Rebellion,* 123–29.

21. G. M. D. Bloss, *Life and Speeches of George Hunt Pendleton* (Cincinnati, Ohio: Miami, 1868), 34.

22. Charles R. Wilson, "Cincinnati A Southern Outpost in 1860–1861?" *Mississippi Valley Historical Review* 24 (1938): 473–82.

23. *Congressional Globe,* 37th Cong., 1st sess., 1861, 95; Bloss, *Life of Pendleton,* 35.

24. *Congressional Globe,* 37th Cong., 1st sess., 1861, 95; George H. Pendleton, *Hear Hon. George H. Pendleton* (n.p., n.d.), 1–2; Bloss, *Life of Pendleton,* 35, 37. Pendleton's pamphlet contains letters to Hon. John B. Haskin and Hon. C. L. Ward in which Pendleton states his belief that he remained consistent to his July 1861 speech throughout the Civil War. These letters and an additional message to an unnamed Missouri Democrat can also be found in McPherson, *History of the Rebellion,* 422.

25. *Congressional Globe,* 37th Cong., 1st sess., 1861, 7–8, ICPSR.

26. Ibid.

27. *Congressional Globe,* 37th Cong., 1st sess., 1861, 195–96, 365. Pendleton also supported increasing regular army pay. *Congressional Globe,* 37th Cong., 1st sess., 1861, 10, ICPSR; *Cincinnati Enquirer,* July 19, 1861.

28. *Congressional Globe,* 37th Cong., 1st sess., 1861, 9, ICPSR; Leonard P. Curry, *Blueprint for Modern America: Nonmilitary Legislation of the First Civil War Congress* (Nashville, Tenn.: Vanderbilt Univ. Press, 1968), 29–30. Pendleton's position on the regular army was in marked contrast to his earlier call for enlarging the army to protect the frontier and crush Indian and Mormon rebellions. His explanation appeared in his earlier comments concerning the war effort. He did not wish to increase Lincoln's patronage. In addition, he cited the incredible public response to the outbreak of hostilities as being sufficient to meet the needs. Another explanation may be found in the common misconception, or perhaps hope, that the war would be short-lived. Finally, Pendleton's earlier support of military expansion shows that he was no pacifist. Yet, in the earlier situations, he saw no constitutional conflict as he did with coercion of the South. Further evidence of Pendleton's desire to prevent the growth of Lincoln's power with regard to the army is seen in his vote against a bill to give the president power to dismiss volunteer or regular army officers without proper court martial. *Congressional Globe,* 37th Cong., 1st sess., 1861, 9, ICPSR.

29. Pendleton's increased activity in this Congress as compared with previous sessions shows his gain in reputation. He was even spoken of as a possible candidate for speaker. *Congressional Globe,* 37th Cong., 1st sess., 1861, 4, ICPSR; Floyd Oliver Rittenhouse, "George Hunt Pendleton: With Special Reference to His Congressional Career" (M.A. thesis, Ohio State University, 1932), 25; Curry, *Blueprint for Modern America,* 31–32.

30. *Congressional Globe,* 37th Cong., 1st sess., 1861, 376–77.

31. *Cincinnati Enquirer,* July 27, 1861.

32. *Congressional Globe,* 37th Cong., 1st sess., 1861, 6, ICPSR; *Cincinnati Enquirer,* July 18, 1861. At the Ohio state Democratic Convention near the end of the first session of Congress, the Democrats called for a similar national conference to discuss how to restore peace. *American Annual Cyclopedia and Register of Important Events of the Year 1861* (New York: D. Appleton and Co., 1862), 559.

33. *Cincinnati Enquirer,* Aug. 4, 1861.

34. *Congressional Globe,* 37th Cong., 1st sess., 1861, 8–10, ICPSR; *Cincinnati Enquirer,* Aug. 4, 1861.

35. *Congressional Globe,* 37th Cong., 1st sess., 1861, 176, 202–3; *Congressional Globe,* 37th Cong., 1st sess., 1861, 7, ICPSR; F. W. Taussig, *The History of the Present Tariff, 1860–1883,* Questions of the Day (New York: G. P. Putnam's Sons, 1885), 4–32; Edward Stanwood, *American Tariff Controversies in the Nineteenth Century* (1903; repr., New York: Russell and Russell, 1967), 2:126–27; Curry, *Blueprint for Modern America,* 149–53.

36. *Congressional Globe,* 37th Cong., 1st sess., 1861, 409–15; ibid., 37th Cong., 1st sess., 1861, 9–10, ICPSR; Rittenhouse, "George Hunt Pendleton," 29; Curry, *Blueprint for Modern America,* 75–77; Patricia M. L. Lucie, "Confiscation: Constitutional Crossroads," *Civil War History* 23 (Dec. 1977): 307–16.

37. Dean B. Mahin, *One War at a Time: The International Dimensions of the American Civil War* (Washington, D.C.: Brassey's, 1999), 58–82. See also Gordon H. Warren, *Fountain of Discontent: The Trent Affair and Freedom of the Seas* (Boston: Northeastern Univ. Press, 1981).

38. *Evening Star,* Jan. 9, 1862, Jan. 20, 1860.

39. *Congressional Globe,* 37th Cong., 2d sess., 1861, 40.

40. Ibid.; McPherson, *History of the Rebellion,* 179. Alexander Groth notes that of the close to fourteen thousand people arrested during the war, most were held only a short time. Groth argues that Lincoln was no dictator and that even in these actions he acted without malice and tried to ensure at least "some form of due process in terms of trials and avenues of appeal in the more substantial, serious cases." Herman Belz agrees, as does Cowden, who noted that "Lincoln's actual record reveals considerable restraint." Cowden, *"Heaven Will Frown,"* 11; Alexander Groth, *Lincoln: Authoritarian Savior* (Lanham, Md.: Univ. Press of America, 1996), 138–51; Herman Belz, *Abraham Lincoln, Constitutionalism, and Equal Rights in the Civil War Era* (New York: Fordham Univ. Press, 1998), 19–43. See also Mark E. Neely Jr., *The Fate of Liberty: Abraham Lincoln and Civil Liberties* (New York: Oxford Univ. Press, 1991); Jennifer M. Lowe, *The Supreme Court and the Civil War* (Washington, D.C.: Supreme Court Historical Society, 1996).

41. Abraham Lincoln, "Special Session Message," in *A Compilation of the Messages and Papers of the Presidents, 1789–1907,* ed. James D. Richardson (Washington, D.C.: Bureau of National Literature and Art, 1908), 6:20–31; McPherson, *History of the Rebellion,* 126.

42. George H. Pendleton, *Power of the President to Suspend the Privilege of Habeas Corpus, Speech of Hon. George H. Pendleton, of Ohio, in the House of Representatives, December 10, 1861* (n.p., n.d.), 2–3.

43. D. A. Mahony, *The Prisoner of State* (New York: Carleton, 1863), 46–74; James G. Randall, *Constitutional Problems under Lincoln* (New York: D. Appleton and Co., 1926), 120–25; Kenneth A. Bernard, "Lincoln and Civil Liberties," *The Abraham Lincoln Quarterly* 6 (Sept. 1951): 380–81; Klement, *Copperheads of the Middle West,* 17–18.

44. Bernard, "Lincoln and Civil Liberties," 5.

45. Pendleton, *Suspend Habeas Corpus,* 7–8.

46. Ibid., 1, 7–8; McPherson, *History of the Rebellion,* 180. For an opposing perspective on Democratic motives, see Neely, *Fate of Liberty.*

47. *Congressional Globe,* 37th Cong., 2d sess., 1861, 15; Ibid., 1862, 617, 760, 3367; Ibid., 37th Cong., 2d sess., 1861, 11, ICPSR; Ibid., 1862, 20, 21, 25, ICPSR.

48. George H. Pendleton, *The Power to Make Treasury Notes a Legal Tender? Speech of Hon. George H. Pendleton, of Ohio, in the House of Representatives, January 29, 1862* (n.p., n.d.), 1–5; *Cincinnati Enquirer,* Jan. 4, 1862; E. G. Spaulding, *History of the Legal Tender Paper Money Issued during the Great Rebellion Being a Loan without Interest and a National Currency* (Buffalo, N. Y.: Express, 1869), 43–45; Robert P. Sharkey, *Money, Class, and Party: An Economic Study of Civil War and Reconstruction* (Baltimore, Md.: Johns Hopkins Press, 1959), 37–38.

49. Pendleton, *Treasury Notes,* 6.

50. *Congressional Globe,* 37th Cong., 2d sess., 1862, 17, ICPSR; Pendleton, *Treasury Notes,* 7; Henry Brooks Adams, "The Legal Tender Act," *North American Review* 110 (Apr. 1870): 308–21; Sharkey, *Money, Class, and Party,* 41–42; Curry, *Blueprint for Modern America,* 187–88.

51. *Congressional Globe,* 37th Cong., 2d sess., 1862, 1116; *Cincinnati Enquirer,* Mar. 8, 1862; Spaulding, *History of the Legal Tender,* 140; James Ford Rhodes, *History of the United States from the Compromise of 1850 to the End of the Roosevelt Administration* (New York: MacMillan, 1928), 3:450–51.

52. *Congressional Globe,* 37th Cong., 2d sess., 1862, 1345.

53. Each industry gave Pendleton reasons why they were unfairly taxed. Ibid., 1439–41, 1463–64; *Cincinnati Enquirer,* Apr. 8, 11, 1862; Curry, *Blueprint for Modern America,* 173.

54. *Congressional Globe,* 38th Cong., 2d sess., 1862, 1364–66.

55. Ibid., 1545.

56. Ibid.; Rittenhouse, "George Hunt Pendleton," 33–34.

57. *Congressional Globe,* 37th Cong., 2d sess., 1862, 1226–27; ibid., 23, 38–39, ICPSR.

58. *Congressional Globe,* 37th Cong., 2nd sess., 1862, 1682.

59. Samuel S. Cox, *Three Decades of Federal Legislation, 1855 to 1885: Personal and Historical Memories of Events Preceding, During, and Since the American Civil War, Involving Slavery and Secession, Emancipation and Reconstruction, with Sketches of Prominent Actors during These Periods* (1885; repr., New York: Books for Libraries Press, 1970), 249; Lindsey, *"Sunset" Cox,* 81.

60. *Congressional Globe,* 37th Cong., 2d sess., 1862, 11–13, 19–20, 26, 31–36, 42–43, 46, ICPSR; Randall, *Constitutional Problems,* 69–70, 286–88, 356–58; Rhodes, *History of the United States,* 4:60–64; Curry, *Blueprint for Modern America,* 60–64; Dell, *Lincoln and the War Democrats,* 142; Silbey, *Respectable Minority,* 50–51; Lucie, "Confiscation," 317–21.

61. *Congressional Globe,* 37th Cong., 2d sess., 1862, 21–24, 29–30, 37, ICPSR; McPherson, *History of the Rebellion,* 209–18; Rhodes, *History of the United States,* 3:518–22; James A. Rawley, *The Politics of Union: Northern Politics during the Civil War* (Hinsdale, Ill.: Dryden Press, 1974), 80–81; Dell, *Lincoln and The War Democrats,* 141; Silbey, *Respectable Minority,* 50.

62. *Cincinnati Enquirer,* May 9, 1862.

63. David R. Roediger, "Irish-American Workers and White Racial Formation in the Antebellum United States," in *Racial Classification and History,* ed. E. Nathaniel Gates (New York: Garland Press, 1997), 254–55.

64. *Cincinnati Enquirer,* July 19, Aug. 24, 1861; Apr. 22, 26, May 9, June 21, 26, Aug. 28, 1862; Roseboom, *Civil War Era,* 401–3; William F. Zornow, "The Ohio Democrats and the 'Africanization' Issue in 1862," *Negro History Bulletin* 11 (June 1948): 211–14; Klement, *Copperheads in the Middle West,* 13–14; Jacque Voegeli, "The Northwest and the Race Issue, 1861–1862," *Mississippi Valley Historical Review* 50 (1963): 237–49; Alexander Saxton, *The Rise and Fall of the White Republic: Class Politics and Mass Culture in Nineteenth-Century America,* with a new foreword by David Roediger (London: Verso, 2003), 385–91.

65. McPherson, *History of the Rebellion,* 227–28; Randall, *Constitutional Problems,* 367–68; Gray, *Hidden Civil War,* 98–100.

66. Whitelaw Reid, *Ohio in the War: Her Statesmen, Her Generals, and Soldiers* (New York: Moore, Wilstach and Baldwin, 1868), 1:83–98; Rittenhouse, "George Hunt Pendleton," 36.

67. Reid, *Ohio in the War,* 1:84.

68. George H. Pendleton to [J. Sterling] Morton, Oct. 5, 1862, Morton Family Papers, Chicago Historical Society, Chicago.

69. *Proceedings of the Democratic Convention, Held at Columbus, Ohio, Friday, July 4, 1862: Containing the Speeches of Hon. Samuel Medary, Hon. C. L. Vallandigham, Hon. Rufus P. Ranney, and Hon. Allen G. Thurman. The Address and Platform, Ballotings for Candidates, and Names of Delegates in Attendance* (Dayton, Ohio: Press of the Dayton Empire, 1862), 9–12; Roseboom, *Civil War Era,* 400–404.

70. *Cincinnati Enquirer,* Oct. 5, 1862.

71. *Cincinnati Commercial,* Sept. 27, Oct. 6, 8, 13, 14, 1862.

72. Abraham Lincoln, *Speeches and Presidential Addresses: 1859–1865 Together with Conversations and Anecdotes, Related by F. B. Carpenter in "Six Months at the White House"* (New York: Current Literature, 1907), 170–74; *Cincinnati Enquirer,* Oct. 7, 9, 1862.

73. *Cincinnati Enquirer,* July 8, 1862.

74. Ibid., Oct. 16–18, 29, 1862; Vallandigham, *Life of Vallandigham,* 215–16; Bloss, *Life of Pendleton,* 46–48; Zornow, "Ohio Democrats and the 'Africanization' Issue," 211; Voegeli, "Northwest and the Race Issue," 249.

75. *Cincinnati Enquirer,* Oct. 11, 1862, Abstract of speech printed in newspaper and quoted in Bloss, *Life of Pendleton,* 36.

76. *Cincinnati Enquirer,* Oct. 11, 1862; Rawley, *Politics of Union,* 75.

Pendleton the Obstructionist

1. Richard F. Bensel, *Yankee Leviathan: The Origins of Central State Authority in America, 1859–1877* (Cambridge: Cambridge Univ. Press, 1990), 94–237.

2. *Congressional Globe,* 37th Cong., 3d sess., 1863, 1354; *Cincinnati Enquirer,* Feb. 6, 1863.

3. *Cincinnati Enquirer,* Dec., 27, 1862. Pendleton also expressed concern about the oath the president required of political prisoners before their parole, in which they promised not to sue the government for damages resulting from imprisonment. Stevens successfully tabled Pendleton's request that the president respond to the House about the oath's facilitation of the public interest. Along with most Democrats, Pendleton would not condone the removal of redress as provided by the Constitution for wrongs done to citizens by the government. *Congressional Globe,* 37th Cong., 3d sess., 1962, 49–50, ICPSR; *Cincinnati Enquirer,* Dec. 19, 1862.

4. *Congressional Globe,* 37th Cong., 3d sess., 1863, 165–66; ibid., 1862, 48, ICPSR; *Cincinnati Enquirer,* Dec. 27, 1862. Not a month earlier, Pendleton and several other Ohio Democrats had written the president to condemn the arrest of Honorable Edson B. Olds, of Lancaster, Ohio, for a speech he made in August. He was held in solitary confinement and, in spite of an order of the judge advocate, had not yet been released. *Cincinnati Enquirer,* Dec. 16, 1862.

5. *Congressional Globe,* 37th Cong., 3d sess., 1863, 1357; James G. Randall, *Constitutional Problems under Lincoln* (New York: D. Appleton and Co., 1926), 189–93; Frank L. Klement, *The Copperheads in the Middle West* (Chicago: Univ. of Chicago Press, 1960), 81–83.

6. *Congressional Globe,* 37th Cong., 3d sess., 1862–63, 48, 50, 65–67, 71–73, ICPSR. The Supreme Court did not rule constitutional the fifth section of the bill that allowed for a second trial of a habeas corpus case, removing the trial from a state court to a circuit court. The justices ruled that this was a violation of the Seventh Amendment of the Constitution. Randall, *Constitutional Problems,* 211–14. Another example of Pendleton's concern regarding unlawful arrests pertained to Gen. Grant's exclusion of all Jews from within army lines because a few had disobeyed trade laws. Pendleton brought resolutions before the House condemning this restriction of rights of the Jews who operated legally.

Congressional Globe, 37th Cong., 3d sess., 1863, 222; G. M. D. Bloss, *Life and Speeches of George Hunt Pendleton* (Cincinnati, Ohio: Miami, 1868), 48–50.

7. *Congressional Globe,* 37th Cong., 3d sess., 1863, 1234, 1255; *The Record of Hon. Clement L. Vallandigham on Abolition, the Union, and the Civil War* (Columbus, Ohio: J. Walter and Co., 1863), 204–10; Randall, *Constitutional Problems,* 268–74; James W. Geary, *We Need Men: The Union Draft in the Civil War* (Dekalb: Northern Illinois Univ. Press, 1991), 49–59.

8. *Congressional Globe,* 37th Cong., 3d sess., 1863, 68–69, ICPSR; *Record of Vallandigham,* 205; George Fort Milton, *Abraham Lincoln and the Fifth Column* (New York: Vanguard Press, 1942), 128–30; Klement, *Copperheads in the Middle West,* 76–77; Geary, *We Need Men,* 60–64.

9. Iver Bernstein, *The New York City Draft Riots: Their Significance for American Society and Politics in the Age of the Civil War* (New York: Oxford Univ. Press, 1990), 10–11.

10. *Congressional Globe,* 37th Cong., 3d sess., 1863, 54, 56–61, ICPSR; Leonard P. Curry, "Congressional Democrats: 1861–1863," *Civil War History* 12 (Sept. 1966): 225; Leonard P. Curry, *Blueprint for Modern America: Nonmilitary Legislation of the First Civil War Congress* (Nashville, Tenn.: Vanderbilt Univ. Press, 1968), 61–67; Joseph T. Glatthaar, *Forged in Battle: The Civil War Alliance of Black Soldiers and White Officers* (New York: Free Press, 1990), 7.

11. George H. Pendleton, *Speech of Hon. George H. Pendleton, of Ohio, on the Enlistment of Negro Soldiers; Delivered during the Debate in the House of Representatives, January 31, 1863* (Washington, D.C.: n.p., 1863), 7.

12. Ibid., 1–8; Klement, *Copperheads in the Middle West,* 82–83.

13. Curry, "Congressional Democrats," 225; Curry, *Blueprint for Modern America,* 66–67; Glatthaar, *Forged in Battle,* 205–6.

14. George H. Pendleton to R. C. Wood, Feb. 24, 1863, and R. C. Wood to Honorable Montgomery Blair, Mar. 5, 1863, Abraham Lincoln Papers, Manuscript Division, Library of Congress; *Congressional Globe,* 37th Cong., 3d sess., 1863, 1029.

15. John Jay Knox, *A History of Banking in the United States* (1903; repr., New York: Augustus M. Kelley, 1969), 91–111; Bensel, *Yankee Leviathan,* 172–73, 226–27.

16. Randall, *Constitutional Problems,* 499–502.

17. *Congressional Globe,* 37th Cong., 3d sess., 1863, appendix, 163–67; *Cincinnati Enquirer,* Mar. 7, 1863.

18. *Congressional Globe,* 37th Cong., 3d sess., 1863, appendix, 166.

19. *Cincinnati Enquirer,* Nov. 7, 19, 1862. The paper later praised Pendleton as being, next to Vallandigham, the most abused Democrat by the abolitionists. The *Enquirer* cited articles in other papers expressing support for Pendleton's bid, such as the *Indianapolis Sentinel, Stark County Democrat,* and *Erie County News. Cincinnati Enquirer,* Oct. 21, 28, 31, Nov. 14, Dec. 2, 1863.

20. George H. Pendleton to Alexander Long, Jan. 6, 1863, Alexander Long Papers, Mss fL848, Cincinnati Historical Society, Cincinnati.

21. George H. Pendleton to J. Sterling Morton, Nov. 20, 1862, Morton Family Papers, Chicago Historical Society, Chicago; George H. Pendleton to Alexander Long, Dec. 7, 1862, Long Papers; Samuel S. Cox to Alexander Long, Apr. 21, 1863, Long Papers; Samuel S. Cox to Manton Marble, Nov. 29, Dec. 5, 1863, Manton Marble Papers, Manuscript Divi-

sion, Library of Congress; J. J. Faran to Alexander Long, Dec. 7, 1863, Long Papers. Long carried on some correspondence on Pendleton's behalf as well. J. F. McKinney to Alexander Long, Dec. 18, 1862, and John McNating to Alexander Long, Jan. 14, 1863, Long Papers. After failing to obtain caucus approval, Pendleton nominated Cox for House Speaker. Cox lost to Schuyler Colfax. *Congressional Globe,* 38th Cong., 1st sess., 1863, 6; ibid., 3, ICPSR; *Cincinnati Enquirer,* Dec. 10, 1863.

22. James L. Vallandigham, *A Life of Clement L. Vallandigham* (Baltimore, Md.: Turnbull Brothers, 1872), 241–60; Union Congressional Committee, *Copperhead Conspiracy in the North-West: An Expose of the Treasonable Order of the "Sons of Liberty"* (New York: John A. Gray & Green, ca. 1864); *Mount Vernon Democratic Banner,* May 9, 1863; James Ford Rhodes, *History of the United States from the Compromise of 1850 to the End of the Roosevelt Administration* (New York: MacMillan, 1928), 4:247–48; Milton, *Abraham Lincoln,* 160–66; Wood Gray, *The Hidden Civil War: The Story of the Copperheads* (New York: Viking Press, 1942), 145; Carl M. Becker, "Picture of a Young Copperhead," *Bulletin of the Historical and Philosophical Society of Ohio* 71 (Jan. 1962): 12–23; *The Limits of Dissent* (Lexington: Univ. Press of Kentucky, 1970), 148–60; Michael Les Benedict, "Vallandigham: Constitutionalist and Copperhead," *Timeline* 3 (Feb.–Mar. 1986): 16–25.

23. George H. Pendleton to J. Sterling Morton, May 29, 1863, Morton Family Papers; Vallandigham, *Life of Vallandigham,* 284–88; *Cincinnati Enquirer,* May 17, 19, 30, June 9, July 10, Aug. 13, Sept. 23, 1863; *New York Times,* July 6, 1863; George H. Pendleton, "Address at Ovation at the Academy of Music," in *Handbook of the Democracy, 1863–1864* (New York: n.p., 1864), 109–111; Joanna Cowden, *"Heaven Will Frown on Such a Cause As This": Six Democrats Who Opposed Lincoln's War* (Lanham, Md.: Univ. Press of America, 2001), 173–80. While Pendleton supported the nomination, Cox did not think Vallandigham a wise choice. Clement Vallandigham to Manton Marble, May 15, Aug. 13, 1863, and Samuel S. Cox to Manton Marble, June 1, 1863, Marble Papers; *The War of the Rebellion: A Compilation of the Official Records of the Union and Confederate Armies,* ser. 2, vol. 7 (Washington, D.C.: GPO, 1880–87), 280–82 (hereafter cited as *OR).*

24. *OR,* ser. 2, vol. 6, 48–68; Vallandigham, *Life of Vallandigham,* 305–11.

25. *New York Tribune,* June 12, 1863; *Cincinnati Enquirer,* May 23, 1863; Klement, *Limits of Dissent,* 180–83.

26. *Cincinnati Enquirer,* Apr. 6, 8, 12, 26, Aug. 29, Sept. 7, 19, 1863; *State Convention of War Democrats: Address to the Democrats of Ohio* (n.p., n.d.), 1–4. Peace men attacked the War Democrats, too, for their support of Union candidate John Brough. The war men saw Vallandigham as inimical to the Union.

27. *Cincinnati Enquirer,* May 22, 1863.

28. *Papers from the Society for the Diffusion of Political Knowledge: Speech of Mr. Pugh to 50,000 Voters, Who Nominated Vallandigham and Resolved to Elect Him Governor of Ohio* (New York: n.d.), 4.

29. George H. Pendleton to J. Sterling Morton, May 29, 1863, Morton Family Papers.

30. Samuel S. Cox to Manton Marble, Aug. 17, 1863, Marble Papers; *Cincinnati Enquirer,* Oct. 9, 20, 1863; Vallandigham, *Life of Vallandigham,* 333–34. Pendleton's speeches improved his reputation. The *Enquirer* reported a column in the *Columbus Statesman* that Pendleton was "beyond question, one of the ablest speakers in the State." As Vallandigham's star faded, Pendleton's continued to rise. *Cincinnati Enquirer,* Oct. 6, 1863; Floyd Oliver

Rittenhouse, "George Hunt Pendleton: With Special Reference to His Congressional Career" (M.A. thesis, Ohio State University, 1932), 44. In the soldier vote, 41,467 voted for Brough, and only 2,298 for Vallandigham. Overall, Brough won 288,761 to 186,672. Arnold Shankman, "Soldier Votes and Clement L. Vallandigham in the 1863 Ohio Gubernatorial Election," *Ohio History* 82 (Winter/Spring 1973): 88–104.

31. Long's resolution failed 22 to 96, whereas Pendleton's lost 47 to 77. *Congressional Globe,* 38th Cong., 1st sess., 1864, 21–22, ICPSR. There were many other peace resolutions as well. See ibid., 1863–64, 5, 9, ICPSR; *Congressional Globe,* 38th Cong., 2d sess., 1865, 67, 71; *New York Times,* Mar. 1, 1864; *Cincinnati Enquirer,* Mar. 5, 1864; Christopher Dell, *Lincoln and the War Democrats: The Grand Erosion of Conservative Tradition* (London: Associated Univ. Press, 1975), 276–77.

32. *Cincinnati Enquirer,* Apr. 13, 1864.

33. *Congressional Globe,* 38th Cong., 1st sess., 1864, 1517–19; *New York Times,* Apr. 13, 1864; Gray, *Hidden Civil War,* 160–62; Klement, *Copperheads in the Middle West,* 229–30; Dell, *Lincoln and the War Democrats,* 278.

34. George H. Pendleton, *The Resolution to Expel Mr. Long, of Ohio. Speech of Hon. George H. Pendleton, of Ohio, Delivered in the House of Representatives, April 11, 1864* (n.p., n.d.), 1.

35. Ibid., 2–8; *Congressional Globe,* 38th Cong., 1st sess., 1864, 1584–86, 1624–26; *Cincinnati Enquirer,* Apr. 18, May 3, 1864. Shortly after these events, the *Enquirer* lamented the division of the Democratic Party, which it blamed on the War Democrats. *Cincinnati Enquirer,* May 24, 1864.

36. Cox disdained Long, his views, and the Extreme Peace views as well. Yet he sustained Long's right to express his opinion. Samuel S. Cox to Manton Marble, May 7, 1864, Marble Papers; J. J. Faran to Alexander Long, Feb. 7, 1864, Long Papers; *Congressional Globe,* 38th Cong., 1st sess., 1864, 30–32, ICPSR; Gray, *Hidden Civil War,* 162; David Lindsey, *"Sunset" Cox: Irrepressible Democrat* (Detroit: Wayne State Univ. Press, 1959), 82–83; Klement, *Copperheads of the Middle West,* 230; Dell, *Lincoln and the War Democrats,* 278–80.

37. *Congressional Globe,* 38th Cong., 1st sess., 1864, 659, 2612–13; ibid., 1st sess., 1863–64, 6, 11, 18, 27, 46, ICPSR; Rhodes, *History of the United States,* 4:472–74; Dell, *Lincoln and the War Democrats,* 274.

38. George H. Pendleton, *Speech of Hon. George H. Pendleton, of Ohio, in the House of Representatives, June 15, 1864* (n.p., n.d.), 1–4; *Congressional Globe,* 38th Cong., 1st sess., 1864, 2992–95.

39. Pendleton, *Speech of Pendleton on June 15, 1864,* 7.

40. *Congressional Globe,* 38th Cong., 1st sess., 1864, 890–92; ibid., 22, ICPSR; Glatthaar, *Forged in Battle,* 310–16.

41. William Frank Zornow, *Lincoln and the Party Divided* (Norman: Univ. of Oklahoma Press, 1954), 108–9; Michael Les Benedict, *A Compromise of Principle: Congressional Republicans and Reconstruction, 1863–1869* (New York: W. W. Norton and Co., 1974), 70–83.

42. *Congressional Globe,* 38th Cong., 1st sess., 1864, 2105–107.

43. Ibid., 2107. Pendleton also found unconstitutional the restrictions on voting and representation rights for reconstructed Southern states. *Congressional Globe,* 38th Cong., 1st sess., 1863–64, 5–6, 33, 37–38, 41, 51, ICPSR.

44. *Congressional Globe,* 38th Cong., 1st sess., 1864, 2107; ibid., 38, ICPSR, Rhodes, *History of the United States,* 4:484–87. When the Radicals introduced legislation to allow African Americans to testify in courts, Pendleton opposed it as a domestic question to be considered at the state level. He also resisted attempts to bring the pay of black soldiers up to that of whites, fearing white disaffection. Constitutional scruples and racism explain his positions. *Congressional Globe,* 38th Cong., 1st sess., 1863–64, 5, 43–44, 51, 60–61, ICPSR. For a more detailed explanation of the early Reconstruction plans, see Herman Belz, *A New Birth of Freedom: The Republican Party and Freedmen's Rights, 1861–1866* (Westport, Conn.: Greenwood Press, 1976).

45. *Congressional Globe,* 38th Cong., 1st sess., 1864, 13, 23, 29, ICPSR.

46. *Congressional Globe,* 38th Cong., 1st sess., 1864, 731–37, 994–95, 2788–93; ibid., 23–24, ICPSR. He continued to oppose the use of greenbacks as legal tender. *Congressional Globe,* 38th Cong., 2d sess., 1865, 81.

47. *Congressional Globe,* 38th Cong., 1st sess., 1864, 30, 33, 59.

48. Ibid., 315–16, 2251–53; ibid., 15–18, 42, 55–56, 58–63, ICPSR.

49. *Congressional Globe,* 38th Cong., 1st sess., 1864, 1389, 1395–96; ibid., 32, 34, 42, ICPSR.

50. Notes of Julia Frances Brice, Misc. Personal Papers of Julia Frances Cox, San Jose, California; *Evening Star,* Mar. 29, 1864.

From Victory Came Defeat

1. James L. Vallandigham, *A Life of Clement L. Vallandigham* (Baltimore, Md.: Turnbull Brothers, 1872), 366; Elizabeth F. Yager, "The Presidential Campaign of 1864 in Ohio," *Ohio History* 34 (1925): 562–63; David Lindsey, *"Sunset" Cox: Irrepressible Democrat* (Detroit: Wayne State Univ. Press, 1959), 84–91. In this chapter, the War and Moderate Peace Democrats will be called "War Democrats" and the Extreme Peace and peace-at-any-price Democrats will be referred to as "Peace Democrats."

2. George W. Morgan to General [George B. McClellan], Mar. 25, Apr. 12, 1864, George B. McClellan Papers, Manuscript Division, Library of Congress, Washington, D.C.; *New York Times,* Mar. 24, 1864; Yager, "Campaign of 1864," 556–58; Wood Gray, *The Hidden Civil War: The Story of the Copperheads* (New York: Viking Press, 1942), 162; William Frank Zornow, "Clement L. Vallandigham and the Democratic Party in 1864," *Historical and Philosophical Society of Ohio Bulletin* 19 (Jan. 1961): 26–27.

3. Harold M. Dudley, "The Election of 1864," *Mississippi Valley Historical Review* 28 (Mar. 1932): 500; Zornow, "Vallandigham and the Democratic Party," 21.

4. Richard Smith to Joseph H. Barrett, Aug. 14, 1864, William H. Smith Papers, Ohio Historical Society, Columbus; Yager, "Campaign of 1864," 551–53; James Ford Rhodes, *History of the United States from the Compromise of 1850 to the End of the Roosevelt Administration* (New York: MacMillan, 1928), 4:458–64; Dudley, "Election of 1864," 501–3; Harold M. Hyman, ed., *The Radical Republicans and Reconstruction, 1861–1870* (Indianapolis, Ind.: Bobbs-Merrill, 1967), 150, 159, 168; Hans L. Trefousse, *Radical Republicans: Lincoln's Vanguard for Racial Justice* (Baton Rouge: Louisiana State Univ. Press, 1968), 266–304; Frederick J. Blue, *Salmon P. Chase: A Life of Politics* (Kent, Ohio: Kent State Univ. Press, 1987), 221–26; David

E. Kyvig, *Explicit and Authentic Acts: Amending the U.S. Constitution, 1776–1995* (Lawrence: Univ. Press of Kansas, 1996), 156–63.

5. Edward McPherson, *The Political History of the United States during the Great Rebellion . . .* (Washington, D.C.: Philip and Solomons, 1865), 410–16; Rhodes, *History of the United States,* 4:463–65; William Frank Zornow, "The Cleveland Convention, 1864, and Radical Democrats," *Mid-America* 36 (1954): 39–53.

6. McPherson, *History of the Rebellion,* 385–86; William Frank Zornow, "McClellan and Seymour in the Chicago Convention of 1864," *Illinois State Historical Society Journal* 43 (Winter 1950): 283, 289. McClellan's lack of success on the battlefield played a significant role in his dismissal as well. For more information on McClellan's military career, see also George B. McClellan, *McClellan's Own Story: The War for the Union, the Soldiers Who Fought It, the Civilians Who Directed It, and His Relations to It and to Them* (New York: Charles L. Webster and Co., 1887); T. Harry Williams, *McClellan, Sherman and Grant* (Westport, Conn.: Greenwood Press, 1962); Stephen W. Sears, *George B. McClellan: The Young Napoleon* (New York: Ticknor and Fields, 1988).

7. Stephen W. Sears, *The Civil War Papers of George B. McClellan: Selected Correspondence, 1860–1865* (New York: Ticknor and Fields, 1989), 586; George W. Morgan to McClellan, Aug. 4, 14, 17, 1864, McClellan Papers. Many pushed McClellan away from the Peace Democrat position as well. Allan Pinkerton to McClellan, Apr. 19, 1864, Max Langenschwartz to McClellan, Aug. 10, 1864, R. B. Marcy to McClellan, Aug. 21, 1864, McClellan Papers; *Cincinnati Enquirer,* Jan. 5, 1864; Zornow, "Vallandigham and the Democratic Party," 28–29.

8. Alexander Long to Alexander Boys, Aug. 9, 1864, Thomas Trimble to D. Houck, Mar. 4, 1864, Alexander Boys Papers, Ohio Historical Society, Columbus; Charles S. Medary to "Father" [Samuel Medary], July 20, 1864, Samuel Medary Papers, Ohio Historical Society, Columbus; Thomas Key to Samuel Barlow, Aug. 24, 1864, Samuel L. M. Barlow Papers, Henry E. Huntington Library, San Marino, California; George F. Hoeffer to Alexander Long, June 8, 1864, Long Papers, Cincinnati Historical Society, Cincinnati; *Cincinnati Gazette,* Aug. 24, 27, 1864; *Cincinnati Enquirer,* Aug. 29, 1864; Frank L. Klement, *The Copperheads in the Middle West* (Chicago: Univ. of Chicago Press, 1960), 279–81; Jerome Mushkat, *Fernando Wood: A Political Biography* (Kent, Ohio: Kent State Univ. Press, 1990), 147–49.

9. Samuel Cox feared delay would harm McClellan's chances, but the general did not prevent the postponement. Samuel S. Cox to McClellan, June 9, Aug. 14, 1864, McClellan Papers; Klement, *Copperheads in the Middle West,* 233–34; Irving Katz, *August Belmont: A Political Biography* (New York: Columbia Univ. Press, 1968), 126–27; Mushkat, *Fernando Wood,* 145–49.

10. John H. James to Samuel Cox, July 13, 1864, James Family Papers, Ohio Historical Society, Columbus; Charles M. Reed to Samuel Randall, Samuel J. Randall Papers, The Historical Society of Pennsylvania, Philadelphia; James Sydney Rollins to Samuel Cox, Aug. 19, 1864, Cox Papers, Ohio Historical Society, Columbus; Manton Marble to James W. Wall, Mar. 30, 1864, Marble Papers, Manuscript Division, Library of Congress; Eugene H. Roseboom, *The Civil War Era, 1850–1873,* vol. 4 of *The History of the State of Ohio,* ed. Carl Wittke (Columbus: Ohio State Archaeological and Historical Society, 1944), 431–45; Lindsey, *"Sunset" Cox,* 84–87; Frank L. Klement, *The Limits of Dissent*

(Lexington: Univ. Press of Kentucky, 1970), 280–83, Joel H. Silbey, *A Respectable Minority: The Democratic Party in the Civil War Era, 1860–1868* (New York: W. W. Norton and Co., 1977), 124–30.

11. Klement, *Limits of Dissent,* 284–85; Silbey, *Respectable Minority,* 130; Sears, *George B. McClellan,* 372–73.

12. *Official Proceedings of the Democratic National Convention, Held in 1864 at Chicago* (Chicago: Times Steam Book and Job Printing House, 1864), 27; *Cincinnati Enquirer,* Sept. 6, 1864.

13. August Belmont to McClellan, Sept. 1, 1864, McClellan Papers; McPherson, *History of the Rebellion,* 423; Klement, *Limits of Dissent,* 282; Silbey, *Respectable Minority,* 129–30. Stephen Sears suggests that Vallandigham threatened to bolt the convention if he did not get the plank he desired in the platform. Klement and Silbey indicate that the Daytonite was not holding that threat over the heads of his adversaries. Vallandigham had committed himself to the nominee of the convention and disavowed the rumors of a bolt. Sears, *George B. McClellan,* 373.

14. *Official Proceedings,* 27–29; *Cincinnati Enquirer,* Aug. 31, 1864; *Cincinnati Gazette,* Aug. 31, 1864; Klement, *Limits of Dissent,* 283–87.

15. *Cincinnati Enquirer,* Aug. 30, 1864; *Cincinnati Gazette,* Aug. 31, 1864; *Harper's Weekly,* Sept. 3, 1864; Vallandigham, *Life of Vallandigham,* 366–67. DeAlva Alexander suggested that some Democrats, such as New Yorker Samuel J. Tilden, may have feared a split in the convention, similar to that of 1860, if the Peace men did not get their way. William Zornow agreed and added that many delegates did not recognize all of the ramifications of its wording because of the abbreviated debate on the plank. Zornow's latter point seems suspect considering the length of time the party had been divided and that convention delegates must have known Vallandigham wrote the plank. Finally, Harold Dudley and Charles Wilson asserted that a prior arrangement could have existed to allow the Peace men to have their say in the platform if the war men obtained their candidate for the presidency. Again, there seems to be little support for this assertion. DeAlva S. Alexander, *A Political History of the State of New York* (1909; repr., Port Washington, N.Y.: Ira J. Friedman, 1969), 3:112–24; Dudley, "Election of 1864," 512–13; Charles R. Wilson, "The Cincinnati *Daily Enquirer* and Civil War Politics: A Study in 'Copperhead' Opinion" (Ph.D. diss., University of Chicago, 1934), 284–85; Zornow, "Vallandigham and the Democratic Party," 30–34; Klement, *Limits of Dissent,* 283–87; Silbey, *Respectable Minority,* 130–34.

16. August Belmont to McClellan, Sept. 3, 1864, McClellan Papers; Rhodes, *History of the United States,* 4:522–23; Zornow, "Vallandigham and the Democratic Party," 32–33; Klement, *Limits of Dissent,* 284–86; Silbey, *Respectable Minority,* 130–34.

17. Samuel Barlow to Manton Marble, Aug. 21, 1864, Marble Papers; *Official Proceedings,* 29–53; McPherson, *History of the Rebellion,* 420; *Cincinnati Gazette,* Aug. 27, 28, 30, Sept. 1, 1864; *Cincinnati Enquirer,* Sept. 1, 1864; *New York Times,* Sept. 1, 1864; *Dayton Empire,* Sept. 6, 1864; Yager, "Campaign of 1864," 563–64; George Fort Milton, *Abraham Lincoln and the Fifth Column* (New York: Vanguard Press, 1942), 227–29; Zornow, "McClellan and Seymour," 293; Zornow, "Vallandigham and the Democratic Party," 30–31; Frank L. Klement, "Clement L. Vallandigham," in *For the Union: Ohio Leaders in the Civil War,* ed. Kenneth W. Wheeler (Columbus: Ohio State Univ. Press, 1968), 58–63; Klement, *Limits of Dissent,* 286; Sears, *George B. McClellan,* 373–75.

18. *Official Proceedings,* 54.

19. Ibid., 54–56; McPherson, *History of the Rebellion,* 420; G. M. D. Bloss, *Life and Speeches of George Hunt Pendleton* (Cincinnati, Ohio: Miami, 1868), 78–82. A *Gazette* article said that Cox had vocally sought the vice-presidential nomination while Pendleton had refrained from promoting himself. The Republican paper expressed respect for Pendleton's consistency to principle, in spite of their disagreement with it, and criticized Cox for his political wavering during the war. *Cincinnati Gazette,* Sept. 1, 3, 1864; *Cincinnati Enquirer,* Sept. 1–2, 1864; *New York Times,* Sept. 1, 1864; Zornow, "Vallandigham and the Democratic Party," 30–31; Klement, *Limits of Dissent,* 286; Harold M. Hyman, "Election of 1864," in *The Coming to Power: Critical Presidential Elections in American History,* ed. Arthur M. Schlesinger Jr. (New York: McGraw-Hill, 1971), 160–61; John C. Waugh, *Reelecting Lincoln: The Battle for the 1864 Presidency* (New York: Crown, 1997), 291–92. Sears believed that Pendleton's nomination was the final blow to an already hopeless ticket. He blamed the compromise fashioned by war men who accepted the peace plank and the Pendleton nomination for the failure of the ticket. Sears believed that the attempts for party unity were "ill-considered," apparently meaning that the Peace men should not have been given any voice. Though a fairly recent work, Sears's approach appears to return to the traditional interpretation of historians who viewed Peace Democrats with disdain. Sears, *George B. McClellan,* 374. For this approach, see also David E. Long, *The Jewel of Liberty: Abraham Lincoln's Re-Election and the End of Slavery* (Mechanicsburg, Pa.: Stackpole Books, 1994), 41–42, 103–5, 111–13, 134–52.

20. *Official Proceedings,* 55–56.

21. *Cincinnati Enquirer,* Sept. 1, 1864; *New York Times,* Sept. 1, 1864.

22. Gideon Welles, *Diary of Gideon Welles: Secretary of the Navy under Lincoln and Johnson* (Boston: Houghton Mifflin, 1911), 2:129–36.

23. *Cincinnati Commercial,* Nov. 10, 1864.

24. Samuel Johnson to McClellan, Sept. 9, 1864, Amator Patriae to Mrs. George B. McClellan, Aug. 31, 1864, newspaper clipping in J. J. Moulton to McClellan, Sept. 5, 1864, McClellan Papers; *Harper's Weekly,* Sept. 10, 1864; Rhodes, *History of the United States,* 4:524–25; Zornow, "Cleveland Convention," 51; Zornow, "Vallandigham and the Democratic Party," 32–33.

25. Samuel Barlow to McClellan, Sept. 3, 1864, Clement L. Vallandigham to McClellan, Sept. 4, 1864, Thomas M. Key to McClellan, Sept. 4, 1864, McClellan Papers; Dudley, "Election of 1864," 513–14; Charles R. Wilson, "McClellan's Changing View on the Peace Plank of 1864," *American Historical Review* 38 (Apr. 1933): 498–500; William Starr Myers, *General George B. McClellan: A Study in Personality* (New York: D. Appleton-Century, 1934) 455; Klement, *Limits of Dissent,* 287; Zornow, "Vallandigham and the Democratic Party," 33–34.

26. Undated draft of McClellan's acceptance letter, McClellan Papers; Myers, *General George B. McClellan,* 455–57. Charles Wilson detailed only four drafts of McClellan's letter, asserting that the general wavered significantly from one draft to the next. Sears found that there were actually six drafts and that Wilson exaggerated the variance between them, but Wilson was correct that the general understood that subtle variations in wording sent signals to the differing factions of the party. Wilson, "McClellan's Changing View," 498–505; Stephen Sears, "McClellan and the Peace Plank of 1864: A Reappraisal," *Civil War History* 36 (Mar. 1990): 57–64.

27. Stephen L. Mershon to McClellan, Sept. 12, 1864, "Your Affectionate Brother" to McClellan, Sept. 14, 1864; Unknown to McClellan, Sept. 14, 1864, Henry Liebeman to McClellan, Sept. 19, 1864, McClellan Papers.

28. Samuel S. Cox to McClellan, Sept. 9, 21, 1864, George W. Morgan to McClellan, Sept. 12, 1864, William S. Garvin to McClellan, Sept. 18, 1864, McClellan Papers; Samuel S. Cox to Marble, July 25, Aug. 9, Sept. 6, 1864, Marble Papers; Yager, "Campaign of 1864," 565–66; Zornow, "Vallandigham and the Democratic Party," 34–35.

29. Samuel Barlow to McClellan, Sept. 12, 1864, John A. Trimble to George H. Pendleton, Sept. 10, 1864, John A. Trimble Papers, Ohio Historical Society, Columbus; Zornow, "Vallandigham and the Democratic Party," 34–35; Klement, *Limits of Dissent,* 288–90; Silbey, *Respectable Minority,* 135–39.

30. William J. Flagg to McClellan, Sept. 11, 1864, Unknown to McClellan, Sept. 23, 1864, McClellan Papers.

31. Robert J. Wright to McClellan, Oct. 13, 1864, McClellan Papers.

32. J. N. Baldwin to Marble, Sept. 5, 1864, Marble Papers; "Venice" to McClellan, Sept. 18, 1864, H. S. Lansing to McClellan, Sept. 22, 1864, C. S. Miller to McClellan, Sept. 24, 1864, McClellan Papers; Sears, *Papers of McClellan,* 603; Waugh, *Reelecting Lincoln,* 332. For a corresponding negative historical perspective of the Peace men, see Long, *Jewel of Liberty,* 62, 174, 231–32.

33. *The Congressional Record of George H. Pendleton: Candidate for Vice President* (Philadelphia: Crissey and Markly, 1864), 1–8; *How the Copperheads Would Preserve the Union: Record of George H. Pendleton, in the Congress of the United States during the Rebellion,* Union Campaign Documents, No. 2 (n.p.: Weed, Parsons and Co., n.d.), 9–14; *Spirit of the Chicago Convention: Extracts from All the Notable Speeches Delivered In and Out of the National "Democratic" Convention,* Union Campaign Documents, No. 6 (n.p.: Weed, Parsons and Co., n.d.), 57–69; *The Votes of the Copperheads in the Congress of the United States* (n.p.: L. Towers, n.d.), 1–8; *The Copperhead Catechism: For the Instruction of Such Politicians as Are of Tender Years* (New York: Sinclair Tousey, 1864), 1–30; *Issues of the Campaign: Shall the North Vote for a Disunion Peace?,* Chicago Tribune Campaign Document, No. 2 (n.p., n.d.), 1–16. George Morgan wrote to Marble about rebutting the Union pamphlets with a Democratic version of Pendleton's record. If the following is the result of his efforts, it is not clear. George W. M[organ] to Marble, Sept. 27, 1864, Marble Papers; George H. Pendleton, *George H. Pendleton and the Volunteers: Behold the Record!* (n.p., n.d.), 1–4.

34. The *Cincinnati Gazette* pushed for a Pendleton response as well. *Cincinnati Gazette,* Sept. 19, 24, Oct. 4, 24, 28, 1864; *New York Times,* Oct. 3, 16, 28, 1864; Katz, *August Belmont,* 135–36.

35. C. C. Hazewell, "The Twentieth Presidential Election," *Atlantic Monthly: A Magazine of Literature, Art and Politics* 14 (Nov. 1864): 635; *Harper's Weekly,* Sept. 3, 10, 24, Oct. 1, 15, Nov. 5, 1864; *New York Times,* Sept. 23, 1864.

36. Pendleton to [August Belmont], Sept. 27, 1864, copy of original apparently sent to McClellan and found in the McClellan Papers.

37. Ibid.

38. Ibid. Pendleton was serenaded twice in Cincinnati and Dayton, but made no substantive statements regarding the ticket or platform of the party. *Ohio Statesman,* Sept. 8, 22, 1864; *Cincinnati Commercial,* Sept. 19, 1864; Myers, *General George B. McClellan,* 458.

39. Samuel S. Cox to McClellan, Sept. 21, Oct. 11, 21, 1864, George W. Morgan to McClellan, Oct. 9, 13, 1864, McClellan Papers; *Cincinnati Enquirer,* Sept. 8, 1864; *Ohio Statesman,* Oct. 18, 1864; *Harper's Weekly,* Oct. 22, 1864; Hazewell, "Twentieth Presidential Election," 641; James A. Rawley, *The Politics of Union: Northern Politics during the Civil War* (Hinsdale, Ill.: Dryden Press, 1974), 160–61; Dudley, "Election of 1864," 514–15; Roseboom, *Civil War Era,* 434–35. Yager compared the numbers to the election for governor. The turn-out for the October election of 1864 was 12 percent lighter than for the 1863 gubernatorial election. The Unionist home vote fell by 17 percent, while its soldier vote dropped 25 percent. The Democrats lost only 2 percent at home and gained 71 percent among soldiers. While Yager suggested that Ohio Democrats look ahead to the November election with re-newed hope, there was little optimism in the letters of Cox and Morgan, who often briefed McClellan on events in Ohio. Yager, "Campaign of 1864," 582.

40. Katz, *August Belmont,* 141.

41. George H. Pendleton, *Hear Honorable George H. Pendleton* (n.p., n.d.), 1–2. In a letter to an unknown recipient, Pendleton clearly expressed concern about the campaign. He asked about the state situation and spoke of the willingness of Gov. Joel Parker of New Jersey and Gov. William A. Richardson of Illinois to speak during the canvass. George H. Pendleton to Unknown, Sept. 21, 1864, Pendleton Miscellaneous Manu-scripts, Rutherford B. Hayes Presidential Library, Fremont, Ohio.

42. Pendleton, *Hear Honorable George H. Pendleton,* 1.

43. Ibid., 4.

44. Ibid., 3–4; *New York Times,* Oct. 25, 1864; *Cincinnati Commercial,* Oct. 27, 1864; *Cincinnati Enquirer,* Oct. 27, 1864.

45. Pendleton's ambivalence was not lost on Republican editors, who vociferously criticized his speech as smoke and mirrors. *New York Times,* Oct. 26, 30, 1864; *Harper's Weekly,* Nov. 5, 1864.

46. *Cincinnati Enquirer,* Nov. 3, 1864.

47. *Cleveland Plain Dealer,* Nov. 2, 1864; *Cincinnati Enquirer,* Nov. 3, 1864.

48. For example, Horatio Seymour, "Speech of Governor Seymour at Philadelphia," Campaign Document, No. 21 in *Handbook of the Democracy* (New York: n.p., 1864), 1–8; The *Handbook* abounds with others.

49. *Cleveland Plain Dealer,* Sept. 7, Oct. 29, 1864; *Cincinnati Enquirer,* Oct. 4, 12, Nov. 3, 1864.

50. Faran quoted the *New York Tribune,* Sept. 30, 1864. *Cincinnati Enquirer,* Oct. 4, 1864. Democratic papers agreed. *The Crisis,* Sept. 28, 1864; *Dayton Empire,* Nov. 14, 1864.

51. *New York Times,* Sept. 4, 1864; *Harper's Weekly,* Sept. 17, 1864.

52. Manton Marble to McClellan, Sept. 12, 1864, McClellan Papers; *Cincinnati Con-vention, October 18, 1864, for the Organization of a Peace Party, upon State-Rights, Jefferso-nian, Democratic Principles and for the Promotion of Peace and Independent Nominations for President and Vice-President of the United States* (n.p., n.d.), 1–16; Joanna Cowden, *"Heaven Will Frown on Such a Cause As This": Six Democrats Who Opposed Lincoln's War* (Lanham, Md.: Univ. Press of America, 2001), 188–90.

53. Yager, "Campaign of 1864," 583; Roseboom, *Civil War Era,* 435; Oscar Osburn Winther, "The Soldier Vote in the Election of 1864," *Quarterly Journal of the New York State Historical Association* 25 (Oct. 1944): 457.

54. Yager, "Campaign of 1864," 583.

55. Dudley, "Election of 1864," 517.

56. A. B. Norton to McClellan, Jan. 2, 1865, McClellan Papers; Earl J. Hess, *Liberty, Virtue, and Progress: Northerners and Their War for the Union,* 2d ed. (New York: Fordham Univ. Press, 1997), 81–102.

57. Hess, *Liberty, Virtue, and Progress,* 81–102; James F. Young to McClellan, Nov. 10, 1864, James Stokes to McClellan, Nov. 10, 1864, McClellan Papers. The strength of the peace element was evidenced by the actions of the congressional caucus, the concern of eastern War Democrats about the midwestern vote, the adoption of a peace platform by the party, and the selection of Pendleton as the vice-presidential candidate.

58. *Cincinnati Gazette,* Aug. 30, 1864.

59. *Congressional Globe,* 38th Cong., 2d sess., 1865, 221–23.

60. Cox's position on this issue is somewhat difficult to understand but was illustrative of his ambivalence throughout the war. In the First Session, he opposed the amendment. In the Second Session, he decided that the Constitution did not forbid the amendment and that slavery had to be removed as a political issue to reunite the nation. He intended to support the proposal on that basis, but at the last minute voted against it, fearing that it would hurt the peace negotiations. Cox attacked Pendleton's speech and leadership in a letter to Manton Marble. By this time, it is apparent that he viewed Pendleton as a threat to his desire to be seen as the state's leading Democrat. Cox suggested that Democrats needed to support the amendment just to "get rid of the element, which ever keeps us in the minority and on the defense." He had referred to that "element" earlier in the letter as Pendleton's wing of the party—the Extreme Peace men. Whatever his reasoning, Cox's sometime support of the amendment played a key role in its passing, according to William H. Seward. S. S. Cox to Marble, Jan. 7, 1865, Marble Papers; Samuel S. Cox, *Three Decades of Federal Legislation, 1855 to 1885: Personal and Historical Memories of Events Preceding, During, and Since the American Civil War, Involving Slavery and Secession, Emancipation and Reconstruction, with Sketches of Prominent Actors during These Periods* (1885; repr., New York: Books for Libraries Press, 1970), 320–27; *Congressional Globe,* 38th Cong., 2d sess., 1865, 222, 238–42; Lindsey, *"Sunset" Cox,* 93–95.

61. Cox, *Three Decades of Federal Legislation,* 322.

62. Ibid., 325.

63. Ibid., 321; *Congressional Globe,* 38th Cong., 2d sess., 1865, 70, ICPSR; McPherson, *History of the Rebellion,* 590; *Cincinnati Enquirer,* Jan. 19, 20, 26, 1865; Lindsey, *"Sunset" Cox,* 92–95; LaWanda Cox and John H. Cox, *Politics, Principle, and Prejudice, 1865–1866* (London: Free Press of Glencoe, 1963), 1–30. One listener in the gallery was a soldier in the 11th U.S. Infantry. He noted in a letter to his parents his impression of Pendleton's speech: "He has a shrill voice—nothing forcible about it." Most commentators lauded Pendleton's "oratorical prowess." George Merryweather to "Parents," Jan. 15, 1865, Merryweather Civil War Letters, Chicago Historical Society, Chicago.

64. In the end, Pendleton was more than just an obstructionist. He sought the return of Cincinnatians held as prisoners of war and the timely pay of Cincinnati quartermasters. He also continued to support peace negotiations. George Pendleton to George Harrington, Assistant Secretary [of the Treasury], Feb. 7, 1865, Pendleton to Barlow, Jan. 16, 31, Feb. 1, 6, 1865, Pendleton Papers, Henry E. Huntington Library, San Marino, California; *Congressional Globe,* 38th Cong., 2d sess., 1865, 3, 6, 99–100; *OR,* ser. 2, vol. 7:1199.

65. *Congressional Globe,* 38th Cong., 1st sess., 1864, 1448, 2575. Pendleton had not abandoned reform ideas in the previous Congress in spite of the war concerns. After seeing the deplorable conditions of the Washington, D.C., jail, he introduced a resolution to investigate means of improvement and later favored building a new jail. *Congressional Globe,* 37th Cong., 2d sess., 1862, 229; Floyd Oliver Rittenhouse, "George Hunt Pendleton: With Special Reference to His Congressional Career" (M.A. thesis, Ohio State University, 1932), 35.

66. *Congressional Globe,* 38th Cong., 2d sess., 1865, 414, 1335; *Cincinnati Enquirer,* Mar. 12, 26, Dec. 23, 1864, Jan. 6, 1865; Bloss, *Life of Pendleton,* 83.

67. Concerning the bill to give cabinet officers seats in the House, both parties were divided. Immediately after Pendleton's speech on May 3, Republican James F. Wilson of Iowa spoke against the bill for reasons similar to those expressed by Cox. *Congressional Globe,* 38th Cong., 2d sess., 1865, appendix, 106–8.

68. *Congressional Globe,* 38th Cong., 2d sess., 1865, 437–44; Lindsey, *"Sunset" Cox,* 88–89.

69. *Congressional Globe,* 38th Cong., 2d sess., 1865, 104–6.

70. Ibid., 103–6.

Pendleton and Party Unity: The Ohio Idea

1. George H. Pendleton to Robert G. Barnwell, Oct. 17, 1866, James D. B. DeBow Papers, William R. Perkins Library, Duke University, Durham, North Carolina; *Cincinnati Enquirer,* Feb. 12, 1866. The extent of Pendleton law activities is unknown. He was frequently available, however, for political speeches in and out of the state. A portion of this chapter was previously published as "George Hunt Pendleton, The Ohio Idea and Political Continuity in Reconstruction America," *Ohio History* 108 (Summer–Autumn 1999): 125–144, and is reproduced here with permission from *Ohio History,* copyright 1999 by the Ohio Historical Society.

2. Eric L. McKitrick, *Andrew Johnson and Reconstruction* (Chicago: Univ. of Chicago Press, 1960), 67–76; Martin E. Mantell, *Johnson, Grant, and the Politics of Reconstruction* (New York: Columbia Univ. Press, 1973), 9–20; Jerome Mushkat, *The Reconstruction of the New York Democracy, 1861–1874* (Rutherford, N.J.: Fairleigh Dickinson Univ. Press, 1981), 66. See also Hans L. Trefousse, *Andrew Johnson: A Biography* (New York: W.W. Norton and Co., 1989).

3. Howard K. Beale, *The Critical Year: A Study of Andrew Johnson and Reconstruction* (New York: Harcourt, Brace and Co., 1930; repr., New York: Frederick Ungar, 1958), 30–47; McKitrick, *Andrew Johnson and Reconstruction,* 48–52; Robert D. Sawrey, *Dubious Victory: The Reconstruction Debate in Ohio* (Lexington: Univ. Press of Kentucky, 1992), 29–46.

4. *Cincinnati Enquirer,* Aug. 25, 1865.

5. George H. Pendleton to Andrew Johnson, Jan. 28, 1866, Andrew Johnson Papers, Manuscript Division, Library of Congress, Washington, D.C. Pendleton wrote the president several times to give references for men seeking government offices, including a letter for Maj. Gen. J. B. Steedman seeking to replace Secretary of War Stanton. Pendleton demonstrated his willingness to work with Unionists on Reconstruction issues with this

letter because Steedman was not a Democrat. See ibid.; Pendleton to Johnson, Aug. 6, 1866, R. Morrow to Pendleton, Johnson Papers; *Cincinnati Enquirer,* Aug. 25, 1865; La-Wanda Cox and John H. Cox, *Politics, Principle, and Prejudice, 1865–1866* (London: Free Press of Glencoe, 1963), 176–77; Sawry, *Dubious Victory,* 67.

6. *Cincinnati Enquirer,* Aug. 25, Oct. 5, 1865; *American Annual Cyclopedia and Register of Important Events of the Year 1861* (New York: D. Appleton and Co., 1862), 5:685–86; George H. Porter, *Ohio Politics during the Civil War Period,* Columbia University Studies in the Social Sciences (1911; repr., New York: Ams Press, 1968), 214–19; Clifford H. Moore, "Ohio in National Politics, 1865–1896," *Ohio Archaeological and Historical Society Publications* 37 (Apr. 1928): 232–36; Eugene H. Roseboom, *The Civil War Era, 1850–1873,* vol. 4 of *The History of the State of Ohio,* ed. Carl Wittke (Columbus: Ohio State Archaeological and Historical Society, 1944), 451–53.

7. *Cincinnati Enquirer,* Jan. 10, 17, Feb. 12, Mar. 9, 1866; *Boston Daily Courier,* Jan. 20, 1866. See also Paul A. Cimbala and Randall M. Miller, eds., *The Freedmen's Bureau and Reconstruction: Reconsiderations* (New York: Fordham Univ. Press, 1999).

8. Porter, *Ohio Politics,* 221; James Ford Rhodes, *History of the United States from the Compromise of 1850 to the End of the Roosevelt Administration* (New York: MacMillan, 1928), 6:53–74; McKitrick, *Andrew Johnson and Reconstruction,* 274–325; Cox and Cox, *Politics, Principle, and Prejudice,* 172–232; W. R. Brock, *An American Crisis: Congress and Reconstruction, 1865–1867* (London: MacMillan and Co., 1963), 105–22; Mantell, *Politics of Reconstruction,* 9–26; Sawrey, *Dubious Victory,* 59–67.

9. *American Annual Cyclopedia,* 6:603; *Cincinnati Enquirer,* May 25, 1866; *New York Times,* May 25, 1866; *Evening Post,* May 29, 1866; *New York Herald,* May 26, 1866.

10. The *Boston Daily Courier* reported earlier that the *New York Herald* advised the Democratic Party to form an alliance with conservative Union men and surrender its name. *Boston Daily Courier,* Feb. 5, 1866; M. H. Mitchell to William Allen, Aug. 8, 1866, William Allen Papers, Manuscript Division, Library of Congress, Washington, D.C.; Henry W. Raymond, ed., "Extracts from the Journal of Henry J. Raymond, Fourth Paper: The Philadelphia Convention of 1866," *Scribner's Monthly* 20 (June 1880): 275–77; Thomas Wagstaff, "The Arm-in-Arm Convention," *Civil War History* 14 (June 1968): 101–5; James M. McPherson, *Ordeal by Fire: The Civil War and Reconstruction* (New York: Alfred A. Knopf, 1982), 518–20.

11. George H. Pendleton, *Address Delivered in Rosse Chapel, Before the Nu Pi Kappa Society of Kenyon College* (Cincinnati, Ohio: Moore, Wilstach and Baldwin, 1866), 1–24; *Cincinnati Enquirer,* July 21, 26, 31, Aug. 2, 1866; *Cincinnati Commercial: Speeches of the Campaign of 1866 in the States of Ohio, Indiana, and Kentucky* (Cincinnati, Ohio: n.p., 1866), 4–5. Vallandigham expressed the concern of some Ohio Democrats that the convention would seek the formation of a new party and disband the Democratic Party. Only after the state central committee was convinced that this was not the aim of the Philadelphia gathering did they sanction it. Three other Ohio Democrats were elected delegates-at-large: William Allen, Gen. George Morgan, and W. R. Willett. *Cincinnati Gazette,* Aug. 16, 1866; Porter, *Ohio Politics,* 228–29; Roseboom, *Civil War Era,* 454–55; Glyndon G. Van Deusen, *William Henry Seward* (New York: Oxford Univ. Press, 1967), 458–61.

12. J. D. Cox to Lewis Campbell, Lewis Campbell Papers, Ohio Historical Society, Columbus; Belmont to Marble, July 17, 1866, Manton Marble Papers, Manuscript Division,

Library of Congress; *New York World,* Aug. 15, 1866; Duane Mowry, ed., "Some Political Letters of Reconstruction Days Succeeding the Civil War," *American Historical Magazine* 4 (May 1909): 332.

13. *Cincinnati Commercial,* Aug. 14–15, 1866; *Cincinnati Enquirer,* Aug. 14–15, 1866; *Cleveland Plain Dealer,* Aug. 14–16, 1866; Raymond, "Journal of Henry J. Raymond," 276–78; James G. Blaine, *Twenty Years of Congress: From Lincoln to Garfield, With a Review of the Events which Led to the Political Revolution of 1860* (Norwich, Conn.: Henry Bill, 1886), 220–22; Bloss said Pendleton did not attend the convention, but most secondary sources assume he did, and the *Times* verified his presence. G. M. D. Bloss, *Life and Speeches of George Hunt Pendleton* (Cincinnati, Ohio: Miami, 1868), 96–97; *New York Times,* Aug. 13–16, 1866; Porter, *Ohio Politics,* 231; Beale, *Critical Year,* 130–34; Roseboom, *Civil War Era,* 454–55; Wagstaff, "Arm-in-Arm Convention," 108–15; Jerome Mushkat, *Fernando Wood: A Political Biography* (Kent, Ohio: Kent State Univ. Press, 1990), 158–60.

14. *American Annual Cyclopedia,* 6:757; *Cincinnati Commercial,* Aug. 16, 1866; *Cincinnati Gazette,* Aug. 17, 1866; *Cincinnati Enquirer,* Aug. 17, 1866; Beale, *Critical Year,* 123–38; Wagstaff, "Arm-in-Arm Convention," 110–19.

15. *Cincinnati Enquirer,* Aug. 31, 1866; *Cincinnati Gazette,* Sept. 3, 1866; *The Crisis,* Sept. 12, 1866.

16. *Cincinnati Enquirer,* Sept. 25, 1866; *Cincinnati Commercial,* Oct. 9, 1866.

17. *Cincinnati Enquirer,* Sept. 5, 1866; *Cincinnati Commercial,* Sept. 5, 1866; *Cincinnati Gazette,* Sept. 5, 1866; *Cleveland Plain Dealer,* Sept. 6, 1866. The desire to concentrate on the present and forget the past was shared by other Democrats. Porter, *Ohio Politics,* 217–18; Frank L. Klement, *The Limits of Dissent* (Lexington: Univ. Press of Kentucky, 1970), 304–5; Felice A. Bonadio, *North of Reconstruction: Ohio Politics, 1865–1870* (New York: New York Univ. Press, 1970), 69.

18. *Cincinnati Commercial,* Sept. 13, 18, 24, 26, 29, 1866; *Cincinnati Enquirer,* Sept. 18, 27, Oct. 2, 1866; *Cincinnati Gazette,* Sept. 17, 25, 26, 28, 1866.

19. *Cincinnati Commercial,* Sept. 21, 22, Oct. 6, 1866; *Cleveland Plain Dealer,* Sept. 22, 26, 1866; *Cincinnati Enquirer,* Oct. 1, 1866. Republican papers tried to portray the race as an aristocrat (Pendleton) versus a commoner (Eggleston). Democrats used this to their advantage, also citing Pendleton's superior education, intellect, and experience. Pendleton responded by stressing the issue of Republican expenditures and the resulting high taxation that burdened the laboring class. *Cincinnati Commercial: Speeches of the Campaign of 1866,* 4–5, 24–25, 38; *Cincinnati Enquirer,* Sept. 27, Oct. 25, 1866.

20. McKitrick, *Andrew Johnson and Reconstruction,* 421–27; Sawrey, *Dubious Victory,* 76.

21. J. D. Cox to Lewis D. Campbell, Apr. 28, 1866, Campbell Papers; Gideon Welles, *Diary of Gideon Welles: Secretary of the Navy under Lincoln and Johnson* (Boston: Houghton Mifflin, 1911), 2:588–96; Porter, *Ohio Politics,* 132–33; Rhodes, *History of the United States,* 6:102–6; Roseboom, *Civil War Era,* 456; McKitrick, *Andrew Johnson and Reconstruction,* 428–47; Hans L. Trefousse, *The Radical Republicans: Lincoln's Vanguard for Racial Justice* (Baton Rouge: Louisiana State Univ. Press, 1968), 330–31.

22. *Cincinnati Enquirer,* Oct. 18, 1866; Bloss, *Life of Pendleton,* 99–100; *Speeches of the Campaign of 1866, in the States of Ohio, Indiana and Kentucky: The Most Remarkable Speeches on Both Sides* (Cincinnati: Cincinnati Commercial, n.d.), 52.

23. Moore, "Ohio in National Politics," 236–40, 250–59; Floyd O. Rittenhouse, "George Hunt Pendleton: With Special Reference to His Congressional Career" (M.A. thesis, Ohio State University, 1932), 53–55; McKitrick, *Andrew Johnson and Reconstruction*, 274–325; Brock, *American Crisis*, 105–22; Sawrey, *Dubious Victory*, 59–67. See also Edward L. Gambill, *Conservative Ordeal: Northern Democrats and Reconstruction, 1865–1868* (Ames: Iowa State Univ. Press, 1981).

24. Max L. Shipley, "The Background and Legal Aspects of the Pendleton Plan," *Mississippi Valley Historical Review* 24 (Sept. 1937): 329–32; Robert P. Sharkey, *Money, Class, and Party: An Economic Study of Civil War and Reconstruction* (Baltimore, Md.: Johns Hopkins Press, 1959), 56–80; Chester M. Destler, *American Radicalism, 1865–1901: Essays and Documents* (New York: Octagon Books, 1963), 32–34; Irwin Unger, *The Greenback Era: A Social and Political History of American Finance, 1865–1879* (Princeton, N. J.: Princeton Univ. Press, 1964), 15–17, 41–43; Michael Les Benedict, *A Compromise of Principle: Congressional Republicans and Reconstruction, 1863–1869* (New York: W. W. Norton and Co., 1974), 262–64; Heather Cox Richardson, *The Greatest Nation of the Earth: Republican Economic Policies during the Civil War* (Cambridge, Mass.: Harvard Univ. Press, 1997), 75–89. See also Wesley Clair Mitchell, *A History of the Greenbacks: With Special Reference to the Economic Consequences of Their Issue: 1862–1865* (Chicago: Univ. of Chicago Press, 1903; repr., Chicago: Univ. of Chicago Press, 1960).

25. *Cincinnati Enquirer*, July 22, 1867; George H. Pendleton, *Payment of the Public Debt in Legal Tender Notes!! Speech of Hon. George H. Pendleton, Milwaukee, November 2, 1867* (n.p., n.d.), 11–12; George H. Pendleton, "Speech of Hon. George H. Pendleton, of Ohio, at Grafton, West Virginia, July 16, 1868," in *Democratic Speaker's Handbook* (Cincinnati, Ohio: Miami, 1868), 310–15; Shipley, "Background of the Pendleton Plan," 329–32; Albert V. House, "Northern Congressional Democrats as Defenders of the South during Reconstruction," *Journal of Southern History* 6 (Feb. 1940): 46–48; George L. Anderson, "The South and Problems of Post-Civil War Finance," *Journal of Southern History* 9 (Aug. 1943): 181–95; Sharkey, *Money, Class, and Party*, 56–80; Destler, *American Radicalism*, 32–34.

26. Don C. Barrett, *The Greenbacks and Resumption of Specie Payments, 1862–1879*, Harvard Economic Studies, vol. 36 (Cambridge, Mass.: Harvard Univ. Press, 1931), 161–69; Edward S. Perzel, "Alexander Long, Salmon P. Chase, and the Election of 1868," *Bulletin of the Cincinnati Historical Society* 23 (Jan. 1965): 3–5; Destler, *American Radicalism*, 49; David Montgomery, *Beyond Equality: Labor and the Radical Republicans, 1862–1872* (New York: Knopf, 1967; repr., Urbana: Univ. of Illinois Press, 1981), 65–66; Sawrey, *Dubious Victory*, 107–9.

27. *Cincinnati Enquirer*, Apr. 19, June 6, 1867; Roseboom, *Civil War Era*, 459; Sharkey, *Money, Class, and Party*, 98–101; Destler, *American Radicalism*, 37–38.

28. *Cincinnati Enquirer*, Jan. 9, 10, May 8, Sept. 18, 1867; *New York Times*, Jan. 9, 13, 1867; Porter, *Ohio Politics*, 238–43; Roseboom, *Civil War Era*, 459. For Republican activities in the 1867 election, see Michael Les Benedict, "The Rout of Radicalism: Republicans and the Elections of 1867," *Civil War History* 18 (Dec. 1972): 334–44.

29. John H. James Jr. to Pendleton, Feb. 31, Mar. 29, Apr. 15, 1867, James Family Papers, Ohio Historical Society, Columbus; *Cincinnati Enquirer*, Apr. 26, May 3, 1867; *New York Times*, Apr. 29, 1867.

30. *Taxing National Currency, Etc.* (Apr. 16, 1866), 39th Cong., 1st sess., H. Miscellaneous Document 87 (serial 1271); *Letter of the Secretary of the Treasury to the Chairman of the Committee on Finance, Transmitting a Statement Relative to the Apportionment of National Currency* (Apr. 23, 1866), 39th Cong., 1st sess., S. Miscellaneous Document 100 (serial 1239); *Cincinnati Enquirer,* July 17, 1867; *New York Times,* July 17, 1867; *Government Funds in National Banks* (Jan. 9, 1868), 40th Cong., 2d sess., H. Executive Document 87 (serial 1332); Destler, *American Radicalism,* 38–39.

31. Pendleton argued that the Republican contraction program would add $48 million in yearly interest payments. Destler suggested that Pendleton adopted Jewett's sinking fund idea. George H. Pendleton, *Speech of Hon. George H. Pendleton, Delivered at Lima, Allen County, Ohio, Thursday, August 15, 1867* (Columbus, Ohio: Crisis Office, 1867), 4–5; *Extracts from Hon. George H. Pendleton's Speeches at Lima and Cleveland* (n.p., n.d.), 2–4; *Cincinnati Enquirer,* Aug. 16, 1867; *New York Times,* Aug. 18, 1867. Pendleton's figures were rounded off estimates but may be somewhat low. One government document shows him to be pretty accurate and may have been his source of information. Wesley Mitchell and Irwin Unger figure the total debt to be closer to $2.8 billion, with $800 million in five-twenties sold by war's end. Pendleton tended to focus on the $400 million in five-twenties held by branches of the National Bank. *Statement of the Public Debt of the United States* (Mar. 3, 1868), 40th Cong., 2d sess., H. Misc. Doc. 87 (serial 1350); Moore, "Ohio in National Politics," 250; Destler, *American Radicalism,* 39; Unger, *Greenback Era,* 16–17; Mitchell, *Greenbacks,* 419; Benedict, *Compromise of Principle,* 262–63.

32. *Extracts from Speeches at Lima and Cleveland,* 2–4; *New York Times,* Sept. 22, 1867. Thaddeus Stevens and Oliver P. Morton, two other Republicans, agreed with Sherman that the five-twenties were indeed legally payable in greenbacks. John Sherman, *Funding of the National Debt, Speech of Hon. John Sherman, of Ohio, in the United States Senate, May 22, 1866* (n.p., n.d.), 1–15. Sherman later recanted, saying he had not favored the payment of the debt in greenbacks until they were at par with gold, which he said was stipulated in the original legal tender act. In essence, the bonds were payable in greenbacks, but only when they were at par. John Sherman, *John Sherman's Recollections of Forty Years in the House, Senate and Cabinet: An Autobiography* (Chicago: Werner, 1895), 2:624–25; Shipley, "Background of the Pendleton Plan," 334–35. See also *Interview between the United States Senate Committee on Finance and the Hon. John Sherman, Sec. of the Treasury, on Refunding, Resumption, Legal-Tenders for Customs Dues, Sinking Fund, and Kindred Subjects* (n.p., 1880).

33. Pendleton, *Payment of the Public Debt,* 1–12; *Cincinnati Enquirer,* Nov. 7, 1867; Destler, *American Radicalism,* 39–41.

34. The *Times* reluctantly accepted the correction of a subscriber that Pendleton was being misrepresented in the paper. While the paper acknowledged that Pendleton was not the inflationist that others were, it doubted whether his plan could be accomplished without some inflation. *New York Times,* Nov. 18, 1867. Pendleton wrote to Manton Marble of the *New York World* hoping Marble would print a portion of Pendleton's Milwaukee speech in a response to the *Times.* Marble was cordial to Pendleton and complied with his request, but was not a supporter of the plan. Nonetheless, Marble defended Pendleton from critics who called him an inflationist. Pendleton to Marble, Nov. 13, 1867, Marble to Pendleton, Nov. 23, 1867, Marble Papers; *New York World,* Nov. 19, 1867;

Feb. 1, 4, May 6, 29, 1868; Pendleton to Horace Greeley, Nov. 13, 1867, Horace Greeley Papers, Manuscript Division, Library of Congress, Washington, D.C.; Destler, *American Radicalism,* 40–41.

35. Pendleton, *Payment of the Public Debt,* 9; Edward McPherson, *A Handbook of Politics for 1868* (1868; repr., New York: Negro Univ. Press, 1969), 354.

36. McPherson, *Handbook of Politics for 1868,* 354; Pendleton, *Payment of the Public Debt,* 9; Benjamin E. Green to Samuel J. Randall, Jan. 2, 1868, Samuel J. Randall Papers, Historical Society of Pennsylvania, Philadelphia; Joseph Medill to Sherman, Jan. 7, 1868, John Sherman Papers, Manuscript Division, Library of Congress, Washington, D.C.; *Cincinnati Enquirer,* Feb. 5, 1868. While Sharkey and Sawrey tend to dismiss Pendleton's ideas as politically expedient and philosophically inconsistent with Jacksonianism, other historians disagree. One of the earliest to note Pendleton's focus on special privilege was Max Shipley. Chester M. Destler followed Shipley's work, calling Pendleton "at the worst, . . . a re-inflationist." Irwin Unger echoes Destler's comments, noting that while hard-money Democrats accused Pendleton of inconsistency, their charges that he was an inflationist were "unfair." One of the most recent studies of the era concurs that Pendleton was essentially consistent to long-held Jacksonian ideals. Gretchen Ritter notes that under the Pendleton Plan, Jacksonian principle was reinterpreted to advocate paper money while maintaining the traditional opposition to the banking system and special status for bondholders. Yet none of these historians takes a strong enough stand on the basic consistency of Pendleton's plan with Jacksonianism. Even Ritter, who speaks the most forthrightly in her comparison of the plan with Jacksonian ideas, classifies Pendleton as an antimonopolist rather than a conservative. She places Jacksonianism within her "conservative" category, but not the Pendleton Plan, because she fails to emphasize Pendleton's ultimate goal of specie resumption. Charles H. Coleman, *The Election of 1868: The Democratic Effort to Regain Control* (New York: Columbia Univ. Press, 1933; repr., New York: Octagon Books, 1971), 25–33; Shipley, "Background of the Pendleton Plan," 339; Sharkey, *Money, Class, and Party,* 99–107, 197, 219, 282–85; Destler, *American Radicalism,* 40; Unger, *Greenback Era,* 84; Montgomery, *Beyond Equality,* 101–2; Richard G. Thompson, *Expectations and the Greenback Rate, 1862–1878* (New York: Garland, 1985), 40–45; Gretchen Ritter, *Goldbugs and Greenbacks: The Antimonopoly Tradition and the Politics of Finance in America* (New York: Cambridge Univ. Press, 1997), 1–9, 41–44.

37. Destler and Unger emphasize the importance of the currency issue while Jerome Mushkat and Sawrey point to race issues. Benedict notes both issues but concluded, "In Ohio the money question had damaged Republicans." Destler, *American Radicalism,* 32–40; Unger, *Greenback Era,* 80–87; Benedict, *Compromise of Principle,* 272–73; Mushkat, *Reconstruction of the New York Democracy,* 113–20; Sawrey, *Dubious Victory,* 105–7.

38. *Cincinnati Enquirer,* Oct. 2, 1867; *New York Herald,* Oct. 7, 9, 10, 12, 1867; *Boston Daily Courier,* Oct. 11, 17, 18, 1867; *New York Leader,* Oct. 12, 1867; *New York World,* Oct. 14, 1867; *New York Tribune,* Oct. 14, 1867; Pendleton to Horatio Seymour, Oct. 21, 1867, Fairchild Collection, New York Historical Society, New York. A Sherman correspondent noted that the currency question had eclipsed the amendment issue by the time of the election. J. C. Devin to John Sherman, Sept. 30, 1867, Schuyler Colfax to Sherman, Oct. 12, 1867, Sherman Papers; Edward McPherson, *The Political History of the United States of America during the Period of Reconstruction, From April 15, 1865, to July 15, 1870* (Washington,

D.C.: Philip and Solomons, 1871), 257–58; McPherson, *Handbook of Politics for 1868,* 354–55; Porter, *Ohio Politics,* 235–48; Moore, "Ohio in National Politics," 240–44; Roseboom, *Civil War Era,* 457–63.

39. *New York Times,* Sept. 22, 1867; Sherman, *Funding of the National Debt,* 1–15; Sherman, *Recollections of Forty Years,* 624–25.

40. R. J. to Sherman, Nov. 11, 1867, Joseph Medill to Sherman, Nov. 22, 1867, Jan. 7, 1868, David Wilder to Sherman, Dec. 20, 1867, C. Davenport to Sherman, Dec. 27, 1867, Sherman Papers; Samuel S. Cox to Marble, Oct. 1, 1867, Marble Papers; *New York Leader,* Aug. 24, 1867; *Cincinnati Enquirer,* May 20, June 3, 6, 26, July 12, 18, 29, Aug. 24, Oct. 17, 18, Nov. 1, 1867; Jan. 4, 1868; Shipley, "Background of the Pendleton Plan," 330–35; Sharkey, *Money, Class, and Party,* 96–97; Destler, *American Radicalism,* 34–35; Montgomery, *Beyond Equality,* 340–56.

41. *Evening Post,* Sept. 7, 1867; "Repudiation Again," *Nation* 5 (Oct. 10, 1867): 294–96; "Correspondence," *Nation* 5 (Oct. 24, 1867): 338–39; "What Inflation Means," *Nation* 5 (Dec. 12, 1867): 480–81; *New York World,* Nov. 19, 1867; Sharkey, *Money, Class, and Party,* 168–69.

42. Jay Cooke to John Sherman, Mar. 2, 1868, Sherman Papers; Pendleton, *Payment of the Public Debt,* 5, 8–9; John Sherman, *The Funding Bill, Speech of Hon. John Sherman, of Ohio, Delivered in the Senate of the United States, Feb. 27, 1868* (Washington, D.C.: F. and J. Rives and George A. Bailey, 1868), 7–8.

43. Benedict, *Compromise of Principle,* 257–78; Montgomery, *Beyond Equality,* 340–56; Terry L. Seip, *The South Returns to Congress: Men, Economic Measures, and Intersectional Relationships, 1868–1879* (Baton Rouge: Louisiana State Univ. Press, 1983), 171–97.

44. *New York Herald,* Oct. 21, 1867; *Cincinnati Enquirer,* Oct. 22, 25, 28, Nov. 9, 11, 14, Dec. 24, 26, 30, 1867; Jan. 6, 1868; *New York Times,* Oct. 24, 1867; Samuel S. Cox to Marble, Nov. 11, 1867, Marble Papers; Roseboom, *Civil War Era,* 464–65.

45. Pendleton to J. Sterling Morton, Jan. 23, Apr. 9, 1868, Morton Family Papers; Pendleton to M. W. Cluskey, May 24, June 2, 8, 16, 1868, Pendleton Miscellaneous Manuscripts, Kentucky Library and Museum, Western Kentucky University, Bowling Green.

46. Pendleton to J. Sterling Morton, Dec. 3, 1867, Morton Family Papers; Pendleton to Unknown, Dec. 25, 1867, Pendleton Miscellaneous Manuscripts, Boston Public Library, Boston; Pendleton to Sylvanus Cadwallader, Feb. 2, 1868, Sylvanus Cadwallader Papers, Manuscript Division, Library of Congress, Washington, D.C. U. S. Grant expressed concern about the potential of Pendleton becoming president due to his peace views during the Civil War. Brooks D. Simpson, *Let Us Have Peace: Ulysses S. Grant and the Politics of War and Reconstruction, 1861–1868* (Chapel Hill: Univ. of North Carolina Press, 1991), 242–43.

47. *Cincinnati Enquirer,* Jan. 9, 1868; *New York Times,* Jan. 12, 1868.

48. *Cincinnati Enquirer,* Jan. 9, 10, 1868; *American Annual Cyclopedia,* 8:601–3; Roseboom, *Civil War Era,* 466; Destler, *American Radicalism,* 41–42.

49. Alexander D. Noyes, *Forty Years of American Finance: A Short History of the Government and People of the United States since the Civil War, 1865–1907* (New York: G. P. Putnam's Sons, 1909), 15–16; Barrett, *Greenbacks and Resumption,* 167–68; Unger, *Greenback Era,* 43.

50. Sherman, *Funding Bill,* 1–16; Joseph Medill to Sherman, Mar. 9, 1868, Sherman Papers; McPherson, *Handbook of Politics for 1868,* 382; *New York Times,* Dec. 26, 1868;

Barrett, *Greenbacks and Resumption,* 168–69; Walter T. K. Nugent, *Money and American Society, 1865–1880* (New York: Free Press, 1968), 131–39.

51. *New York World,* Jan. 8–9, 1868; *Cincinnati Enquirer,* Jan. 11, 14, 20, 31, 1868; Gambill, *Conservative Ordeal,* 123–36.

52. The "swallow-tail" Democrats were upper-class New Yorkers such as Samuel Tilden, Samuel Barlow, and August Belmont who favored a hard-money policy and the National Bank System. Irving Katz, *August Belmont: A Political Biography* (New York: Columbia Univ. Press, 1968), 170–71; Mushkat, *Reconstruction of the New York Democracy,* 34–35, 121.

53. *East Oregonian,* Nov. 4, 1935; Sept. 17, 1937; Lewis A. McArthur, *Oregon Geographic Names,* 5th ed. (n.p.: Western Imprints, 1982), 579–80.

54. Pendleton to J. Sterling Morton, Jan. 23, Mar. 12, 25, Apr. 9, June 20, 1868, Morton Family Papers; *New York Herald,* June 11, 1868; Destler, *American Radicalism,* 42; David Black, *King of Fifth Avenue: The Fortunes of August Belmont* (New York: Dial Press, 1981), 303–4.

55. Alexander Long to Salmon P. Chase, Apr. 6, 11, 1868, Chase to Long, Apr. 8, 19, 1868, J. W. Schuckers to Long, Apr. 30, June 15, 1868, M. S. Hawley to Long, June 18, 1868, Long Papers, Cincinnati Historical Society, Cincinnati; *New York World,* June 9, 1868. The Pendleton escort invited Long, in spite of his outspoken dissent, to join them in their trek to the convention. He undoubtedly declined. Invitation, May 22, 1868, Long Papers; J. W. Schuckers, *The Life and Public Services of Salmon Portland Chase, United States Senator and Governor of Ohio; Secretary of the Treasury, and Chief-Justice of the United States* (New York: D. Appleton and Co., 1874), 578, 589; Coleman, *Election of 1868,* 68–80, 119, 129–40; Perzel, "Alexander Long," 6; Frederick J. Blue, *Salmon P. Chase: A Life of Politics* (Kent, Ohio: Kent State Univ. Press, 1987), 286–91.

56. James L. Vallandigham, *A Life of Clement L. Vallandigham* (Baltimore, Md.: Turnbull Brothers, 1872), 422–24; *Cincinnati Commercial,* Feb. 7, 1868; *New York World,* Feb. 5, 1868; *Cincinnati Enquirer,* May 13, 1923; Moore, "Ohio in National Politics," 258–60; Horace Samuel Merrill, *Bourbon Leader: Grover Cleveland and the Democratic Party,* The Library of American Biography, ed. Oscar Handlin (Boston: Little, Brown and Co., 1957), 24–46; Katz, *August Belmont,* 167–71; Mushkat, *Reconstruction of the New York Democracy,* 113–42; Montgomery, *Beyond Equality,* 351.

57. *New York Times,* July 10, 1868; DeAlva S. Alexander, *A Political History of the State of New York,* vol. 3 (1909; repr., Port Washington, N.Y.: Ira J. Friedman, 1969), 89–97; Coleman, *Election of 1868,* 21–35, 149–86; Stewart Mitchell, *Horatio Seymour of New York* (New York: Da Capo Press, 1970), 383–411; Montgomery, *Beyond Equality,* 346; Blue, *Salmon P. Chase,* 292.

58. R. W. Clelland to Marble, Jan. 24, 1868; R. Gillet to Marble, Feb. 22, 1868; Horace White to Marble, Feb. 25, 1868; McLean to Marble, Mar. 22, Apr. 5, 1868; James R. Doolittle to Marble, May 30, 1868; Belmont to Marble, June 1868; Winslow Pierce to Marble, June 15, 1868, all in Marble Papers. W. F. Allen to Samuel Tilden, May 25, 1868; Frank Blair to Tilden, June 2, 1868; Montgomery Blair to Tilden, June 5, 1868; E. Casserly to Tilden, June 6, 1868; Samuel Ward to Tilden, June 9, 1868, all in Samuel J. Tilden Papers, Manuscripts and Archives Division, New York Public Library, Astor, Lenox and Tilden Foundations. J. W. Schuckers to Long, Apr. 30, June 15, 1868, Long Papers; McLean to

Samuel Barlow, Jan. 14, 1868, Samuel Barlow Papers, Henry E. Huntington Library, San Marino, California; *New York World,* Feb. 1, May 9, June 9, July 22, 1868; *Cincinnati Enquirer,* May 21, June 1, 10, 1868; *Cincinnati Gazette,* July 1–3, 6, 1868.

59. Marble to Pendleton, Nov. 23, 1867, Pendleton to Marble, Dec. 5, 1867; Mar. 3, 1868, Marble Papers; Samuel Ward to Salmon P. Chase, June 26, 1868, Salmon P. Chase Papers, Manuscript Division, Library of Congress, Washington, D.C.; *New York Herald,* Jan. 10, 27, Apr. 25, 1868; *New York World,* Feb. 1, May 9, June 1, 9, 26, July 2–4, 22, 1868; *Cincinnati Commercial,* Feb. 8, July 2–4, 1868; *New York Evening Post,* Feb. 13, 1868; *Cincinnati Gazette,* Feb. 27, July 1–3, 6, 1868; *New York Leader,* Mar. 28, Apr. 11, 18, 1868; *Cincinnati Enquirer,* May 2, 21, 29, June 1, 10, 1868; *Boston Daily Courier,* June 11, 22, 1868.

60. *Cincinnati Enquirer,* July 5–6, 1868; *Cincinnati Commercial,* July 6, 1868; Coleman, *Election of 1868,* 194–96.

61. *Official Proceedings of the National Democratic Convention, held at New York, July 4–9, 1868* (Boston: Rockwell and Rollins, 1868), 22–30; Coleman, *Election of 1868,* 196–98.

62. *Official Proceedings, 1868,* 58.

63. The National Labor Union endorsed these principles. *Official Proceedings, 1868,* 58–59; *New York World,* July 8, 1868; Coleman, *Election of 1868,* 200–202; Katz, *August Belmont,* 172–73; Black, *King of Fifth Avenue,* 303–5.

64. *Official Proceedings, 1868,* 59–61; *Cincinnati Commercial,* July 6, 1868; *Cleveland Plain Dealer,* July 7, 1868. Though it certainly was not the equivalent of a hard-money position, the Ohio Idea was aimed at restoring the country to the specie standard as soon as possible. The party, in large part due to Jackson, had long focused on the laboring element of the country. Pendleton's plan emphasized their concerns. In addition, it sought to destroy the National Bank System, though the platform did not include this provision, which was certainly a Jacksonian principle. Finally, Pendleton was a realist. He believed the best way, the least painful way, to reinstate the long-held party position on hard money was to make use of the Republican creation to its fullest advantage. Historians differ on the consistency of the platform with Jacksonianism. Coleman, *Election of 1868,* 201–5; Roseboom, *Civil War Era,* 466–67; Mitchell, *Horatio Seymour,* 417–20.

65. *Official Proceedings, 1868,* 58.

66. In the years prior to 1837, land speculation expanded due to a flurry of railroad and canal building. Banks fueled this growth with expanded credit. President Andrew Jackson, fearing runaway speculation, issued the Specie Circular in 1836 requiring all public lands to be purchased in gold. Jackson's action, combined with tightened credit in Europe and poor harvests among American farmers, created a significant depression in the late 1830s and early 1840s. Kellogg's writings encouraged some Americans to view paper currency as the means of preventing such economic problems. Peter Temin, *The Jacksonian Economy* (New York: W. W. Norton and Co., 1969), 113–47. See also Reginald C. McGrane, *The Panic of 1837: Some Financial Problems of the Jacksonian Era* (1924; repr., Chicago: Univ. of Chicago Press, 1965).

67. *New York World,* Sept. 22, 25, 30–31, 1868; T. V. Powderly, *Thirty Years of Labor, 1859–1889, in which the History of the Attempts to Form Organizations of Workingmen for the Discussion of Political, Social, and Economic Questions Is Traced, the National Labor Union of 1866, the Industrial Brotherhood of 1874, and the Order of the Knights of Labor of America and the World, the Chief and Most Important Principles in the Preamble of the*

Knights of Labor Discussed and Explained with Views of the Author on Land, Labor and Transportation (Columbus, Ohio: n.p., 1889), 48–89; Barrett, *Greenbacks and Resumption,* 161–73; Destler, *American Radicalism,* 44–49; Unger, *Greenback Era,* 81–91; Foster Rhea Dulles, *Labor in America: A History,* 3d ed. (New York: Crowell, 1966), 109–11; Joseph G. Rayback, *A History of American Labor,* exp. ed. (New York: MacMillan, 1966), 103–28.

68. *New York World,* Sept. 22, 25, 30–31, 1868; Montgomery, *Beyond Equality,* vii–xi, 335–60.

69. *Official Proceedings, 1868,* 68.

70. Ibid., 66–174; *Cincinnati Commercial,* July 9, 10, 1868; *Cleveland Plain Dealer,* July 9–11, 1868; *Cincinnati Enquirer,* July 10, 14, 1868; *New York Times,* July 10, 1868; *New York World,* July 10, 1868; *Diary and Correspondence of Salmon P. Chase* (New York: n.p., 1971), 520–21; Coleman, *Election of 1868,* 208–12; Mitchell, *Horatio Seymour,* 422–32; Gambill, *Conservative Ordeal,* 137–54; Blue, *Salmon P. Chase,* 294–95.

71. Blue, *Salmon P. Chase,* 303.

72. *Cincinnati Gazette,* July 10, 1868; *Cincinnati Commercial,* July 10–11, 1868; *Cincinnati Enquirer,* May 13, 1923; Charles R. Williams, ed., *Diary and Letters of Rutherford B. Hayes: Nineteenth President of the United States* (Columbus: Ohio Archaeological and Historical Society, 1926), 3:53–54; Coleman, *Election of 1868,* 212–14; Seip, *South Returns to Congress,* 171–218; Blue, *Salmon P. Chase,* 294–95.

73. Montgomery, *Beyond Equality,* 346–48.

74. Pendleton, "Speech at Grafton," 310–15; George H. Pendleton, *Common Sense for the People: Our Country and Its Condition, Speech of Hon. George H. Pendleton at Bangor, Thursday, August 20th, 1868* (n.p., n.d.), 1–8; Long to Seymour, July 14, 1868, Long to Chase, Oct. 15, 1868, Long Papers; Pendleton to Morton, Oct. 11, 1868, Morton Family Papers; *Cincinnati Enquirer,* July 25–Nov. 6, 1868; *Cincinnati Commercial,* Aug. 21–Sept. 16, 1868; *Cincinnati Gazette,* Aug. 22, Sept. 1, 1868.

75. Pendleton to Morton, May 2, 1868, Morton Family Papers; *Cincinnati Gazette,* Aug. 28, 1868; *Cincinnati Enquirer,* Aug. 31, 1868.

76. *Cincinnati Gazette,* Sept. 23, 1868; *New York Times,* Sept. 24, Oct. 1, 19, 1868.

77. *Harper's Weekly,* July 25, 1868; *Cincinnati Gazette,* Sept. 24, 25, 30, Oct. 6, 8, 14, 1868; *Cincinnati Commercial,* Oct. 19, 1868; *New York Times,* Oct. 21, 1868; "More About Bonds, Greenbacks, and Gold," *Nation* 7 (Sept. 10, 1868): 209.

78. Long to Chase, Oct. 15, 1868, Long Papers; Long to Chase, Sept. 10, Oct. 3, 1868, Chase Papers; Long to Marble, Oct. 17, 1868, Marble Papers; Samuel Ward to Samuel Barlow, July 16, 1868, Barlow Papers; *Cincinnati Enquirer,* Oct. 16, 19, 22, 1868; *Cincinnati Gazette,* Oct. 17, 1868. Coleman recorded a rumored deal between Barlow and McLean in which McLean agreed to the ticket changes for 1868. In return, Barlow pledged support for Pendleton in 1872. Coleman doubts the accuracy of this hearsay due to the lack of corroborating evidence. Coleman also suggests that Seymour was willing to accept the change in ticket, but Mitchell denies this suggestion. Coleman, *Election of 1868,* 344–59; Perzel, "Alexander Long," 11–18; Mitchell, *Horatio Seymour,* 468–71.

79. Letter cited in Coleman, *Election of 1868,* 336–39, 362–79; *Cincinnati Gazette,* Nov. 4, 1868; *Cincinnati Commercial,* Nov. 4, 1868; *Cincinnati Enquirer,* Nov. 22, 1868.

80. *Cincinnati Enquirer,* July 15, 1868.

81. Pendleton to John T. Stuart, Jan. 24, 1867, Pendleton to C. L. Ward, Apr. 16, 1867,

Pendleton to Schuyler Colfax, June 10, 1867, Pendleton Miscellaneous Manuscripts, Pendleton Miscellaneous Manuscripts, Rutherford B. Hayes Presidential Library, Fremont, Ohio; *Cincinnati Enquirer*, Apr. 20, 1866; Mar. 9, 1867.

82. Pendleton to Schuyler Colfax, June 7, 1869, Pendleton to Thomas H. Foulds, July 3, 1869, Pendleton Miscellaneous Manuscripts, Hayes Library; *Cincinnati Enquirer*, May 21, 25, 29, 1869; *Cincinnati Commercial*, Aug. 10, 12, 1868.

83. Thomas E. Powell, ed., *The Democratic Party of the State of Ohio: A Comprehensive History of Democracy in Ohio from 1803 to 1912, Including Democratic Legislation in the State, the Campaigns of a Century, History of Democratic Conventions, the Reverses and Successes of the Party, Etc.* (Columbus: Ohio Publishing, 1913), 191–95; Roseboom, *Civil War Era*, 473–76; Klement, *Limits of Dissent*, 304–5; Lawrence Grossman, *The Democratic Party and the Negro: Northern and National Politics, 1868–1892* (Urbana: Univ. of Illinois Press, 1976), 15–21.

84. McPherson, *Period of Reconstruction*, 399, 496–97; *New York Times*, Mar. 17, 1869; *Cincinnati Enquirer*, Mar. 18, May 12, 20, 20, 26, June 26, 30, 1869; *American Annual Cyclopedia*, 9:549; Moore, "Ohio in National Politics," 263–71.

85. *American Annual Cyclopedia*, 9:550; *Cleveland Plain Dealer*, July 9, 1869; Roseboom, *Civil War Era*, 469.

86. *American Annual Cyclopedia*, 9:550.

87. McPherson, *Period of Reconstruction*, 412–13; *Cincinnati Enquirer*, July 8, 1869; *New York Times*, July 8, 1869; *Cleveland Plain Dealer*, July 8, 1869; *Crisis*, July 14, 1869; Roseboom, *Civil War Era*, 469–70.

88. *Cincinnati Enquirer*, Jan. 11, July 8, 1869; *Cleveland Plain Dealer*, July 8, 1869; *New York Times*, July 10, 1869; *Crisis*, July 14, 1869; Roseboom, *Civil War Era*, 460.

89. *Cincinnati Commercial*, Aug. 7, 9, 10, 1869; *Cincinnati Enquirer*, Aug. 10, 12, 26, 1869; *Crisis*, Aug. 18, Sept. 1, 1869; Roseboom, *Civil War Era*, 470.

90. *Cincinnati Enquirer*, Aug. 20, 1869.

91. Ibid., Aug. 12, 14, 16, 17, 23, 1869; *Cincinnati Gazette*, Aug. 16, 1869; *Cincinnati Commercial*, Aug. 23, 24, Oct. 11, 1869.

92. *Cincinnati Enquirer*, Aug. 20, 1869.

93. Pendleton to George W. Morgan, Aug. 23, 30, 1869, Pendleton Miscellaneous Manuscripts, Western Reserve Historical Society, Cleveland, Ohio; *Cincinnati Enquirer*, Aug. 19, 23, Sept. 20, 23, 25, Oct. 5, 8, 9, 1869.

94. George H. Pendleton, *Speech of Hon. George H. Pendleton, at Clifton, Friday, September 10, 1869* (n.p., n.d.), 1–7; *Cincinnati Enquirer*, Aug. 23, 1869; Charles R. Williams, *The Life of Rutherford B. Hayes: Nineteenth President of the United States* (Boston: Houghton Mifflin, 1914), 338–39.

95. Pendleton to M. W. Cluskey, Oct. 16, 1869, Pendleton Miscellaneous Manuscripts, Kentucky Library and Museum; *Cincinnati Enquirer*, Sept. 30, 1869.

96. Rutherford B. Hayes to Sardis Birchard, Aug. 16, 1869, W. M. Dickson to Hayes, Sept. 15, 1869, Rutherford B. Hayes Papers, Rutherford B. Hayes Presidential Library, Fremont, Ohio; *Cincinnati Enquirer*, Aug. 13, 18, 26, Sept. 8, 15, 20, 1869; *Cincinnati Gazette*, Aug. 21, 1869; *Cincinnati Commercial*, Aug. 25, 28, Sept. 2, 4, 14, Oct. 6, 7, 11, 1869; "Hays [*sic*] and Pendleton," *Fremont Weekly Journal* 17 (Oct. 1, 1869): 1.

97. *Cincinnati Commercial*, Oct. 13, 14, 16, 20, 1869; *Cincinnati Gazette*, Oct. 13, 14,

18, 1869; *Cincinnati Enquirer,* Oct. 15, 20, Nov. 1, 1869; Powell, *Democratic Party,* 195–96; Roseboom, *Civil War Era,* 470–71; Unger, *Greenback Era,* 43.

    98. *Cincinnati Enquirer,* Nov. 11, 1869.

The Great Railroad Case and the Road to the Senate

    1. Joseph F. Gastright, "The Making of the Kentucky Central," *Kenton County Historical Society Quarterly Review* (July 1983): pt. 1, pp. 1–2; Joseph F. Gastright, "The Making of the Kentucky Central," *Kenton County Historical Society Quarterly Review* (Spring 1984): pt. 2, p. 1.

    2. Gastright, "Kentucky Central," pt. 1, pp. 1–2.

    3. Ibid., pp. 2–3.

    4. Ibid., p. 3; Lewis Collins, *Collins' Historical Sketches of Kentucky, History of Kentucky: By the Late Lewis Collins, Judge of the Mason County Court, Revised, Enlarged Fourfold, and Brought Down to the Year 1874 by His Son, Richard H. Collins, A.M., LL.B. . . .* (n.p., 1874; repr., n.p., 1976), 81.

    5. Peter Zinn, *Leading and Select Cases on Trusts: With Extended Abstracts of Important Cases; Explanatory and Critical Notes; and Numerous Citations of Authorities Bearing on Every Branch of the Law of Trusts. Also, a Full Report of the Great Case of the Covington and Lexington Railroad Company, against the Robert B. Bowler's Heirs and Others, Just Decided at the Winter Term, 1873, of the Court of Appeals of the State of Kentucky* (Cincinnati, Ohio: Robert Clarke and Co., 1873), 589–90.

    6. Collins, *Collins' Historical Sketches,* 81; Joseph F. Gastright, "The Making of the Kentucky Central," *Kenton County Historical Society Quarterly Review* (Spring 1985): pt. 3, pp. 1–2.

    7. Gastright, "Kentucky Central," pt. 3, 1–3.

    8. *Covington Journal,* Nov. 6, 20, 1869; Henry V. Poor, *Manual of the Railroads of the United States, for 1868–69, Showing Their Mileage, Stocks, Bonds, Cost, Earnings, Expenses, and Organizations; with a Sketch of Their Rise, Progress, Influence, etc. Together with an Appendix, Containing a Full Analysis of the Debts of the United States, and of the Several States* (New York: H. V. and H. W. Poor, 1876), 170; Henry V. Poor, *Manual of the Railroads of the United States, for 1868, Showing Their Mileage, Stocks, Bonds, Cost, Earnings, Expenses, and Organizations; with a Sketch of Their Rise, Progress, Influence, etc. Together with an Appendix, Containing a Full Analysis of the Debts of the United States, and of the Several States* (New York: H. V. and H. W. Poor, 1876), 839; Henry V. Poor, *Manual of the Railroads of the United States, for 1869–70, Showing Their Mileage, Stocks, Bonds, Cost, Earnings, Expenses, and Organizations; with a Sketch of Their Rise, Progress, Influence, etc. Together with an Appendix, Containing a Full Analysis of the Debts of the United States, and of the Several States* (New York: H. V. and H. W. Poor, 1876), 237.

    9. *Covington Journal,* Aug. 14, Oct. 2, 16, 1869; Apr. 16, Sept. 24, 1870; Gastright, "Kentucky Central," pt. 3, pp. 2–3.

    10. Edward W. Hines, *Corporate History of the Louisville and Nashville Railroad Company and Roads in Its System* (Louisville, Ky.: John P. Morton and Co., 1905), 253–55.

    11. *Covington Journal,* Nov. 18, 25, 1871; May 3, 1873. The *Covington Journal* trumpeted

Zinn's "underdog" victory. Zinn defeated what the paper described as "an able array of lawyers . . . a powerful corporation . . . the influence of Bowler's relatives, including George H. Pendleton . . . [and] a muzzled press, silent through Pendleton's appeals not to injure the family, but leave the matter to the courts." *Covington Journal,* May 24, 1873; "Old and New Roads," *Railroad Gazette* 5 (May 3, 1873): 183; Gastright, "Kentucky Central," pt. 3, p. 3.

12. *Covington Journal,* Aug. 16, 23, 1873; Apr. 25, May 2, 1874; *Cincinnati Enquirer,* Oct. 10, 1873; Apr. 17, 1874.

13. "Old and New Roads," *Railroad Gazette* 7 (Feb. 27, 1875): 90; Gastright, "Kentucky Central," pt. 3, p. 3.

14. *Covington Journal,* Aug. 23, 1873.

15. Ibid.; *Cincinnati Enquirer,* Aug. 21, 1873. In another instance, Pendleton defended his honor against the charge that he used bribery of Covington and Lexington board members to obtain a favorable compromise. Once again, the claims were baseless. *Cincinnati Enquirer,* May 25, 1874.

16. *Covington Journal,* Feb. 6, May 1, 1875; *Cincinnati Enquirer,* Feb. 6, Apr. 30, May 7, 1875.

17. *Covington Journal,* May 8, 29, June 5, July 10, 1875; *Cincinnati Enquirer,* May 8, July 7, 1875; "Old and New Roads," *Railroad Gazette* 7 (May 29, 1875): 224–25; Gastright, "Kentucky Central," pt. 3, p. 3.

18. *Cincinnati Enquirer,* July 6, 1875; Nicole Etcheson, "Private Interest and Public Good: Upland Southerners and Antebellum Midwestern Political Culture," in *The Pursuit of Public Power: Political Culture in Ohio, 1787–1861,* ed. Jeffrey P. Brown and Andrew R. L. Cayton (Kent, Ohio: Kent State Univ. Press, 1994), 28–39.

19. *Cincinnati Enquirer,* Nov. 11, 1869; *Covington Journal,* Nov. 20, 1869, Mar. 19, Sept. 17, Dec. 18, 1870; Feb. 11, Nov. 18, 1871; Apr. 13, 27, July 27, 1872, Nov. 27, 1875; *Daily Commonwealth,* May 28, Sept. 15, 1879, Aug. 5, Nov. 26, Dec. 29, 1880; Jan. 26, 1881; "Old and New Roads," *Railroad Gazette* 8 (Jan. 14, 1876): 29; "Old and New Roads," *Railroad Gazette* 9 (May 4, 1877): 207; "Old and New Roads," *Railroad Gazette* 12 (Oct. 29, 1880): 577; "Old and New Roads," *Railroad Gazette* 12 (Dec. 31, 1880):703; Maury Klein, *History of the Louisville and Nashville Railroad,* Railroads of America, ed. Thomas B. Brewer (New York: MacMillan, 1972), 102–11.

20. Though newspapers in this time period were becoming increasingly independent, Frank Mott suggested that the *Herald* was sympathetic with the Republican cause on most issues. This partisan affiliation was somewhat different from the paper's position during the Civil War. Frank L. Mott, *American Journalism, A History: 1690–1960,* 3d ed. (New York: MacMillan, 1962), 348–50, 413–21.

21. House Committee on Expenditures in War Department, *The Management of the War Department,* 44th Cong., 1st sess., 1876, H. Rept. 779, 279. Sources refer to both an "Amanda Bower" and an "Amanda Bowers." She will be referred to in this discussion as "Amanda Bower" until her marriage to Gen. Belknap because that was the name her husband's former partner, Ezra Leonard, used in describing her to the *Enquirer's* reporter. House Committee, *War Department,* 279; *Cincinnati Enquirer,* Mar. 18, 1876; Geoffrey Perret, *Ulysses S. Grant: Soldier and President* (New York: Modern Library, 1999), 436–37.

22. For the Belknap impeachment articles and report of the House on the impeachment proceedings, see House Committee on the Judiciary, *Impeachment of William W.*

Belknap, 44th Cong., 1st sess., 1876, H. Rept. 345, 1–8; *Report of the House Managers on the Impeachment of W. W. Belknap, Late Secretary of War*, 44th Cong., 1st sess., 1876, H. Rept. 791, 1–2; *Cincinnati Enquirer*, Mar. 3, 13, 1876. For a secondary accounting of the Belknap scandal, see William B. Hesseltine, *Ulysses S. Grant: Politician*, American Classics (1935; repr., New York: Frederick Unger, 1957), 395–96; Allan Nevins, *Hamilton Fish: The Inner History of the Grant Administration*, rev. ed., vol. 2, American Classics (New York: Frederick Unger, 1957), 805; Roger Dean Bridges, "The Impeachment and Trial of William Worth Belknap, Secretary of War" (M.A. thesis, State College of Iowa, 1963); William S. McFeely, *Grant: A Biography* (New York: W. W. Norton, 1981), 426–40.

23. *Cincinnati Enquirer*, Mar. 6, 18, 1876; *The Record of George H. Pendleton: Why He is Unfit for Any Government Position* (n.p.: 1885), 23; Notes of Julia Frances Brice, Misc. Personal Papers of Julia Frances Cox; Collins, *Collins' Historical Sketches*, 246; Mott, *American Journalism*, 413. Pendleton's relationship was apparently more than just business, however, though not inappropriate. On December 11, 1873, Pendleton "gave away" Bower at her wedding to William Belknap. Bridges's version is slightly different, with Pendleton turning $20,000 of life insurance money into $92,000 for Mrs. Bower. Bridges, "Impeachment of Belknap," 10.

24. *Record of Pendleton*, 41–43.

25. Ibid., 12–14, 43–45.

26. *Cincinnati Enquirer*, Mar. 7, 1876.

27. Ibid.

28. House Committee, *War Department*, 279–81, 295; Notes of Julia Frances Brice; *New York Times*, Mar. 11, 1876; Mark Wahlgren Summers, *The Era of Good Stealings* (New York: Oxford Univ. Press, 1993), 68.

29. House Committee, *War Department*, 281.

30. Ibid., 281–82; *Cincinnati Enquirer*, Mar. 15, 1876; *New York Times*, Mar. 15, 1876; *Covington Journal*, Mar. 18, 1876; Poor, *Manual of the Railroads for 1869–70*, 237.

31. House Committee, *War Department*, 282–83; *Cincinnati Enquirer*, Mar. 15, 1876; *Covington Journal*, Mar. 18, 1876.

32. The *Covington Journal* suggested that Meigs was motivated by political factors in opposing the claim. *Covington Journal*, Apr. 8, 1876; House Committee, *War Department*, 286–87, 340–41. A letter to Hayes sheds some light not only on Pendleton's thoughts but also on the political morality of the era. "Nor did it even occur to Pendleton that there was anything wrong in him turning his aristocratic social position to account. That has been his stock in trade for many years, and while toadies throng about him why not use it?" William M. Dickson to Rutherford B. Hayes, May 23, 1876, Rutherford B. Hayes Papers, Rutherford B. Hayes Presidential Library, Fremont, Ohio. One source seems to bolster Pendleton's claim, as it noted that the government did not use the line on at least one occasion because the different gauge necessitated soldiers to transfer from that line to another. Thomas Weber, *The Northern Railroads in the Civil War, 1861–1865* (Bloomington: Indiana Univ. Press, 1999), 182.

33. House Committee, *War Department*, 287–89; *New York Times*, Mar. 15, 1876.

34. Mrs. Marsh refused to return from hiding in Canada with her husband, Caleb Marsh, until they were granted immunity. Mr. Marsh was involved in the Indian Post scandal, which proved to be Secretary Belknap's downfall. *Record of Pendleton*, 17.

35. House Committee, *War Department,* 328–29.

36. Ibid., 293–353; *Cincinnati Enquirer,* May 17, 1876; *New York Times,* Mar. 17, Apr. 14, 1876; *Covington Journal,* May 20, 27, 1876.

37. The Democrats had gained control of the House by the 44th Congress, beginning in December 1875, by a margin of sixty seats.

38. *Cincinnati Enquirer,* Mar. 15, 1876.

39. *Record of Pendleton,* 11–12, 27–28, 32–34; House Committee, *War Department,* 281–89, 293–94, 339; *New York Times,* Mar. 22, 1876; *Cincinnati Enquirer,* Apr. 26, July 31, 1876; *Covington Journal,* Apr. 29, 1876. Mrs. Bowler knew the story about Pendleton's trip into Spain did not involve an affair. Mrs. Pendleton was to join them, but there were difficulties at the border between France and Spain, and she wanted to be sure that she could return to her children without delay. As a result, she decided to stay in France. Notes of Julia Frances Brice; Summers, *Era of Good Stealings,* 68–71, 327.

40. *Record of Pendleton,* 5–49; House Committee, *War Department,* 279–80, 295–96; *New York Times,* Mar. 8, 10, 18, 26, 1876; *Cincinnati Enquirer,* Mar. 18, 1876; *Covington Journal,* Apr. 8, 29, 1876.

41. Albert V. House, "Republicans and Democrats Search for New Identities, 1870–1890," *Review of Politics* 13 (Oct. 1969): 466–68. House tended to overemphasize the willingness of midwestern Democrats to change in light of a new political milieu. He was correct in asserting that the Democrats sought new issues, but not all of them were willing to adopt new political positions. While Bourbon Democrats seemed to be willing to do so, Pendleton was not.

42. Horace Samuel Merrill, *Bourbon Democracy of the Middle West, 1865–1896* (Baton Rouge: Louisiana State Univ. Press, 1953), 42–44, 98; Horace Samuel Merrill, *Bourbon Leader: Grover Cleveland and the Democratic Party* (Boston: Little, Brown and Co., 1957), 44–47; Morton Keller, *Affairs of State: Public Life in Late Nineteenth Century America* (Cambridge, Mass.: Belknap Press of Harvard Univ. Press, 1977), 245–47.

43. Morton Keller asserts that the Democratic Party as a whole emphasized organizational reform. That seems to ring more true for Bourbons in the East than Democrats in the Midwest. Keller's implication that Pendleton accepted the new focus on organization does not seem to be evidenced through an examination of Pendleton's stalwart opposition to the Bourbons. The relative lack of political bosses in the Midwest tends to discredit that idea as well. Merrill points out that the eastern Bourbon organization hampered the efforts of midwestern Democrats, such as Pendleton, because they were able to unite their supporters more efficiently than the loosely organized Midwest. Merrill, *Bourbon Democracy,* 60–64; Keller, *Affairs of State,* 254–58.

44. *Cincinnati Enquirer,* Feb. 21, May 11, July 1–2, 1870; Thomas E. Powell, ed., *The Democratic Party of the State of Ohio: A Comprehensive History of Democracy in Ohio from 1803 to 1912, Including Democratic Legislation in the State, the Campaigns of a Century, History of Democratic Conventions, the Reverses and Successes of the Party, Etc.* (Columbus: Ohio Publishing, 1913), 196.

45. *Cincinnati Enquirer,* June 2, 1870.

46. *Cincinnati Enquirer,* Jan. 30, June 2, Aug. 19, 1870; June 1–2, 1871; Powell, *Democratic Party of Ohio,* 196–97; Reginald Charles McGrane, *William Allen: A Study in Western Democracy* (Columbus: Ohio State Archaeological and Historical Society, 1925), 184;

Clifford H. Moore, "Ohio in National Politics, 1865–1896," *Ohio Archaeological and Historical Society Publications* 37 (Apr.–June 1928): 265–68; Eugene H. Roseboom, *The Civil War Era, 1850–1873*, vol. 4 of *The History of the State of Ohio*, ed. Carl Wittke (Columbus: Ohio State Archaeological and Historical Society, 1944), 472–475.

47. *American Annual Cyclopedia and Register of Important Events of the Year 1861* (New York: D. Appleton and Co., 1862), 11:611.

48. *Cincinnati Enquirer*, June 2, 1871; Moore, "Ohio in National Politics," 269; Roseboom, *Civil War Era*, 475–76.

49. *Cincinnati Enquirer*, June 2–5, July 8, Aug. 23, 30, 1871; *Speech of Hon. George H. Pendleton, at Loveland, O., August 22, 1871* (n.p., n.d.), 1–8.

50. *Cincinnati Enquirer*, June 17, 1871.

51. William H. Worthington to William Allen, n.d., William Allen Papers, Manuscript Division, Library of Congress, Washington, D.C.

52. Powell, *Democratic Party of Ohio*, 197–98; Roseboom, *Civil War Era*, 478–79; Merrill, *Bourbon Democracy*, 69–70.

53. *Letter of Hon. Thomas Ewing, of Ohio to the Finance Committee of the Senate, on the Public Debt and Currency* (Washington, D.C.: Judd and Detweiler, 1869), 3–17; Thomas Ewing to J. Maguire, Apr. 18 1870, transcription, Thomas Ewing and Family Papers, Manuscript Division, Library of Congress, Washington, D.C.; *Letter from Hon. Thomas Ewing* (n.p., n.d.), 1–16; Thomas Ewing to Friedrich Hassaurek, May 28, June 2, 7, 1873, Frederick Hassaurek Papers, Ohio Historical Society, Columbus; McGrane, *William Allen*, 190–92; Irwin Unger, *The Greenback Era: A Social and Political History of American Finance, 1865–1879* (Princeton, N.J.: Princeton Univ. Press, 1964), 182–87; Mark A. Lause, *The Civil War's Last Campaign: James B. Weaver, the Greenback-Labor Party and the Politics of Race and Section* (Lanham, Md.: Univ. Press of America, 2001), 20.

54. The Liberal Republicans held to a hard-currency position but advocated fair taxation and the end of land grants to railroads and corporations, positions most Democrats maintained. Richard Allen Gerber postulates that the Republicans who became Liberals were motivated primarily by a desire to bring order to society. Following the Civil War, they believed that the freedmen needed a measure of equality to promote stability in the South. When further programs to benefit African Americans produced a white backlash, Liberals left the Republican fold for the same reason that they had supported such measures in the first place—maintenance of stability. Joined by a free trade element, these men saw in peace with the South, civil service reform, and tariff reform a means to promote harmony in the age of industrial development. From this perspective, it seems likely that the Democrats agreed on these key issues enough to support the Liberals, even if they differed on currency. The South desired lower tariffs, and all Democrats opposed Grant's administration. Richard Allen Gerber, "The Liberal Republicans of 1872 in Historiographical Perspective," *Journal of American History* 62 (June 1975): 40–73. See also Matthew T. Downey, "Horace Greeley and the Politicians: The Liberal Republican Convention in 1872," *Journal of American History* 53 (Mar. 1967): 727–50, and Earle Dudley Ross, *The Liberal Republican Movement*, 2d ed. (New York: AMS Press, 1971).

55. *Cincinnati Enquirer*, May 4, 14, 25, July 24, 1872; Lurton D. Ingersoll, *The Life of Horace Greeley* (Chicago: Union, 1873; rep., New York: Beekman, 1974), 530–65; *American Annual Cyclopedia*, 14:668; Roseboom, *Civil War Era*, 480–82; Henry Luther Stoddard,

Horace Greeley: Printer, Editor, Crusader (New York: G. P. Putnam's Sons, 1946), 305–16; Glyndon G. Van Deusen, *Horace Greeley: Nineteenth-Century Crusader,* American Century Series (New York: Hill and Wang, 1964), 294–99, 400–427; Unger, *Greenback Era,* 163–94; Ross, *Liberal Republican Movement,* 93–104.

56. *Cincinnati Enquirer,* Jan. 9, 1872; Keller, *Affairs of State,* 272–75; Ari Hoogenboom, *The Presidency of Rutherford B. Hayes* (Lawrence: Univ. Press of Kansas, 1988), 102. Pendleton supported the ideas embodied in the Jenckes Bill of 1865, which called for professionalizing the civil service through competitive examinations.

57. *Official Proceedings of the National Democratic Convention, Held at Baltimore, July 9, 1872* (Boston: Rickwell and Churchill, 1872): 40–81; *American Annual Cyclopedia,* 12:656–57; *Cincinnati Enquirer,* May 31, July 24, Aug. 1, Sept. 11, 28, Oct. 1, 16, 23, 31, 1872; Ingersoll, *Horace Greeley,* 542; *Roseboom, Civil War Era,* 483–85; Merrill, *Bourbon Democracy,* 74; Unger, *Greenback Era,* 193–94; Ross, *Liberal Republican Movement,* 129–46, 183.

58. Philip D. Jordan, *Ohio Comes of Age, 1873–1900,* vol. 5 of *The History of the State of Ohio,* ed. Carl Wittke (Columbus: Ohio State Archaeological and Historical Society, 1943), 21–29; Roseboom, *Civil War Era,* 484–85; Unger, *Greenback Era,* 213–30.

59. Powell, *Democratic Party of Ohio,* 218; McGrane, *William Allen,* 193–94; Jordan, *Ohio Comes of Age,* 27–29.

60. *Cincinnati Enquirer,* Aug. 7, 9, 1873; *American Annual Cyclopaedia,* 13:610.

61. Thomas Ewing to Friedrich Hassaurek, May 28, June 2, 7, 1873, Hassaurek Papers; John H. O'Neill to Rutherford B. Hayes, Aug. 9, 1873, Hayes Papers; *Cincinnati Enquirer,* July 3, 30–31, 1873; Powell, *Democratic Party of Ohio,* 218–19; McGrane, *William Allen,* 195–207; Moore, "Ohio in National Politics," 273–80.

62. *Cincinnati Enquirer,* Sept. 19, 29, Oct. 3, 8, 1873.

63. George H. Pendleton to William Allen, Dec. 29, 1873, Allen Papers.

64. Charles W. Calhoun, "Reimagining the 'Lost Men' of the Gilded Age: Perspectives on the Late Nineteenth-Century Presidents," *Journal of the Gilded Age and Progressive Era* 1 (July 2002): 236–37; Walter T. K. Nugent, *Money and American Society, 1865–1880* (New York: Free Press, 1968), 221–25.

65. Powell, *Democratic Party of Ohio,* 225–26; Moore, "Ohio in National Politics," 291–94; Unger, *Greenback Era,* 213–43.

66. *New York Times,* Apr. 13, 1874; *Cincinnati Enquirer,* Apr. 16, Oct. 5, 1874.

67. *Cincinnati Enquirer,* Apr. 7, Mar. 26, 31, 1874; *New York Times,* Apr. 11, 13, 1874.

68. *Cincinnati Enquirer,* Apr. 17, 24, July 22, 27, Aug. 11, 1874; *New York Times,* Aug. 27, Oct. 28, 1874; *American Annual Cyclopedia,* 14:667–68.

69. *Cincinnati Enquirer,* Sept. 11, 1874.

70. Ibid., Oct. 31, 1874.

71. *Cincinnati Enquirer,* July 27, Sept. 11, 14, Oct. 5, 13, 16, Nov. 2, 1874; *New York Times,* Sept. 13, 1874; *Cincinnati Enquirer,* Oct. 21, 31, 1874; *American Annual Cyclopedia,* 14:668; Powell, *Democratic Party of Ohio,* 226.

72. Merrill, *Bourbon Democracy,* 105; Unger, *Greenback Era,* 249–51.

73. Moore, "Ohio in National Politics," 294–98; Unger, *Greenback Era,* 249–55; Terry L. Seip, *The South Returns to Congress: Men, Economic Measures, and Intersectional Relationships, 1868–1879* (Baton Rouge: Louisiana State Univ. Press, 1983), 202–6, 215–18.

74. Banks actually began to retire notes in some areas. Regardless of the net change, however, for each $100 of new banknotes, the Treasury contracted $80 in greenbacks. The overall result was contraction. Unger, *Greenback Era,* 264–69.

75. Allen Thurman's position on the Ohio Idea principles had not been consistent. In 1867, he accepted the plan hoping to use midwestern distaste for government policies that benefited bondholders to his advantage. By 1875, however, he opposed the principles of Pendleton's plan. The Democrats also attempted to solidify their labor and farm support by nominating Samuel F. Cary as their candidate for lieutenant governor. Cary had been involved in previous independent labor and reform movements in Ohio and was more inflationary than Pendleton. *New York Times,* May 2, June 18, July 26, Dec. 19, 1875; *Cincinnati Enquirer,* June 18, July 20, 31, Aug. 2, 14, 17, 1875; Powell, *Democratic Party of Ohio,* 226; McGrane, *William Allen,* 208–45; Moore, "Ohio in National Politics," 289–98; Jordan, *Ohio Comes of Age,* 41–49; Merrill, *Bourbon Democracy,* 99; Unger, *Greenback Era,* 83–84, 265–85. The Republican focus on the Catholic influence in public schools demonstrated a possible answer to the question of what issues kept the various factions of each party committed to their political affiliation. In other words, such ethnocultural factors kept Bourbon and midwestern Democrats within the Democratic Party rather than allowing it to splinter over financial questions. Paul Kleppner suggests that "ethnoreligious and political communications reinforced each other." Paul Kleppner, *Who Voted? The Dynamics of Electoral Turnout, 1870–1980,* American Political Parties and Elections (New York: Praeger, 1982), 43–54.

76. W. H. Dakin to Rutherford B. Hayes, Oct. 20, 1875, Hayes Papers; *Speech of Hon. George H. Pendleton, Delivered at Gallipolis, Ohio, July 21, 1875* (n.p., n.d.), 1–7; *Cincinnati Enquirer,* Jan. 9, June 18, July 22, 26, Aug. 14, 17, 19, 28, 30, Sept. 20, Oct. 26, Nov. 6, 1875; *New York Times,* July 22, Aug. 27, Sept. 1, Dec. 19, 1875.

77. Gen. Morgan recognized the importance of key issues in the election. "Outside of the financial issues we did not make a vote, and all we lost, and they were not a few, was [*sic*] on the church question." George W. Morgan to William Allen, Oct. 16, 1875, James J. Faran to William Allen, May 15, 1875, Allen Papers; W. H. Dakin to Rutherford B. Hayes, 20 Oct. 1875, Hayes Papers; *American Annual Cyclopedia,* 15:606–7; *New York Times,* Aug. 27, Sept. 1, 1875; *Cincinnati Enquirer,* Aug. 30, 1875; McGrane, *William Allen,* 228–34; Moore, "Ohio in National Politics," 288–89.

78. Remarking to Hayes early that year, Republican Edwin Cowles said, "Pendleton saved us." Edwin Cowles to R. B. Hayes, Apr. 3, 1876, Hayes Papers; Peter Cooper, *An Open Letter to the Republican and Democratic Candidates for the Presidency, by Peter Cooper, Together with the Platform of the Independent Party and Mr. Cooper's Letter of Acceptance* (New York: n.p., 1876), 1–8; *New York Times,* May 17–18, 1876; *Cincinnati Enquirer,* Nov. 6, Dec. 17, 1875; Feb. 5, 1876; *American Annual Cyclopedia,* 16:647–49; Powell, *Democratic Party of Ohio,* 226–27; Unger, *Greenback Era,* 286–308.

79. *New York Times,* May 17–18, 1876; *Appleton's Annual Cyclopedia and Register of Important Events of the Year 1876: Embracing Political, Civil, Military, and Social Affairs; Public Documents; Biography, Statistics, Commerce, Finance, Literature, Science, Agriculture, and Mechanical Industry,* vol. 16 (New York: D. Appleton and Co., 1877), 648; Powell, *Democratic Party of Ohio,* 227–28; McGrane, *William Allen,* 253–55.

80. *Official Proceedings of the National Democratic Convention, Held in St. Louis, Mo.,*

June 27th, 28th and 29th, 1876, with an Appendix Containing the Letters of Acceptance of Gov. Tilden and Gov. Hendricks (St. Louis, Mo.: Woodward, Tiernan, and Hale, 1876), 94–98; *Cincinnati Enquirer,* May 18, July 10, Sept. 18, 1876; Unger, *Greenback Era,* 307–11; House, "Search for New Identities," 474–75.

81. *Cincinnati Enquirer,* Nov. 23, 1876; Hoogenboom, *Rutherford B. Hayes,* 1–51.

82. *Cincinnati Enquirer,* Dec. 17, 1875; Feb. 10, Nov. 11, 16, 1876; Jan. 19, Feb. 10, 13, 17, Mar. 3, 6, 1877; Powell, *Democratic Party of Ohio,* 227–31; Moore, "Ohio in National Politics," 303–6; Brooks D. Simpson, *The Reconstruction Presidents* (Lawrence: Univ. Press of Kansas, 1998), 199–228.

"Kicking Against the Goads": Pendleton and Civil Service Reform

1. *Cincinnati Enquirer,* June 1, 4, 5, 1877; *New York Times,* June 1, 1877; Clifford H. Moore, "Ohio in National Politics, 1865–1896," *Ohio Archaeological and Historical Society Publications* 37 (Apr.–June 1928): 303–13; Philip D. Jordan, *Ohio Comes of Age, 1873–1900,* vol. 5 of *The History of the State of Ohio,* ed. Carl Wittke (Columbus: Ohio State Archaeological and Historical Society, 1943), 154–57.

2. *Cincinnati Enquirer,* July 23–24, 1877.

3. Pendleton explained his decision in a rare interview with a newspaper reporter. Pendleton chastised the reporter for what he thought a "blunt and impudent" question, but then answered: "It is asserted that I have combined with candidates from other parts of the state, and against candidates at home, in order to make strength for the Senatorship. This is utterly false. I have denied it in public and in private, but the lie is still repeated. I have sometimes felt that the most effective way to refute it, and to manifest my own opinion of the manifest inexpediency of obtruding the Senatorial question into this canvass, is to stay away from the Convention." *Cincinnati Enquirer,* July 23, 1877; *New York Times,* July 25, 26, 28, 1877.

4. George H. Pendleton, *Speech of Hon. George H. Pendleton, at the Opening of the Democratic Campaign, at Columbus, Ohio, Thursday Evening, August 23, 1877* (n.p., n.d.), 1.

5. *Cincinnati Enquirer,* May 4, 15, July 24, 26, Sept. 4, 6, 7, 27, Oct. 2, 9, 1877; *New York Times,* July 25, 26, 28, Aug. 24, 30, 1877; Pendleton, *Opening of the Democratic Campaign,* 1–7.

6. James A. Garfield to Lucretia Garfield, Sept. 11, 1877, in Harry James Brown and Frederick D. Williams, eds., *The Diary of James A. Garfield, 1875–77,* vol. 3 (Lansing: Michigan State Univ. Press, 1973), 514.

7. Theodore Clarke Smith, ed., *The Life and Letters of James Abram Garfield,* vol. 2 (New Haven, Conn.: Yale Univ. Press, 1925), 656–57; Brown and Williams, *Diary of Garfield,* 3:514–22; *Cincinnati Enquirer,* Sept. 13, 26, 29, 1877; Floyd Oliver Rittenhouse, "George Hunt Pendleton: With Special Reference to His Congressional Career" (M.A. thesis, Ohio State University, 1932), 58–59.

8. *Cincinnati Enquirer,* Oct. 11, 1877; Smith, *Life and Letters of Garfield,* 656–57; Thomas E. Powell, ed., *The Democratic Party of the State of Ohio: A Comprehensive History of Democracy in Ohio from 1803 to 1912, Including Democratic Legislation in the State, the Campaigns of a Century, History of Democratic Conventions, the Reverses and Successes*

of the Party, Etc. (Columbus: Ohio Publishing, 1913), 235–37; Moore, "Ohio in National Politics," 312–14; Jordan, *Ohio Comes of Age,* 158–59.

9. *Cincinnati Enquirer,* Oct. 11, 15, 16, 18, Nov. 16, Dec. 20, 22, 25, 1877; Jan. 5, 7–10, 1878; Rittenhouse, "George Hunt Pendleton," 60.

10. George H. Pendleton to W. W. Armstrong, Oct. 27 1877, Pendleton Miscellaneous Manuscripts, Rutherford B. Hayes Presidential Library, Fremont, Ohio; John H. James Jr. to George H. Pendleton, Dec. 21, 1877, James Family Papers, Ohio Historical Society, Columbus. "Pendleton and Morgan are both corresponding with members of the Legislature in their own interest." John Irvine to Thomas Ewing, Nov. 3, Dec. 29, 1877, Thomas Ewing and Family Papers, Manuscript Division, Library of Congress, Washington, D.C.

11. Irvine Dungan to Thomas Ewing, Dec. 9, 1877, C. Bonsall to Thomas Ewing, Jan. 3, 1878, Thomas Ewing and Family Papers.

12. [Illegible] Beebe to Thomas Ewing, Oct. 16, 1877, Frank [no last name] to Thomas Ewing, Jan. 6, 1878, Mile Forbes to Thomas Ewing, Jan. 7, 1878, Thomas Ewing and Family Papers; *Cincinnati Enquirer,* Jan. 11, 12, 17, 18, 1878; *New York Times,* Jan. 11, 13, 22, 1878; Powell, *Democratic Party of Ohio,* 237; Rittenhouse, "George Hunt Pendleton," 61.

13. Pendleton had laid the groundwork for this unity prior to his receiving the nomination. In a letter to Ewing, he denied any association with those men who were publicly criticizing him. "I have entertained for you a sincere respect and friendly regard." George H. Pendleton to Thomas Ewing, Dec. 2, 1877, Thomas Ewing and Family Papers.

14. George H. Pendleton to Rutherford B. Hayes, July 2, 1877, George H. Pendleton to Lysander Spooner, May 1, 1878, Pendleton Miscellaneous Manuscripts, Hayes Library; Henry V. Poor, *Manual of the Railroads of the United States, for 1879, Showing their Mileage, Stocks, Bonds, Cost, Earnings, Expenses, and Organizations; with a Sketch of Their Rise, Progress, Influence, etc. Together with an Appendix, Containing a Full Analysis of the Debts of the United States, and of the Several States* (New York: H. V. and H. W. Poor, 1880), 464–465; Henry V. Poor, *Manual of the Railroads of the United States, for 1880, Showing their Mileage, Stocks, Bonds, Cost, Earnings, Expenses, and Organizations; with a Sketch of Their Rise, Progress, Influence, etc. Together with an Appendix, Containing a Full Analysis of the Debts of the United States, and of the Several States* (New York: H. V. and H. W. Poor, 1881), 463–65; *Newport Local,* Mar. 7, 1878; *Daily Commonwealth,* May 28, July 8, 22, Aug. 13–18, 27, 1879; Dec. 29, 1880; Jan. 26, 1881; H. H. Hancock, "High Lights of History on the Kentucky Central during the Eighties," *The L. & N. Employees Magazine,* Oct. 1926, 18–20; K. A. H., "The Old Reliable Purchases a Bluegrass 'Thoroughbred,'" *The L. & N. Employees Magazine,* June 1940, 11–14; Cerinda W. Evans, *Collis Porter Huntington,* vol. 2 (Newport News, Va.: Mariners' Museum, 1954), 538–39, 578–83; Maury Klein, *History of the Louisville and Nashville Railroad,* Railroads of America, ed. Thomas B. Brewer (New York: MacMillan, 1972), 299–308, 360; Joseph F. Gastright, "The Making of the Kentucky Central," *Kenton County Historical Society Quarterly Review* (July 1983): pt. 3, pp. 3–4; William B. Friedricks, *Henry E. Huntington and the Creation of the Southern California* (Columbus: Ohio State Univ. Press, 1992), 20–43.

15. *Cincinnati Enquirer,* Aug. 23, Sept. 11, Oct. 2, 9, 11, Nov. 6, 27, Dec. 31, 1878; *New York Times,* Sept. 11, 14, Nov. 9, 1878; Jordan, *Ohio Comes of Age,* 161–65.

16. *Cincinnati Enquirer,* Aug. 14, Oct. 14, Dec. 28, 1878; Powell, *Democratic Party of Ohio,* 237–39.

17. *Congressional Record,* 46th Cong., 1st sess., 1879, 14–15, 19, 24, ICPSR; ibid., 46th Cong., 1st sess., 1879, 1331–32, 2380; Rittenhouse, "George Hunt Pendleton," 63–64; Ari Hoogenboom, *The Presidency of Rutherford B. Hayes* (Lawrence: Univ. Press of Kansas, 1988), 73–76.

18. *Evening Star,* June 2, 10, 18, 30, 1879.

19. Ibid., Mar. 15, 1879.

20. Ibid., Mar. 10, 17, 20, Apr. 28, May 5, 1879.

21. George H. Pendleton, *The Heads of Departments on the Floors of Congress: Speech of Hon. George H. Pendleton, of Ohio, in the Senate of the United States, April 28, 1879* (Washington, D.C.: n.p., 1879), 1–16; *Congressional Record,* 46th Cong., 1st sess., 1879, 72, 141, 967–74, 1659, 1683; *Cincinnati Enquirer,* Apr. 24, 1879, Nov. 14, 1881. Pendleton was particularly pleased to learn that President Hayes had expressed interest in the concept of cabinet officers holding seats in Congress. George H. Pendleton to Rutherford B. Hayes, Apr. 2, 1878, Pendleton Miscellaneous Manuscripts, Hayes Library. One correspondent wanted Hayes to take the idea and make it his policy. Issues such as "specie payments, the tariff, civil service reform and the Southern question are too complex and the party lines too much broken upon all of them." The correspondent, Gamaliel Bradford, believed that Hayes could unify the Republican Party around this concept. Gamaliel Bradford to Rutherford B. Hayes, Feb. 18, 1878, Hayes Papers.

22. *Evening Star,* May 20, 1879; *Cincinnati Enquirer,* June 4, 5, 17–19, 25, 26, Aug. 8, 12, 21, Sept. 18, 22, Oct. 9, 11, Nov. 27, 1879; *New York Times,* June 5, Aug. 8, Sept. 22–23, 1879; Ari Hoogenboom, *Outlawing the Spoils: A History of the Civil Service Reform Movement, 1865–1883* (1961; repr., Urbana: Univ. of Illinois Press, 1968), 163–67.

23. *Official Proceedings of the National Democratic Convention, Held in St. Louis, Mo., June 27th, 28th and 29th, 1876* (St. Louis: Woodward, Tiernan and Hale, 1876), 94–98; *The Reconstruction Epoch—Official Proceedings of the National Republican Conventions of 1868, 1872, 1876, and 1880* (Minneapolis, Minn.: Charles W. Johnson, 1903), 279–81; Paul P. Van Riper, *History of the United States Civil Service* (Evanston, Ill.: Row, Peterson and Co., 1958), 75–88; Hoogenboom, *Outlawing the Spoils,* 135–78; Ari Hoogenboom, "Rutherford B. Hayes and Reform of the Spoils System," *Hayes Historical Journal* 4 (Spring 1984): 16–27.

24. *Appleton's Annual Cyclopedia and Register of Important Events of the Year 1876: Embracing Political, Civil, Military, and Social Affairs; Public Documents; Biography, Statistics, Commerce, Finance, Literature, Science, Agriculture, and Mechanical Industry* (New York: D. Appleton and Co., 1877), 18:667–68; Jordan, *Ohio Comes of Age,* 48, 165–69.

25. *Congressional Record,* 46th Cong., 2d sess., 1880, 20, 135, 718, 2032–35, 2303, 3611, 3852, 3964; *Cincinnati Enquirer,* Jan. 5, Feb. 12, 1880.

26. Making Medicine was baptized "David Pendleton" and later became an Episcopalian minister on a reservation. Making Medicine named his son Frank after Pendleton's own son. Karen Daniels Petersen, *Plains Indian Art from Fort Marion* (Norman: Univ. of Oklahoma Press, 1971), 68, 188, 225–26. Culture and faith were closely associated in nineteenth-century America, and Pendleton's own faith commitments influenced his desire to help Making Medicine. Though Pendleton supported a policy that would ultimately destroy Indian culture, his motives should be judged by nineteenth-century perspectives. Pendleton, and Dawes for that matter, believed that this policy would improve the life of

Native Americans. Pendleton demonstrated his concern for the well being of the Native Americans by initiating a bill to invest the funds of Indian tribes in government bonds rather than in private stocks and bonds. The government bonds, he argued, were more stable and gave a consistent rate of return. *Congressional Record,* 46th Cong., 2d sess., 1880, 12, 212–15, 646, 719–20.

27. *Congressional Record,* 46th Cong., 2d sess., 1880, 2152–59, 2201, 4308–9, 4464–65; *Congressional Record,* 46th Cong., 2d sess., 1880, 38–39, 42–43, ICPSR; George H. Pendleton, *Speech of Hon. George H. Pendleton, of Ohio, on the Bill to Increase the Army; Delivered in the House of Representatives, March 17, 1858* (Washington, D.C.: Congressional Globe Office, 1858), 4; Claude Moore Fuess, *Carl Schurz: Reformer, 1829–1906* (New York: Dodd, Mead and Co., 1932), 252–78; Rittenhouse, "George Hunt Pendleton," 65–66; Mark W. Summers, *The Gilded Age or The Hazard of New Functions* (Upper Saddle River, N.J.: Prentice Hall, 1997), 71–73.

28. *Congressional Record,* 46th Cong., 2d sess., 1880, 4049–50; Rittenhouse, "George Hunt Pendleton," 66–67.

29. *Evening Star,* Feb. 16, 1880.

30. *Newport Journal,* Jan. 24, 1877.

31. Russel B. Nye, *George Bancroft: Brahmin Rebel* (New York: Alfred A. Knopf, 1945), 282.

32. George Bancroft to Matthew Arnold, Dec. 26, 1883, Massachusetts Historical Society, Boston, as cited in Robert H. Canary, *George Bancroft* (New York: Twayne, 1974), 102.

33. M. A. DeWolfe Howe, *The Life and Letters of George Bancroft,* vol. 2 (1908; repr., Port Washington, N.Y.: Kennikat Press, 1971), 156–58, 278–82; Nye, *George Bancroft,* 280–95; Canary, *George Bancroft,* 101–2, 129; Jerome Mushkat, *The Reconstruction of the New York Democracy, 1861–1874* (Rutherford, N.J.: Fairleigh Dickinson Univ. Press, 1981), 29, 61–62, 85.

34. *Evening Star,* Jan. 8, Feb. 16, 21, 24, 27, Mar. 15, 29, Apr. 12, May 24, 1880; *Cincinnati Enquirer,* Feb. 27, Mar. 31, 1880; Rittenhouse, "George Hunt Pendleton," 65; David J. Rothman, *Politics and Power: The Unites States Senate, 1869–1901* (Cambridge, Mass.: Harvard Univ. Press, 1966), 130–60.

35. *Official Proceedings of the National Democratic Convention, Held in Cincinnati, O., June 22d, 23d, and 24th, 1880* (Dayton, Ohio: Daily Journal Book and Job Rooms, 1882), 81–114; Moore, "Ohio in National Politics," 343–49; Jordan, *Ohio Comes of Age,* 172–73; Herbert J. Clancy, *The Presidential Election of 1880* (Chicago: Loyola Univ. Press, 1959), 122–56.

36. *National Democratic Proceedings, 1880,* 128.

37. The Pendleton home at Newport was rented out for the season. *New York Times,* May 5–7, 1880; *Evening Star,* June 2, 1880; *Cincinnati Enquirer,* June 28, July 22, 26, Sept. 5, 9, 13, 1880; William Dudley Foulke, *Fighting the Spoilsmen: Reminiscences of the Civil Service Reform Movement* (New York: G. P. Putnam's Sons, 1919), 127–29, 295–98. Because of past differences, Pendleton could not be expected to lobby hard for either Ohio candidate, which explains his meager contribution to the meeting.

38. *New York Times,* July 26, Oct. 13, 15, Nov. 3, 1880; *Reconstruction Epoch,* 535–41; James Ford Rhodes, *History of the United States from the Compromise of 1850 to the End of the Roosevelt Administration* (New York: MacMillan, 1928), 8:128–38; Clancy, *Presidential Election of 1880,* 167–239.

39. *Cincinnati Enquirer,* Dec. 3, 1880.

40. Ibid., Dec. 13, 15, 16, 1880; *Congressional Record,* 46th Cong., 3d sess., 1880, 72, 144; *New York Times,* Dec. 16, 1880; A. Bower Sageser, *The First Two Decades of the Pendleton Act: A Study of Civil Service Reform,* University Studies, vols. 34–35 (Lincoln: Univ. of Nebraska Press, 1935), 37–38.

41. *Cincinnati Enquirer,* Jan. 9, 1879.

42. George H. Pendleton to Nahum Caper, Nov. 12, 1881, Pendleton Miscellaneous Manuscripts, Ohio Historical Society, Columbus.

43. George H. Pendleton, *Civil Service Reform: Speech of Hon. George H. Pendleton, of Ohio, delivered in the Senate of the United States, December 13, 1881* (n.p., n.d.), 1–7, 13–15; George H. Pendleton, *The Dead Lock in the Senate: Speech of Mr. Pendleton, of Ohio, in the United States Senate, April 13, 1881* (Washington, D.C.: n.p., 1881), 1–13; George H. Pendleton, *Improvement of the Subordinate Civil Service: Speech of Hon. George H. Pendleton, of Ohio, in the Senate of the United States, Tuesday, December 12, 1882* (n.p., n.d.), 1–8; Rittenhouse, "George Hunt Pendleton," 69; Sageser, *Pendleton Act,* 37–38; Hoogenboom, *Outlawing the Spoils,* 200. Historians have long debated the motivations of the civil service reformers. Most interpretations shed little light on why Pendleton fostered the idea. Early historians tended to view the reform movement as simply a struggle between "good" and "evil." Paul Van Riper continued this perspective in his 1958 book. Matthew Josephson sees the struggle as an attempt on the part of businessmen to wrest political power from the hands of political bosses. E. E. Schattschneider argues that the presidents were primary movers in the reform movement because they too wished to reduce the power of party spoilsmen. Carl R. Fish and Leonard D. White utilize administrative frameworks resulting in a view of reform movements dedicated to adapting new business management programs to improve efficiency in government. Richard Hofstadter offers a slightly different perspective, suggesting that reformers tended to be members of an older aristocratic class within the country. This "displaced class" was afraid that its influence on society was being eroded by a rising class of wealthy, politically ambitious politicians. One of the more recent historical studies of civil service reform, Ari Hoogenboom's *Outlawing the Spoils,* takes Hofstadter's thesis a step further, contending that the reform struggle was between those who were "out" of power and those who were "in." The "outs" hoped to use civil service reform to aggrandize political power. Pendleton, like most individuals involved in this reform effort, was not motivated by only one factor. For Pendleton, there was a moral element. He had often demonstrated his desire to see efficiency in government. He did not fit Schattschneider's model because he was not a president, but he did desire to see the power of political bosses diminished. While technically a member of Hofstadter's aristocratic class, he was hardly "displaced" as a member of the Senate. Nor was he technically out of power, as Hoogenboom's model would suggest. Though the Democrats had been a minority party for more than twenty years, they were, by 1884, on the verge of returning to power. Pendleton did not come from the aristocratic, New England–born, abolition-minded stock from which most reformers came, according to Hoogenboom. No, Pendleton was motivated by numerous factors as discussed in the text. His story sheds light on the movement as a whole. Pendleton demonstrates a commitment to principle and partisanship that adds a new dimension to the historiography of the civil service reform movement. He is too instrumental in its success

to be dismissed as an anomaly, as most historians have done. Carl Russell Fish, *The Civil Service and the Patronage,* vol. 11 (New York: Longmans, Green and Co., 1905); Matthew Josephson, *The Politicos, 1865–1896* (New York: Harcourt, Brace and World, 1938); Elmer E. Schattschneider, *Party Government* (New York: n.p., 1942); Richard Hofstadter, *The Age of Reform: From Bryan to F.D.R.* (New York: Alfred A. Knopf, 1955); Van Riper, *History of the Civil Service*; Leonard D. White, *The Republican Era: A Study in Administrative History, 1869–1901* (New York: Macmillan, 1958); Hoogenboom, *Outlawing the Spoils.*

44. *New York Times,* Jan. 15, 1881.

45. George H. Pendleton to Edward M. Shepard, Jan. 31, 1881, Edward Morse Shepard Papers, Rare Book and Manuscript Library, Columbia University, New York; George H. Pendleton to Nahum Caper, Nov. 12, 1881, Pendleton Miscellaneous Manuscripts, Ohio Historical Society; Pendleton, *Civil Service Reform,* 1–5, 16; Pendleton, *Dead Lock,* 1–13; George H. Pendleton, *Political Assessments by the Republican Party: Speech of Hon. George H. Pendleton, of Ohio, in the Senate of the United States, June 26, 1882* (Washington, D.C.: n.p., 1882), 1–13; Pendleton, *Subordinate Civil Service,* 6–11; H. Wayne Morgan, *From Hayes to McKinley: National Party Politics, 1877–1896* (Syracuse, N.Y.: Syracuse Univ. Press, 1969), 162–63.

46. George H. Pendleton to Malcolm Hay, Jan. 6, 1871, Southard Hay Autograph Collection, Manuscripts and Archives, Yale University Library, New Haven, Connecticut.

47. John M. Dobson, *Politics in the Gilded Age: A New Perspective on Reform* (New York: Praeger, 1972), 65–67.

48. Pendleton, *Civil Service Reform,* 5–6, 11–12; Pendleton, *Subordinate Civil Service,* 13–16; Van Riper, *History of the Civil Service,* 63; David H. Rosenbloom, ed., *Centenary Issues of the Pendleton Act of 1883: The Problematic Legacy of Civil Service Reform* (New York: Marcel Dekkex, 1982), 107, 117; Robert Maranto and David Schultz, *A Short History of the United States Civil Service* (Lanham, Md.: Univ. Press of America, 1991), 27–38. A more cynical analysis might suggest that Jackson was much less a democrat than a Democrat. In other words, he was only seeking power for his party. In some ways, Pendleton, too, was motivated to advance his party's position.

49. Pendleton, *Speech on the Bill to Increase the Army,* 3–5; Thomas A. Jenckes, *Speech of Hon. Thomas A. Jenckes, of Rhode Island, on the Bill to Regulate the Civil Service of the United States and Promote the Efficiency Thereof; Delivered in the House of Representatives, May 14, 1868* (Washington, D.C.: F. and J. Rives and Geo. A. Bailey, 1868), 1–15; Joint Select Committee, *Civil Service of the United States,* 39th Cong., 2d sess., 1867, H. Rept. 8; *Report Concerning Civil Service in Great Britain Being Part of the Messages and Documents Communicated to the Two Houses of Congress at the Beginning of the Second Session of the Forty-Sixth Congress,* 46th Cong., 2d sess., 1879, H. Ex. Doc. 1, pt. 7, pt. 8; Dorman B. Eaton, *Civil Service in Great Britain: A History of Abuses and Reforms and Their Bearing upon American Politics* (New York: Harper and Brothers, 1880); Henry W. Bellows, "Civil Service Reform," *North American Review* 130 (1880): 247–60; *Cincinnati Enquirer,* Jan. 5, Mar. 9, 1869, Dec. 16, 1880; Sageser, *Pendleton Act,* 38; Van Riper, *History of the Civil Service,* 60–70; Hoogenboom, *Outlawing the Spoils,* 14–16, 33–69, 200–201; John Y. Simon, "Ulysses S. Grant and Civil Service Reform," *Hayes Historical Journal* 4 (Spring 1984): 9–15. For more on the first Civil Service Commission, see also Lionel V. Murphy, "The First Federal Civil Service Commission, 1871–1875, Parts I–III," *Public Personnel Review* 3 (Jan., July 1942 and Oct. 1943): 29–39, 218–31, 299–323.

50. In 1876, Eaton believed the Democrats were incapable of fostering reform, leaving him only the Republican Party as the means of achieving it. Pendleton proved him wrong. Dorman B. Eaton, *The Cincinnati Convention* (New York: n.p., 1876), 1–46; Edward Cary to Carl Schurz, Jan. 22, 1881, Carl Schurz Papers, University of Georgia Libraries, Athens; *New York Times*, Dec. 18, 1880; Sageser, *Pendleton Act*, 38–39; Hoogenboom, *Outlawing the Spoils*, 201.

51. Pendleton also replaced his bill against political assessments with a version written by the reform association. William Potts to Carl Schurz, Aug. 3, 1881, Schurz Papers; *Congressional Record*, 46th Cong., 3d sess., 1880, 285; Select Committee to Examine the Several Branches of the Civil Service, *The Regulation and Improvement of the Civil Service*, 46th Cong. 3d sess., 1881, S. Rept. 872; *Dorman B. Eaton, 1823–1899* (n.p., 1900), 3–6, 25–30; Sageser, *Pendleton Act*, 39–40.

52. *Regulation and Improvement of the Civil Service*, 4–6; Dorman B. Eaton, "A New Phase of the Reform Movement," *North American Review* 132 (1881): 554–56; Sageser, *Pendleton Act*, 40–41; Rittenhouse, "George Hunt Pendleton," 82; O. Glenn Stahl, *Public Personnel Administration*, 7th ed. (New York: Harper and Row, 1976), 40–47.

53. *Cincinnati Enquirer*, Jan. 12, 20, Feb. 2, 5–6, Mar. 8, 10, 13, 1881.

54. George H. Pendleton to Simeon E. Baldwin, Oct. 2, 15, 1881, Baldwin Family Papers, Yale University Library, New Haven, Connecticut; *Congressional Record*, 46th Cong., 3d sess., 1880–81, 285, 1443; *Evening Star*, Jan. 7, 13, 15, 29, Feb. 4, 10, 15, 22, 25, 28, Mar. 7, 8, 15, 18, 23, May 22, 1881; George Frederick Howe, *Chester Alan Arthur: A Quarter Century of Machine Politics* (New York: Frederick Ungar, 1935), 134; Thomas C. Reeves, *Gentleman Boss: The Life of Chester Alan Arthur* (New York: Alfred A. Knopf, 1975), 220–21.

55. George H. Pendleton to Lucius Q. C. Lamar, Sept. 27, 1881, Lucius Quintus Cincinnatus Lamar and Edward Mayes Papers, Mississippi Department of Archives and History, Jackson, Mississippi; *Congressional Record*, 47th Cong., spec. sess., 1881, 41–42, 122, 274–79. The *Enquirer* covered the debate in Congress. At one point, it blamed the patronage system for the delay in meaningful activity. *Cincinnati Enquirer*, Mar. 15, 27, Apr. 8, 27, May 2, 1881; Rittenhouse, "George Hunt Pendleton," 70.

56. *Evening Star*, Apr. 13, 1881; Readjuster-Democrats opposed Bourbon control of Virginia and sought repudiation of the state's debt. Howe, *Chester Alan Arthur*, 136–37.

57. *Evening Star*, Apr. 13, 1881.

58. Ibid.; Howe, *Chester Alan Arthur*, 136–38; Reeves, *Gentleman Boss*, 222–23.

59. J. H. C. Nevins to Roscoe Conkling, July 5, 1881, Schurz Papers; *Reconstruction Epoch*, 532–41, 648–53; Thomas C. Platt, *The Autobiography of Thomas Collier Platt*, ed. Louis J. Lang (New York: Arno Press, 1974), 139–66; *Cincinnati Enquirer*, May 17–18, June 25, 1881. Of Conkling, Pendleton said, "He is a man of great ability, but his influence rested almost wholly upon the spoils at his disposal. Shorn of these, he loses all power." *New York Times*, June 21, 1881; Rittenhouse, "George Hunt Pendleton," 69–71; Howe, *Chester Alan Arthur*, 141, 196; Kenneth R. Rossman, "Chester A. Arthur and Civil Service Reform" (M.A. thesis, Ohio State University, 1936), 27–30; Van Riper, *History of the Civil Service*, 75–78; Reeves, *Gentleman Boss*, 220–23; Allan Peskin, *Garfield* (Kent, Ohio: Kent State Univ. Press, 1978), 555–72; Justus D. Doenecke, *The Presidencies of James A. Garfield and Chester A. Arthur* (Lawrence: Regents Press of Kansas, 1981), 38–45.

60. *Cincinnati Enquirer*, July 4, 1881.

61. *Congressional Record,* 47th Cong., 2d spec. sess., 1881, 505, 538; *Cincinnati Enquirer,* July 4, Oct. 9, 11, 14, 1881. Correspondents of Carl Schurz noted the importance of public support. Silas W. Burt to Carl Schurz, July 12, 1881, Henry Hitchcock, Sept. 23, 1881, Schurz Papers; Ari Hoogenboom, ed., *Spoilsmen and Reformers* (New York: Rand McNally and Co., 1964), 30–35; Peskin, *Garfield,* 594–607; Doenecke, *Garfield and Arthur,* 53–54.

62. *Cincinnati Enquirer,* July 14, 22, 26, Oct. 13–14, Nov. 14, 1881.

63. Chester A. Arthur, "First Annual Message," in *A Compilation of the Messages and Papers of the Presidents, 1789–1907,* ed. James D. Richardson (Washington, D.C.: Bureau of National Literature and Art, 1908), 8:37–65; *Cincinnati Enquirer,* Dec. 7, 1881; Sageser, *Pendleton Act,* 41–42; Howe, *Chester Alan Arthur,* 160–64, 199, 203; Reeves, *Gentleman Boss,* 258–67.

64. *Congressional Record,* 47th Cong., 1st sess., 1881, 80.

65. Ibid., 79–85; Pendleton, *Civil Service Reform,* 1–16; *Cincinnati Enquirer,* Dec. 13–16, 1881; Jan. 1, 1882; *New York Times,* Dec. 14, 1881; Jan. 3, 1882. In an interview in the *Enquirer* dated January 1, Pendleton snapped at those who claimed his bill would act to keep Republicans in government offices. Drawing his critics' attention to the wording of the bill, he said to the reporter, "I showed plainly therein that no fixed term of office was established by it, and that there was no limitation of the power of removal as it now exists."

66. *Congressional Record,* 47th Cong., 1st sess., 1882, 1086.

67. Silas W. Burt to Carl Schurz, July 22, 1881, Everett P. Wheeler to Carl Schurz, Dec. 12, 1882, Schurz Papers; *Congressional Record,* 47th Cong., 1st sess., 1882, 1086–87; *Cincinnati Enquirer,* Mar. 10, 1882; Dorman B. Eaton and Everett P. Wheeler, *The Pendleton Bill and the Dawes Bill: Compared by the Committee on Legislation of the Civil-Service Reform Association* (New York: G. P. Putnam's Sons, 1882), 1–37; Frank Mann Stewart, *The National Civil Service Reform League: History, Activities, and Problems* (Austin: University of Texas, 1929), 32–33; Hoogenboom, *Outlawing the Spoils,* 219–22.

68. Committee on Civil Service and Retrenchment, *Report: To Accompany Bill S. 133,* 47th Cong., 1st sess., 1882, S. Rept. 576; *Congressional Record,* 47th Cong., 1st sess., 1882, 2357; Sageser, *Pendleton Act,* 44–45.

69. *Cincinnati Enquirer,* Dec. 16, 1881; Sageser, *Pendleton Act,* 43–45; Hoogenboom, *Outlawing the Spoils,* 219.

70. George H. Pendleton, *To Gain Political Power under the Guise of a Bill for the Punishment of Polygamy: Remarks of Hon. George H. Pendleton, of Ohio, in the Senate of the United States, Thursday, February 16, 1882* (n.p., n.d.), 7–8.

71. Ibid., 1–8; *Congressional Record,* 47th Cong., 1st sess., 1882, 1209–11; Rittenhouse, "George Hunt Pendleton," 73–74; Doenecke, *Garfield and Arthur,* 84–85.

72. George H. Pendleton, *The Funding Bill—Three Per Cent. Bonds: Speech of Hon. George H. Pendleton, of Ohio, Delivered in the Senate of the United States, January 17, 1882* (n.p., n.d.), 2, 7, 8; *Congressional Record,* 47th Cong., 1st sess., 1882, 450–52; *Cincinnati Enquirer,* Apr. 4, 1882.

73. George H. Pendleton, *The Reform of the Tariff: Speech of Hon. George H. Pendleton, of Ohio, in the Senate of the United States, Friday, March 17, 1882* (Washington, D.C.: R. O. Polkinhorn, 1882), 6.

74. Ibid., 3–8; *Congressional Record,* 47th Cong., 1st sess., 1882, 2000–2001; *Cincinnati Enquirer,* Mar. 18, 20, 1882.

75. George H. Pendleton, *Chinese Immigration: Speech of Hon. George H. Pendleton, of Ohio, Delivered in the Senate of the United States, April 28, 1882* (Washington, D.C.: n.p., 1882), 7.

76. Ibid., 3–8; *Congressional Record,* 47th Cong., 1st sess., 1882, 3408–10; *Cincinnati Enquirer,* Apr. 6, 1882. George William Curtis, noted civil service reformer, agreed with Arthur, who vetoed the initial exclusion bill because he believed it was undemocratic. Reeves, *Gentleman Boss,* 277–79; Doenecke, *Garfield and Arthur,* 81–84.

77. *Congressional Record,* 47th Cong., 1st sess., 1882, 4510–11, 5329–32; Rittenhouse, "George Hunt Pendleton," 76–77; Sageser, *Pendleton Act,* 49–51; Van Riper, *History of the Civil Service,* 90–94; Hoogenboom, *Outlawing the Spoils,* 233–35.

78. *Evening Star,* Jan. 19, 20, 24, Feb. 10, Mar. 15, Apr. 6, 19, May 5, 6, 8, 1882.

79. *Cincinnati Enquirer,* July 24, 1882; Benjamin Patton to Allen G. Thurman, Mar. 30, 1883, Allen Thurman Papers, Ohio Historical Society, Columbus.

80. *Cincinnati Enquirer,* July 21, 1882.

81. Ibid., July 16–20, Sept. 12, 1882; *New York Times,* Jan. 3, 9, July 17, 18, 20, 21, 27, 1882. Pendleton, according to the *Times,* had stepped aside for Thurman, who sought the presidential nomination in 1880, and now Pendleton was in competition with him for control of the Ohio Party. Contrary to the reporter's view, Pendleton was aligned more with Thurman than with other party leaders. He had opposed the nomination of John Bookwalter in 1881 and had developed some political enemies in spite of his involvement in the campaign. In addition, some Ohio Democrats smarted over Pendleton's vote in favor of confirming Ohio Republican Stanley Matthews for the Supreme Court. Pendleton said he voted for him as a matter of "courtesy." W. U. Hensel, *Life and Public Services of Grover Cleveland, Twenty-Second President of the United States and Democratic Nominee for Re-election, 1888. An Introductory Sketch by the Late Wm. Dorsheimer, Enlarged and Continued through the Present Administration to the Date of Publication. Together with A Sketch of the Life and Public Services of Allen G. Thurman, Ex-United States Senator from Ohio and Democratic Nominee for Vice-President* (Philadelphia: Hubbard Brothers, 1888), 440–42.

82. *Cincinnati Enquirer,* Mar. 10, Aug. 12, 15, 29, 1882; *New York Times,* July 21, 22, Aug. 6, Sept. 25, 1882; Hoogenboom, *Outlawing the Spoils,* 219. Many reformers opposed the direct election of government officers, fearing that political bosses would control those elections in many cities.

83. *Cincinnati Enquirer,* July 22, 1882.

84. Ibid., July 24, 1882. The *Enquirer,* though suspect in its interpretation of the convention, did not hesitate to print articles and editorials from papers with which it disagreed.

85. *New York Times,* Sept. 25, Oct. 21, 1882; *Cincinnati Enquirer,* Sept. 28, Oct. 1, 1882.

86. Fuess, *Carl Schurz,* 144; Hoogenboom, *Outlawing the Spoils,* 233–35.

87. *Cincinnati Enquirer,* Dec. 9, 1881; Jan. 24, July 20, Nov. 6, 1882; *New York Times,* July 24, 1882; *Cincinnati Gazette,* Dec. 13, 22, 1882; Pendleton, *Subordinate Civil Service,* 4–7; "'Voluntary Contributions' and the Republican Party," *Nation* 35 (Aug. 31, 1882): 170; Dorman B. Eaton, "Patronage Monopoly and the Pendleton Bill," *Princeton Review* 9 (Mar. 1882): 185–207. Pendleton attributed the election of Democratic governors in New York, Massachusetts, Kansas, Michigan, and other states as well as the rather large Democratic majority in the House for the coming Congress to the civil service reform issue. Howe, *Chester Alan Arthur,* 204; Sageser, *Pendleton Act,* 45–51; Rossman, *Chester A. Arthur,* 55;

Van Riper, *History of the Civil Service*, 90–94; Hoogenboom, *Outlawing the Spoils*, 234–35; Reeves, *Gentleman Boss*, 322.

88. *Evening Star*, Dec. 11, 1882; Jan. 12, 1883; Allen Nevins, *Grover Cleveland: A Study in Courage* (New York: Dodd, Mead and Co., 1964), 299.

89. Pendleton, *Subordinate Civil Service*, 5; *Cincinnati Enquirer*, Dec. 2, 1882; Edward McPherson, *Handbook of Politics, III, 1884–1888, Being a Record of Important Political Action, National and State, July 31, 1884–August 31, 1888* (1884–88; repr., New York: Da Capo Press, 1972), 3–6. See also Marion Mills Miller, ed., *Great Debates in American History: From the Debates in the British Parliament on the Colonial Stamp Act (1764–1765) to the Debates in Congress at the Close of the Taft Administration (1912–1913)*, vol. 9 (New York: Current Literature, 1913), 331–39.

90. Pendleton, *Subordinate Civil Service*, 1–8.

91. Ibid., 9.

92. The actual figure was probably closer to 14,000 out of a total of 131,000 government jobs. Still, it was only about 11 percent of the total. Ari Hoogenboom, "The Pendleton Act and the Civil Service," *American Historical Review* 64 (Jan. 1959): 303.

93. Pendleton, *Subordinate Civil Service*, 11–13; Hoogenboom asserts that reformers were essentially conservative in their movement and wanted to return to "the good old days before Jacksonian democracy and the industrial revolution—days when men with their background, status, and education were the unquestioned leaders of society." In some respects, this is an appropriate description of the paternalistic Pendleton, perhaps reflecting his Whig antecedents. In other ways, Pendleton could place reform well within Jacksonianism. Hoogenboom, *Outlawing the Spoils*, 186–97. Hoogenboom also notes the role of partisanship in Democrats supporting reform early on in an attempt to attract reformers of any political stripe. Hoogenboom, *Spoilsmen and Reformers*, 20–24.

94. Pendleton, *Subordinate Civil Service*, 14–15.

95. *Cincinnati Commercial*, Dec. 12, 13, 1882; *Cincinnati Gazette*, Dec. 15, 1882; *Cincinnati Enquirer*, Dec. 15, 20, 27, 1882; Jan. 11, 1883. McLean noted after the bill passed that the Ohio Assembly did not support reform.

96. Pendleton, *Subordinate Civil Service*, 14. McLean continued a daily campaign against reform throughout the debates. *Cincinnati Enquirer*, Dec. 4–7, 12–21, 23–31, 1882; C. B. Galbreath, "Ohio's Contribution to National Civil Service Reform," *Ohio Archaeological and Historical Society Publications* 33 (1924): 176–204. Pendleton caucused with Senate Democrats to garner support.

97. George H. Pendleton to William W. Armstrong, Jan. 8, 1883, William Wirt Armstrong Miscellaneous Manuscripts, Rutherford B. Hayes Presidential Library, Fremont, Ohio; Pendleton, *Subordinate Civil Service*, 16; *Cincinnati Enquirer*, Dec. 18, 1882; *Congressional Record*, 47th Cong., 2d sess., 1882, 202–10; Hoogenboom, *Outlawing the Spoils*, 236–38, 242.

98. *Congressional Record*, 47th Cong., 2d sess., 1882, 247–48, 461–71; Sageser, *Pendleton Act*, 52–53. Logan had been no friend of reform in the past, but the elections of 1882 apparently gave him a push in that direction. Senator Morgan also played an important role in passing the amendment opening entry to the service at any level. Hoogenboom, *Outlawing the Spoils*, 236–43.

99. *Cincinnati Gazette*, Dec. 12, 1882; Sageser, *Pendleton Act*, 53–54; Hoogenboom, *Outlawing the Spoils*, 245–46.

100. *Congressional Record,* 47th Cong., 2d sess., 1882, 616–17; Hoogenboom, *Outlawing the Spoils,* 243.

101. *Congressional Record,* 47th Cong., 2d sess., 1882, 604–5; Pendleton, *Subordinate Civil Service,* 16; Hoogenboom, *Outlawing the Spoils,* 245.

102. *Congressional Record,* 47th Cong., 2d sess., 1882, 322–24, 353, 362–68, 461–71, 527, 601–6, 615–17; Sageser, *Pendleton Act,* 54.

103. Rutherford B. Hayes to Silas W. Burt, Jan. 12, 1883, transcript, Rutherford B. Hayes Papers, Rutherford B. Hayes Presidential Library, Fremont, Ohio; *New York Times,* Dec. 28, 29, 1882; Jan. 18, 1883; *Cincinnati Commercial,* Dec. 28, 1882; *Cincinnati Enquirer,* Jan. 7, 9, 1883; *Evening Star,* Jan. 17, Feb. 21, 1883; John Sherman, *John Sherman's Recollections of Forty Years in the House, Senate and Cabinet: An Autobiography* (Chicago: Werner, 1895), 2:855. Hayes noted the Democracy's attitude in Ohio: "The Democracy in this state are reading Mr. Pendleton savage lectures. *They* will try to drive him out of public life." McLean added that Pendleton had simply been duped by the Republicans and Dorman Eaton. Pendleton's chances for the White House, he believed, were gone. At the annual January 8 Andrew Jackson Day meeting, Pendleton was not present. He telegraphed an apology. McLean believed he was too embarrassed to come. Moorfield Storey, *The Democratic Party and Civil Service Reform: A Paper Prepared for the Annual Meeting of the National Civil Service Reform League at Cincinnati, Ohio, December 17, 1897* (n.p.: National Civil Service Reform League, 1897), 6–8; Galbreath, "Ohio's Contribution," 198–99; Rittenhouse, "George Hunt Pendleton," 81–82; Sageser, *Pendleton Act,* 57–60; Howe, *Chester Alan Arthur,* 208–9; Hoogenboom, *Outlawing the Spoils,* 246–53; Reeves, *Gentleman Boss,* 324–35; Thomas C. Reeves, "The Irony of the Pendleton Act," *Hayes Historical Journal* 4 (Spring 1984): 37–43. The third member of the Civil Service Commission was John M. Gregory, president of the Illinois Board of Health.

104. *Evening Star,* Mar. 3, 4, 6, 12, 14, 1883; *Congressional Record,* 47th Cong., 2d sess., 1883, 2476; ibid., 47th Cong., 2d sess., 1883, 32, 38–51, ICPSR; Rittenhouse, "George Hunt Pendleton," 79, 83–84.

105. *New York Times,* June 18, 20, 1883; *Cincinnati Enquirer,* June 22, 1883; Moore, "Ohio in National Politics," 352–54.

106. *Cincinnati Enquirer,* June 22, 1883; *Appleton's Annual Cyclopaedia,* 23:608.

107. *New York Times,* June 22, 1883; *Cincinnati Enquirer,* June 24–25, 1883. Payne's son, Oliver, was treasurer of the Standard Oil Company in Cleveland. Rumors of immense amounts of money coming through him from the company surfaced throughout the campaign and especially during Henry Payne's Senate bid. Payne provided a couple of ironic paradoxes. First, he represented those Democrats who, in spite of years of platform planks to the contrary, opposed civil service reform. Second, he was largely associated with a monopoly, which the party had been condemning for years as well.

108. Ida M. Tarbell, *The History of the Standard Oil Company* (New York: McClure, Phillips and Co., 1904), 1:54–59, 2:111–12.

109. *Cincinnati Enquirer,* July 6, 1883. See also *New York Times,* June 23, 28, 30, July 2, 8, 11, Aug. 4, 17, 22, 1883. Thurman later commented on the irony of Pendleton having succeeded in accomplishing what the Democratic platforms had demanded for years and then being ostracized. Thurman could attribute it to only one thing: the desire to develop a political machine in Ohio led by McLean and Payne. Moore, "Ohio in National Politics," 357–58.

110. McLean even accused Pendleton of mismanagement and embezzlement of funds from the Bowler estate over which he presided. *Cincinnati Enquirer,* Jan. 10, Apr. 21, 1882. McLean became so powerful in Cincinnati that many viewed him as a political boss. Rumors circulated that Hoadly had made a deal with McLean. In return for his support, Hoadly was to work to destroy Pendleton's Senate hopes. *New York Times,* Sept. 9, 1883; Rittenhouse, "George Hunt Pendleton," 91–94.

111. *New York Times,* Sept. 8–11, 1883; Jan. 11, 1884; *Cincinnati Enquirer,* Sept. 10, 12, 14, 21, 24, 28, 1883. Hoadly came out in favor of the Highland House ticket, "not because it is better than the reform ticket, but because party discipline must be maintained." A longtime associate of Pendleton, William S. Groesbeck, delivered a speech in College Hall early in August (about a month before the Reform Convention) in support of Pendleton's Civil Service Reform Act. Though there is no connection between the two events, the public speech demonstrated that there were some Ohio Democrats who supported Pendleton's reform. William S. Groesbeck, *Speech Delivered by W. S. Groesbeck, at College Hall, Cincinnati, August 2, 1883* (Cincinnati, Ohio: Robert Clarke and Co., 1883), 1–26.

112. *Cincinnati Enquirer,* Sept. 29, Oct. 1–2, 4, 7, 10–11, 18, 1883; Jordan, *Ohio Comes of Age,* 179–82.

113. *Cincinnati Enquirer,* Nov. 5, 12, 26, Dec. 5, 1883; Jan 13, 1884; Galbreath, "Ohio's Contribution," 199; Rittenhouse, "George Hunt Pendleton," 85.

114. *Cincinnati Enquirer,* Dec. 6–7, 1883.

115. Ibid., Dec. 17–19, 24, 26, 28–29, 31, 1883; Jan. 1–2, 1884; Moore, "Ohio in National Politics," 355–56; Rittenhouse, "George Hunt Pendleton," 94–95.

116. George H. Pendleton to Andrew I. Williams, Nov. 12, 1883, George H. Pendleton Papers, Henry E. Huntington Library, San Marino, California; *New York Times,* Nov. 14, 1883; Jan. 2, 4–5, 1884; *Cincinnati Enquirer,* Jan. 3–6, 1884. Though Pendleton men claimed thirty-two votes, they were not secure. They needed ten more. Payne men claimed that ten of the votes Pendleton counted on were not yet decided. Perhaps the most telling tale of this pre-caucus prognostication was that the Hamilton County votes were said to be under McLean's control.

117. *New York Times,* Jan. 9, 1884; *Cincinnati Enquirer,* Jan. 9–10, 1884.

118. *Cincinnati Enquirer,* Dec. 9, 1881; Jan. 11, 12, 17, 24, Mar. 7, 20, Apr. 6, Oct. 11, 16, 21, Nov. 6, Dec. 25, 1882; Jan. 22, 27, Mar. 16, 1883.

119. *Evening Star,* Jan. 15, 1884.

120. *Cincinnati Enquirer,* Jan. 11, 13, 18, 1884; Miller, *Great Debates,* 339–40; Charles R. Williams, ed., *Diary and Letters of Rutherford B. Hayes: Nineteenth President of the United States* (Columbus: Ohio Archaeological and Historical Society, 1926), 4:135–36; Frank G. Carpenter, *Carp's Washington* (New York: McGraw-Hill, 1960), 119–22; Galbreath, "Ohio's Contribution," 199–202. Allen Thurman issued a public letter the day of the caucus vote: "I hear Payne men say: 'We can not support Pendleton because we disapprove of his civil service reform bill,' forgetting that convention after convention of the Democratic Party, both State and National, had resolved in favor of civil service reform, and also forgetting that the Republicans now in office are just as liable to be turned out as if the Pendleton bill had never passed. I do not advocate that bill. I think it ought to be amended or repealed; but I would not slaughter a life-long Democrat because in a long public service he happened to make one mistake." *Columbus Evening Dispatch,* Jan. 8, 1884, cited in Galbreath, "Ohio's Contribution," 200.

121. *Columbus Evening Dispatch,* Jan. 8, 1884, cited in Galbreath, "Ohio's Contribution," 200.

122. *New York Times,* Jan. 7, 1884.

123. *The Week: Illustrated* 1 (Jan. 1884): 321; *New York Times,* Jan. 10, 1884; Jordan, *Ohio Comes of Age,* 183–85; Nevins, *Grover Cleveland,* 344.

124. *New York Times,* Jan. 10–11, 1884; Henry Demarest Lloyd, *Wealth against Commonwealth* (New York: Harper and Brothers, 1894), 370–88; Tarbell, *Standard Oil Company,* 2:111–20; *The Week: Illustrated* 1 (Jan. 1884): 326; Galbreath, "Ohio's Contribution," 200–203; Moore, "Ohio in National Politics," 356–59; Rittenhouse, "George Hunt Pendleton," 98–100; Josephson, *Politicos,* 322–23; Jordan, *Ohio Comes of Age,* 183; Nevins, *Grover Cleveland,* 343–44.

125. Robert W. Cherny and William L. Barney, "The Gilded Age, 1878–1900," in *A Companion to Nineteenth-Century America,* ed. William L. Barney (Oxford: Blackwell, 2001), 68–71. See also Robert D. Marcus, *Grand Old Party: Political Structure in the Gilded Age, 1880–1896* (New York: Oxford Univ. Press, 1971), and Stephen Skowronek, *Building a New American State: The Expansion of National Administration Capacities, 1897–1920* (New York: Cambridge Univ. Press, 1982).

126. *Congressional Record,* 48th Cong., 1st sees., 1884, 588, 1583–85, 1614–19, 1647–48; ibid., 48th Cong., 1st sess., 1884, 6, ICPSR.

127. Ibid., 48th Cong., 1st sess., 1884, 8, ICPSR; *Congressional Record,* 48th Cong., 1st sess., 1884, 2534–48; McPherson, *Handbook of Politics, III, 1884–1888,* 144–47. Pendleton used similar reasoning for opposing the government's use of eminent domain to procure land for the Library of Congress. *Congressional Record,* 48th Cong., 1st sess., 1884, 1051–54; ibid., 48th Cong., 1st sess., 1884, 4–5, ICPSR; Rittenhouse, "George Hunt Pendleton," 86–90.

128. *Evening Star,* Feb. 19, 1884.

129. Ibid., Dec. 20, 1883; Jan. 11, 15, 19, 25, Feb. 11, 19, 26, 29, 1884.

130. *New York Times,* June 24–27, 1884; *Cincinnati Enquirer,* June 26, 1884.

131. *New York Times,* Sept. 7, 1884. Pendleton was very pleased with the improvement seen during Arthur's term as a result of this act and was optimistic concerning Cleveland, saying he was "above all a man who believes that public office is a public trust." George H. Pendleton to James F. Colby, Dec. 10, 1884, 2 Jan. 1885, National Civil Service Reform League Papers, Cornell University Library, Ithaca, New York.

132. *New York Times,* Apr. 6, July 17, Sept. 7, 1884; *Cincinnati Enquirer,* July 5, 7, 12–13, 1884; *Official Proceedings of the National Democratic Convention, Held in Chicago, Ill., July 8th, 9th, 10th, and 11th, 1884, Containing also the Preliminary Proceedings of the National Democratic Committee and the Committee of Arrangements . . .* (New York: Douglas Taylor's Democratic Printing House, 1884), 195–202, 247, 293–96; Powell, *Democratic Party of Ohio,* 295–96; Robert McElroy, *Grover Cleveland: The Man and the Statesman, An Authorized Biography,* vol. 1 (New York: Harper and Brothers, 1923), 82–83; Horace Samuel Merrill, *Bourbon Leader: Grover Cleveland and the Democratic Party,* The Library of American Biography, ed. Oscar Handlin (Boston: Little, Brown and Co., 1957), 32, 38, 44–58; Nevins, *Grover Cleveland,* 123.

133. McElroy, *Grover Cleveland,* 97, 107–9; Merrill, *Bourbon Leader,* 44; Nevins, *Grover Cleveland,* 195–201.

134. *Cincinnati Enquirer,* Sept. 26, Oct. 11, 16, 19, 1884; Jordan, *Ohio Comes of Age,* 187.

135. Grover Cleveland, *Letter of Grover Cleveland to the National Civil Service Reform League* (n.p., n.d.), 1–3, in Schurz Papers; *Cincinnati Enquirer,* Nov. 18, 20, 26, Dec. 19, 20–21, 1884; Jan. 9–10, 1885; *Evening Star,* Dec. 3, 30, 1884; *Congressional Record,* 48th Cong., 2d sess., 1885, 826–27, 1050, 2461, 426–27, 1706; Rittenhouse, "George Hunt Pendleton," 102–3; Sageser, *Pendleton Act,* 60–89; McElroy, *Grover Cleveland,* 103–4; Nevins, *Grover Cleveland,* 195, 200–201. Republicans feared that Pendleton might obtain a cabinet seat and published a lengthy pamphlet with newspaper excerpts detailing his Kentucky Central claim scandal. *The Record of George H. Pendleton: Why He Is Unfit for Any Government Position* (n.p.: 1885), 1–49.

Minister Plenipotentiary . . . to Germany

1. Wade Hampton, et. al., to Grover Cleveland, Mar. 14, 1885, John T. Morgan to Grover Cleveland, Mar. 9, 1885, Application and Recommendation Letters of Grover Cleveland Administration, 1885–1889, National Archives, Washington, D.C.; William S. Groesbeck to Thomas Bayard, Mar. 19, 1885, Thomas F. Bayard Papers, Manuscript Division, Library of Congress; *New York Times,* Aug. 19, 1886. Pendleton had the money necessary to sustain himself and the legation in spite of the low pay of the position. David J. Rothman, *Politics and Power: The United States Senate, 1869–1901* (Cambridge, Mass.: Harvard Univ. Press, 1966), 157.

2. *Congressional Record,* 48th Cong., 1st. sess., 1884, 373; ibid., 48th Cong., 1st sess., 1884, 3, ICPSR; *Evening Star,* Mar. 23, 1885; *Cincinnati Graphic* 3 (Mar. 28, 1885): 198; "The Diplomatic Service," *Nation* 40 (June 11, 1885): 476; Charles C. Tansill, *The Foreign Policy of Thomas F. Bayard, 1885–1897* (New York: Fordham Univ. Press, 1940), xx; Mark A. Lause, *The Civil War's Last Campaign: James B. Weaver, the Greenback-Labor Party and the Politics of Race and Section* (Lanham, Md.: Univ. Press of America, 2001), 52.

3. Everett P. Wheeler to Thomas Bayard, Apr. 22, 1885, Bayard Papers; *Cincinnati Graphic* 3 (Apr. 25, 1885): 261–70; ibid. (May 2, 1885): 278; *Cincinnati Commercial Gazette,* Nov. 23, 1889.

4. Pendleton to Bayard, Aug. 9, 1885, Bayard Papers.

5. Pendleton to Bayard, July 23, 1886, Bayard Papers.

6. Pendleton to Bayard, June 8, Aug. 9, Sept. 6, 1885, Bayard to Pendleton, Oct. 21, 1885, Bayard Papers; George H. Pendleton to Thomas Bayard, May 21, 1885, Despatches from United States Ministers to the German States and Germany, 1799–1801, 1835–1906, vol. 38, National Archives, Washington, D.C.; Bayard to Pendleton, June 15, Sept. 9, Nov. 21, 1885, Carl Schurz to Bayard, May 22, 1886, Bayard Papers; Pendleton to Grover Cleveland, Sept. 24, 1885, Grover Cleveland Papers, Manuscript Division, Library of Congress; Pendleton to John W. Harper, Apr. 14, 1886, Rutherford B. Hayes Papers, Rutherford B. Hayes Presidential Library, Fremont, Ohio; *Cincinnati Enquirer,* Mar. 24, May 18, July 14, 1885; "One View of Civil-Service Reform," *Nation* 41 (July 9, 1885): 31; "The Civil Service and the Soldiers," *Nation* 40 (June 11, 1885): 476–77. John McLean of the *Cincinnati Enquirer* was one of the editors who continued to attack reform. McLean noted that Pendleton's acceptance of the Berlin post left his supporters in Ohio without a leader.

7. Pendleton to Bayard, Aug. 30, 1885, Bayard Papers.

8. This material came from an article written by Jane Pendleton Brice, Pendleton's daughter, titled "Recollections of Court Life in Berlin, 1885–1889." It was probably published in a newspaper or periodical. Frances C. Cox, Brice's granddaughter, later edited the manuscript for publication in 1988 under a new title. Jane Pendleton Brice, "The Year of the Three Kaisers," *Foreign Service Journal* (Dec. 1988): 44–46.

9. Miscellaneous notes, Aug. 24, 1885, Sept. 4, 1885, Records of Foreign Service Posts-Germany, vol. 140, *U.S. Legation in Berlin: Notes from the German Government, Jan. 1, 1884–Dec. 28, 1886,* vol. 13, National Archives, Washington, D.C.; Pendleton to Bayard, Sept. 10, 1885, Bayard to Pendleton, Oct. 21, 1885, Pendleton to Prince Bismarck, Jan. 4, 1886, Bayard Papers; Pendleton to Grover Cleveland, June 14, Sept. 11, 1885, Cleveland Papers; Tansill, *Foreign Policy of Bayard,* 28–30.

10. Bayard to Pendleton, Sept. 9, 1885, Bayard Papers.

11. Pendleton to Bayard, Sept. 10, Nov. 9, 1885, Bayard Papers; Pendleton to Bayard, Sept. 23, Oct. 6, 1885, Despatches, vol. 39.

12. Pendleton to Bayard, Dec. 25, 1885, Bayard Papers.

13. Pendleton to Bayard, Dec. 25, 1885, Bayard Papers; Thomas F. Bayard to George H. Pendleton, July 7, 9, Aug. 4, 5, 1885, Diplomatic Instructions of the Department of State, 1885, vol. 17, National Archives, Washington, D.C. According to the documents and letters provided to Congress, Pendleton spent most of the first two years in Berlin dealing with these types of cases. *Message and Foreign Relations, 1885,* 49th Cong., 1st sess., 1885, H. Ex. Doc. 1 (serial 2368), 390–440; *Message and Foreign Relations, 1886,* 49th Cong., 2d sess., 1885–86, H. Ex. Doc. 1 (serial 2460), 309–35; Pendleton to Bayard, Apr. 7, 1887, Despatches, vol. 44; Count Henry Bismarck to George H. Pendleton, Dec. 21, 1885; Mar. 26, 1886, Records of Foreign Service Posts, vol. 140, *Notes from the German Government,* vol. 13; Miscellaneous note, Records of Foreign Service Posts—Germany, vol. 141, *U.S. Legation in Berlin: Notes from the German Government, Jan. 6, 1887–Dec. 25, 1888,* vol. 14, National Archives, Washington, D.C.; "Emigration from Germany," *Nation* 43 (Mar. 24, 1887): 245; *Cincinnati Enquirer,* Aug. 8, 1887.

14. Stuart Anderson, "'Pacific Destiny' and American Policy in Samoa, 1872–1899," *Hawaiian Journal of History* 12 (1978): 46–50. For more on the history of international interest in Samoa, see Sylvia Masterman, *The Origins of the International Rivalry in Samoa, 1845–1884* (Stanford, Calif.: Stanford Univ. Press, 1934). For more on Samoa, see R. P. Gilson, *Samoa, 1830 to 1900: The Politics of a Multi-Cultural Community,* with an introduction and conclusion by J. W. Davidson (Melbourne: Oxford Univ. Press, 1970).

15. C. Brunsdon Fletcher, *Stevenson's Germany: The Case against Germany in the Pacific* (New York: Charles Scribner's Sons, 1920), 40–55; Tansill, *Foreign Policy of Bayard,* preface, 1–15; Anderson, "'Pacific Destiny,'" 49–51.

16. Tensions between Germany and France continued throughout much of 1887. *Cincinnati Enquirer,* Jan. 21, 25, 29, Feb. 1, 6, 9, Mar. 1, May 18–19, June 1, 5, 12, Dec. 26, 1887; "A French View of Bismarck's Speech," *Nation* 46 (Mar. 1, 1888): 172; Tansill, *Foreign Policy of Bayard,* 9–21. In February 1887, Pendleton returned to the United States on a leave of absence. He visited with the president to discuss events in Germany. Some speculated at the time that he would replace Secretary of the Treasury Daniel Manning. Pendleton disavowed that rumor.

17. *Commercial Relations of United States, 1884–1885,* 49th Cong., 1st sess., 1885, II. Ex. Doc. 253 (serial 2402), 198–200; *Cincinnati Enquirer,* July 25, 1887; Tansill, *Foreign Policy of Bayard,* 22–30.

18. Miscellaneous note, Apr. 6, 1886, Records of Foreign Service Posts, vol. 140, *Notes from the German Government,* vol. 13; *American Rights in Samoa: Message from the President of the United States with Inclosures [sic], In Response to the Resolution of the House of Representatives in Relation to Affairs in Samoa,* 50th Cong., 1st sess., 1888, H. Ex. Doc. 238 (serial 2560), 12–20; George Herbert Ryden, *The Foreign Policy of the United States in Relation to Samoa* (New Haven, Conn.: Yale Univ. Press, 1933), 301–21; Tansill, *Foreign Policy of Bayard,* 31–34.

19. *Cincinnati Enquirer,* May 21–26, 1886; *New York Times,* May 21, 23, 26, 1886; *Cincinnati Graphic* 5 (May 29, 1886): 351. The *Graphic* called for a monument to Mrs. Pendleton in Cincinnati due to her charitable work in "bettering the condition of the children of the poor."

20. Pendleton to Bayard, July 23, 1886, Bayard Papers.

21. Pendleton to Bayard, June 2, July 2, 3, Sept. 10, 1886, Despatches, vols. 41–42; *Cincinnati Enquirer,* May 26, 1886.

22. Tansill, *Foreign Policy of Bayard,* 52–81; Anderson, "'Pacific Destiny,'" 48–55.

23. Pendleton to Bayard, Oct. 13, 1887, Despatches, vol. 45; Pendleton to Bayard, Oct. 17, 1887, Bayard to Pendleton, Oct. 29, 1887, Bayard Papers; *Message and Foreign Relations, 1888,* 50th Cong., 2d sess., 1887, H. Ex. Doc. 1 (serial 2626–2627), 570–78; *Message from the President of the United States Transmitting Documents Relating to the Condition of Affairs in Samoa,* 50th Cong., 2d sess., 1888, S. Ex. Doc. 31 (serial 2610), 1–157; *Message from the President of the United States Transmitting Information Touching Affairs in Samoa,* 50th Cong., 2d sess., 1889, S. Ex. Doc. 68 (serial 2611), 1–22; *Affairs at Samoa: Message from the President of the United States in Relation to Affairs in the Samoa Islands,* 50th Cong., 2d sess., 1889, H. Ex. Doc. 118 (serial 2651), 1–15; *Samoa: Message from the President of the United States, Transmitting Additional Information Relating to Affairs in Samoa,* 50th Cong., 2d sess., 1889, H. Ex. Doc. 119 (serial 2651), 1–3; *Message from the President of the United States, Transmitting Information Relative to Affairs in Samoa,* 50th Cong., 2d sess., 1889, S. Ex. Doc. 102 (serial 2612), 1–10; Tansill, *Foreign Policy of Bayard,* 76–85.

24. Pendleton to Bayard, Nov. 12, 1887, Bayard Papers; Bayard to Pendleton, Jan. 17, 1888, Diplomatic Instructions of the Department of State, 1888, vol. 18, National Archives, Washington, D.C.; *Message and Foreign Relations, 1888,* 579–662; *American Rights in Samoa,* 106–36; *Cincinnati Commercial Gazette,* Jan. 24, 1888; "The Samoan Affair," *Nation* 48 (Jan. 31, 1889): 84–85; Tansill, *Foreign Policy of Bayard,* 86–119; Anderson, "'Pacific Destiny,'" 55; Matthew Frye Jacobson, *Barbarian Virtues: The United States Encounters Foreign Peoples at Home and Abroad, 1876–1917* (New York: Hill and Wang, 2000), 23.

25. Bayard to Chapman Coleman, June 25, 1888, Bayard Papers.

26. Fred Crosby to Bayard, Apr. 20–21, 23, 1888, Pendleton to Bayard, Mar. 9, Nov. 9, 1888, Despatches, vol. 46; Coleman to Bayard, May 7, June 11, Oct. 30, 1888, Bayard to Coleman, May 19, June 25, 1888, Pendleton to Bayard, May 21, 1888, Bayard to Pendleton, June 7, 1888, Bayard Papers; Ryden, *Foreign Policy of the United States,* 429; Tansill, *Foreign Policy of Bayard,* 114, 118.

27. Lambert Tree to Bayard, Dec. 23, 1888, Bayard Papers.

28. Pendleton to Bayard, Dec. 25, 1888; Feb. 11, 1889, Bayard Papers; W. G. Roberts to Benjamin Harrison, Apr. 5, 1889, Application and Recommendation Letters of Benjamin Harrison Administration, 1889–1893, National Archives, Washington, D.C.; Pendleton to James G. Blaine, Apr. 25, 1889, Despatches, vol. 48; *Cincinnati Commercial Gazette,* Mar. 10, 1888; Rittenhouse, "George Hunt Pendleton," 105.

29. Anderson, "'Pacific Destiny,'" 56–58.

30. *Evening Star,* Nov. 23, 25, 26, 1889; *Cincinnati Commercial Gazette,* Nov. 23, 26, 1889; *New York Times,* Nov. 23, 26, 1889; Rittenhouse, "George Hunt Pendleton," 106.

31. John B. Mosby to Rutherford B. Hayes, Mar. 3, 1890, Hayes Papers; *Cincinnati Enquirer,* Nov. 26, 1889; *Cincinnati Commercial Gazette,* Nov. 26, 1889, Mar. 8–9, 1890; *Evening Star,* Mar. 6, 8, 1890; Rittenhouse, "George Hunt Pendleton," 107.

32. Isaac Jordan, *George Hunt Pendleton, Music Hall, Cincinnati* (Cincinnati, Ohio: n.p., 1890), 22.

33. Ibid., 46.

34. Ibid., 47.

35. Ibid., 40.

36. *Evening Star,* Nov. 26, 1889.

37. *Cincinnati Commercial Gazette,* Nov. 23, 1889.

Conclusion

1. Stephen Skowronek, *The Politics That Presidents Make: Leadership from John Adams to Bill Clinton,* 2d ed. (Cambridge, Mass.: Belknap Press of Harvard Univ. Press, 1997), 129–96.

2. Woodrow Wilson, *Congressional Government,* with an introduction by Walter Lippmann (1885; repr., Gloucester: Peter Smith, 1973).

3. Morris P. Fiorina, "The Decline of Collective Responsibility in American Politics," Working Paper Number 50 (St. Louis, Mo.: Center for the Study of American Business, 1980).

4. John H. Aldrich, *Why Parties: The Origin and Transformation of Political Parties in America,* American Politics and Political Economy Series, ed. Benjamin I. Page (Chicago: Univ. of Chicago Press, 1995).

5. Paul Kleppner, *The Third Electoral Party System, 1853–1892: Parties, Voters, and Political Cultures* (Chapel Hill: Univ. of North Carolina Press, 1979).

6. Joel Silbey, *A Respectable Minority: The Democratic Party in the Civil War Era, 1860–1868* (New York: W. W. Norton and Co., 1977).

Bibliography

Government Documents

Affairs at Samoa: Message from the President of the United States in Relation to Affairs in the Samoan Islands. 50th Cong., 2d sess., 1889. H. Executive Doc. 118, serial 2651.

American Rights in Samoa: Message from the President of the United States with Inclosures [sic], In Response to the Resolution of the House of Representatives in Relation to Affairs in Samoa. 50th Cong., 1st sess., 1888. H. Executive Doc. 238, serial 2560.

Biographical Directory of the American Congress, 1774–1949. Washington, D.C.: GPO, 1950.

Commercial Relations of United States, 1884–1885. 49th Cong., 1st sess., 1885. H. Executive Doc. 253, serial 2402.

Congressional Globe. 46 vols. Washington, D.C., 1834–73.

Congressional Globe. 46 vols. Inter-University Consortium for Political and Social Research. Washington, D.C., 1834–73. Computer database, University of Michigan, Ann Arbor.

Congressional Record. Washington, D.C., 1873–85.

Congressional Record. Inter-University Consortium for Political and Social Research. Washington, D.C., 1873–85. Computer database, University of Michigan, Ann Arbor.

Despatches [sic] from United States Ministers to the German States and Germany, 1799–1801, 1835–1906. Vols. 38–48. National Archives, Washington, D.C. Microfilm at National Archives and Records Administration, Kansas City.

House Committee on the Judiciary, *Impeachment of William W. Belknap.* 44th Cong., 1st sess., 1876. H. Rept. 345.

Message and Foreign Relations, 1885. 49th Cong., 1st sess., 1885. H. Executive Doc. 1, serial 2368.

Message and Foreign Relations, 1886. 49th Cong., 2d sess., 1885–86. H. Executive Doc. 1, serial 2460.

Message and Foreign Relations, 1888. 50th Cong., 2d sess., 1887. H. Executive Doc. 1, serial 2626–27.

Message from the President of the United States Transmitting Documents Relating to the Condition of Affairs in Samoa. 50th Cong., 2d sess., 1888. S. Executive Doc. 31, serial 2610.

Message from the President of the United States, Transmitting Information Relative to Affairs in Samoa. 50th Cong., 2d sess., 1889. S. Executive Doc. 102, serial 2612.

Message from the President of the United States Transmitting Information Touching Affairs in Samoa. 50th Cong., 2d sess., 1889. S. Executive Doc. 68, serial 2611.

Ohio. General Assembly. Senate. *Journal of the Senate of the State of Ohio.* 51st Assembly, 1st sess., 1854.

Papers Relating to Civil Service in the United States; Being Part of the Messages and Documents Communicated to the Two Houses of Congress at the Beginning of the Second Session of the Forty-Sixth Congress. 46th Cong., 2d sess., 1879. H. Executive Doc. 1, pt. 8.

Population Schedules of the Seventh Census of the United States, 1850. Roll 687. Washington, D.C: National Archives Microfilm Publications, 1964.

Population Schedules of the Eighth Census of the United States, 1860. Roll 973. Washington, D.C: National Archives Microfilm Publications, 1967.

Population Schedules of the Ninth Census of the United States, 1870. Roll 1209. Washington, D.C: National Archives Microfilm Publications, 1965.

Records of the Foreign Service Posts—Germany. Vol. 140. *U.S. Legation in Berlin: Notes from the German Government, Jan. 1, 1884–Dec. 28, 1886.* Vol. 13. National Archives, Washington, D.C.

Records of the Foreign Service Posts—Germany. Vol. 141. *U.S. Legation in Berlin: Notes from the German Government, Jan. 6, 1887–Dec. 25, 1888.* Vol. 14. National Archives, Washington, D.C.

Report Concerning Civil Service in Great Britain Being Part of the Messages and Documents Communicated to the Two Houses of Congress at the Beginning of the Second Session of the Forty-Sixth Congress. 46th Cong., 2d sess., 1879. H. Executive Doc. 1, pt. 7.

Report of the House Managers on the Impeachment of W. W. Belknap, Late Secretary of War. 44th Cong., 1st sess., 1876. H. Rept. 791.

Samoa: Message from the President of the United States, Transmitting Additional Information Relating to Affairs in Samoa. 50th Cong., 2d sess., 1889. H. Executive Doc. 119, serial 2651.

U.S. Congress. House. Committee on Expenditures in War Department. *The Management of the War Department.* 44th Cong., 1st sess., 1876. H. Rept. 779.

———. House. Committee on the Judiciary. *Impeachment of William W. Belknap.* 44th Cong., 1st sess., 1876. H. Rept. 345.

———. House. *Government Funds in National Banks.* 40th Cong., 2d sess., 1868. H. Executive Doc. 87, serial 1332.

———. House. *Report of the House Managers on the Impeachment of W. W. Belknap, Late Secretary of War.* 44th Cong., 1st sess., 1876. H. Rept. 791.

———. House. *Statement of the Public Debt of the United States.* 40th Cong., 2d sess., 1868. H. Misc. Doc. 87, serial 1350.

———. House. *Taxing National Currency, Etc.* 39th Cong., 1st sess., 1866. H. Misc. Doc. 87, serial 1271.

———. Joint Select Committee. *Civil Service of the United States.* 39th Cong., 2d sess., 1867. H. Rept. 8.

———. Senate. Committee on Civil Service and Retrenchment. *Report: To Accompany Bill S. 133.* 47th Cong., 1st sess., 1882. S. Rept. 576.

———. Senate. *Letter of the Secretary of the Treasury to the Chairman of the Committee on*

Finance, Transmitting a Statement Relative to the Apportionment of National Currency. 39th Cong., 1st sess., 1866. S. Misc. Doc. 100, serial 1239.

————. Senate. Select Committee to Examine the Several Branches of the Civil Service. *The Regulation and Improvement of the Civil Service.* 46th Cong., 3d sess., 1881. S. Rept. 872.

U.S. Department of State. Diplomatic Instructions of the Department of State, Germany. Vols. 17–18. National Archives, Washington, D.C.

The War of the Rebellion: A Compilation of the Official Records of the Union and Confederate Armies. 128 vols. Washington, D.C.: GPO, 1880–1901.

Newspapers

Boston Daily Courier, 1866–68.
Cincinnati Commercial, 1854–69, 1882.
Cincinnati Commercial Gazette, 1888–90.
Cincinnati Enquirer, 1847–89, 1923–24.
Cincinnati Gazette, 1864–69, 1882.
Cleveland Plain Dealer, 1864–69.
Columbus Evening Dispatch, 1884.
Covington Journal, 1869–76.
The Crisis, 1864–66, 1869.
Daily Commonwealth, 1879–81.
Dayton Empire, 1864.
Evening East Oregonian, 1935, 1937.
Harper's Weekly, 1864, 1868.
Mount Vernon Democratic Banner, 1863.
New York Evening Post, 1866–68.
New York Herald, 1866–68.
New York Leader, 1867–68.
New York Times, 1859–69, 1874–89.
New York Tribune, 1864, 1867.
New York World, 1866–68.
Newport Journal, 1877.
Newport Local, 1878.
Ohio Statesman, 1853–56, 1864.
Washington Evening Star, 1857–66, 1878–90.

Manuscripts

Allen, William. Papers. Manuscript Division, Library of Congress, Washington, D.C.
Armstrong, William W. Miscellaneous Manuscripts. Rutherford B. Hayes Presidential Library, Fremont, Ohio.
Barlow, Samuel L. M. Papers. Henry E. Huntington Library, San Marino, California.
Bayard, Thomas F. Papers. Manuscript Division, Library of Congress, Washington, D.C.

Boys, Alexander. Papers. Ohio Historical Society, Columbus.

Cadwallader, Sylvanus. Papers. Manuscript Division, Library of Congress, Washington, D.C.

Campbell, Lewis. Papers. Ohio Historical Society, Columbus.

Chase, Salmon P. Papers. Manuscript Division, Library of Congress, Washington, D.C.

Cleveland, Grover. Application and Recommendation Letters of Grover Cleveland Administration, 1885–1889. National Archives, Washington, D.C.

Cleveland, Grover. Papers. Manuscript Division, Library of Congress, Washington, D.C.

Cox, Jane Frances. Miscellaneous Personal Papers. San Jose, California.

Cox, Samuel S. Papers. Ohio Historical Society, Columbus.

DeBow, James D. B. Papers. William R. Perkins Library, Duke University, Durham, N.C.

Ewing, Thomas. Family Papers. Manuscript Division, Library of Congress, Washington, D.C.

Greeley, Horace. Papers. Manuscript Division, Library of Congress, Washington, D.C.

Gunther Collections. Chicago Historical Society, Chicago.

Harrison, Benjamin. Application and Recommendation Letters of Benjamin Harrison Administration, 1889–1893. National Archives, Washington, D.C.

Hassaurek, Frederick. Papers. Ohio Historical Society, Columbus.

Hayes, Rutherford B. Papers. Rutherford B. Hayes Presidential Library, Fremont, Ohio.

James Family. Papers. Ohio Historical Society, Columbus.

Johnson, Andrew. Papers. Manuscript Division, Library of Congress, Washington, D.C.

King, Rufus. Papers. Mss K54c. Cincinnati Historical Society, Cincinnati, Ohio.

Lamar, Lucius Quintus Cincinnatus, and Edward Mayes. Papers. Mississippi Department of Archives and History, Jackson.

Lane, Eben. Papers. Chicago Historical Society, Chicago.

Lincoln, Abraham. Papers. Manuscript Division, Library of Congress, Washington, D.C.

Long, Alexander. Papers. Mss fL848. Cincinnati Historical Society, Cincinnati.

Marble, Manton. Papers. Manuscript Division, Library of Congress, Washington, D.C.

McClellan, George B. Papers. Manuscript Division, Library of Congress, Washington, D.C.

Medary, Samuel. Papers. Ohio Historical Society, Columbus.

Merryweather Civil War Letters. Chicago Historical Society, Chicago.

Morton Family. Papers. Chicago Historical Society, Chicago.

National Civil Service Reform League. Papers. Department of Manuscripts and Archives, Cornell University Library, Ithaca, New York. Microfilm at Ohio Historical Society.

Pendleton, George H. Miscellaneous Manuscripts. Boston Public Library, Boston.

Pendleton, George H. Miscellaneous Manuscripts. Ohio Historical Society, Columbus.

Pendleton, George H. Miscellaneous Manuscripts. Rutherford B. Hayes Presidential Library, Fremont, Ohio.

Pendleton, George H. Miscellaneous Manuscripts. Western Kentucky University Library, Bowling Green.

Pendleton, George H. Miscellaneous Manuscripts. Western Reserve Historical Society, Cleveland, Ohio.

Pendleton, George H. Papers. Henry E. Huntington Library, San Marino, California.

Randall, Samuel J. Papers. The Historical Society of Pennsylvania, Philadelphia.

Rice, Charles E. Collection. Ohio Historical Society, Columbus.

Schurz, Carl. Papers. University of Georgia Libraries, Athens.

Shepard, Edward Morse. Papers. Rare Book and Manuscript Library, Columbia University, New York.

Sherman, John. Papers. Manuscript Division, Library of Congress, Washington, D.C.

Smith, William H. Papers. Ohio Historical Society, Columbus.

Thurman, Allen. Papers. Ohio Historical Society, Columbus.

Tilden, Samuel J. Papers. Manuscripts and Archives Division, New York Public Library, Astor, Lenox and Tilden Foundations, New York.

Trimble, John A. Papers. Ohio Historical Society, Columbus.

Contemporary Works and Published Diaries, Letters, and Memoirs

Adams, Henry Brooks. "The Legal Tender Act." *North American Review* 110 (Apr. 1870): 308–21.

American Annual Cyclopedia and Register of Important Events of the Year . . . 25 vols. New York: D. Appleton and Co., 1862–86. (As of 1875 known as *Appleton's Annual Cyclopedia and Register of Important Events of the Year . . .*)

Bellows, Henry W. "Civil Service Reform." *North American Review* 130 (1880): 247–60.

Blaine, James G. *Twenty Years of Congress: From Lincoln to Garfield, With a Review of the Events which Led to the Political Revolution of 1860.* Norwich, Conn.: Henry Bill, 1886.

Bloss, G. M. D. *Life and Speeches of George Hunt Pendleton.* Cincinnati, Ohio: Miami Printing and Publishing Co., 1868.

Brown, Harry James, and Frederick D. Williams, eds. *The Diary of James A. Garfield, 1875–77.* Vol. 3. Lansing: Michigan State Univ. Press, 1973.

Calhoun, John C. *"A Disquisition on Government" and Selections from the "Discourse."* The American Heritage Series, ed. C. Gordon Post, vol. 10. New York: Liberal Arts Press, 1953.

Carpenter, Frank G., ed. *Carp's Washington.* New York: McGraw-Hill, 1960.

Cincinnati Commercial: Speeches of the Campaign of 1866 in the States of Ohio, Indiana, and Kentucky. Cincinnati: n.p., 1866.

Cincinnati Convention, October 18, 1864, for the Organization of a Peace Party, upon States-Rights, Jeffersonian, Democratic Principles and for the Promotion of Peace and Independent Nominations for President and Vice-President of the United States. n.p., n.d.

Cincinnati Graphic 3 (Mar. 28, 1885): 198.

Cincinnati Graphic 3 (Apr. 25, 1885): 261–70.

Cincinnati Graphic 5 (May 29, 1886): 351.

"The Civil Service and Soldiers." *Nation* 40 (June 11, 1885): 476–77.

Cleave's Biographical Cyclopaedia of the State of Ohio: City of Cincinnati and Hamilton County. Philadelphia: J. B. Lippincott and Co., 1873.

Collins, Lewis. *Collins' Historical Sketches of Kentucky, History of Kentucky: By the Late Lewis Collins, Judge of the Mason County Court, Revised, Enlarged Four-fold, and Brought Down to the Year 1874 by His Son, Richard H. Collins, A.M., LL.B. . . .* 1874. Reprint, n.p., 1976.

The Congressional Record of George H. Pendleton: Candidate for Vice President. Philadelphia: Crissey and Markly, 1864.

The Copperhead Catechism. For the Instruction of Such Politicians as are of Tender Years. Carefully Compiled by Divers [sic] Learned and Designing Men. Authorized and with Admonitions by Fernando the Gothamite, High Priest of the Order of Copperheads. New York: Sinclair Tousey, 1864.

"Correspondence." *Nation* 5 (Oct. 24, 1867): 338–39.

Cox, Samuel S. *Three Decades of Federal Legislation. 1855 to 1885. Personal and Historical Memories of Events Preceding, During, and Since the American Civil War, Involving Slavery and Secession, Emancipation and Reconstruction, with Sketches of Prominent Actors during These Periods.* 1885. Reprint, New York: Books for Libraries Press, 1970.

DeBow, J. D. B. *Statistical View of the United States, 1850.* Washington, D.C.: n.p., 1854.

Diary and Correspondence of Salmon P. Chase. 1903. Reprint, New York: Da Capo Press, 1971.

"The Diplomatic Service." *Nation* 40 (June 11, 1885): 476.

Eaton, Dorman B. *The Cincinnati Convention.* New York: n.p., 1876.

———. *Civil Service in Great Britain: A History of Abuses and Reforms and Their Bearing upon American Politics.* New York: Harper and Brothers, 1880.

———. "A New Phase of the Reform Movement." *North American Review* 132 (1881): 546–58.

———. "Patronage Monopoly and the Pendleton Bill." *Princeton Review* 9 (Mar. 1882): 185–207.

———, and Everett P. Wheeler. *The Pendleton Bill and the Dawes Bill: Compared by the Committee on Legislation of the Civil-Service Reform Association.* New York: G. P. Putnam's Sons, 1882.

"Emigration from Germany." *Nation* 43 (Mar. 24, 1887): 245.

Ewing, Thomas. *Letter from Hon. Thomas Ewing.* n.p., n.d.

———. *Letter of Hon. Thomas Ewing, of Ohio to the Finance Committee of the Senate, on the Public Debt and Currency.* Washington, D.C.: Judd and Detweiler, 1869.

Ford, Henry A., and Kate B. Ford. *History of Cincinnati, Ohio, With Illustrations and Biographical Sketches.* Cleveland, Ohio: L. A. Williams and Co., 1881.

Foulke, William Dudley. *Fighting the Spoilsmen: Reminiscences of the Civil Service Reform Movement.* New York: G. P. Putnam's Sons, 1919.

"A French View of Bismarck's Speech." *Nation* 46 (Mar. 1, 1888): 172.

George H. Pendleton and the Volunteers: Behold the Record! n.p., n.d.

Groesbeck, William S. *Speech Delivered by W. S. Groesbeck, at College Hall, Cincinnati, August 2, 1883.* Cincinnati, Ohio: Robert Clarke and Co., 1883.

"Hays [sic] and Pendleton." *Fremont Weekly Journal* 17 (Oct. 1, 1869): 1.

Hazewell, C. C. "The Twentieth Presidential Election." *Atlantic Monthly: A Magazine of Literature, Art and Politics* 14 (Nov. 1864): 633–41.

Helper, Hinton R. *Compendium of the Impending Crisis of the South.* 1860. Reprint, Miami, Fla.: Mnemosyne, 1969.

How the Copperheads Would Preserve the Union: Record of George H. Pendleton, in the Congress of the United States during the Rebellion. Union Campaign Documents, No. 2. n.p.: Weed, Parsons and Co., n.d.

Interview between the United States Senate Committee on Finance and the Hon. John Sher-

man, Sec. of the Treasury, on Refunding, Resumption, Legal-Tenders for Customs Dues, Sinking Fund, and Kindred Subjects. n.p., 1880.

Issues of the Campaign: Shall the North Vote for a Disunion Peace? Chicago Tribune Campaign Document, No. 2. n.p., n.d.

Jenckes, Thomas A. *Speech of Hon. Thomas A. Jenckes, of Rhode Island, on the Bill to Regulate the Efficiency Thereof; Delivered in the House of Representatives, May 14, 1868.* Washington, D.C.: F. and J. Rives and Geo. A. Bailey, 1868.

Jordan, Isaac M. *George Hunt Pendleton.* Cincinnati: n.p., 1890.

Lincoln, Abraham. *Speeches and Presidential Addresses: 1859–1865. Together with Conversations and Anecdotes, Related by F. B. Carpenter in "Six Months at the White House."* New York: Current Literature, 1907.

Mahony, D. A. *The Prisoner of State.* New York: Carleton, 1863.

Malone, Dumas, ed. *Directory of American Biography.* New York: Charles Scribner's Sons, 1934.

Mansfield, Edward Derring. *Personal Memories, Social, Political, and Literary, 1803–1843.* 1879. Reprint, New York: Arno and New York Times, 1970.

McClellan, George B. *McClellan's Own Story: The War for the Union, the Soldiers Who Fought It, the Civilians Who Directed It, and His Relations to It and to Them.* New York: Charles L. Webster and Co., 1887.

McPherson, Edward. *A Handbook of Politics for 1868.* 1868. Reprint, New York: Negro Univ. Press, 1969.

———. *Handbook of Politics, III, 1884–1888, Being a Record of Important Political Action, National and State, July 31, 1884–August 31, 1888.* 1884–88. Reprint, New York: Da Capo Press, 1972.

———. *The Political History of the United States during the Great Rebellion . . .* Washington, D.C.: Philip and Solomons, 1865.

———. *The Political History of the United States of America during the Period of Reconstruction, from April 15, 1865, to July 15, 1870.* Washington, D.C.: Philip and Solomons, 1871.

Miller, Marion Mills, ed. *Great Debates in American History: From the Debates in the British Parliament on the Colonial Stamp Act (1764–1765) to the Debates in Congress at the Close of the Taft Administration (1912–1913).* Vol. 9. New York: Current Literature, 1913.

"More about Bonds, Greenbacks, and Gold." *Nation* 7 (Sept. 10, 1868): 209.

Official Proceedings of the Democratic National Convention, Held in 1860, at Charleston and Baltimore. Cleveland, Ohio: Nevins Print, Plain Dealer Job Office, 1860.

Official Proceedings of the Democratic National Convention, Held in 1864 at Chicago. Chicago: Times Steam Book and Job Printing House, 1864.

Official Proceedings of the National Democratic Convention, Held at New York, July 4–9, 1868. Boston: Rockwell and Rollins, 1868.

Official Proceedings of the National Democratic Convention, Held at Baltimore, July 9, 1872. Boston: Rockwell and Churchill, 1872.

Official Proceedings of the National Democratic Convention, Held in St. Louis, Mo., June 27th, 28th and 29th, 1876, with an Appendix Containing the Letters of Acceptance of Gov. Tilden and Gov. Hendricks. St. Louis, Mo.: Woodward, Tiernan and Hale, 1876.

Official Proceedings of the National Democratic Convention, Held in Cincinnati, O., June 22d, 23d, and 24th, 1880. Dayton, Ohio: Daily Journal Book and Job Rooms, 1882.

Official Proceedings of the National Democratic Convention, Held in Chicago, Ill., July 8th, 9th, 10th, and 11th, 1884, Containing also the Preliminary Proceedings of the National Democratic Committee and the Committee of Arrangements . . . New York: Douglas Taylor's Democratic Printing House, 1884.

"Old Roads and New Roads." *Railroad Gazette* 5 (May 3, 1873): 183.

"Old Roads and New Roads." *Railroad Gazette* 7 (Feb. 27, 1875): 90.

"Old Roads and New Roads." *Railroad Gazette* 7 (May 29, 1875): 224–25.

"One View of Civil-Service Reform." *Nation* 41 (July 9, 1885): 31.

Papers from the Society for the Diffusion of Political Knowledge: Speech of Mr. Pugh to 50,000 Voters, Who Nominated Vallandigham and Resolved to Elect Him Governor of Ohio. New York: n.p., n.d.

Pendleton, George Hunt. *Address Delivered in Rosse Chapel, before the Nu Pi Kappa Society of Kenyon College.* Cincinnati, Ohio: Moore, Wilstach, and Baldwin, 1866.

———. "Address at Ovation at the Academy of Music." In *Handbook of the Democracy, 1863–1864.* New York: n.p., 1864.

———. *Chinese Immigration: Speech of Hon. George H. Pendleton, of Ohio, Delivered in the Senate of the United States, April 28, 1882.* Washington, D.C.: n.p., 1882.

———. *Civil Service Reform: Speech of Hon. George H. Pendleton, of Ohio, Delivered in the Senate of the United States, December 13, 1881.* n.p., n.d.

———. *Common Sense for the People: Our Country and Its Condition, Speech of Hon. George H. Pendleton at Bangor, Thursday, August 20th, 1868.* n.p., n.d.

———. *The Deadlock in the Senate: Speech of Hon. George H. Pendleton, of Ohio, in the United States Senate, April 13, 1881.* Washington, D.C.: n.p., 1881.

———. *Extracts from Hon. George H. Pendleton's Speeches at Lima and Cleveland.* n.p., n.d.

———. *The Funding Bill-Three Per Cent. Bonds: Speech of Hon. George H. Pendleton, of Ohio, Delivered in the Senate of the United States, January 17, 1882.* n.p., n.d.

———. *The Heads of Departments on the Floors of Congress: Speech of Hon. George H. Pendleton, of Ohio, in the Senate of the United States, April 28, 1879.* Washington, D.C.: n.p., 1879.

———. *Hear Hon. George H. Pendleton.* n.p., n.d.

———. *Improvement of the Subordinate Civil Service: Speech of Hon. George H. Pendleton, of Ohio, in the Senate of the United States, Tuesday, December 12, 1882.* n.p., n.d.

———. *Letter of George H. Pendleton, of Ohio, to His Constituents.* Washington, D.C.: n.p., 1858.

———. *Payment of the Public Debt in Legal Tender Notes!! Speech of Hon. George H. Pendleton, Milwaukee, November 2, 1867.* n.p., n.d.

———. *Political Assessments by the Republican Party: Speech of Hon. George H. Pendleton, of Ohio, in the Senate of the United States, June 26, 1882.* Washington, D.C.: n.p., 1882.

———. *Power of the President to Suspend the Privilege of Habeas Corpus, Speech of Hon. George H. Pendleton, of Ohio, in the House of Representatives, December 10, 1861.* n.p., n.d.

———. *The Power to Make Treasury Notes a Legal Tender? Speech of Hon. George H. Pendleton, of Ohio, in the House of Representatives, January 29, 1862.* n.p., n.d.

———. *The Reform of the Tariff: Speech of Hon. George H. Pendleton, of Ohio, in the Senate of the United States, Friday, March 17, 1882.* Washington, D.C.: R. O. Polkinhorn, 1882.

————. *The Resolution to Expel Mr. Long, of Ohio. Speech of Hon. George H. Pendleton, of Ohio, Delivered in the House of Representatives, April 11, 1864.* n.p., n.d.

————. *Speech of Hon. George H. Pendleton, at Clifton, Friday, September 10, 1869.* n.p., n.d.

————. *Speech of Hon. George H. Pendleton, at Loveland, O., August 22, 1871.* n.p., n.d.

————. *Speech of Hon. George H. Pendleton, at the Opening of the Democratic Campaign, at Columbus, Ohio, Thursday Evening, August 23, 1877.* n.p., n.d.

————. *Speech of Hon. George H. Pendleton, Delivered at Gallipolis, Ohio, July 21, 1875.* n.p., n.d.

————. *Speech of Hon. George H. Pendleton, Delivered at Lima, Allen County, Ohio, Thursday, August 15, 1867.* Columbus, Ohio: Crisis Office, 1867.

————. "Speech of Hon. George H. Pendleton, of Ohio at Grafton, West Virginia, July 16, 1868." In *Democratic Speaker's Handbook.* Cincinnati, Ohio: Miami Print and Publishing Co., 1868.

————. *Speech of Hon. George H. Pendleton, of Ohio, in the House of Representatives, June 15, 1864.* n.p., n.d.

————. *Speech of Hon. George H. Pendleton, of Ohio, on The Admission of Kansas; Delivered in the House of Representatives, June 9, 1858.* Washington, D.C.: Congressional Globe Office, 1858.

————. *Speech of Hon. George H. Pendleton, of Ohio, on the Bill to Increase the Army; Delivered in the House of Representatives, March 17, 1858.* Washington, D.C.: Congressional Globe Office, 1858.

————. *Speech of Hon. George H. Pendleton, of Ohio, on the Enlistment of Negro Soldiers; Delivered during the Debate in the House of Representatives, January 31, 1863.* Washington: n.p., 1863.

————. *Speech of Hon. George H. Pendleton, of Ohio, on the State of the Union; Delivered in the House of Representatives, January 18, 1861.* n.p.: Lemuel Towers, 1861.

————. *To Gain Political Power under the Guise of a Bill for the Punishment of Polygamy: Remarks of Hon. George H. Pendleton, of Ohio, in the Senate of the United States, Thursday, February 16, 1882.* n.p., n.d.

Pendleton, Nathaniel Greene. *Letter on Our Political Troubles.* Washington, D.C.: H. Polkinhorn, 1861.

Poor, Henry V. *Manual of the Railroads of the United States, for 1868–86, Showing Their Mileage, Stocks, Bonds, Cost, Earnings, Expenses, and Organizations; with a Sketch of Their Rise, Progress, Influence, etc. Together with an Appendix, Containing a Full Analysis of the Debts of the United States, and of the Several States.* 19 vols. New York: H. V. and H. W. Poor, 1868–86.

Powderly, T. V. *Thirty Years of Labor, 1859–1889, in which the History of the Attempts to Form Organizations of Workingmen for the Discussion of Political, Social, and Economic Questions Is Traced, the National Labor Union of 1866, the Industrial Brotherhood of 1874, and the Order of the Knights of Labor of America and the World, the Chief and Most Important Principles in the Preamble of the Knights of Labor Discussed and Explained with Views of the Author on Land, Labor and Transportation.* Columbus, Ohio: n.p., 1889.

Proceedings of the Democratic Convention, held at Columbus, Ohio, Friday, July 4, 1862. Containing the Speeches of Hon. Samuel Medary, Hon. C. L. Vallandigham, Hon. Rufus

P. Ranney, and Hon. Allen G. Thurman. *The Address and Platform, Ballotings for Candidates, and Names of Delegates in Attendance.* Dayton, Ohio: Press of the Dayton Empire, 1862.

Proceedings of the Republican National Convention Held at Chicago, Illinois, Wednesday, Thursday, Friday, Saturday, Monday, and Tuesday, June 2d, 3d, 4th, 5th, 7th, and 8th, 1880. Chicago: Jno. B. Jeffrey, 1881.

Pugh, George E. *Speech of George E. Pugh, of Ohio, in the Democratic National Convention at Charleston, Friday, April 27, 1860.* n.p.: Lemuel Towers, 1860.

Raymond, Henry W., ed. "Extracts from the Journal of Henry J. Raymond, Fourth Paper: The Philadelphia Convention of 1866." *Scribner's Monthly* 20 (June 1880): 275–77.

The Record of George H. Pendleton: Why He Is Unfit for Any Government Position. n.p., 1885.

The Record of Hon. Clement L. Vallandigham on Abolition, the Union, and the Civil War. Columbus, Ohio: J. Walter and Co., 1863.

Reid, Whitelaw. *Ohio in the War: Her Statesmen, Her Generals, and Soldiers.* 2 vols. New York: Morre, Wilstach, and Baldwin, 1868.

"Repudiation Again." *Nation* 5 (Oct. 10, 1867): 294–96.

Richardson, James D., ed. *A Compilation of the Messages and Papers of the Presidents, 1789–1907.* Washington, D.C.: Bureau of National Literature and Art, 1908.

"The Samoan Affair." *Nation* 48 (Jan. 31, 1889): 84–85.

Schuckers, J. W. *The Life and Public Services of Salmon Portland Chase, United States Senator and Governor of Ohio; Secretary of the Treasury, and Chief-Justice of the United States.* New York: D. Appleton and Co., 1874.

Sears, Stephen W., ed. *The Civil War Papers of George B. McClellan: Selected Correspondence, 1860–1865.* New York: Ticknor and Fields, 1989.

Seymour, Horatio. "Speech of Governor Seymour at Philadelphia." Campaign Document, No. 21. In *Handbook of the Democracy.* New York: n.p., 1864.

Sherman, John. *The Funding Bill, Speech of Hon. John Sherman, of Ohio, Delivered in the Senate of the United States, February 27, 1868.* Washington, D.C.: F. and J. Rives and George A. Bailey, 1868.

———. *John Sherman's Recollections of Forty Years in the House, Senate and Cabinet. An Autobiography.* 2 vols. Chicago: Werner Co., 1895.

Smith, Theodore Clarke, ed. *The Life and Letters of James Abram Garfield.* Vol. 2. New Haven, Conn.: Yale Univ. Press, 1925.

Spaulding, E. G. *History of the Legal Tender Paper Money Issued during the Great Rebellion Being a Loan without Interest and a National Currency.* Buffalo, N.Y.: Express, 1869.

Speeches of the Campaign of 1866, in the States of Ohio, Indiana and Kentucky: The Most Remarkable Speeches on Both Sides. Cincinnati, Ohio: Cincinnati Commercial, n.d.

Spirit of the Chicago Convention: Extracts from All the Notable Speeches Delivered In and Out of the National "Democratic" Convention, Union Campaign Documents, No. 6. n.p.: Weed, Parsons and Co., n.d.

State Convention of War Democrats: Address to the Democrats of Ohio. n.p., n.d.

Taussig, F. W. *The History of the Present Tariff, 1860–1883.* Questions of the Day. New York: G. P. Putnam's Sons, 1885.

Union Congressional Committee. *Copperhead Conspiracy in the North-West: An Expose of the Treasonable Order of the "Sons of Liberty."* New York: John A. Gray and Green, ca. 1864.

Vallandigham, James L. *A Life of Clement L. Vallandigham.* Baltimore, Md.: Turnbull Brothers, 1872.

"'Voluntary Contributions' and the Republican Party." *Nation* 35 (Aug. 31, 1882): 170.

The Votes of the Copperheads in the Congress of the United States. n.p.: L. Towers, n.d.

The Week: Illustrated 1 (Jan. 1884): 321–26.

Welles, Gideon. *Diary of Gideon Welles: Secretary of the Navy under Lincoln and Johnson.* 3 vols. Boston: Houghton Mifflin, 1911.

"What Inflation Means." *Nation* 5 (Dec. 12, 1867): 480–81.

Williams, Charles R., ed. *Diary and Letters of Rutherford B. Hayes: Nineteenth President of the United States.* 5 vols. Columbus: Ohio State Archaeological and Historical Society, 1926.

Williams Cincinnati Directory and Business Advertiser. 37 vols. Cincinnati, Ohio: C. S. Williams, 1849–87.

Zinn, Peter. *Leading and Select Cases on Trusts: With Extended Abstracts of Important Cases; Explanatory and Critical Notes; and Numerous Citations of Authorities Bearing on Every Branch of the Law of Trusts. Also, a Full Report of the Great Case of the Covington and Lexington Railroad Company, against the Robert B. Bowler's Heirs and Others, Just Decided at the Winter Term, 1873, of the Court of Appeals of the State of Kentucky.* Cincinnati, Ohio: Robert Clarke and Co., 1873.

Secondary Sources

Aldrich, John H. *Why Parties: The Origin and Transformation of Political Parties in America.* American Politics and Political Economy Series, ed. Benjamin I. Page. Chicago: Univ. of Chicago Press, 1995.

Alexander, DeAlva S. *A Political History of the State of New York.* 3 vols. 1909. Reprint, Port Washington, N.Y.: Ira J. Friedman, 1969.

Anbinder, Tyler. *Nativism and Slavery: The Northern Know Nothings and the Politics of the 1850s.* New York: Oxford Univ. Press, 1992.

Ashworth, John. *"Agrarians" and "Aristocrats": Party Political Ideology in the United States, 1837–1846.* Cambridge: Cambridge Univ. Press, 1983.

Barney, William L., ed. *A Companion to Nineteenth-Century America.* Malden, Mass.: Blackwell, 2001.

Barrett, Don. C. *The Greenbacks and Resumption of Specie Payments, 1862–1879.* Cambridge, Mass.: Harvard Univ. Press, 1931.

Beale, Howard K. *The Critical Year: A Study of Andrew Johnson and Reconstruction.* New York: Harcourt Brace, 1930. Reprint, New York: Frederick Ungar, 1958.

Belz, Herman. *Abraham Lincoln, Constitutionalism, and Equal Rights in the Civil War Era.* New York: Fordham Univ. Press, 1998.

———. *A New Birth of Freedom: The Republican Party and Freedmen's Rights, 1861–1866.* Westport, Conn.: Greenwood Press, 1976.

Benedict, Michael Les. *A Compromise of Principle: Congressional Republicans and Reconstruction, 1863–1869.* New York: W. W. Norton and Co., 1974.

Bensel, Richard Franklin. *Yankee Leviathan: The Origins of Central State Authority in America, 1859–1877.* Cambridge: Cambridge Univ. Press, 1990.

Benson, Lee. *Concept of Jacksonian Democracy: New York as a Test Case.* Princeton, N.J.: Princeton Univ. Press, 1961.

Benton, Elbert J. *The Movement for Peace without Victory during the Civil War.* Cleveland, Ohio: Western Reserve Historical Society, 1918.

Bernstein, Iver. *The New York City Draft Riots: Their Significance for American Society and Politics in the Age of the Civil War.* New York: Oxford Univ. Press, 1990.

Black, David. *King of Fifth Avenue: The Fortunes of August Belmont.* New York: Dial Press, 1981.

Blue, Frederick J. *Salmon P. Chase: A Life of Politics.* Kent, Ohio: Kent State Univ. Press, 1987.

Bonadio, Felice A. *North of Reconstruction: Ohio Politics, 1865–1870.* New York: New York Univ. Press, 1970.

Brock, W. R. *An American Crisis: Congress and Reconstruction, 1865–1867.* London: MacMillan and Co., 1963.

Brown, Jeffrey P., and Andrew R. L. Cayton, eds. *The Pursuit of Public Power: Political Culture in Ohio, 1787–1861.* Kent, Ohio: Kent State Univ. Press, 1994.

Catton, William, and Bruce Catton. *Two Roads to Sumter.* New York: McGraw-Hill, 1963.

Cimbala, Paul A., and Randall M. Miller, eds. *The Freedmen's Bureau and Reconstruction: Reconsiderations.* New York: Fordham Univ. Press, 1999.

Clancy, Herbert J. *The Presidential Election of 1880.* Jesuit Studies. Chicago: Loyola Univ. Press, 1959.

Coit, Margaret L. *John C. Calhoun: American Portrait.* Boston: Houghton Mifflin, 1950.

Cole, Arthur C. *The Whig Party in the South.* Washington, D.C.: American Historical Association, 1913.

Coleman, Charles H. *The Election of 1868: The Democratic Effort to Regain Control.* 1933. Reprint, New York: Octagon Books, 1971.

Collins, Bruce. *The Origins of America's Civil War.* New York: Holmes and Meier, 1981.

Cowden, Joanna D. *"Heaven Will Frown on Such a Cause as This": Six Democrats Who Opposed Lincoln's War.* Lanham, Md.: Univ. Press of America, 2001.

Cox, LaWanda, and John H. Cox. *Politics, Principle, and Prejudice, 1865–1866.* London: Free Press of Glencoe, 1963.

Craven, Avery. *The Coming of the Civil War.* 2d ed. Chicago: Univ. of Chicago Press, 1957.

Current, Richard N. *Daniel Webster and the Rise of National Conservatism.* Boston: Little, Brown and Co., 1955.

Curry, Leonard P. *Blueprint for Modern America: Nonmilitary Legislation of the First Civil War Congress.* Nashville, Tenn.: Vanderbilt Univ. Press, 1968.

DeChambrun, Clara Longworth. *Cincinnati: Story of the Queen City.* New York: Charles Scribner's Sons, 1939.

Dell, Christopher. *Lincoln and the War Democrats: The Grand Erosion of Conservative Tradition.* London: Associated Univ. Press, 1975.

Destler, Chester M. *American Radicalism, 1865–1901: Essays and Documents.* New York: Octagon Books, 1963.

Dobson, John M. *Politics in the Gilded Age: A New Perspective on Reform.* New York: Praeger, 1972.

Doenecke, Justus D. *The Presidencies of James A. Garfield and Chester A. Arthur.* Lawrence: Regents Press of Kansas, 1981.

Dulles, Foster Rhea. *Labor in America: A History.* 3d ed. New York: Crowell, 1966.

Eaton, Clement. *Henry Clay and the Art of American Politics.* Boston: Little, Brown and Co, 1957.

Etcheson, Nicole. *Bleeding Kansas: Contested Liberty in the Civil War Era.* Lawrence: Univ. Press of Kansas, 2004.

————. *The Emerging Midwest: Upland Southerners and the Political Culture of the Old Northwest, 1787–1861.* Bloomington: Indiana Univ. Press, 1996.

Fiorina, Morris P. "The Decline of Collective Responsibility in American Politics." Working Paper Number 50. St. Louis, Mo.: Center for the Study of American Business, 1980.

Fish, Carl Russell. *The Civil Service and the Patronage.* New York: Longmans, Green and Co., 1905.

Fletcher, C. Brunsdon. *Stevenson's Germany: The Case against Germany in the Pacific.* New York: Charles Scribner's Sons, 1920.

Formisano, Ronald P. *The Birth of Mass Political Parties: Michigan, 1827–1861.* Princeton, N.J.: Princeton Univ. Press, 1972.

Fox, Dixon Ryan. *The Decline of Aristocracy in the Politics of New York, 1801–1840.* New York: Columbia Univ. Press, 1919.

Fox, Stephen C. *The Group Bases of Ohio Political Behavior, 1803–1848.* New York: Garland, 1989.

Fuess, Claude Moore. *Carl Schurz: Reformer, 1829–1906.* New York: Dodd, Mead and Co., 1932.

Gambill, Edward L. *Conservative Ordeal: Northern Democrats and Reconstruction, 1865–1868.* Ames: Iowa State Univ. Press, 1981.

Gates, E. Nathaniel, ed. *Racial Classification and History.* New York: Garland, 1997.

Geary, James W. *We Need Men: The Union Draft in the Civil War.* DeKalb: Northern Illinois Univ. Press, 1991.

Gienapp, William E. *The Origins of the Republican Party, 1852–1856.* New York: Oxford Univ. Press, 1987.

Gilson, R. P. *Samoa, 1830 to 1900: The Politics of a Multi-Cultural Community.* With an introduction and conclusion by J. W. Davidson. Melbourne: Oxford Univ. Press, 1970.

Glatthaar, Joseph T. *Forged in Battle: The Civil War Alliance of Black Soldiers and White Officers.* New York: Free Press, 1990.

Gray, Wood. *The Hidden Civil War: The Story of the Copperheads.* New York: Viking Press, 1942.

Grossman, Lawrence. *The Democratic Party and the Negro: Northern and National Politics, 1868–1892.* Urbana: Univ. of Illinois Press, 1976.

Groth, Alexander J. *Lincoln: Authoritarian Savior.* Lanham, Md.: Univ. Press of America, 1996.

Gunderson, Robert Gray. *Old Gentlemen's Convention: The Washington Peace Conference of 1861.* Madison: Univ. of Wisconsin Press, 1961.

Haas, Garland A. *The Politics of Disintegration: Political Party Decay in the United States, 1840–1900.* Jefferson, N.C.: McFarland and Co., 1994.

Harlow, Alvin F. *The Serene Cincinnatians.* n.p., 1950.

Hess, Earl J. *Liberty, Virtue, and Progress: Northerners and Their War for the Union.* 2d ed. New York: Fordham Univ. Press, 1997.

Hesseltine, William B., ed. *Three Against Lincoln: Murat Halstead Reports the Caucuses of 1860*. Baton Rouge: Louisiana State Univ. Press, 1960.

————, *Ulysses S. Grant: Politician*. American Classics. 1935. Reprint, New York: Frederick Unger, 1957.

Hines, Edward W. *Corporate History of the Louisville and Nashville Railroad Company and Roads in Its System*. Louisville, Ky.: John P. Morton and Co., 1905.

Hofstadter, Richard. *The Age of Reform: From Bryan to F.D.R.* New York: Alfred A. Knopf, 1955.

Holt, Michael F. *The Political Crisis of the 1850s*. Critical Episodes in American Politics Series, ed. Robert A. Divine. New York: John Wiley and Sons, 1978.

————. *Political Parties and American Political Development from the Age of Jackson to the Age of Lincoln*. Baton Rouge: Louisiana State Univ. Press, 1992.

————. *The Rise and Fall of the American Whig Party*. New York: Oxford Univ. Press, 1999.

Hoogenboom, Ari. *Outlawing the Spoils: A History of the Civil Service Reform Movement, 1865–1883*. Urbana: Univ. of Illinois Press, 1961.

————. *The Presidency of Rutherford B. Hayes*. Lawrence: Univ. Press of Kansas, 1988.

————, ed. *Spoilsmen and Reformers*. New York: Rand McNally and Co., 1964.

Howe, Daniel Walker. *The Political Culture of the American Whigs*. Chicago: Univ. of Chicago Press, 1979.

Hubbart, Henry Clyde. *The Older Middle West, 1840–1880: Its Social, Economic, and Political Life and Sectional Tendencies Before, During, and After the Civil War*. New York: D. Appleton-Century, 1936.

Huggins, Walter. *Jacksonian Democracy in the Working Class: A Study of the Workingmen's Movement, 1829–1837*. Stanford, Calif.: Stanford Univ. Press, 1960.

Hyman, Harold M. "Election of 1864." In *The Coming to Power: Critical Presidential Elections in American History*, ed. by Arthur M. Schlesinger Jr. New York: McGraw-Hill, 1971.

Johannsen, Robert W. *The Frontier, The Union, and Stephen A. Douglas*. Urbana: Univ. of Illinois Press, 1989.

————. *Stephen A. Douglas*. New York: Oxford Univ. Press, 1973.

Jordan, Philip D. *Ohio Comes of Age, 1873–1900*. Vol. 5 of *The History of the State of Ohio*, ed. Carl Wittke. Columbus: Ohio State Archaeological and Historical Society, 1943.

Josephson, Matthew. *The Politicos, 1865–1896*. New York: Harcourt, Brace and World, 1938.

Katz, Irving. *August Belmont: A Political Biography*. New York: Columbia Univ. Press, 1968.

Keller, Morton. *Affairs of State: Public Life in Late Nineteenth Century America*. Cambridge, Mass.: Belknap Press of Harvard Univ. Press, 1977.

Klein, Maury. *History of the Louisville and Nashville Railroad*. Railroads of America, ed. Thomas B. Brewer. New York: MacMillan, 1972.

Klein, Philip S. *President James Buchanan: A Biography*. University Park: Pennsylvania State Univ. Press, 1962.

Klement, Frank L. "Clement L. Vallandigham." In *For the Union: Ohio Leaders in the Civil War*, ed. by Kenneth W. Wheeler. Columbus: Ohio State Univ. Press, 1968.

————. *The Copperheads in the Middle West*. Chicago: Univ. of Chicago Press, 1960.

————. "The Democrats as Sectionalists." In *Lincoln and Civil War Politics*, ed. James A. Rawley. Huntington, N.Y.: Robert E. Krieger, 1977.

————. *The Limits of Dissent.* Lexington: Univ. Press of Kentucky, 1970.

————. *Lincoln's Critics: The Copperheads of the North.* Edited with an introduction by Steven K. Rogstad. Shippensburg, Pa.: White Maine Books, 1999.

Kleppner, Paul. *Who Voted? The Dynamics of Electoral Turnout, 1870–1980.* New York: Praeger, 1982.

Knox, John Jay. *A History of Banking in the United States.* 1903. Reprint, New York: Augustus M. Kelley, 1969.

Kohl, Lawrence F. *The Politics of Individualism: Parties and the American Character in the Jacksonian Era.* New York: Oxford Univ. Press, 1989.

Kyvig, David E. *Explicit and Authentic Acts: Amending the U.S. Constitution, 1776–1995.* Lawrence: Univ. Press of Kansas, 1996.

Lause, Mark A. *The Civil War's Last Campaign: James B. Weaver, the Greenback-Labor Party and the Politics of Race and Section.* Lanham, Md.: Univ. Press of America, 2001.

Lindsey, David. *"Sunset" Cox: Irrepressible Democrat.* Detroit: Wayne State Univ. Press, 1959.

Long, David E. *The Jewel of Liberty: Abraham Lincoln's Reelection and the End of Slavery.* Mechanicsburg, Pa.: Stackpole Books, 1994.

Lowe, Jennifer M. *The Supreme Court and the Civil War.* Washington, D.C.: Supreme Court Historical Society, 1996.

Mahin, Dean B. *One War at a Time: The International Dimensions of the American Civil War.* Washington, D.C.: Brassey's, 1999.

Maizlish, Stephen E. *The Triumph of Sectionalism: The Transformation of Ohio Politics, 1844–1856.* Kent, Ohio: Kent State Univ. Press, 1983.

Mantell, Martin F. *Johnson, Grant, and the Politics of Reconstruction.* New York: Columbia Univ. Press, 1973.

Maranto, Robert, and David Schultz. *A Short History of the United States Civil Service.* Lanham, Md.: Univ. Press of America, 1991.

Marshall, Carrington T. *A History of the Courts and Lawyers of Ohio.* Vol. 4. New York: American Historical Society, 1934.

Masterman, Sylvia. *The Origins of the International Rivalry in Samoa, 1845–1884.* Stanford, Calif.: Stanford Univ. Press, 1934.

McArthur, Lewis A. *Oregon Geographic Names.* 5th ed. n.p.: Western Imprints, 1982.

McFeeley, William S. *Grant: A Biography.* New York: W. W. Norton, 1981.

McGrane, Reginald C. *The Panic of 1837: Some Financial Problems of the Jacksonian Era.* 1924. Reprint, Chicago: Univ. of Chicago Press, 1965.

————. *William Allen: A Study in Western Democracy.* Columbus: Ohio State Archaeological and Historical Society, 1925.

McKitrick, Eric L. *Andrew Johnson and Reconstruction.* Chicago: Univ. of Chicago Press, 1960.

McPherson, James M. *Ordeal by Fire: The Civil War and Reconstruction.* New York: Alfred A. Knopf, 1982.

Merrill, Horace Samuel. *Bourbon Democracy of the Middle West, 1865–1896.* Baton Rouge: Louisiana State Univ. Press, 1953.

————. *Bourbon Leader: Grover Cleveland and the Democratic Party.* Boston: Little, Brown and Co., 1957.

Meyers, Marvin. *The Jacksonian Persuasion: Politics and Belief.* Stanford, Calif.: Stanford Univ. Press, 1957.

Milton, George Fort. *Abraham Lincoln and the Fifth Column.* New York: Vanguard Press, 1942.

Mitchell, Stewart. *Horatio Seymour of New York.* 1938. Reprint, New York: Da Capo Press, 1970.

Mitchell, Wesley Clair. *A History of the Greenbacks: With Special Reference to the Economic Consequences of Their Issue: 1862–1865.* Chicago: Univ. of Chicago Press, 1903. Reprint, Chicago: Univ. of Chicago Press, 1960.

Montgomery, David. *Beyond Equality: Labor and the Radical Republicans, 1862–1872.* New York: Knopf, 1967. Reprint, Urbana: Univ. of Illinois Press, 1981.

Moorman, Donald R., and Gene A. Sessions. *Camp Floyd and the Mormons: The Utah War.* Salt Lake City: Univ. of Utah Press, 1992.

Morgan, H. Wayne. *From Hayes to McKinley: National Party Politics, 1877–1896.* Syracuse, N.Y.: Syracuse Univ. Press, 1969.

Mott, Frank L. *American Journalism, A History: 1690–1960.* 3d ed. New York: MacMillan, 1962.

Mueller, Henry R. *The Whig Party in Pennsylvania.* New York: Columbia Univ. Press, 1922.

Mushkat, Jerome. *Fernando Wood: A Political Biography.* Kent, Ohio: Kent State Univ. Press, 1990.

————. *The Reconstruction of the New York Democracy, 1861–1874.* Rutherford, N.J.: Fairleigh Dickinson Univ. Press, 1981.

Myers, William Starr. *General George B. McClellan: A Study in Personality.* New York: D. Appleton-Century, 1934.

National Cyclopaedia of American Biography. New York: James T. White and Co., 1931.

Neely, Jr., Mark E. *The Fate of Liberty: Abraham Lincoln and Civil Liberties.* New York: Oxford Univ. Press, 1991.

Nevins, Allan. *Hamilton Fish: The Inner History of the Grant Administration.* 2 vols. Rev. ed. New York: Frederick Unger, 1957.

Nichols, Alice. *Bleeding Kansas.* New York: Oxford Univ. Press, 1954.

Nichols, Roy F. *The Disruption of American Democracy.* New York: MacMillan, 1948.

Niven, John. *John C. Calhoun and the Price of Union: A Biography.* Baton Rouge: Louisiana State Univ. Press, 1988.

Noyes, Alexander D. *Forty Years of American Finance: A Short History of the Government and People of the United States since the Civil War, 1865–1907.* New York: G. P. Putnam's Sons, 1909.

Nugent, Walter T. K. *Money and American Society, 1865–1880.* New York: Free Press, 1968.

Oates, Stephen B. *To Purge This Land with Blood: A Biography of John Brown.* New York: Harper and Row, 1970.

Perret, Geoffrey. *Ulysses S. Grant: Soldier and President.* New York: Modern Library, 1999.

Peskin, Allan. *Garfield.* Kent, Ohio: Kent State Univ. Press, 1978.

Petersen, Karen Daniels. *Plains Indian Art from Fort Marion.* Norman: Univ. of Oklahoma Press, 1971.

Peterson, Norma Lois. *The Presidencies of William Henry Harrison and John Tyler.* Lawrence: Univ. Press of Kansas, 1989.

Porter, George H. *Ohio Politics during the Civil War Period.* 1911. Reprint, New York: Ams Press, 1968.

Powell, Thomas E., ed. *The Democratic Party of the State of Ohio: A Comprehensive History of Democracy in Ohio from 1803 to 1912, Including Democratic Legislation in the State, the Campaigns of a Century, History of Democratic Conventions, the Reverses and Successes of the Party, Etc.* 2 vols. Columbus: Ohio Publishing, 1913.

Randall, James G. *Constitutional Problems under Lincoln.* New York: D. Appleton and Co., 1926.

Rawley, James A. *The Politics of Union: Northern Politics during the Civil War.* Hinsdale, Ill.: Dryden Press, 1974.

———. *Race and Politics: "Bleeding Kansas" and the Coming of the Civil War.* Philadelphia: J. B. Lippincott, 1969.

Rayback, Joseph G. *A History of American Labor,* exp. ed. New York: MacMillan, 1966.

Rayback, Robert J. *Millard Fillmore: Biography of a President.* New York: Henry Stewart, 1959.

Reeves, Thomas C. *Gentleman Boss: The Life of Chester Alan Arthur.* New York: Alfred A. Knopf, 1975.

Remini, Robert V. *The Life of Andrew Jackson.* New York: Penguin Books, 1988.

Rhodes, James Ford. *History of the United States from the Compromise of 1850 to the End of the Roosevelt Administration.* 9 vols. New York: MacMillan, 1928.

Richardson, Heather Cox. *The Death of Reconstruction: Race, Labor, and Politics in the Post-Civil War North, 1865–1901.* Cambridge, Mass.: Harvard Univ. Press, 2001.

———. *The Greatest Nation on the Earth: Republican Economic Policies during the Civil War.* Cambridge, Mass.: Harvard Univ. Press, 1997.

Ritter, Gretchen. *Goldbugs and Greenbacks: The Antimonopoly Tradition and the Politics of Finance in America.* New York: Cambridge Univ. Press, 1997.

Roseboom, Eugene H. *The Civil War Era, 1850–1873.* Vol. 4 of *The History of the State of Ohio,* ed. Carl Wittke. Columbus: Ohio State Archaeological and Historical Society, 1944.

Rosenbloom, David H. *Centenary Issues of the Pendleton Act of 1883: The Problematic Legacy of Civil Service Reform.* New York: Marcel Dekkex, 1982.

Ross, Earle Dudley. *The Liberal Republican Movement.* 2d ed. New York: AMS Press, 1971.

Rothman, David J. *Politics and Power: The United States Senate, 1869–1901.* Cambridge, Mass.: Harvard Univ. Press, 1966.

Ryan, Daniel J. *Lincoln and Ohio.* Cleveland: Ohio State Archaeological and Historical Society, 1923.

Ryden, George Herbert. *The Foreign Policy of the United States in Relation to Samoa.* New Haven, Conn.: Yale Univ. Press, 1933.

Sageser, A. Bower. *The First Two Decades of the Pendleton Act: A Study of Civil Service Reform.* Lincoln: Univ. of Nebraska Press, 1935.

Sawrey, Robert D. *Dubious Victory: The Reconstruction Debate in Ohio.* Lexington: Univ. Press of Kentucky, 1992.

Saxon, Alexander. *The Rise and Fall of the White Republic: Class Politics and Mass Culture in Nineteenth-Century America.* London: Verso, 1990.

Schattschneider, Elmer E. *Party Government.* New York: n.p., 1942.

Schlesinger, Jr., Arthur M. *The Age of Jackson.* Boston: Little, Brown and Co., 1945.

Sears, Stephen W. *George B. McClellan: The Young Napoleon.* New York: Ticknor and Fields, 1988.

Seip, Terry L. *The South Returns to Congress: Men, Economic Measures, and Intersectional Relationships, 1868–1879.* Baton Rouge: Louisiana State Univ. Press, 1983.

Sellers, Charles. *The Market Revolution: Jacksonian America, 1815–1846.* New York: Oxford Univ. Press, 1991.

SenGupta, Gunja. *For God and Mammon: Evangelists and Entrepreneurs, Masters and Slaves in Territorial Kansas, 1854–1860.* Athens: Univ. of Georgia Press, 1996.

Shafer, Byron E., and Anthony J. Badger, eds. *Contesting Democracy: Substance and Structure in American Political History, 1775–2000.* Lawrence: Univ. Press of Kansas, 2001.

Sharkey, Robert P. *Money, Class, and Party: An Economic Study of the Civil War and Reconstruction.* Baltimore, Md.: Johns Hopkins Press, 1959.

Silbey, Joel H. *The American Political Nation, 1838–1893.* Stanford, Calif.: Stanford Univ. Press, 1991.

———. *A Respectable Minority: The Democratic Party in the Civil War Era, 1860–1868.* New York: W. W. Norton and Co., 1977.

Simms, Henry H. *The Rise of the Whigs in Virginia, 1824–1840.* Richmond, Va.: William Byrd Press, 1929.

Simpson, Brooks D. *Let Us Have Peace: Ulysses S. Grant and the Politics of War and Reconstruction, 1861–1868.* Chapel Hill: Univ. of North Carolina Press, 1991.

Skowronek, Stephen. *The Politics Presidents Make: Leadership from John Adams to Bill Clinton.* 2d ed. Cambridge, Mass.: Belknap Press of Harvard Univ. Press, 1997.

Smith, Clifford Neal. *Early Nineteenth-Century German Settlers in Ohio (Mainly Cincinnati and Environs), Kentucky, and Other States . . .* McNeal, Ariz.: Westland, 1984.

Stahl, O. Glenn. *Public Personnel Administration.* 7th ed. New York: Harper and Row, 1976.

Stampp, Kenneth M. *And the War Came: The North and the Secession Crisis, 1860–1861.* Binghamton, N.Y.: Vail-Ballou Press, 1950.

Stanwood, Edward. *American Tariff Controversies in the Nineteenth Century.* 2 vols. 1903. Reprint, New York: Russell and Russell, 1967.

Stewart, Frank Mann. *The National Civil Service Reform League: History, Activities, and Problems.* Austin: University of Texas, 1929.

Storey, Moorfield. *The Democratic Party and Civil Service Reform: A Paper Prepared for the Annual Meeting of the National Civil Service Reform League at Cincinnati, Ohio, December 17, 1897.* n.p.: National Civil Service Reform League, 1897.

Summers, Mark Wahlgren. *The Era of Good Stealings.* New York: Oxford Univ. Press, 1993.

———. *The Gilded Age or the Hazard of New Functions.* Upper Saddle River, N.J.: Prentice Hall, 1997.

Tansill, Charles C. *The Foreign Policy of Thomas F. Bayard, 1885–1897.* New York: Fordham Univ. Press, 1940.

Temin, Peter. *The Jacksonian Economy.* New York: W. W. Norton and Co., 1969.

Thompson, Richard G. *Expectations and the Greenback Rate, 1862–1878.* New York: Garland, 1985.

Trefousse, Hans L. *The Radical Republicans: Lincoln's Vanguard for Racial Justice.* Baton Rouge: Louisiana State Univ. Press, 1968.

Unger, Irwin. *The Greenback Era: A Social and Political History of American Finance, 1865–1879*. Princeton, N.J.: Princeton Univ. Press, 1964.

Van Duesen, Glyndon G. *William Henry Seward*. New York: Oxford Univ. Press, 1967.

Van Riper, Paul P. *History of the United States Civil Service*. Evanston, Ill.: Row, Peterson and Co., 1958.

Voss-Hubbard, Mark. *Beyond Party: Cultures of Antipartisanship in Northern Politics before the Civil War*. Baltimore, Md.: Johns Hopkins Univ. Press, 2002.

Warren, Gordon H. *Fountain of Discontent: The Trent Affair and Freedom of the Seas*. Boston: Northeastern Univ. Press, 1981.

Watson, Harry L. *Liberty and Power: The Politics of Jacksonian America*. American Century Series, ed. Eric Foner. New York: Hill and Wang, 1990.

Waugh, John C. *Reelecting Lincoln: The Battle for the 1864 Presidency*. New York: Crown, 1997.

Weber, Thomas. *The Northern Railroads in the Civil War, 1861–1865*. Bloomington: Indiana Univ. Press, 1999.

Weisenburger, Francis P. "A Brief History of the Immigrant Groups in Ohio." In *In the Trek of the Immigrants: Essays Presented to Carl Wittke*. Rock Island, Ill.: Augustana College Library, 1964.

———. *The Passing of the Frontier, 1825–1850*. Vol. 3 of *The History of the State of Ohio*, ed. Carl Wittke. Columbus: Ohio State Archaeological and Historical Society, 1941.

Wells, Damon. *Stephen Douglas: The Last Years, 1857–1861*. Austin: Univ. of Texas Press, 1971.

White, Leonard D. *The Republican Era: A Study in Administrative History, 1869–1901*. New York: MacMillan, 1958.

Williams, Charles R. *The Life of Rutherford B. Hayes: Nineteenth President of the United States*. Boston: Houghton Mifflin Co., 1914.

Williams, T. Harry. *McClellan, Sherman and Grant*. Westport, Conn.: Greenwood Press, 1962.

Wilson, Woodrow. *Congressional Government*. Introduction by Walter Lippmann. 1885. Reprint, Gloucester: Peter Smith, 1973.

Wilson, Woodrow. *Congressional Government*. Introduction by Walter Lippman. 1885. Reprint, Gloucester: Peter Smith, 1973.

Zornow, William Frank. *Lincoln and the Party Divided*. Norman: Univ. of Oklahoma Press, 1954.

Articles

Anderson, George L. "The South and Problems of Post-Civil War Finance." *Journal of Southern History* 9 (Aug. 1943): 181–95.

Anderson, Stuart. "'Pacific Destiny' and American Policy in Samoa, 1872–1899." *Hawaiian Journal of History* 12 (1978): 45–60.

Baker, Jean H. "A Loyal Opposition: Northern Democrats in the Thirty-seventh Congress." *Civil War History* 25 (June 1979): 139–55.

Becker, Carl M. "Picture of a Young Copperhead." *Bulletin of the Historical and Philosophical Society of Ohio* 71 (Jan. 1962): 3–23.

Benedict, Michael Les. "The Rout of Radicalism: Republicans and the Elections of 1867." *Civil War History* 18 (Dec. 1972): 334–44.

———. "Vallandigham: Constitutionalist and Copperhead." *Timeline* 3 (Feb.–Mar. 1986): 16–25.

Bernard, Kenneth A. "Lincoln and Civil Liberties." *The Abraham Lincoln Quarterly* 6 (Sept. 1951): 375–99.

Brice, Jane Pendleton. "The Year of the Three Kaisers." *Foreign Service Journal* (Dec. 1988): 44–46.

Brown, David. "Slavery and the Market Revolution: The South's Place in Jacksonian Historiography." *Southern Studies* 4 (1993): 189–207.

Calhoun, Charles W. "Reimagining the 'Lost Men' of the Gilded Age: Perspectives on the Late Nineteenth Century Presidents." *Journal of the Gilded Age and Progressive Era* 1 (July 2002): 225–57.

Cardinal, Eric J. "The Ohio Democracy and the Crisis of Disunion, 1860–1861." *Ohio History* 86 (Winter 1977): 19–40.

Curry, Leonard P. "Congressional Democrats, 1861–1863." *Civil War History* 12 (Sept. 1966): 213–29.

Curry, Richard O. "The Union as It Was: A Critique of Recent Interpretations of the 'Copperheads.'" *Civil War History* 13 (Mar. 1967): 25–39.

Downey, Matthew T. "Horace Greeley and the Politicians: The Liberal Republican Convention in 1872." *Journal of American History* 53 (Mar. 1967): 727–50.

Dudley, Harold M. "The Election of 1864." *Mississippi Valley Historical Review* 28 (Mar. 1932): 500–518.

Galbreath, C. B. "Ohio's Contribution to National Civil Service Reform." *Ohio Archaeological and Historical Society Publications* 33 (1924): 176–204.

Gastright, Joseph F. "The Making of the Kentucky Central." *Kenton Country Historical Society Quarterly Review* (July 1983): pt. 1, pp. 1–2.

———. "The Making of the Kentucky Central." *Kenton Country Historical Society Quarterly Review* (Spring 1984): pt. 2, pp. 1–3.

———. "The Making of the Kentucky Central." *Kenton Country Historical Society Quarterly Review* (Spring 1985): pt. 3, pp. 1–4.

Gerber, Richard Allen. "The Liberal Republicans of 1872 in Historiographical Perspective." *Journal of American History* 62 (June 1975): 40–73.

Hoogenboom, Ari. "The Pendleton Act and the Civil Service." *American Historical Review* 64 (Jan. 1959): 301–18.

House, Albert V. "Northern Congressional Democrats as Defenders of the South during the Southern Reconstruction." *Journal of Southern History* 6 (Feb. 1940): 46–71.

———. "Republicans and Democrats Search for New Identities, 1870–1890." *Review of Politics* 13 (Oct. 1969): 466–76.

Hubbell, John T. "The Douglas Democrats and the Election of 1860." *Mid-America* 54 (1973): 108–33.

———. "Politics as Usual: The Northern Democracy and Party Survival, 1860–1861." *Illinois Quarterly* 36 (1973): 22–35.

Hyman, Harold M. "Election of 1864." In *The Coming to Power: Critical Presidential Elections in American History,* ed. Arthur M. Schlesinger Jr., 160–61. New York: McGraw Hill, 1971.

Klement, Frank L. "Clement L. Vallandigham." In *For the Union. Ohio Leaders in the Civil War,* ed. Kenneth W. Wheeler, 58–63. Columbus: Ohio State Univ. Press, 1968.

———. "Sound and Fury: Civil War Dissent in the Cincinnati Area." *Cincinnati Historical Society Bulletin* 35 (1977): 99–114.

Lucie, Patricia M. L. "Confiscation: Constitutional Crossroads." *Civil War History* 23 (Dec. 1977): 307–16.

Mach, Thomas S. "Family Ties, Party Realities, and Political Ideology: George Hunt Pendleton and Partisanship in Antebellum Cincinnati." *Ohio Valley History* 3 (Summer 2003): 17–30.

———. "George Hunt Pendleton, the Ohio Idea and Political Continuity in Reconstruction America." *Ohio History* 108 (Summer–Autumn 1999): 125–44.

Moore, Clifford H. "Ohio in National Politics, 1865–1896." *Ohio Archaeological and Historical Society Publications* 37 (Apr.–June 1928): 200–427.

Mowry, Duane, ed. "Some Political Letters of Reconstruction Days Succeeding the Civil War." *American Historical Magazine* 4 (May 1909): 332.

Perzel, Edward S. "Alexander Long, Salmon P. Chase, and the Election of 1868." *Bulletin of the Cincinnati Historical Society* 23 (Jan. 1965): 3–18.

Pessen, Edward. "Did Labor Support Jackson?" *Political Science Quarterly* 64 (June 1949): 262–74.

Peterson, Owen M. "Ohio Leaders in the Democratic Convention of 1860." *Historical and Philosophical Society of Ohio Bulletin* 13 (Apr. 1955): 99–113.

Ratcliffe, Donald J. "The Market Revolution and Party Alignments in Ohio, 1828–1840." In *The Pursuit of Public Power: Political Culture in Ohio, 1787–1861,* ed. Jeffrey P. Brown and Andrew R. L. Cayton, 99–116. Kent, Ohio: Kent State University Press, 1994.

Reeves, Thomas C. "The Irony of the Pendleton Act." *Hayes Historical Journal* 4 (Spring 1984): 37–43.

Roseboom, Eugene H. "Southern Ohio and the Union in 1863." *Mississippi Valley Historical Review* 39 (1952): 29–44.

Sears, Stephen. "McClellan and the Peace Plank of 1864: A Reappraisal." *Civil War History* 36 (Mar. 1990): 57–64.

Shipley, Max L. "The Background and Legal Aspects of the Pendleton Plan." *Mississippi Valley Historical Review* 24 (Sept. 1937): 329–40.

Sullivan, William A. "Did Labor Support Andrew Jackson?" *Political Science Quarterly* 62 (Dec. 1947): 569–80.

Voegeli, Jacque. "The Northwest and the Race Issue, 1861–1862." *Mississippi Valley Historical Review* 50 (1963): 235–51.

Wagstaff, Thomas. "The Arm-in-Arm Convention." *Civil War History* 14 (June 1968): 101–19.

Wilson, Charles R. "Cincinnati: A Southern Outpost in 1860–1861?" *Mississippi Valley Historical Review* 24 (1938): 473–82.

———. "McClellan's Changing View on the Peace Plank of 1864." *American Historical Review* 38 (Apr. 1933): 498–500.

Winther, Oscar Osburn. "The Soldier Vote in the Election of 1864." *Quarterly Journal of the New York State Historical Association* 25 (Oct. 1944): 440–58.

"Woodward High School in Cincinnati." *American Journal of Education* 4 (Sept. 1957): 520–25.

Wubben, H. H. "Copperhead Charles Mason: A Question of Loyalty." *Civil War History* 24 (Mar. 1978): 46–65.

Yager, Elizabeth F. "The Presidential Campaign of 1864 in Ohio." *Ohio History* 34 (1925): 548–89.

Zornow, William Frank. "Clement L. Vallandigham and the Democratic Party in 1864." *Historical and Philosophical Society of Ohio Bulletin* 19 (Jan. 1961): 21–37.

———. "The Cleveland Convention, 1864, and Radical Democrats." *Mid-America* 36 (1954): 39–53.

———. "McClellan and Seymour in the Chicago Convention of 1864." *Illinois State Historical Society Journal* 43 (Winter 1950): 282–95.

———. "The Ohio Democrats and the 'Africanization' Issue in 1862." *Negro History Bulletin* 11 (June 1948): 211–14.

Reference Works

Dictionary of American Biography Base Set. American Council of Learned Societies, 1928–1936. Reproduced in *Biography Resource Center,* Farmington Hills, Mich.: Thomson Gale, 2005. http://galenet.galegroup.com/servlet/BioRC.

Encyclopedia of World Biography. 2d ed. 17 vols. Gale Research, 1998. Reproduced in *Biography Resource Center.* Farmington Hills, Mich.: Thomson Gale. 2005. http://galenet.galegroup.com/servlet/BioRC.

Dissertations and Theses

Bridges, Roger Dean. "The Impeachment and Trial of William Worth Belknap, Secretary of War." Master's thesis, State College of Iowa, 1963.

Cardinal, Eric J. "The Democratic Party of Ohio and the Civil War: An Analysis of a Wartime Political Minority." Ph.D. diss., Kent State University, 1981.

Hemmer, Jr., Joseph John. "The Democratic National Conventions of 1860: Discourse of Disruption in Rhetorical-Historical Perspective." Ph.D. diss., University of Wisconsin, 1969.

Johns, Lee. "The Peace Democrats of Ohio in the 1862 and 1863 Ohio Elections." Master's thesis, Kent State University, 1975.

Rittenhouse, Floyd Oliver. "George Hunt Pendleton: With Special Reference to His Congressional Career." Master's thesis, Ohio State University, 1932.

Wilson, Charles R. "The *Cincinnati Daily Enquirer* and Civil War Politics: A Study in 'Copperhead' Opinion." Ph.D. diss., University of Chicago, 1934.

Index